D1154572

International African Library 33
General Editors: J. D. Y. Peel, Colin Murray and Suzette Heald

ETHNICITY AND THE MAKING OF HISTORY IN NORTHERN GHANA

The *International African Library* is a major monograph series from the International African Institute and complements its quarterly periodical *Africa*, the premier journal in the field of African studies. Theoretically informed ethnographies, studies of social relations 'on the ground' which are sensitive to local cultural forms, have long been central to the Institute's publications programme. The *IAL* maintains this strength but extends it into new areas of contemporary concern, both practical and intellectual. It includes works focused on problems of development, especially on the linkages between the local and national levels of society; studies along the interface between the social and environmental sciences; and historical studies, especially those of a social, cultural or interdisciplinary character.

International African Library

General Editors

J. D. Y. Peel, Colin Murray *and* Suzette Heald

ETHNICITY AND THE MAKING OF HISTORY IN NORTHERN GHANA

CAROLA LENTZ

EDINBURGH UNIVERSITY PRESS
for the International African Institute, London

GN
655
.G45
L46
2006

© Carola Lentz, 2006

Edinburgh University Press Ltd
22 George Square, Edinburgh

Typeset in Plantin
by Koinonia, Bury, and
printed and bound in Great Britain
by MPG Books Ltd, Bodmin, Cornwall

A CIP record for this book is available
from the British Library

ISBN-10 0 7486 2401 5 (hardback)
ISBN-13 978 0 7486 2401 0

The right of Carola Lentz to be identified
as author of this work has been asserted in
accordance with the Copyright, Designs
and Patents Act 1988.

For other publications of the International
African Institute, please visit their web site at
www.iaionthe.net

CONTENTS

LIST OF MAPS AND PLATES

PREFACE

Tuonianuo, 'Bitterness is sweetness': this name, given to me by Anselmy Bemile, my Dagara father, was intended to encourage me to be patient and persevere. Like all Dagara personal names it expressed the name-giver's life experience and was to guide its recipient through life. As one of the first Catholic converts in his family and in his village in North-Western Ghana, Anselmy had courageously worked for many years as a catechist and farmer, and sent all seven sons and one daughter to school. Conflicts with chiefs, imprisonment, the malicious gossip of his enemies – this was the bitterness, the hardship, as Anselmy would often tell me. And the joy? Well, now in his old age, he had little cause for complaint. One of his sons worked his fields, and all children visited home regularly – never with empty hands. Thus, his own name had proven true: *Bemile*, let them talk, never mind what others may think. *Tuonianuo*: Were not all his efforts rewarded in that his eldest son Paul became Bishop of the Wa Diocese and that Sebastian, after many years of study in Germany, had finally come home, together with me and so many other students, to study the Dagara culture? That I was now a part of the family was no coincidence, Anselmy continued, his father Yob was not baptised with the name Carolus for nothing. And Yob, actually *yɔb-bʋm*, means: the rewards of travel.

It was on my very first trip to Ghana in 1987, that I got to know Anselmy and his wife Catherina, his brothers Jonas Nifaasie and Gervase Waka with their families, his son Barth and his wife Cordelia and the extended family of the house of Yob in Hamile. To make Ghana the place where I would do my future research was in effect an armchair decision, when the Department of Social Anthropology of the Free University of Berlin asked me to organise student fieldwork in a West African country. Back then I had no idea that I would become so attached to Northern Ghana so as today to consider it to be a second home. But after having spent a week of my first trip at Anselmy and Catherina's compound in Hamile I knew this was where I wanted to conduct my research. It was particularly the long conversations with Anselmy that impressed me: he, who had never been to school, spoke with great authority about the Dagara way of life and about their neighbours, about the history of his family and the Kpiele clan, about his earlier role in local politics and his estimation of the current government. And when he asked about the various customs in Germany, as he often did, and I responded, he would be amused by how 'uncivilised' we were. Of course in his eyes Christianity and the wisdom of the ancestors, local knowledge and greater politics, and the enjoyment of modern consumer goods and pride in one's traditions did not contradict or undermine each other, but were part of one greater reality. I would later come to know more such old men and women, who with great dignity knew how to balance 'tradition' with 'modernity'. And I made friends among the younger generation, the labour migrants and the educated elite, who impressed me no less; under the most arduous circumstances they would try to reconcile the expectations of their relatives back home with the requirements and constraints of modern professional and family life in the city.

The present work is the product of my many stays in Ghana and would not have been possible without the support of a great many people, only a few of whom can be named here. First and foremost I would like to thank Anselmy Bemile and Catharina Kuunifaa, Barth Bemile and Cordelia Yelkekpi and of course Dr Sebastian Bemile and his wife Kate Kuuire as well as my other brothers and sisters for their love, friendship and support. With gratitude I will always remember the instructive conversations with Archbishop Peter Dery, Bishop Dr Paul Bemile and Dr Edward Tengan. To Father Gervase Sentuu and Father Richard Abba-Kugbeh I owe thanks for their heartfelt hospitality and their continuous encouragement. Without the kind support of Nandom Naa Dr Charles Imoro, Lambussie Kuoro K. Y. Baloro, Lawra Naa Abayifaa Karbo and Jirapa Naa Bapenyiri Yelpoe my research would not have been possible. Conducting 'multi-ethnic' research is a tricky endeavour, and it was not always easy to proceed through the thicket of older and more recent conflicts, some of them still quite virulent, with the requisite diplomatic sensitivity. Some have accused me of being too 'pro-Dagara', others of being much too understanding of the Sisala perspective. But in the house of the Nandom Naa and of the Lambussie Kuoro, where I had the privilege of being a frequent guest, my research was followed critically, but quite benevolently. I owe a great many thanks also to the other members of the Nandom chiefly family, particularly Rear-Admiral (Gn. rtd) Kevin Dzang Chemogoh and Gbeckature Boro, as well as to W. K. Dibaar from the earth-priestly family in Nandomkpee for their readiness to speak with me. Dr Daniel Delle, also a member of the Nandom chiefly family and a surgeon in Trier, Germany, who kindly supported my work from the very beginning, often provided me in our many conversations with just the information and the advice I needed to be able to continue writing. Heartfelt thanks also go out to Kumbonoh Gandah, who was so generous with his wealth of expertise on tradition and politics in Lawra District, and Salifu Bawa Dy-Yakah, from the chiefly house of Lambussie, who was always ready to explain the intricacies involved in the politics of North-West Ghana.

Thanks also go out to the former District Secretaries of Lawra-Nandom, Raymond Maaldu and Isaac Dasoberi, and of Jirapa-Lambussie, Jacob Boon and Ivan Angbing, Regional Secretary Y. Antunmini, his successor Yelechire and the employees of the regional archives in Tamale as well as those at the Ghana National Archive in Accra. Professor Nana Kwame Arhin Birempon and the Institute of African Studies at the University of Ghana, Legon, welcomed me as a research associate and extended their generous support. I am also grateful to the assistants who have worked with me over the years: Anthony Baloro, Cornelius Debpuur, Isidor Lobnibe, Gregory Sullibie and Dominique Ziniel. And last, but not least, I would like to name at least some of those friends, whose many conversations contributed greatly to my work: John-Bosco Baanuo, Aloysius Denkabe, Peter and Claire Der, Ben Kunbuor, Dr Edward N. and Prudence Gyader, Linus Kabobah, Ambrose and Lucy Kokoro, Alexis Nakaar, Bruno Ninnang, Jacob Songsore, John Sotenga and Jacob Yirerong.

Far too many of my most important Ghanaian interview partners have passed away in recent years: Y. Antunmini, Anselmy and Barth Bemile, Dr Daniel Delle, Peter Der, Bawa Dy-Yakah, Lambussie Kuoro K. Y. Baloro, Jirapa Naa Bapenyiri Yelpoe, S. W. D. K. Gandah, Lawra Naa Abayifaa Karbo ... Their deaths have been a great loss. It is in their memory that I would like to dedicate this book.

Like the research itself, this book has a long history, during each phase of which I incurred many debts of gratitude. The initial manuscript was written between 1995 and 1996 and submitted as a post-doctoral thesis to the Free University of Berlin. Here I would like to thank first and foremost the staff of the Department of Social Anthropology and especially Georg Elwert for their faithful support. A grant from the *Deutsche Forschungsgemeinschaft* financed part of the field research and made the write-up possible. During my time as Professor at the Department of Historical Ethnology at the Johann Wolfgang Goethe University Frankfurt, the manuscript, more than one thousand pages in length, was shortened and published in 1998 by the Köppe-Verlag in Cologne, appearing in the series 'Studien zur Kulturkunde' under the title *Die Konstruktion von Ethnizität. Eine politische Geschichte Nord-West Ghanas, 1870–1990*. Only generous financing by the *Deutsche Forschungsgemeinschaft* made the publication possible. I owe many thanks particularly to Karl-Heinz Kohl and Beatrix Heintze, the editors of the series, as well as to Rüdiger Köppe, who approved the generous distribution of free copies so that German-speaking Ghanaians could read it and together with reviewers push for its translation into English. This marked the beginning of a long odyssey through the world of English-language publishing, which ended with the realisation that there simply was no market and therefore no publisher for such an extensive monograph about such a small spot on the African continent. It took me four years to get used to the idea that I would have to sacrifice much of the historical detail that was so dear to me and shorten the book to less than half its original length, i.e. to make an altogether new book out of it. Without the encouragement and editorial support of John Peel I would most likely have never embarked on such an undertaking. A great many thanks to Robert Parkin for his competence as translator, to Stephanie Delfs for her assistance with the technical aspects of producing the new manuscript, and to Richard Kuba for his great help with the maps in this book. In addition, without Katja Rieck's tireless editorial commitment, wonderful feel for the subtleties of language and skill in identifying argumentative snags the English text would never have become as readable as I hope it now is. And finally I would like to mention the names of at least a few of those who supported me throughout the writing process and in innumerable conversations helped further clarify my thoughts: Emmanuel Akyeampong, Andrea Behrends, Thomas Bier-schenk, Artur Bogner, John Comaroff, Mamadou Diawara, Andreas Eckert, Peter Geschiere, Axel Harneit-Sievers, Beatrix Heintze, Richard Kuba, John Lonsdale, Tom MacCaskie, Birgit Meyer, Paul Nugent, Achim von Oppen, Mike Rowlands, Gerd Spittler, Katja Werthmann, Ivor Wilks and Albert Wirz, who unfortunately also left us far too soon.

Finally I would like to send this book on its way with a Dagara proverb and ask my friends and interlocutors for forgiveness should – despite all my efforts at preserving historical accuracy and balance – half-truths, ignorance, imbalances or errors have crept into the text:

> *Saan zi bàɲnɛ yààrì kpa-puo tèrv ɛ.*
> A guest who knows his way around, often wounds the back of his head.

In other words: the better a visitor or a researcher thinks he knows his way around and the more confidently he moves about in the house, the more often he will in the dimness of the interior whack his head on the low ceiling, reminding him that he does not know the place as well as he thought he did.

NOTE ON SPELLING, TERMINOLOGY AND ETHNIC NAMES

Because of the variances in both Dagara and Sisala spelling, place names and indigenous terms pose problems. There are attempts at standardisation, but many people still use their personally preferred orthographies as does much of the archival and other written material quoted in this book. When using my own words, I have, with some simplification in the use of diacritical signs, mainly relied on the orthography proposed by Sebastian Bemile (1990), which has been adopted by many Ghanaian Dagara intellectuals. However, when quoting, I have retained the original spelling.

I hope that readers are not offended by my use of words such as 'tribe' and colonial ethnic names such as 'Dagarti', 'Grunshi' or 'Lobi' without always employing quotation marks or italics. The use of these terms and names, even if not set off in direct quotation, are part of a particular historical discourse, be it of colonial administrators or local actors, of which I am by no means uncritical. But since the subject of this book requires that I use these terms and names in almost every other sentence, I have often omitted the quotation marks in the interests of readability.

A final problem concerns the use of the terms 'Dagara' and 'Dagaba', which are currently the most common, but also controversial ethnic self-designations, as is discussed in further detail in the final chapter of this book. Some believe that the people living around Wa, Nadawli and Jirapa form a distinct group, the Dagaba (the British 'Dagarti'), who speak Dagaare, and that they should not be confounded with the Dagara, who speak Dagara and live around Lawra and Nandom and in parts of South-Western Burkina Faso (the British 'Lobi' and 'Lobi-Dagarti'). Although some would admit that these two groups together actually form a single large ethnic community, they still insist that the correct name for this large community is Dagaba. Others hold that Dagara is the only correct term for both the language and the entire ethnic group. According to the available evidence, neither Dagaba (sing. Dagao) nor Dagara are neologisms but rather long-standing indigenous ethnonyms which the local people themselves generally use when speaking in their own language. However, in English-language conversations, and particularly when addressing Ghanaians unfamiliar with the North-West, one often also hears the colonial term 'Dagarti' or 'Lobi'. In any case, Sean Hawkins' (2002: 6, 41, 102–3) decision to adopt Jack Goody's nomenclature that refers to the Dagara/Dagaba as 'LoDagaa', because of a purported lack of consensus on which name to use and because 'these terms are of little concern to the people themselves' (Hawkins 1996: 233 fn. 3), is highly problematic. Unlike Hawkins, I *did* encounter a 'strong sense of collective consciousness' (ibid.) and a lively interest in the issue of which name to use. The lack of agreement on the part of locals regarding the choice of terms does not justify simply imposing an observer's name, particularly when it is one that the locals themselves actually reject. Because most of my discussions refer to the area around Nandom and Lawra, I have in this book decided to use the term Dagara unless referring specifically to the residents of the 'Dagaba' area and unless, of course, when quoting from other discourses.

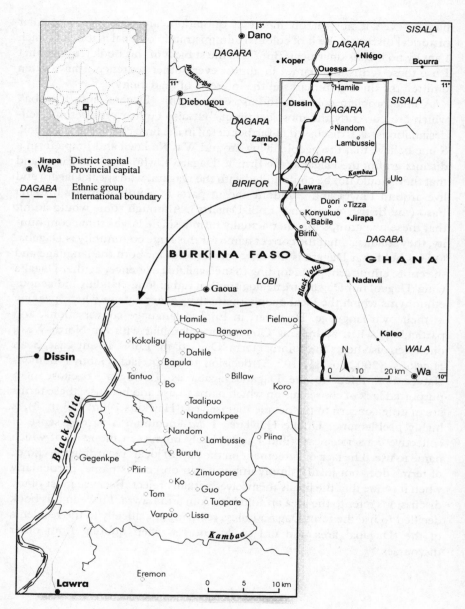

Map 1 The Black Volta region today

INTRODUCTION

'The loyalties of the people are still extremely local', wrote Lawra-Tumu District Commissioner Mead in 1947 in support of a chief's demand for political independence from a neighbouring chiefdom, and strongly recommended that British administrative reforms draw on this 'local patriotism ... rather than suppress it'.[1] Like his predecessors, however, Mead harboured no doubts that beyond their attachments to kin, village and chiefdom, the Africans living under his administration also belonged to 'tribes' which, though these had not (yet) developed into self-conscious political communities, were clearly identifiable by historical roots, language and 'custom'. The British anthropologist Jack Goody, on the other hand, who began research in Lawra District during the early 1950s, was convinced that North-West Ghana was inhabited by congeries of peoples who had linguistically and culturally so much in common that such ethnic boundaries could not be drawn unequivocally. Goody insisted that ethnonyms such as 'Sisala', 'Dagarti' and 'Lobi' or 'Lobi-Dagarti' were colonial constructions and that the indigenous population employed a small-scale, context-dependent, flexible system of referents for themselves and their neighbours, evincing no 'consciousness of unity sufficient to give rise to ... tribal name[s]' (1956: 20).

Some forty years later, Peter Dery, Archbishop of Tamale and the first ordained Dagara priest, drew a very different picture of his home region's history and culture. Calling for ethnic unity and the preservation of the 'uniqueness of Dagara culture', he insisted that the Dagara, despite their many dialectal and cultural variations, were 'originally one single group of people of common origin with one common language', who had, in their quest for autonomy and dignity, broken away from the Dagomba kingdom.[2] Although not everyone in the North-West shares Dery's political and cultural views or his broad definition of Dagara ethnicity, all would agree that ethnic categories and a sense of belonging to an ethnic group are part and parcel of local reality.

These quotations reflect the far-reaching political, social and cultural transformations that have taken place since the end of the nineteenth century in North-Western Ghana, a region which in the pre-colonial period was neither politically centralised nor inhabited by distinct 'tribes'. One of the most momentous innovations was the colonial introduction of chieftaincy which gradually re-ordered, or at least overlaid, older local concepts of belonging and authority. To legitimate their claims to authority and expand their influence, these new chiefs not only re-interpreted oral traditions but also appropriated the British 'tribal' discourse. Another decisive change was labour migration which came to play an increasingly important role in the regional economy. To cope with the situation, these young men initiated new idioms of solidarity, often containing ethnic overtones, that emphasised ties extending beyond the boundaries of the patriclan or home village. Furthermore, the mission of the White Fathers, which since the 1930s had converted thousands of North-Westerners to Christianity, helped to anchor this new ethnic awareness by putting the Dagara language into writing. This created an 'imagined community' (Anderson 1983) of Dagara/Dagaare speakers that reached far beyond the colonial boundaries of local 'tribes', chiefdoms, districts, even beyond the Protectorate. Mission and state schools, finally, brought forth an educated elite who were socialised to think ethnically, even though loyalties to the patriclan, the village, the chiefdom, the local Christian congregation or their peers from other parts of the country both complemented and competed with these new ethnic identifications.

Like many anthropologists of his time, however, Goody was less interested in such contemporary transformations, than in the study of social organisation as it supposedly existed in the pre-colonial period. Yet insistence on a lack of ethnic consciousness may also reflect that in village daily life the new ethnic identifications at this time were so vaguely defined that an anthropologist could easily overlook them. However, by the late 1980s, when I began my research, the situation was quite different: education and labour migration were even more widespread than they had been forty years earlier, linking local, national and even international discourses concerning 'ethnicity' and 'tradition'. The educated elite not only repeatedly mobilised ethnicity politically, but also worked out a whole repertoire of cultural material constituting Dagara (and also Sisala and Wala) identity, a repertoire that included folk tales, songs, proverbs and migration histories, studies of language, kinship and religion, and lavishly celebrated cultural festivals that were covered by the national media. Archbishop Dery's views aptly articulate this recent cultural work to constitute ethnicity.

This book, then, aims at providing a social and political history of North-Western Ghana, paying particular attention to the creation of new ethnic and territorial boundaries, categories and forms of self-understanding. It explores how, and in which contexts, ethnic distinctions and commonalities were created and continually re-defined by colonial officials, missionaries, anthropologists, chiefs, migrant workers, catechists, peasants, and educated elites. It also addresses the tensions between territorial, linguistic and cultural criteria for drawing ethnic boundaries, and discusses the links between ethnic and other collective identifications.

Ethnicity is an enigmatic, unstable and problematic notion. Like other key terms in the social sciences and history, it is at once a category 'of social and political *analysis*' and a category 'of social and political *practice*' (Brubaker and Cooper 2000: 4). It belongs not only to the theoretical repertoire of social scientists but also to the vocabulary of chiefs, politicians, local intellectuals, labour migrants and social movements. Unlike other bases of group cohesion such as class, religion or membership of a political community, it is a protean and polythetic category which rests on no single essential trait (Fardon 1996). It may draw on traditions of origin or descent, possession of any number of cultural and social traits, language, region, membership of (or opposition to) a polity or religion, or any combination of these; but at the same time it need not involve any particular one of these bases. This is why ethnicity, while having immense power to command subjectivities and hence to generate highly 'real' social and political effects, is also a 'shadow theatre', as Bayart (1993: 41–59) put it. Thus while ethnic discourses argue in an essentialist manner and naturalise social relationships, the 'content' of any particular ethnicity is historically contingent. As I will show in this book, it is the product both of particular – mainly political – contexts and of the materials which history has made available. The ethnicity's power rests precisely on this inherent contradiction: ethnic identifications claim to be primordial, dictated by birth, and are thus non-negotiable, creating permanent bonds, stability and security (as well as instability and insecurity among those excluded). At the same time the boundaries of the communities created and the specific traits and practices associated with them are malleable and can be adapted to serve specific interests and contexts.

Ethnicity therefore has to be considered as a specific form of 'totemic consciousness' (Comaroff 1992: 51), that is: an awareness arising in relation to the other ethnicities with which it contrasts itself, typically other ethnic groups within the same colonial and later national state. At the same time, it has to be analysed in relation to the various other bases of identity from which it draws some of its content, or which constitute alternative identifications – these often being 'higher' or 'lower' in the hierarchy of communities (of which the ethnic group is often one) or supra-local bases of self-understanding, such as class, educated versus non-educated, Catholic versus 'pagan' or Muslim, or rural versus urban. The fact that ethnicity itself is not only fluid, but fluidly connected to these non-ethnic bases of identification and commonality makes it necessary to broaden the perspective and explore much more than 'just' ethnicity – namely, the changing role of patriclans and earth-shrine areas, the colonial transformation of the political landscape, the history of chieftaincy, the world of labour migration, the engagement with the Catholic mission and the new forms of social differentiation resulting from the formation of an educated, urban-based elite. Thus, although ethnicity plays a substantial role in the history of North-Western Ghana, it is often eclipsed by other sources of identification or of conflict and therefore 'absent' for long stretches of this book's narrative. In the remainder of this introduction, I will sketch the course of research that resulted in this broader perspective and briefly present the three major themes around which the narrative is organised: the colonial encounter, the construction of ethnicity and the production of history.

THE COURSE OF RESEARCH

Originally, I had not planned to write a political history of North-Western Ghana, but wanted to focus on what ethnicity currently means to different actors. However, as the brief historical chapter which was to set the scene became longer in the writing and required ever more research, I finally had to recast the entire structure of the book and present the material in a diachronic perspective. This move very much reflects my interlocutors' existential interest in history as well as the fact that the complex links between ethnicity and alternative bases of commonality can only be under-stood from a historical perspective. In the end, my research became increasingly preoccupied with the colonial encounter, pre-colonial forms of commonality and categorisation and with the production of history, that is, the ways in which colonial administrators, missionaries and Africans reconstructed, remembered, (re-)interpreted and used history to legitimate their various political (or religious) agendas and to come to terms with new challenges.

This broader interest had methodological implications. Instead of conducting long-term anthropological fieldwork in a single location in a classical fashion, I made repeated trips to Ghana over the course of fifteen years, and conducted fieldwork in various settings – among migrants both in the gold mines and their home villages, among the educated elite in Accra, Kumasi, Tamale, Bolgatanga and Wa, among administrators, civil servants and youth association activists in the district capitals of the North-West, in chiefs' houses and in the simple compounds of 'commoners', among the Dagara and Dagaba, as well as among the Sisala and Wala. In addition, I spent extended periods conducting archival and library research in Accra, Tamale, London, Oxford, Rome and Evanston (USA). Among the advantages of undertaking repeated field trips was that I was able to witness changes in the larger political and economic context. The effects of the structural adjustment programme, the drawing up of new districts, and finally the return to multi-party democracy were some of the changes which affected the political dimensions of ethnicity. I was often intrigued by how, after the return to party politics, informants spoke of the past very differently than they had under the military regime. Repeated discussions and developing friendships with some of my interlocutors also provided an opportunity to discuss preliminary results – discussions which shifted the focus of my research from a rather politico-instrumental understanding of ethnicity to a view that takes more seriously the idea that the invention of ethnic categories is circumscribed by the historically available materials and that the new modes of self-understanding must be anchored in existing social relations and ideas for them to be meaningful.

From this wider historical perspective, however, defining the unit of analysis became a problem, both theoretically and methodologically. The more recent political history of North-Western Ghana is characterised by the growing interconnectedness of kinship and neighbourhood ties with larger political and economic networks. Ethnicity, in particular, is a supra-local phenomenon, and since ethnic categories only develop in the plural, it does not suffice to look at only one of the new ethnic groups trying to distinguish itself from the others, particularly given the contested nature of these boundaries. Furthermore, even if the study were to focus exclusively on the construction of ethnicity, it could not at the outset define its object of enquiry in ethnic terms. One simply cannot take as given the very proposition to be examined. Thus ultimately, a territorial definition of the object of enquiry proved the most appropriate approach.

Interest in a micro-history of ethnicity and complementary or alternative identities, however, required fixing this territorial unit in terms smaller than the entire North-West, especially as Ivor Wilks' seminal study on Wa (1989) already provided an outstanding history of the southern part of the region. Thus although the North-West repeatedly appears in this book as a colonial unit of administration and as a point of reference for political demands presented by the educated elite, for reasons of methodological feasibility, especially as regards interviews and participant observation, a focus on one of its larger chiefdoms proved more meaningful. I chose the Lawra Confederacy (which is territorially coincident with the old Lawra District), and Nandom in particular, one of the 'divisions' (today called 'para-mountcies' or 'traditional areas') created by the colonial administration in 1903/05 and amalgamated into the Lawra Confederacy Native Authority in 1934 along with the three neighbouring divisions of Lawra, Jirapa and Lambussie. As this book shall show, these divisions and the Lawra Confederacy developed into a frame of reference for mobilising local political action and collective identification still relevant today.

The focus on Nandom, however, is not unproblematic. In their study of the Luo in Kenya, Cohen and Odhiambo (1989) have elucidated how the mental maps of commonality shift, depending on whether the focus lies on space and a sense of belonging created through shared neighbourhood, or on the temporally defined referent of descent, resulting in a supra-local network of a 'Luo nation'. On the one hand, Nandom, like Jirapa, Lambussie or Lawra, is a more or less clearly bounded territory encompassing villages, small market towns and an ascertainable number of inhabitants 'subject' to the Nandom Naa. At the same time, however, Nandom constitutes a point of reference for social networks and a sense of belonging that transcends these territorial boundaries. 'Nandome' live in many parts of the world and may not even have been born in Nandom, while conversely not all those who actually reside in Nandom, people like government employees, traders and those who have married in, are considered 'Nandome'. It is these two meanings of Nandom, the historical circumstances that led to their rise and the practices associated with each that are to be discussed in this book. Furthermore, I will look at how the history of Nandom is firmly embedded in that of the Lawra Confederacy, and how ethnic boundaries, kinship ties and political alliances cross-cut chiefdom and district boundaries. Moreover, individual actors participate in other multi-ethnically defined institutions such as unions and professional associations, churches, lodges and political parties. And finally, although ethnicity is certainly a discourse highlighting local particularities, it is by no means a purely local phenomenon. Studying it therefore requires embracing the larger political and cultural contexts also.

THEORETICAL CONCERNS: ETHNICITY, COLONIALISM AND THE PRODUCTION OF HISTORY

When I began studying the history of ethnicity in North-Western Ghana in the late 1980s, the 'colonial invention of tribes' school (e.g. Iliffe 1979, Ranger 1983, Vail 1989) dominated, at least among African historians and anthropologists, and it certainly shaped my perspective.[3] However, I soon found its focus on the role which the newly created ethnic categories and the codification of 'customs' played in cementing (colonial) authority too one-sided to do justice to my multi-faceted material. Lonsdale's (1992) notion of 'moral ethnicity' – the idea that ethnicity creates a moral community, which defines civic virtues and organises the debate over the legitimacy of social differentiation – proved to be more fruitful, particularly for analysing the views of the educated elites and their relations with labour migrants and peasants. Ranger (1993) himself noted critically that the concept of 'invention' over-emphasised the mechanical and authorial, the European initiative, and the fictionality and rigidity of the created tradition. He suggested that a concept such as 'imagination' might do more justice to the complex long-term process of creating new, and rearranging older, elements of (ethnic) identification, in which many actors, diverse motives and a variety of interpretations are involved. In the same vein, Peel – with West

African cases boasting a long tradition of ethnic thinking in mind – has questioned one-sided instrumentalist explanations of ethnicity and convincingly emphasised the limits of its 'invention'. Unless ethnic ideologies make 'a genuine contact with people's actual experience, that is with history that happened', Peel argued, they are 'not likely to be effective' (1989: 200).

Currently the discussion is heading in the other direction, as Spear's recent critique of 'constructionists' shows. '[E]thnic concepts, processes and politics', Spear maintains, 'predated the imposition of colonial rule, developing in the context of conquest states, regional exchange networks, dispersion, migration and settlement and urbanization' and were merely transformed, but 'rarely created ... from scratch' by colonial authorities (2003: 24). But as important as it is to understand the *longue durée* of ethnic identifications in some African societies and regions, we must also pay attention to cases in which ethnicity played no significant role prior to colonialism. Segmentary societies such as those discussed in this book, for instance, were characterised by 'a distinctively relational mode of identification, self-understanding and social location, one that construe[d] the social world in terms of the degree and quality of connection among people rather than in terms of categories, groups, or boundaries' (Brubaker and Cooper 2000: 21–2). Here colonial ethnicisation really did produce new forms of classification and self-understanding which differed considerably from pre-colonial models of belonging.

This book, then, will explore both the colonial 'invention' of ethnic categories, by multiple actors and with diverse interests, and the embeddedness of these new constructs in pre-colonial modes of social positioning and belonging. As in most African languages, in Dagara or Sisala there is no word to correspond exactly to 'tribe' or 'ethnic group'. The rough translations local people make of the English terms thus provide an indication of the older models of identification and commonality to which the new discourses on ethnicity were linked – namely language, locality or kinship, though the ethnic groups defined on the basis of any one of these components never quite amounted to that unit which colonial officers called a 'tribe'. However, not only were local interpretations of ethnicity multi-faceted and contradictory, but so too were British (and French) colonial officials' notions regarding 'tribes' and the North-West's ethnic make-up, depending partly on the administrators' political leanings and partly on their specific interactions with Africans.

Four aspects of colonial 'ethnicisation' can be stated here summarily, which also fit the case of North-West Ghana.[4] First, ethnic re-categorisation usually took place in a context of social inequality, often, indeed – at least initially – as an instrument to stabilise (or provide new legitimation for) these inequities. Second, co-operation between colonial authorities and local cultural intermediaries, mostly chiefs and those educated in state and mission schools, interwove European with local models of belonging. In the process, new practices, symbols and histories were often introduced as 'tradition', while older elements were adapted and transformed through the codification into 'customary law' and other processes of formalisation in writing. However, although colonial ethnic categorisations *appeared* to be more rigid and standardised than pre-colonial modes of belonging, the reality was that these were subject to continuous debate and negotiation. The third aspect is the inculcation of these newly produced identities through everyday (administrative) practice so that they eventually appeared natural. Fourth and finally, the reasons that initially precipitate the creation of (new) ethnicities can differ from the reasons for which they continue to be meaningful. For example, ethnic categories and forms of self-understanding created in the colonial context, administered and perpetuated by chiefs, also provided labour migrants with a much-needed sense of security. In the post-colonial period they then became the idiom of political claims against the state (also giving rise to secession attempts and wars), and they were used to found moral communities, from which the legitimacy of social differences and norms of reciprocity were disputed.

The discovery of the 'complexity of African engagement with imported institutions and constructs' (Cooper 1994: 1534) and an understanding of colonialism as both political project and 'cultural encounter' between colonial administrators and African 'subjects', with profound effects on identity politics in the post-colonial world, have been important insights in recent studies on colonial rule (Pels 1997). It is in this vein that the present book discusses how North-Westerners appropriated the colonial constructs of 'tribe' and chiefdom, and how African strategies forced colonial administrators to reconsider and reshape their political projects. It explores the long-term continuities as well as changes in big-men strategies and local discourses legitimising authority and belonging. More specifically, it analyses conflicts over the relationship between land ownership and political authority, and over the indigenous practices of multi-locality and mobility which challenged British notions of clear-cut membership in a 'native state'. Contrary to British projects of making tribes and chiefdoms congruent administrative entities, there was, and still is, a good deal of tension between political and ethnic boundaries – and thus ample room for local actors to negotiate and contest their political allegiances.

British officers were well aware of this tension. Paradoxically, while they worked at 'village-ising' the landscape (by means of censuses, taxes and the establishment of village headmen) and consolidating larger chiefdoms, they gained deeper insights into indigenous institutions such as the earth-shrine areas which defied distinctly territorial colonial notions. Colonial admin-istrators did not generally prefer 'historical fiction to ethnographic facts', as

Sean Hawkins (2002: 119) asserts in his analysis of Lawra District's colonisation, but often knew an astonishing amount about their African districts. What did present a problem was converting this knowledge into administrative measures. Furthermore, colonial intelligence depended on African informants who, acting in their own interests, exerted a certain degree of control over the knowledge gained by colonial officials and so tried to influence administrative practice (Alexandre 1970, Pels 1996, Osborn 2003). African chiefs, migrants, Christian converts and peasants had their own agendas for which they either sought the support of their local district commissioner, or attempted to avoid his interference, depending on the situation.

The perspective followed in this book is thus actor-oriented and takes as its point of departure the 'non-self-evident nature' of the formation of power and domination in the colonial state, as Trutz von Trotha (1994) has formulated it. Or, as Stoler and Cooper (1997: 6) put it, colonial regimes were 'neither monolithic nor omnipotent', and African responses to them often had profound consequences for the concrete workings of colonial rule. Whether colonial rule in Lawra District can be considered 'conquest', as Hawkins (2002) suggests, and whether the British really intended to subjugate and 'appropriate' the local population, is debatable.[5] Instead, evidence indicates that, individual ambitious officers notwithstanding, the British generally pursued a minimalist project. On the whole, indigenous actors had much latitude to manipulate local affairs in their own interests. This book therefore aims at 'localising' and 'historicising' the colonial encounter (N. Thomas 1994: 3), and the period examined is intentionally set to encompass both the pre- and post-colonial era, in order to counteract the tendency to over-estimate the influence of British rule on the regional political landscape.[6]

The creation of new social categories and modes of belonging is always accompanied by a 'production of history' (Cohen 1989), and this is particularly true of ethnicity, because the argumentation relies particularly heavily on the imagination of historical continuities. This book therefore listens closely to conflicting voices and examines a number of historio-graphical genres, beginning with the recollections of lineage elders regarding migration, settlement and the colonial introduction of the chieftaincy to the colonial ethnographies and debates over tribal versus clan histories to the most recent works written by local intellectuals, who document their cultural work of ethnicity. However, the book also attempts to reconstruct the regional history of ethnicity and chieftaincy itself, because a presentist perspective alone cannot explain the power of historical arguments. The past, as Appadurai (1981) has succinctly argued, is not a 'limitless and plastic symbolic resource', and substantial convictions of what constitutes the past are not purely 'of the present'. A critical analysis of indigenous and colonial discourses and debates on chieftaincy, ethnicity and citizenship which argue historically presupposes some grasp of history 'as it happened'. It needs, as Trouillot put it in his critique of a radically constructivist perspective, a 'second narrative' (and a third, fourth, and so on) which can only exist because 'the historical process has some autonomy vis-à-vis the narrative' (1995: 15).[7] This reconstruction of 'the history' of ethnicity, chieftaincy and other forms of commonality, however, involves thorny methodological problems, in particular the fact that the various types of sources – written documents and oral narratives (mostly interviews I personally conducted) – are not available to the same extent for all periods.

For the pre-colonial period, we need to keep in mind that in the Black Volta region, as in many African societies, social and political boundaries, cultural categories and idioms of belonging, were only fixed in writing during the last decade of the nineteenth century, as an outgrowth of European 'ethnicisation' projects. The views of the pre-colonial past, which local interpreters, chiefs and elders worked out and which colonial officials, missionaries and African intellectuals recorded, often projected newly created ethnic categories and the chiefdoms onto the historical landscape. There are therefore few written documents dating from the pre-colonial period which can relativise such ethnicising historiographies.[8] Moreover, what we do learn about indigenous institutions and oral traditions from colonial documents is filtered through British perceptions, intentions and writing conventions. Recent oral traditions are also problematic, since it is precisely the pre-colonial past and early contacts with the 'white man' that are a popular field for the projection of present interests and the legitimation of political strategies. However, paying particular attention to the ruptures and contradictions in colonial 'tribal' historiographies and exploring the diverging clan and village histories which continue to exist alongside them, do offer some basis for the reconstruction of regional history.[9]

For the colonial period, there exists a wealth of documents for Lawra District written by colonial administrators and, after 1929, also by missionaries. The picture of local society painted by these sources is by no means one-dimensional. The authors' differing perspectives, as well as the motives that stimulated the production of these documents, resulted in different discourses. Thus, annual reports, various memoranda, intelligence reports and amateur ethnographies sketch a rather unified picture of the different 'tribes' and their respective languages, customs, characteristics and migration histories. The monthly and quarterly reports, letters and station diaries, however, testify to the contradictions and conflicts, arising from administrative practice. These documents show how local interests, practices and strategies deviated from administrators' preconceived notions. And, as Sara Berry has shown for colonial Asante, the processes of 'codification and proliferation of narratives about the past', particularly in the context of indirect rule, were 'simultaneous and contradictory'. They resulted neither in 'a master narrative of invented tradition nor a coherent counterhegemonic discourse, but [in] an ongoing process of historiographical debate, which defied contemporary efforts at administrative rationalization' (2001: 10). Nonetheless, although Africans decided what information to give and what to withhold from colonial officials (and missionaries), the latter – and not their African subjects – decided what should be recorded and what should be passed over in silence. Sometimes, historical 'facts' can be reconstructed because they were silenced in the written historiographies only; simply by reading between the lines in the archival sources we can glean alternative historiographies. At other times, the sources provide no clues and we can only make educated guesses about the possible contents of those gaps, such as when an event escaped all conventional categories or was regarded as unimportant.

Regarding the oral history of the colonial period, which can help break these silences, we are still confronted with the problem that present-day interests are projected onto the past. However, the inter-war period and time of post-war local government reforms are so recent that my older interlocutors experienced these developments personally. As a result, the amount of often contradictory information on particular events grows, painting a detailed picture of the actors and their interests, hopes and strategies. In the 1950s, the proportion of 'external' texts, written by Europeans, to oral histories, produced by Africans, was reversed. Moreover, we find an ever greater number of documents authored by chiefs and the educated elite themselves – ethnographic and historical treatises, literary texts and, of course, political and administrative documents (petitions, association by-laws, committee meeting minutes, etc.).

In a certain sense, then, over the course of a century a shift in discourse took place, from an 'outside' to an 'inner' view, a shift which entailed a change in the respective weight of oral and written, contemporary and retrospective sources. However, it is important not to equate such source-dependent 'changes in discourse' with 'changes of actor'. Just because we have more extensive knowledge of the ideologies, strategies and the decisions of particular actors, does not mean the latter also *de facto* dominated and controlled local events (and vice versa). Nevertheless, the increasing number of locally produced African texts does open up an extensive array of documents that allows us to examine the change in oral genres and new forms of self-representation under the influence of a written culture which compels people to embed their communities in a wider geographical and historical context.[10]

THE STRUCTURE OF THE BOOK

The following case study will be presented roughly in chronological order, beginning with the last third of the nineteenth century and covering developments up into the 1990s. The first chapter discusses the multi-layered, ambiguous and locally varied nature of political organisation in the North-West on the eve of colonisation, which was characterised not only by earth-shrine 'parishes' and geographically dispersed patriclans, but also by networks of power, developed by local 'strongmen' in alliance with, or in opposition to, Muslim warlords and slave traders. It is out of these networks, as well as upon the central principles of social belonging (the patriclan and the earth shrine) and the dynamic relationship between first-comers and late-comers, as cast by settlement histories, that the colonial constructions of chieftaincy and ethnicity were later fashioned. The following chapters deal mainly with the colonial transformation of this political landscape. Chapter 2 discusses the creation of the new administrative structures and chiefdoms, a process guided by colonial officials' a priori ideas regarding 'tribes' and 'native states', which, although at odds with local realities, did gradually transform them. The chapter also explores how the chieftaincy was subsequently appropriated locally and analyses the competing paradigms by which the new chiefs were legitimised, as well as the interplay between local 'strongmen's' strategies and British interventions. Chapter 3 focuses on the British production of an ethnic map and the colonial 'invention' of ethnic names, stereotypes and tribal histories. Discussing the changing conditions under which colonial knowledge was produced, it emphasises the fact that the British officers did not speak with one voice, and looks at the influence of African informants, interpreters and employees on British perceptions. The 1930s, the period studied in Chapter 4, constitutes a particularly important period which – through the introduction of 'indirect rule' and the establishment of the Lawra Confederacy – set the stage on which to this day local politics is played, not least because it was during this time that the foundations were laid for the formation of an educated elite which was imbued with this new loyalty to tribe and chief-dom. The chapter explores the contradictions inherent in British policies of indirect rule, and the conflicts surrounding the territorial reconfiguration of Lawra District, the introduction of taxation, and the codification of customary law. Labour migration (Chapter 5) and the Catholic mission (Chapter 6) fostered alternative ethnic communities circumscribed by boundaries that cross-cut those of the chiefdoms and constituted new arenas of debate over local cultural norms.

The second half of the book explores how chiefs and the educated elite in the post-war period appropriated and revised colonial ethnic and political boundaries. In Chapters 7 and 8, my main focus is on the 1950s and early 1960s, the period of important local government reforms and the early days of party politics. During this time, local conflicts merged with national politics, the effects of which can still be felt today. Virtually all present-day disputes over district boundaries, electoral constituencies, taxation and the links between political authority and allodial land titles are foreshadowed in disputes that took place in the 1930s and 1950s. Chapter 9 describes some of these recent debates by analysing the history of the Nandom Youth and Development Association and similar ethno-political associations in the region, which, although founded by the educated elite since the 1970s, labour migrants also support. The cultural work required for ethnicity to become effective and the activities that associations and their members initiate – activities that have a lasting impact on how people in the region think about this concept – is the focus of Chapter 10. This chapter looks particularly at the writings of and debates among Dagara intellectuals who re-evaluate the ethnic constructs produced by outsiders and discuss what 'Dagara culture' was and what it should be in the future.

1

THE NORTH-WEST IN THE NINETEENTH CENTURY

In the pre-colonial period, the dominant reality of the Black Volta region was the existence of small, relatively mobile groups of relatives, overlapping networks and flexible boundaries. There was no local ideology, let alone the social and political reality, corresponding to what British colonial administrators later represented as the ideal tribe, that is a population linked by descent, sharing a single language and culture, living in a particular territory and ruled by a council of elders or a chief. The 'house' (local kin group as well as supra-local clan) and the earth-shrine area were the cornerstones of local societies and are still meaningful today. They could integrate people of different dialects and languages, and required only some core elements of cultural similarity (recognition of the earth deity, the rights of first settlers, etc.).

However, because the region was never isolated from the greater political developments of the Niger Bend, there were also other types of social boundaries that extended beyond local community ideologies and began to resemble an 'ethnic' map. It is in this context that, for instance, the difference between Wala and Dagaba/Dagara must be understood. The distinction marked a religious and political boundary between Wa, as a centre of Islamic learning and state power, and the 'heathen', acephalous population of the surrounding area. When the British (and French) incorporated the Black Volta region into their empires and made their first tours of the area, they began to use these 'ethnic' names. It is this process of embedding colonial ethnic terms in older nomenclatures which made it seem that the newly delimited groups had historical depth; the continuity of names is thus easily (mis)taken for the continuity of communities themselves.

The ideas that colonial officers, anthropologists and local intellectuals held, and still hold, regarding the indigenous political organisation of the Dagara/Dagaba and their neighbours in the pre-colonial period oscillate between two opposing images: at the one end, that of a segmentary, egalitarian, more or less peaceful decentralised society, and at the other extreme that of peoples that came to develop their own chieftaincies at an early stage. The most prominent representative of the first view is Jack Goody, for whom the 'LoDagaa' are the paradigm of a segmentary society, still mostly untouched by colonial influences as late as the 1950s.[1] Sabelli, who is seeking a living anti-capitalist utopia, sees in the Dagara a 'communal society' which has successfully resisted the 'paradigm imposed by the market nation state' even well into the 1980s (1986: 190–2). For Hawkins, on the other hand, who recently declared the 'LoDagaa' once again a textbook example of an acephalous society, the 'colonial tyranny' of the chieftaincy and 'the monster of neo-traditionalism' marginalised authentic political structures long ago (1996: 217, 229). Conversely, Dagara supporters of the 'acephalousness' thesis, like Bozi Somé (1969), emphasise the continued absence of a political hierarchy, which they ascribe to the Dagara's unbroken love of freedom and age-old democratic traditions.[2] Whereas supporters of the second view, namely that Dagara and Sisala chieftaincies existed in pre-colonial times, were once to be found among a minority of colonial officers, today they comprise Ghanaian Dagara intellectuals in particular. The latter firmly distance themselves from the value judgements, which the 'acephalousness' thesis supposedly implies, concerning the primitive nature of chiefless societies. Some of these Dagara authors see the origins of the chieftaincy in defensive alliances against foreign aggressors, while others regard the division of labour between earth priests and secular leaders as being the primary impetus. Yet others have suggested that chieftaincy was introduced by immigrants from the ruling dynasties of neighbouring states (Dasah 1974; Der 1977, 2001; Tuurey 1982; Yelpaala 1983).

In any case, the question of the pre-colonial political organisation of the Dagara (and Sisala) has stimulated lively interest that extends far beyond the circles of the educated elite, not least because it makes possible a critical view of the political present in the idiom of the past, and provides the framework under which a desirable future can be sketched out (Lentz 2003a). In fact, however, large parts of the North-West in the nineteenth century were neither characterised by strict hierarchy with permanent chieftaincies, hereditary succession and ritualised office, nor by a completely acephalous type of polity, let alone an egalitarian one. Beyond the 'house' and the 'earth shrine', the two basic indigenous concepts of belonging, local people and powerful outsiders developed an intricate, flexible network of alliances and enmities between independent villages, individual 'strongmen' and, in the second half of the nineteenth century, Muslim warlords operating locally or supra-regionally. In this chapter, I shall examine this multi-layered pre-colonial political landscape, highlighting in particular the sources of identification and commonality as well as the bases of conflict to which the colonial construction of ethnicity and chieftaincy had to relate.

INDIGENOUS CONCEPTS OF BELONGING

In the absence of contemporary sources, how can we reconstruct pre-colonial local cultures and the nineteenth-century political landscape? One possibility is to turn to the ideas of social order as articulated in the indigenous languages. Although even these were subject to a continuous change in meaning, they are much older than ethnicising discourses in English and are indicative of different social practices. Thus, particularly with regard to the central notions of order – *yir* (house, patriclan) and *tèŋgán* (earth shrine) – it becomes apparent that social and socio-spatial boundaries were drawn differently depending on the context. Yet even within a given context, different interpretations competed with one another. This ambiguity and flexibility was, and continues to be, an important strategic resource.

Yir: *the house and the patriclan*

Yir means, to begin with, simply 'house' and refers to a single mud compound that usually consists of several *dìòŋ* (literally 'rooms') or *logr* (literally 'sides'), each with its own granary. Whoever shares such a granary farms in common, but may eat in different cooking groups. Residence, production and consumption groups overlap with one another without being congruent. *Yir*, however, can also refer to several neighbouring, agnatically linked compounds, in which case the term means 'family' or, more precisely, 'patrilineal kinship'.

Goody (1956, 1957) distinguishes between 'patrilineage', 'patriclan sector' and 'patriclan'. According to him, the patrilineage, consisting of neighbouring compounds whose male inhabitants trace themselves back two to four generations via the patriline to a common ancestor, makes all decisions concerning the inheritance of land and buildings, and constitutes the community that shares food during particular rituals or in an emergency. Neighbouring patrilineages form a 'patriclan sector' that co-operates on the occasion of burials, the *bàgr* initiation and sacrifices at the earth shrine. Patriclans, on the other hand, are territorially unbounded, exogamous descent groups that include all those who regard themselves patrilineally related, without being able to name an actual common ancestor, and who should in the event of a conflict lend one another mutual assistance.

The Dagara language does not differentiate between 'patriclan sector' and 'patrilineage', but operates only with the term *yir*, which is more widely or narrowly defined depending on the context of action. Thus kin who have settled in far-off places may belong to the same *yir* if on particular occasions they sacrifice at the ancestral shrine of the *yi-kpɛ̃ɛ́* (literally 'great house'), the house of origin. Conversely, a spatially nearby compound may be ignored if one's own relations with it are conflictual. Thus the term *yir* can be used to stress the spatial and local as well as the social components of kinship. However, not only patrikin are counted as *yirdèm* ('people of the house'): children of unmarried or divorced daughters, adopted children, guests, and formerly also household slaves were all included in this category, although they did not enjoy the same rights as the members of the narrower patrilineage.

Finally, *yir* can also be understood in the sense of 'patriclan', which can have thousands of members and may transcend linguistic and cultural boundaries. This level of meaning is particularly suitable when abroad and serves to create kinship relations with other migrants in situations where no members of the patrilineage in the narrow sense or matrilateral relatives are available. This capacity of the patriclan to create networks was of strategic significance in the pre-colonial period, when there was an extensive appropriation of land by the Dagara (Kuba and Lentz 2002). Later, in the context of colonial labour migration it became still more important, and kinship relations were claimed to exist even with non-Dagara groups, on the basis of similar taboos and totemic animals, as was the case with the Mossi or the Asante, or on the basis of joking relationships, as was the case with the Frafra or Karaboro.

Certainly practice does not always follow kinship ideology. In central fields of action such as agriculture, marriage, the raising of children and inheritance, the concept of the *yir* as a locally bounded kinship group continues to be relevant, with ancestors who can be named and who have the power to impose sanctions. On the other hand, in many practical affairs each member of the *yir* also resorts to networks that are not derived from the principle of patrilineal descent. In the Nandom and Lawra areas in particular, the mother's brother and sister's son play an important role in matters of inheritance and in many rituals.[3] The mother's patrilineage may be approached for aid, married women maintain close contact with their house of origin, while friendships also constitute an important element of one's personal networks. Although women are excluded from the dominant patriclan ideology, women and relationships made via women play a central role in such networks, as they belong to the patriclan of their father, but also have close ties to that of their husband.

Yir communities can thus be defined more narrowly or more widely, and they are embedded in multiple other social networks, or else are criss-crossed and eclipsed by them. For the present discussion, what is important is that they do not presuppose any linguistic or cultural homogeneity. For one thing, all neighbouring groups, like the Sisala or Birifor, have similar kinship structures. For another, the great mobility of settlements has led to a situation in which individual lineage segments have in the course of their migrations acquired new languages and adopted different cultural practices. As some colonial officers discovered as far back as the 1930s, some groups in the Lambussie Traditional Area, who speak Sisala and are regarded as

Sisala today, were formerly Dagaare-speakers who came from the area around Jirapa and Wa.[4] Even today, the memories of the shared origin of particular clans that have since split into Sisala and Dagara sections, of partly identical migration routes and of the adoption of a new language in the course of past migrations are fixed elements in many lineage traditions.[5] The concept of the *yir* therefore transcends ethnic boundaries.

Tèŋgán: *the earth shrine*

The institution of the *tèŋgán* is also characterised by integrative strength and flexibility. Goody (1956, 1957) translates this term as 'parish' or 'ritual area', because the earth shrine that stands at its centre consolidates the neighbourhood community through communal sacrifices. Generally, *tèŋ* means 'earth' or 'soil', but also refers to a settlement or even a whole region when used in connection with a specific name, such as 'Dagara land' (*Dagara tèŋ*). Yet *tèŋ* also entails a metaphysical meaning: thus the ancestors live in *kpímé tèŋ*, the land of the ancestors, and the *bàgr* myth contrasts *tèŋ* in the sense of the feminine, conception principle to the masculine, fertilising rain (Goody 1972). The word *tèŋgán* (plural *tèŋgáme*; literally 'skin of the earth') refers to the earth deity and the shrine at which sacrifices are performed, as well as to the territory controlled by this shrine and the earth deity. No sharp distinction is made between the earth as a material good and the earth as a spiritual being.[6]

All the land is subject to an earth shrine, which is administered by a *tèŋgánsòb* (plural *tèŋgándèm*; literally 'owner of the earth's skin').[7] Ideally the *tèŋgánsòb* ought to be a descendant of the first settler, who acquired this office through a pact with the earth deity or, in some cases, with the bush spirits (*kɔntɔmɛ*). Narratives relating the migration and settlement of the *tèŋgánsòb* lineage guarantee claims to the office and establish the genea-logical tie between office-holder and first settler. Yet in fact, many of these stories also report that although the individual alleged to be the first Dagara settler originally believed he was settling on uninhabited land, he soon discovered that others had settled there before him and had already set up a *tèŋgán*. In the Nandom area, the Sisala are frequently said to have been the first settlers from whom an earth shrine had to be acquired. These narratives go on to clarify how the new immigrants – sometimes peacefully, but sometimes only after violent conflicts – ultimately came to an agreement with the older settlers regarding sacrifices to the earth deity, the allocation of the spoils of the hunt and the rights over stray animals, in short: an agreement regarding the installation of a new *tèŋgán* and the nature of its relationship to the original shrine.[8]

Later Dagara immigrants had to seek out the new *tèŋgánsòb* in order to have land allocated to them, be awarded permission to build their houses and bury their dead. Land once allocated is under the control of the lineage concerned, which may pass it on to its descendants or yield it to outsiders or neighbours asking for land, either temporarily or for an extended period. However, what control the *tèngánsòb* has over the land after it has been divided among the lineages is disputed, especially in areas like Nandom and Lawra, which are characterised by an increasing land shortage.

Goody sees the significance of the *tèngándèm* above all in their role as guarantors of the earth's fertility and in their capacity to exercise social control. Before the colonial introduction of the chieftaincy, according to Goody, the *tèngánsòb* was 'virtually the only office outside the localised group of agnatic kinsmen' (1957: 79). Within the patrilineal descent group, anti-social behaviour was punished with sanctions imposed by the ancestors. Attacks on members of other patriclans, however, were not only not punishable, but were considered admirable deeds, kept in check only by the fear of violent revenge (ibid.: 94–6). However, the institution of the *tèngán* worked to countervail violent conflicts between patriclans, at least insofar as they lived in the same shrine area. Goody concludes that even in the absence of a central political authority the institutions of neighbourhood and descent, as ritually expressed in the earth cult and the ancestral cult, guaranteed some degree of peaceful co-existence (ibid.: 103).

The same narratives that legitimise the *tèngándèm*'s claim to the office also encode relationships between neighbouring shrines, which, as Goody states with reference to the Dagara, are characterised by historical relations of dependence and by a hierarchy of 'maximal ritual areas', 'major ritual areas' (*tèngánkpɛ̃ɛ́*) and 'minor ritual areas' (*tèngánbile*) (1956: 91–9). This hierarchy had, incidentally, been discovered already by the British District Commissioner Eyre-Smith (1933) in his search for indigenous bases for the indirect rule reforms of the 1930s.[9] According to Goody, the area of Lawra, Nandom and Lambussie is divided into two maximal ritual areas: Nyoor, stretching south of Nandom over the Kambaa River up to Eremon; and Kabir, which includes Lambussie and Nandom and extends to the west far beyond the Black Volta and to the north right up to the border with Burkina Faso. In the course of time, several *tèngan kpɛ̃ɛ́* ('major ritual areas') are said to have split off from the Kabir and Nyoor shrines and become the relevant units for their own sacrifices and loci of social control, eventually further sub-divided by the establishment of numerous *tèngánbile*.

However, the territorial expansion of Nyoor and Kabir and the hierarchies between various levels of shrines that Goody reconstructed are a matter of some controversy, not least because earth shrines are at the same time both territorial institutions and mobile medicine shrines. People came, and still do come, from far and wide to sacrifice at particularly powerful earth shrines, in hopes of being granted protection, healing and fertility. Sometimes, they take ritually 'charged' stones from the area around the earth shrine back home with them so that these may continue to serve them as personal or even village medicine shrines. Only under particular circumstances, however, such a village medicine shrine may be transformed into a (dependent) earth shrine. In any case, the dual nature of the *tèŋgáme* offered and still offers a wide variety of possibilities for the formation of cross-village alliances or, conversely, for secession.

Generally speaking, the installation of a new *tèŋgán* was a conflict-ridden process. Typically the *tèŋgánsòb* of the older shrine claimed to have given a shrine stone to the newcomers voluntarily and thus to have retained the right to a share of each animal sacrificed. The new *tèŋgánsòb*, on the other hand, often claimed that he was no longer bound by such obligations, because the older *tèŋgánsòb* neglected his duty of care. Dagara late-comers sometimes also turned to the neighbouring Sisala in order to acquire a shrine stone from them and thus free themselves from their dependence on the Dagara first-comers. The configuration between first-comers and late-comers was and is therefore relative and depended on the balance of power. Settlement histories might be re-interpreted in order to take proper ideological account of a new balance of power in the event that a lineage, which had arrived later, succeeded in appropriating the office of earth priest through military superiority or skilful kinship politics.

How were, and are, earth-shrine territories delineated in spatial terms? The only indigenous terms for 'boundary' are *turbogr* (Dagara) and *susubuo* (Sisala). These words literally refer to a 'continuous line of holes', i.e. a ditch, and designate the boundaries between fields. Fields owned by different lineages, and within lineages by different individuals, are usually marked off physically, by ditches, paths, shrub hedges or marks on trees. The nature of earth-shrine parish 'boundaries', however, is more difficult to define, and the local population rarely uses the terms *turbogr* or *susubuo* when speaking of these boundaries. The earth shrine was, and still is, perceived not as a flat homogenous territory, but as a field of ritual power. The bush was a zone of contact rather than separation, and earth-shrine borders were not imagined as linear boundaries but as a series of 'meeting points' in the bush (*tuoritaa-zie*) marked by hills, rivers, rocks, ponds or specific trees. As more and more bush was cultivated, the boundaries between earth-shrine parishes had to be defined more precisely. In the border zones, the ritual allegiance and village membership of houses and fields were usually defined according to which earth priest had originally given permission to cultivate or build. This process continues up to the present under the pressure of increasing population.[10]

The boundaries between the earth-shrine areas were and are negotiable. The *tèŋgán* is therefore not only an institution that regulates neighbourly relations, but also adapts to new neighbourhood relationships that are born out of the mobility of the patrilineages. The British commissioner of the Northern Province of the Northern Territories of the Gold Coast discovered how complicated this could make ascertaining which houses and farms territorially belonged to particular *tèŋgán* areas when, in 1928, as part of the preparations for the reform of the native administration, he wanted to know, 'what were the Tribal Administrative Areas at the time of the advent of the European'. He instructed his district commissioners to draw up precise maps of the *tèŋgán* areas, with 'lines showing the boundaries between the areas controlled by the different Tindanas', but at the same time suspected that this would probably not be an easy task.[11] At least for Lawra District, no such map was ever drawn up, nor has it been to this day.

It was not only the fluidity of the boundaries but also the flexibility of the earth-shrine hierarchy that presented a challenge to the colonial officers in their attempts to create a clear territorial order. In the pre-colonial period for what was later to become Lawra District, there were no permanent territorial units that extended beyond the boundaries of the *tèŋgánkpèé* areas. The native states set up by the British, on the other hand, usually included several earth-shrine parishes or else divided a *tèŋgán* area between two chieftaincies. We shall discuss the conflict-ridden process of adaptation between the new and the old territorial orders in the following chapters.

DRAWING SOCIAL BOUNDARIES

Both forms of social belonging and control, *yir* and *tèŋgán*, were and are still to be found throughout the whole Black Volta region in similar manifestations, creating integrative institutions that cross cultural and linguistic boundaries. A *tèŋgán* is capable of integrating a population that speaks different dialects or languages. The mobility induced by land shortages or local conflicts resulted in migrating groups of kin or friends adopting a second language and new cultural practices in their new home, without giving up membership of their original patriclan. However, the new neighbourhood did not always effect cultural adjustment, nor was this really necessary so long as all shared a set of core beliefs (recognition of the earth deity, the rights of first settlers, etc.). Language and culture (in the narrow sense), in European thought the conceptual pillars of ethnic and national community, only played a limited role in the organisation of neighbourly relations and supra-local social belonging.

This becomes evident through the various terms which mark, according to context, the boundary between 'us' and 'them'. Terms for outsiders reflect the two principles of belonging, namely the sacrificial community of an earth shrine and the kin group. Local and kinship criteria of belonging may reinforce each other, constituting a graded, flexible scale of otherness. The Dagara word *saan*, for instance, means both guest and outsider. Even a relative from another village is at first treated as a *saan*, when he arrives. If he stays, he may then gradually become integrated and join the people of the house (*yirdèm*). A non-relative remains a *saan* in the host's house while in the village he gradually comes to be acknowledged as a member of the house and is no longer seen as an outsider. Many proverbs refer to the dangers as well as rewards involved in dealing with the *saan* and the fact that he does not have complete participatory rights in his new home.[12] Anyone who is not a guest, relative or friend of a particular household is referred to as *zaglɛ*, one who is not allowed to interfere. The same goes for a *nvɔra* (literally, 'to push, stick something in'), an adopted member of the family or a slave, who might nonetheless in due time be integrated into the household. Kin who have remained in the original home describe the family's labour migrants as *mvɔpvɔ nıbɛ* or 'bush people', a reference to the difference between the house (and earth-shrine parish) as domesticated nature and the wilderness. Strangers from 'outside' the village, or sometimes even neighbouring groups, are also occasionally called *mvɔpvɔ nıbɛ*, and thus classified as belonging to the non-domesticated wilderness. In any case, *zaglɛ*, *nvɔra* and *mvɔpvɔ nıbɛ* describe social, not necessarily either cultural or linguistic distance.

There are no separate local terms for the configurations of 'first-comers' and 'late-comers' or, as the British would later put it, 'natives' and 'strangers'. In Dagara, as in Sisala, the term *tèŋgándèm* can be used for all first settlers, including the earth-priestly lineage and its closest allies. If the families who settled earlier wish to distinguish themselves from those who in-migrated later, they describe themselves as *tengdem* (owners of the village) or *tengbiir* (children of the land). The 'late-comers' are sometimes described as *saame*, guests or outsiders. In other contexts, however, as when they have finally become integrated into the village's sacrificial community, they are counted as *tengbiir*. Settlers who do not take part in the sacrifices at the earth shrine are always referred to as *saame*. Essentially, however, the integration of migrants was desired, provided they respect the rights of the older settlers.

It should be stressed that the boundaries between 'us' and 'them' were, and continue to be, relative and context-dependent. Language becomes a criterion of distinction in only a few contexts. My informants often translated the English word 'tribe' as *m-bvvrı* (literally 'different types of people') and distinguished the Dagara from the *m-bvh*, literally 'those who stammer or stutter and do not know Dagara' – a general term for 'others' that is found among many groups in the region. Unlike the term *saan*, however, *m-bvh* does not imply any sort of social relationship. Very often it has a negative ring, but does not entail imperatives for dealing with people in this category.

Group labels like 'Dagaba', 'Grunshi' and 'Lobi' which were later taken up by the British and French administrators as ethnonyms were probably originally terms that Muslim scholars, merchants and warriors coined for the non-Muslim population of the region. At any rate, these names, even if they represented local self-designations, were re-interpreted from the perspective of political, religious and economic centres, and began to connote lack of civilisation, political anarchy and nakedness – connotations the colonial masters subsequently adopted. Of these, nakedness was the most visible sign distinguishing infidels from Muslims, which is why Binger, Ferguson and other early commentators on the region inevitably listed this as the first characteristic of the 'barbarous tribes'.[13] This is especially clear from the various colonial explications of the etymology of 'Grunshi'. In 1908 Captain Read reported that Zaberma troops had introduced this name for 'fetish worshippers' into the region they had raided, a derivative of the Sonrai word *grunga*, 'fetish'.[14] District Commissioner Blair later traced 'Grunshi' back to 'Girousi', a Mossi and Dagomba term supposedly meaning 'wearers of leaves'.[15] The government anthropologist Rattray, finally, explained 'Gurinse' to be the Dagbani word for 'foolish ones' and 'bush men' (1932: 398).[16] Similarly, the name 'Lobi' probably arose as a term used by the ruler of Kong and by the Dyula merchants for those gold-mining populations along the Black Volta that they never succeeded in controlling.[17] The term 'Dagaba', as opposed to 'Wala', also connoted the dichotomies bush–civilisation and infidel–Muslim.[18]

However, these collective names, shaped by or at least re-defined by outsiders, hardly corresponded to a large-scale collective self-awareness as Sisala, Dagaba or Dagara comparable to the identities with which these names are associated today. Neither the 'strongmen' networks discussed below nor slavery ceased at ethnic boundaries. Yet the population certainly did develop a sense of belonging to larger communities, beyond the narrow confines of the patriclan and local village. Mobility with respect to settlement and marriage ensured inter-ethnic encounters, while regional markets, burial rites and initiation cults also exposed people to cultural, linguistic and socio-political differences. Particularly in frontier areas where new settlers competed with established first-comers over land ownership and ritual control, community ideologies could develop ethnic overtones if the boundary between first-comers and late-comers coincided with linguistic difference.

This is also reflected in the collective names used locally to refer to neighbours. Sisala are usually called *laŋme* by the Dagara, literally 'people who unite, huddle together, remain together'. This was sometimes explained as a non-judgemental reference to the rather compact building style of Sisala villages that presents a stark contrast to the scattered settlements of the Dagara. On other occasions it was viewed as describing the cowardice of the Sisala who were said to have withdrawn in fear from the onslaught of the slave raiders and the Dagara. In turn, the Sisala often describe the Dagara as *kyielo*, 'eagles', which is also open to several interpretations. From the Sisala perspective this is a reference to the mobility and restlessness of the Dagara, who are immigrants to their area, while from the Dagara perspective it is a reference to their warlike qualities.

It is difficult to reconstruct whether these early conflicts over land did actually mobilise an ethnic solidarity that transcended clans and villages, as many of my informants claimed, or whether this is just a projection of present-day ideas of ethnicity. In any case, ethnic boundaries were permeable, and cultural exchange, assimilation and linguistic flexibility were all more important than the emphasis on difference. We should probably think of pre-colonial ethnicity in the segmentary societies of the Black Volta region as a kind of decentralised sense of unity, nourished by extended kinship networks and clan alliances, and by intersecting and overlapping migration routes. This decentralised and fragmented ethnic consciousness was heightened in frontier areas, zones of encounter between groups that spoke different languages, had different kin networks and followed different migration routes. We should bear in mind, however, that this ethnic consciousness did not at all preclude 'intra-ethnic' feuds, which were as frequent or even more frequent than inter-ethnic conflicts. Also, religion was probably more important than ethnicity when it came to drawing social and political boundaries, particularly when Muslim founders of states and slave raiders declared the *jihad* against 'infidels' in the second half of the nineteenth century.

MUSLIM WARLORDS AND LOCAL STRONGMEN

In pre-colonial times, and in some areas well into the colonial period, the Black Volta region was an 'internal frontier', to use Kopytoff's (1989) term, a politically open area into which frontiersmen of diverse origins moved to found new settlements. From the perspective of neighbouring African states, namely the Mossi, Dagomba and Wala polities, the region was a 'frontier of separation' or 'buffer zone' (Asiwaju 1983) in which the ruling elites of these states occasionally undertook forays for slaves and booty.[19] However, from the perspective of the in-migrating frontiersmen, whose mobility was promoted by these slave-raiding activities as well as by the dynamics of shifting cultivation, it was a zone of contact between different groups of (im)migrants, and a zone of transition between more densely populated farmlands and sparsely inhabited savannah bush land.

During the past 200 or 300 years, or even longer, Dagara-speaking groups have been the most successful frontiersmen in the region. Probably setting out from what is currently the southern parts of North-Western Ghana,[20] small groups of hunters and farmers migrated in a northerly direction, some then turning westwards, across the Black Volta, others remaining east of the Volta and continuing northwards, and yet others crossing the river more than once. The Dagara migrants rarely entered unpopulated, 'empty' territory; instead they tended to settle close to, and eventually displace, Sisala-, Dyane-, Phuie- and Bwamu-speaking groups, who moved further west and north (Dyan, Phuo and Bwaba) or north-east

(Sisala). Violence certainly played a role in the territorial expansion, but so did specific strategies for the ritual appropriation of new territories. The Dagara system of *tèŋgáme*, discussed above, with its characteristic fission of existing shrines and networks of interconnected shrines, supported mobility and helped the migrants bring new territories under their ritual control. The other decisive factor in Dagara expansion was their ability to draw on a wide range of networks, including patriclans, matriclans, clan alliances and institutionalised friendships, in order to mobilise followers. This was a crucial asset for the security of the newly founded settlements and the territorial encroachment onto Phuo and Sisala land (Kuba and Lentz 2002).

In the following section (see pp. 26–32), however, the focus is not the dynamics of this appropriation of land, which lasted into the twentieth century, but rather the transformation of the regional political landscape through the incursions of Muslim warlords in the second half of the nineteenth century. These external developments had far-reaching consequences for local power relations and in many places facilitated the colonial introduction of the chieftaincy. As followers of warlords or successful organisers of the resistance against the Muslim cavalry, local strongmen obtained wealth and power, as reported by the emissary of the British crown, G. E. Ferguson, after his travels through the Gold Coast hinterland in 1892 and 1894 (Arhin 1974: 100). These strongmen created alliances between villages that later became the building blocks of the new paramount chiefdoms. Such alliances with, or in opposition to, the Muslim warlords deepened old lines of conflict both within and between villages. Moreover, easier access to weapons led to ever more conflicts being resolved through violence.

The increased levels of violence also affected settlement dynamics. In the past, the Phuo and Sisala used to opt for 'exit', moving further afield into virtually uninhabited land, when cohabitation with the in-migrating Dagara became difficult. These 'exit options' were now being severely restricted by the Zaberma slave raiders, who had established their headquarters in the region of Leo, and by the incursions of warlords from Ouahabou under the leadership of the Karantao. On the whole, the Dagara seem to have been less affected by the attacks of the Muslim warriors because the Phuo and Sisala settlements served as a kind of buffer zone between them and these mounted raiders. They could therefore devote more energy to the appropriation of land. Particularly towards the end of the nineteenth century, violent disputes with the Sisala and Phuo over land ownership appear to have become more frequent. These conflicts probably sharpened both parties' awareness of 'ethnic' boundaries, an awareness on which the colonial construction of ethnicity could build.

Babatu and Samori in the 'country of Dagarti'

As Ivor Wilks has argued (1989), the relationship of Wala Muslims to their non-believing Dagara neighbours was shaped, during a long period, by the principle of peaceful co-existence, which the dominant Suwari tradition in Wa prescribed. In the mid-nineteenth century, however, following a pilgrimage to Mecca, Mahamudu Karantao of Boromo in the Black Volta region declared a *jihad*, which some Wala groups joined (Levtzion 1968: 147–54). Wa had become involved in the conflict over the succession in Gonja and summoned the Asante army for military assistance, a service for which it had to pay in slaves. For many Wala, therefore, the *jihad* declared by Karantao, and later by the Zamberma, provided a welcome justification for attacks on Dagaba villages.

Wa had formerly been an agricultural town and a centre of Islamic learning. Only from the mid-nineteenth century, through slave raiding and the slave trade, did it become significant as a market and a staging post on the long-distance trade route from Kumasi to both Timbuktu and Hausa country, as reported by the French Captain Louis Binger (1892) and the British representative Ferguson. The demand for food created by Muslim troops and trade caravans allowed commercial agriculture to flourish. Thus, slaves were not only delivered to Asante and other interested parties in the South, they were also put to use in agriculture and trade by Wala entrepreneurs.

In the 1870s, Wa's commercial upswing and the transformation of its relationships with the 'infidel' Dagaba and Sisala were accelerated by trade links with the Zaberma. The first groups of Muslim Zaberma probably arrived in the Dagomba kingdom as horse-traders around 1860 from the area to the east of the Niger bend. Later the Dagomba hired them as mercenaries in order to capture the slaves that the Dagomba owed the Asantehene. Around 1870, the Zaberma began slaving on their own account, ultimately making Kasana, and later Sati (in present-day Burkina Faso), their headquarters. From there, under the leadership of Alfa Gazari and finally under his successor Babatu, they 'conquered' the area between the Black and White Voltas, from Wa to just outside of Boromo. Villages that did not pay any protection money in the form of cattle, cowries and slaves were mercilessly ransacked.[21]

Because the Wa Na no longer provided them with effective protection against attack, the Dagaba settlements rebelled against his rule, severely defeating the Wala troops. The Wa Na finally asked Babatu for military support. However, by the end of the 1880s the latter's troops had sub-jugated not only Issa, Wogu, Busie, Sabuli and other Dagaba settlements in the surroundings of Wa, but even Wa itself, probably because it refused to make the promised remunerations.[22] Babatu made Wa his headquarters for a short time, but then returned to Sati after losing a battle against the

Dagaba of Sankana. In Sati, however, he was soon confronted with an uprising of villages and commanders in the Sisala area, or 'Grunshi', as the British and French called it.

In 1896, two years after concluding a treaty of friendship with the British and one year after signing a similar agreement with the French, the Wa Na finally summoned the assistance of Sofa troops stationed in Bole under Sarankye Mori against the rebellious Dagaba of Kaleo and neighbouring settlements. Like Babatu, however, the Sofa leader Sarankye Mori was not satisfied by his victory over the Dagaba, but eventually also strove to incorporate the North-West, including Wa, into the territory under his rule. He made Sankana his military headquarters and is said to have left minor garrisons in Busie, Nadawli, Issa, Wogu, Sabuli, Jirapa, Ulu and Lambussie, among other places.[23]

While Sarankye Mori was still trying to negotiate with Babatu and Amariya, one of the 'Grunshi' rebels, a French troop under Voulet and Chanoine marched from Ouagadougou to Dasima in September 1896, concluded a defensive agreement with Amariya, who styled himself 'King of Grunshi', and demanded the withdrawal of the Sofa troops. Sarankye Mori, leaving only a governor in Wa, withdrew in December 1896 with his troops from Sankana to Bole and ultimately to Buna. Before that, however, he once again descended on the surrounding Dagaba settlements, together with Wala and Zaberma.[24]

By this time the British had already occupied the Asante kingdom and were seeking to extend their influence northwards, in order to put a stop to further French activities. To this end, a Hausa troop under the command of Lieutenant Henderson marched to Wa in January 1897, where a new agreement, this time a defensive treaty, was signed with the Wa Na and a British fort built. However, Henderson's attempt in April 1897 to expel Samori's governor from Wa provoked an armed conflict with the Sofa and finally ended with the British sustaining an inglorious defeat, their withdrawal from Wa, the death of Ferguson, who had accompanied Henderson, and Henderson's own capture by Sarankye Mori.

After Sarankye Mori's withdrawal from Sankana, Babatu's troops resumed their attacks on Dagaba villages. However, in March 1897 Amariya's troops, backed by French *tirailleurs*, succeeded in pushing Babatu back to Yagaba and finally Ducie, south-east of Wa. In June 1897 the French commander expelled Babatu from Ducie, signed a protection agreement with Wa Na Seidu Takora, and made himself at home in the latter's palace with an escort of two *tirailleurs*. But the British governor of the Gold Coast soon ordered Wa to be reconquered, and in October 1897, Captain Mackworth entered the town with one doctor, one officer, 50 soldiers, 10 Grunshi recruits, a machine gun and a rocket-launcher. In response, the French also strengthened their military presence. In November, further

British troops arrived, and they took the Wa Na into the British fort more or less by force, condemning him to a large fine for treason committed in the form of 'intrigues' with Samori and the French. Negotiations with Wala notables and treaties of protection with Dagaba settlements were intended to strengthen British influence in Wa and 'Dagarti'. For some months, both parties, the British and the French, put forward claims to the North-West, but a military test of strength was impeded at the highest political levels. The Anglo-French Convention of 14 June 1898 finally established the Black Volta and 11th degree of latitude as the new international border, thus deciding the conflict over Wa in favour of the British. However, it was only in September 1898, when Lt-Col Northcott, the first Commissioner and Commandant of the Northern Territories of the Gold Coast, ordered the removal of Wa Na Seidu Takora and had a chief more amenable to him installed, that the Wala and Dagaba realised that they were now subject to the British government.

The 'strongmen' of Lawra District

The area of the later Lawra District formed an internal frontier, as already mentioned, and was characterised by the mobility of small groups of kin. Whether the first Dagara-speaking groups had already settled in Nandom by the end of the seventeenth century, as Benedict Der claims (1989: 13), or whether this only came to pass at the beginning of the nineteenth century, as the British District Commissioner Eyre-Smith thought,[25] must remain an open question. In the course of the Mande migrations to Wa individual Muslim families, who now tend to call themselves Yeri or Yarsi, settled down in Jirapa, Zimuopere near Nandom and in some places west of the Volta.[26] However, such settlements, in the midst of a people engaged in predominantly hunting and subsistence agriculture, did not become bases for inter-regional trade before the second half of the nineteenth century. Stories like those of the Jirapa Naa, according to which the Yeri immigrants buried the Koran upon arriving at their new home, are indicative of cultural, religious and linguistic assimilation.[27] In any case, the 'long-established trade route, passing through Wa, Lawra then crossing the Volta at Menuo to Diébougou', mentioned by Goody (1956: 7), can hardly have existed before 1900. Only in 1903, when local feuds and attacks on caravans were making the trade route west of the Black Volta unsafe, did traders shift over a period of years to the easterly route from Wa to Bobo-Dioulasso, described by Goody.[28] To the north of Lawra, on the now highly frequented route through Nandom and Hamile, inter-regional trade only got going after the First World War. However, occasional peripatetic traders, who found shelter and protection on their travels with locally influential farming families, were already selling cloth, salt, kola nuts and ironware in the region before the turn of the century.[29]

Unlike in 'Dagarti', to which the Wa Na Seidu Takora laid claim in his negotiations with Ferguson, neither a hereditary chiefdom nor permanent cross-village political alliances developed in the settlements of the later Lawra District before the turn of the century, and the area never belonged to the Wala polity or any other state.[30] However, individual men managed to acquire a certain surplus, mostly in the form of cattle, through crafts, local trade and above all successful agriculture. Such powerful, influential men, referred to as kʋ́ɔrbɛ-nàà ('rich farmer', 'chief of farmers'), tuor-naa ('chief of the mortar') or tuor-kpɛ̃ɛ́ ('great mortar'), possessed large herds of cattle that enabled them to afford bridewealth for several women and therefore have more children. With many sons, they could in turn expand their agricultural activities, while through the bridewealth payments for their daughters they could further increase their herds. By taking over bride-wealth payments for poorer relatives or neighbours, they secured them-selves additional labour and loyalty. Merchants and other travellers found accommodation and protection with them, in exchange for presents or magical knowledge and amulets, which increased their hosts' reputation and influence.[31] However, the term 'strongmen', as used by the British negotiator Ferguson, or the term fàŋdèm (literally 'owner of strength'), that many of my informants mentioned, refers to yet another source of power and wealth: violence and the slave trade.

During drought or other crises, poorer families would approach richer houses for aid, sometimes handing over in exchange for food one of their own offspring as a gbàŋgbaar or 'slave', whose labour increased a strongman's wealth even further. In fact, although my informants always spoke of them by using the English word 'slaves', these were pawns rather than slaves in the strict sense.[32] However, such older local dependencies were commercialised in the context of the new regional slave-trade networks that arose in the second half of the nineteenth century. The local strongmen not only sold pawns to the Muslim traders, they also acquired slaves themselves via the market in exchange for cowries. At least two markets in the later Lawra District – Gegenkpe, near a ford over the Volta, and Tuopari, east of Nandom – were known as proper slave markets.[33] Male gbàŋgbaar worked in the fields of their masters, who cared for them and might later marry them off. Girls were adopted as daughters. Outwardly, the gbàŋgbaar, like their descendants today, were regarded as members of the house and the patriclan (in Lawra also the matriclan) of the master of the house. However, internally, slaves and their offspring did not and still do not have the same rights as other yirdèm. The difference was made apparent at burials and other internal family rituals, and they may become neither tèŋgándèm nor chiefs, though this is strongly disputed.[34]

In general, the prosperity and security of a house hinged on securing the largest possible following. In this respect, the acquisition of gbàŋgbaar was only one strategy among many. Another, much older strategy was the exploitation of all conceivable kinship links in order to attract more settlers. In many interviews it was reported that the first settler, the notorious hunter who once founded a new settlement in the thick of the forest, invited his brothers, and especially his sisters' sons, to settle in the area, in order to 'open up' the land and 'tame' or 'cool' the wild animals. However, the first-comers and *tèŋgándèm* were not necessarily 'strongmen' – relatives or friends who were summoned as alliance partners might become stronger than the first settlers. Besides agriculture and hunting, feuds were another important source of wealth and power. Many lineage narratives mention armed attacks by 'enemies' as a reason for migrating, though the extent and frequency of such clashes, which took place further back in the past, can only be an object of speculation. Some families may have fled from slave raids launched by groups from the Gonja and Mande states, which had become more numerous since the mid-eighteenth century. However, even back then there must have been perpetrators as well as victims. For example, one large Dagara patriclan, the Kusiele, is still known as a clan of warriors. The Kusiele seem to have acted as mercenaries for many different interests – for other Dagara settlers as well as regionally active slave raiders.[35]

A more reliable picture emerges for the final decades of the nineteenth century, when local feuds were closely tied to raids by Zaberma troops and slavery found its way deep into the internal social fabric. According to written sources, the first incursion of Zaberma troops into Lawra District took place under Alfa Gazari between 1870 and 1878 and focused on the settlements around Lambussie and possibly also around Nandom.[36] A second wave of looting is said to have hit the area around 1887, following Babatu's conquest and destruction of Wa.[37] It is not clear whether the Zaberma carried out smaller attacks between these two great raids, or whether they demanded regular tribute from the settlements they had defeated. However, what is relatively certain is that Lambussie at first paid tribute to Babatu and then, like other Sisala settlements, joined Amariya's rebellion against Babatu in the early 1890s.[38] In May or June 1896, after their victory over the Dagaba at Sankana, Sarankye Mori's troops, equipped with three thousand guns, finally pushed further north into the Lawra area – a move that, according to a Wala manuscript dating from the turn of the century, allowed the Sofa to capture 2,000 cows, 99 male slaves and countless women and children.[39] The raid undertaken jointly by the Wala, Sofa and Zaberma in December 1896 did not reach so far north, and even Babatu's last operation in early 1897 most likely only grazed the Lawra and Nandom area.

Many of my informants mentioned the fact that the *bɔŋ*, *zabog* or *zebag*, as the mounted Zaberma troops are called in Dagara,[40] raided their settlements more than once. Only a few of them could provide, or wanted to provide, a more precise account, and sometimes their descriptions indicated that what were said to be Zaberma cavalry were actually the first 'white' man with his troops, who appointed as chief that courageous fighter daring enough to remain in the village.[41] However, some interviews confirm those Zaberma campaigns which can be reconstructed from written sources. In Ko, south-east of Nandom, for example, there are accounts of three attacks: the first under Babatu; the second under Issaka, one of Babatu's commanders; and the third by the *ngmāākpaar*, the 'cutters of necks', as Samori's Sofa troops were usually known.[42] Apparently the *zebag* camped near Jirapa or Lambussie during their attacks. Lambussie itself, according to the earth priest Nansie Issifu Tomo, was never conquered by Babatu because Gbeliñu, who was later to become the first chief of Lambussie, had along with a friend joined Babatu's troops:

> They fought on his behalf and then came home and settled. And from that time onwards, any time Babatu came to Bussie [Lambussie], he notified Gbeliñu. Gbeliñu then looked for some small things, goats and food items. At that time, they were still enslaving people and they used to catch the people around those *kyielo* [Dagara] we were talking of, and then give them to Babatu as a bribe. They used to bring them here to Bussie and sell them. They used to pick about five slaves and give them to Babatu, as a thanksgiving, and then Babatu would go back.[43]

In the Sisala settlements of Billaw and Nabaala and the Dagaba villages of Karni, Han and Ulu, informants also reported that individual men who had been recruited by force later returned to their villages, together with the wives and slaves they had acquired during their travels.[44] Some of these mercenaries, like Boyon of Ulu or Sougoulé of Samoa, then became active on their own account as marauders and slave raiders. Sometimes such local mercenaries were referred to as *bòŋ gbɛbaalɛ* ('barefoot *bòŋ*'), and thus distinguished from the mounted Zaberma.[45]

Lawra, which Babatu is said to have tried to plunder three times, reacted differently. At the first sign of approaching Zaberma, women, children and the elderly were taken to safety in the thickly wooded hills on the other side of the Black Volta, while the men armed themselves for battle with bows and arrows:

> Our grandfathers described that first they were always aiming at the horse rider – Babatu was on horseback – but that was a difficult target. So later on they shot the horse first, then the poisoned horse fell quickly and the warrior with his sword couldn't do anything to the bowman. ... They retreated towards the river normally so that if the

battle was so hot, they could cross the river and go to the hills ... You
will find that a lot of those who partook in those Babatu wars wore the
red fez. If you killed a Babatu warrior you took the fez, took his turban
and his sword and cut off the horse's tail.[46]

A similar combination of flight and resistance was also reported to me in
Eremon, Dikpe, Tantuo, Nandom-Burutu and Ko.[47] In Lawra, however,
active resistance also seems to have been supplemented by the payment of a
tribute of 100,000 cowries, in order to avert further attacks.[48]

The reactions to Zaberma attacks, then, were spatially differentiated. In
the western Dagara settlements, flight and resistance were the dominant
responses, while in the eastern Sisala and Dagaba villages it was more
common for tribute to be paid and for individual men to be recruited by the
Zaberma, in some instances voluntarily and in others by force. Slaves were
captured and sold in both areas. Thanks to the Zaberma campaigns a new
market opened here, which may have aggravated local feuds and which was
used by those who had the requisite resources. For most of the inhabitants
of what was to become Lawra District, the attacks launched by the Zaberma
and the Sofa meant forced mobility, increased insecurity and serious losses
in stores, cattle and people. Yet for some they presented an opportunity to
increase their wealth and influence. Many of the strongmen mentioned
earlier, with their large compounds, well-secured with numerous archers,
became protectors for their neighbours and helped victims whose stores had
been looted. On the other hand, many also sold slaves to Muslim traders, in
exchange for weapons, horses and clothing.[49] They built up political
influence, which they were later able to institutionalise under British rule. In
many Dagara settlements it was those strong warriors opposed to Babatu,
and in Sisala villages often the former Zaberma mercenaries – with their
rudimentary knowledge of Hausa or Zabrama and their familiarity with the
world beyond the village – who after the turn of the century became the new
chiefs.

2

THE INTRODUCTION
OF CHIEFTAINCY

In October 1897, H. P. Northcott was appointed Commissioner and Commandant of the Northern Territories, with the task of controlling areas in the hinterland of the Gold Coast that were tied to Great Britain under treaties of friendship or protection. The Anglo-French Convention of 1898 delineated the territorial boundaries of the new protectorate, while the Northern Territories Order in Council of 1901 defined its legal status as formally independent protectorate, though at the same time subject to the Gold Coast Governor. The British had brought the Northern Territories under their control in order to prevent European rivals from establishing themselves along the trade routes from Kumasi to the north. However, neither the Colonial Office nor the Governor of the Gold Coast had a clear idea of what to do with this new appendage of the Gold Coast Colony, except that its administration should cost as little as possible. Northcott and his successors, Morris and Watherston, stated 'opening up the country and facilitating commercial intercourse' to be the main goal. This required the pacification of the region and the mobilisation of labour to carry goods and build roads. In the context of such plans, 'native chiefs' were to be the pillars of a 'scheme of government of the simplest and most economic form'.[1]

This chapter deals with the introduction of chieftaincy in the formerly chiefless societies of the North-West – a process guided by colonial officials' normative ideas of 'tribes' and 'native states', which deliberately denied local realities, while at the same time gradually transforming the latter so that they more closely resembled British expectations. The pre-colonial structures to which the new chiefdoms attached themselves differed from case to case. This question was also intensely debated on the spot, because the new chiefs as well as their competitors and opponents sought to support political claims by referring to pre-colonial traditions and to how the British set up the first chiefs. A typical model appears to have been the recruitment of the first chiefs from the local 'strongmen'. However, not everywhere did these first chiefs also belong to the earth priest's patrilineage, and even where they did, the offices of earth priest and chief were from the very beginning separate. The extent of the new chiefdoms was therefore defined not according to the borders of the earth-shrine areas, but in terms of the size of the kinship, friendship and clientele networks of the chiefs. Establishing the boundaries of the chiefdoms and recruiting effective chiefs was a matter of trial and error, whereby existing local power structures on the one hand and the British model of small, territorial states with an inheritable kingdom on the other were gradually made to correspond to each other. The successful introduction of rituals and symbols of rule and the lasting transformation of the physical infrastructure contributed to the stability of the new political order. Yet, during the first decades of colonial rule, the head chiefs controlled personal networks but no territory, a reality that did not fit the British model. Their 'area' of rule was defined by lists of sub-chiefs and villages subordinate to them. Only with the introduction of a poll tax and the creation of a native treasury in the 1930s, did rule and political belonging become more territorialised, and only then did it become important for the political subordination of each compound to be clearly fixed – a development harbouring new potential for conflict which I will discuss in Chapter 4.

The history of the introduction of the chieftaincy was marked by tactical jockeying between outright resistance, avoidance (fleeing across the international border or to a neighbouring district), acceptance, as well as the active appropriation of new institutions. Ordinary peasants often tried to avoid *corvée* labour and other obligations imposed by the colonial regime and its local agents, the chiefs. Yet at the same time they also took advantage of some of these newly introduced institutions, particularly the chiefs' courts and the right of appeal to the district commissioner, in order to pursue their own interests. Chiefs served as intermediaries between individual compounds and the colonial regime – a role they sometimes exercised for their subjects' benefit and sometimes for their own personal gain. In any event, the older forms of organisation, the patriclan and the earth-shrine parish, were too vague or too exclusive and small in scale to play such an intermediary role effectively. In addition, the adoption of the chieftaincy allowed some groups from the North-West to achieve a certain degree of 'progress' in the colonial context. Whereas earlier members of these stateless societies had been stigmatised as uncivilised or anarchic, often regarded merely as booty for slave-raiders, they were now integrated as equals in the native states of the Northern Territories, at least in principle. Thus, the new political structures, rituals and discourses were attractive not only to chiefs, but also to migrant workers and the first generation of educated elites, who sought the same status and respect as colleagues and fellow pupils from pre-colonial kingdoms.

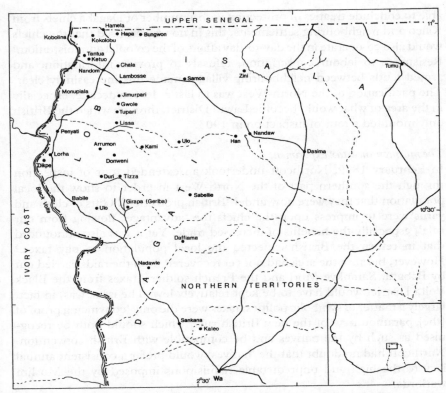

Map 2 North-Western District of the Northern Territories of the Gold Coast, 1905
Source: PRO, CO 1047, Gold Coast 425

THE COLONIAL PACIFICATION OF THE NORTH-WEST

The Native Administrative Ordinance of 1902 stipulated that while the British were to have direct control over prisons, roads, ferries, markets, abattoirs and taxes, most other matters were to be the responsibility of native tribunals chaired by the chiefs, provided they issued no decrees that were 'repugnant to natural justice' and did not resort to any 'barbarous or inhuman method' in enforcing their decisions.[2] However, native chiefs would only provide the desired 'government of the most economic form' if they co-operated with colonial officers and managed, with the aid of loyal sub-chiefs, to effectively control large areas. In this regard, the North-West posed the same problem for the British as it did for the Wala, Zaberma and Sofa: the insubordination of Dagaba settlements once subject to the Wa Na, not to mention the 'outlying districts of Dagarti' further north, which had always been independent of Wa and from which complaints of 'looting, seizing cattle and even murder' often reached Wa.[3] Although Northcott was

able to conclude treaties of protection with a number of Dagaba chiefs from
Kaleo and neighbouring settlements, this in no way ensured that the chiefs
would also co-operate in the day-to-day affairs of the colonial administration.[4]
Resistance to labour conscription, refusals to provide information, and
armed feuds between neighbouring villages made this increasingly clear.
The pacification of the North-West was to last at least a decade, especially
in the area of what would become Lawra District, through which the British
only mounted a tour of inspection in 1903.

The maintenance-tax experiment

In February 1899, Northcott undertook an extended tour of inspection
through the southern part of the North-West in order to show the local
population that they were now under 'British protection'. Gifts of cloth and
yarns were to impress upon the chiefs the 'advantages flowing from our
rule', especially the benefits of increased trade. Yet it was also announced
that in return the British expected the local population to pay taxes.[5]
However, because the area had not yet recovered from the raids carried out
by Babatu, Sarankye Mori and the French soldiers, taxes from the Black
Volta District would have to be kept relatively low. The issue was, in fact,
largely a matter of symbolic politics: taxes were the only 'convincing proof of
[the] paramountcy' of the new British rule, which should both be recognised as such by the natives and be compatible with British convention.
Northcott had no doubt that the 'natives' would prefer a consistent annual
levy to the high and unpredictable requisitions imposed by the Muslim
warlords.[6]

Was the maintenance tax really legitimate, or did it remain entirely alien,
especially to the 'Dagarti' and 'Grunshi', who were averse to any 'central
form of government'? This was the subject of a controversy that blew up
between Northcott's successor, Morris, and the governor of the Gold
Coast. Ultimately, the debate ended in the tax's abolition, having been
actually levied only twice, in 1900 and 1901. As the governor summed up,
the effort required to collect the tax and the political damage involved with
it, namely 'disaffection among the tribes', bore no relation to the modest
income it produced.[7] The most important argument against a tax, later
voiced by Chief Commissioner Irvine, throws a light *ex negativo* on British
notions regarding legitimate rule:

> [I]n the most densely populated parts of these Territories, namely ...
> Fra-Fra, Grunshi, Dagarti, and Lobi-Dagarti, there is no central form
> of Government, and up to the present little has been done to open up
> this part of the country. ... [I]t would be unfair to tax the natives of
> these districts ... until they have ... had an opportunity of seeing the
> benefits which accrued to them from the White man's rule.[8]

Irvine suggested that, instead of a poll or hut tax, the chiefs should provide 'free labour' to build and maintain government buildings and roads. The obligatory road work was later set at twenty-four days per year per adult male and retained until the poll tax was introduced in 1936.

The attempts to levy the maintenance tax made it clear how fragmentary British knowledge of local matters still was, particularly with respect to the Dagarti sub-district in the north of Black Volta District. For the sake of political stability, the census had not been carried out there.[9] District Commissioner Reynolds repeatedly discovered that the tax lists drawn up by his predecessors had no basis in reality. He received tax payments from the chiefs of places that were not even listed, while many listed settlements did not exist at all, or if they did, under different names. Thus, Reynolds was totally reliant on the support of 'Corporal Mama Dagatah', 'who knows the country around very well and has especially a large knowledge of nearly all the towns in Dagarti'.[10] Mama Dagarti – apparently a Dagaba who had fought with Zaberma or maybe Sofa troops, converted to Islam, finally settling in Lawra – became for the British one of the most important local informants and interpreters in these early years.[11] He may well have played a decisive role in shaping the British view of what would become Lawra District.

It is unclear how far north from Wa taxation penetrated.[12] In March 1901, Reynolds was still complaining that the Dagarti sub-district had as yet hardly paid any taxes. In the following months, however, many settlements seem to have heeded Reynolds' 'strong warning' and sent tax payments to Wa. The reports cited, among others, Karni, Oolu (Ulu), Sabulu (Sabuli), Lambusi (Lambussie), Mankuri, Douri (Duori), Hyan (Han), Tempala (Tampala?) and Tissah (Tizza), with Lambussie submitting the highest sum of more than £15, while most settlements only sent in £1 or £2.[13] It was primarily the eastern settlements, which had paid tribute to Babatu in earlier decades, that paid the maintenance tax. Settlements in the immediate vicinity of Lawra and Nandom, on the other hand, appear not to have been taxed at all. Thus, the manner in which taxes were submitted reflected the local political experiences of the prior decades. In any case, as the distance from Wa increased, so did the efforts required to collect tax payments, leaving Reynolds to state wearily that 'the Dagarti people are a very peculiar and difficult people to deal with. ... These people are very hard to "get at" as ... they recognize no big chiefs and consequently each compound is practically a law unto itself.'[14]

The first tour of inspection through 'Lobi country'
The idea that among the Dagarti and Lobi every compound was 'a law unto itself' – alternatively 'a small kingdom'[15] or 'a little republic unto itself',[16] depending on the political inclination of the correspondent – became

among the British a standard turn of phrase, as did the complaint that the
Lobi-Dagarti were 'a powerful turbulent people who for many years
plundered their more peaceful neighbours with impunity'.[17] Captain
Berthon, who took over the administration of Black Volta District in
December 1901, complained repeatedly of the 'very unquiet state of the
Natives in Dagarti'[18] and of attacks of robbery on merchants. Sometimes,
Dagarti or Grunshi messengers came to Wa to report attacks by
neighbouring settlements and to ask for British assistance. Berthon then
usually sent out an escort with orders to bring the guilty parties to Wa,
orders that were never successfully carried out. Instead, soldiers would open
fire on villagers that resisted, burn down huts and granaries, and confiscate
cattle, some of which would then be sold in Wa to fill government coffers,
the rest being returned to those who managed to pass themselves off as
victims most convincingly.[19]

Despite such punitive expeditions, the complaints regarding 'crime and
restlessness' in the 'outlying portions of Dagarti' did not cease.[20] Thus,
towards the end of 1903, Berthon was finally ordered to undertake a
'peaceful tour of inspection' through Dagarti and make recommendations
as to the best place to set up another British district station.[21] Even though
a number of settlements near the border had already been visited by
members of the Anglo-French Boundary Commission, for most of the
villages around Lambussie, Nandom, Lawra and Jirapa, the tour of
inspection of December 1903 by Berthon, who was accompanied by 100
soldiers with ample ammunition, was their first direct encounter with the
colonial regime. This tour, as well as a second one headed by Captain Read
in March 1905, served to lay the groundwork for further political
developments and the drawing of ethnic boundaries.

The first part of the journey, from Wa to Tumu via Funsi, and from there
to Dassima and Nandaw, apparently went off without incident. However,
Berthon then received news that the inhabitants of 'some Lobi compounds
in the vicinity of Nardaw' (Nandom) had attacked Lambussie and killed
eleven people.[22] Berthon camped the troops in Lambussie for two days and
sent messengers to 'Nardaw [Nandom], Chilla,[23] Gu [Guo], Nadowseri
[Nandomser] and Kokologu [Kokoligu] to tell the Chiefs and the Headmen
to come and palaver'. The first message was ignored. Only after a second
summons did 'messengers from Chilla' arrive at the British camp the
following day; 'none of the others came in'. The messengers were told to
fetch their chief, who then received orders to provide a guide so that
Berthon could hold a 'palaver' in Nandom. The guide came, but then ran
away as soon as the party had reached the first compounds just outside
Nandom. Berthon sent soldiers after him, but his escape was covered by
villagers armed with bows and arrows.

Berthon then rode with 25 soldiers as far as Tantuo, whose inhabitants, according to Berthon's report, attacked the troops with bows and arrows. Berthon's men shot back, but quickly broke off their pursuit, 'not wishing to engage these enterprising people on terms where the rifle comes down to being little superior to arrows'. Berthon counted at least three dead Lobi, but believed there to have been many more victims and reported that his men had confiscated all the cattle they could get hold of. Over the next two days there were many more skirmishes and many compounds were burnt down, until the troops finally reached Lawra. In Babile, south of Lawra, where Berthon wished to investigate a murder case, his troops killed at least four 'enemies' and confiscated at least 18 cows as well as over 100 sheep and goats. A reconnaissance mission to Janyea led by Sergeant Mama Dagarti, who also served as Berthon's interpreter, ended with at least seven more dead Lobi. Berthon only ceased resorting to violence on his way back to Wa via Tizza and Dafiama, 'through quite friendly people'. The Governor of the Gold Coast later accused Chief Commissioner Morris of conducting an operation that was 'rather a warlike and punitive expedition, than a peaceful tour of inspection'.[24]

The intensity of the resistance to his orders became Berthon's most important criterion in categorising the population. Summarising matters, he laid down what would be the British view of the 'Lobi' – who were now to be distinguished from the 'Dagarti' and 'Grunshi' – for a long time to come: 'I find the Dagartis as a rule quite friendly, also the Grunshis, but any part where the Lobis and Dagartis are mixed, the former seem invariably to be hostile.'[25] Yet 'Lobi-Dagarti' – another term, at once an ethnonym and a toponym, that was coined by Berthon and adopted by all his successors – was 'densely populated', 'extremely well stocked' and 'nearly wholly under cultivation', in brief 'undoubtedly the richest country in the district'. Apparently the fighting spirit of the local population also earned Berthon's respect, since he stressed that they were a 'very big and strongly built race', among whom it would be worthwhile recruiting troops.

This first tour of inspection contributed little to gaining a better understanding of the local political organisation. Berthon, whose report indulged in military details, harboured not the least doubt that chiefs existed everywhere. It did not occur to him that the chiefs and headmen he summoned in vain might not be obeying him, because there was no clear chain of command. However, Chief Commissioner Morris, who had to justify the excessive violence used on this tour to a very concerned governor, ascribed Berthon's problem, as well as all other administrative difficulties in Lobi-Dagarti District in the North-West and in Fra-Fra District in the North-East, to the fact 'that these countries practically possess no central form of government, as the power of the Kings is purely nominal.'[26]

Appointing head chiefs

Regardless of how little Berthon had grasped of the local political organ-isation, his tour produced some practical results. In any event, Captain Read, Berthon's successor, noted with satisfaction that Lobi country was peaceful and that merchants were travelling through it unmolested. In Dagarti the armed night watches were abolished, while in Grunshi many of the places that were destroyed by Babatu and Amariya had been rebuilt.[27] Even from Nandom there was happy news 'that they had rebuilt their village that was destroyed by Captain Berthon in Dec. 03 and were recognising one of the chiefs appointed by him at Chiriri as their ruler'.[28]

Yet as fresh reports of raids and attacks arrived, Read embarked on a second tour of inspection to Jirapa, Lambussie, Nandom, Lawra and Babile, with an escort of 36 Non-Commissioned Officers, a Maxim gun, 62 porters, a medical officer and two Wala Muslims, Malam Abdulai and Musa, as interpreters. During his two-week tour in March 1905, Read calculated that he had visited over 40 villages in 'Lobi' alone, met with messengers from a good number of additional villages, and contributed a great deal of new information regarding the position, ethnic composition, and customs and habits of villages in Lobi and Dagarti country. Indeed, on this tour of inspection, Read did lay the groundwork for the first accurate map of the North-Western District and collected data for a comprehensive ethnographic report that he was to complete in 1908.[29] Yet Read's primary concern was strengthening the local chiefs.

When Read summoned all 'Lobi chiefs and headmen' to a 'palaver', he was at first no more successful than Berthon had been. Initially only Kyiir and representatives from seven villages came. Only a second summons to the chiefs of all the villages within a ten-mile radius produced the desired result – memories of Berthon's punitive expedition must still have been quite vivid:

> Chief Cheiri [Kyiir] came in with headmen or representatives of 29 Lobi (a few Lobi-Dagarti) villages. ... Some 300 to 400 people were present and orders were given them as to their future good behaviour, obedience to chiefs, roads, markets and prohibition of carrying arms to markets. All these villages, which included nearly every village in the northern part of Lobi, expressed their willingness to serve under Cheiri and he was according appointed head chief of all that district.[30]

In order to strengthen visibly the authority of Kyiir, who had just been appointed head chief, Read had a fine of £10 (as usual in the form of cattle) imposed on the inhabitants of Monyupele, from where the alleged perpetrators of the murder of a Wala merchant had fled to French territory, 'for resisting with arms the chief of Cheriri when he sent to enquire into this murder'.[31] In Lawra, only seventeen Lobi villages sent representatives to the usual palaver, at which they were reminded to recognise 'Chief Daka of Lorha' as head chief – not a very satisfactory outcome, Read was to discover, 'as the villages are very numerous around Lorha'.[32]

One year later, Chief Commissioner Watherston too tried to induce the chiefs to join together to form larger units and recognise the authority of their 'head chiefs', 'paramount chiefs' or 'kings' (the terminology continued to be variable all the way into the 1920s). Yet local strategies to restrict the accumulation of power, like witchcraft or poisonings, greatly limited political centralisation. Lambussie, which was supposedly controlled by a 'big Paramount Chief', is a good example of this. According to Watherston, Lambussie was once a large town, but poisonings by unknown assailants or 'some powerful fetish at work' were said to have provoked the flight of most inhabitants into the bush. The 'King of Lambussie's' compound was reported to be in a sorry state. Only in Bangwon – a settlement bordering on the French colony that should actually have been subject to Lambussie but tended to turn to French Hamile instead – did Watherston finally succeed in assembling the Lambussie sub-chiefs:

> [I] induced them to return to their allegiance to their paramount Chief on the ground that with big chiefs like Nandom, Lorha and Samoa round them I could only look on them as small people unless they combined to form a similar state. This they agreed to but said that these sudden deaths had broken up the country coupled with the removal of the richest man in Lambussie to Samoa country. This man we afterwards found had removed because being so rich he feared that the people would kill him, and apparently with reason as four men had died in his compound in a month from poison.[33]

In the first years of British rule, reports of success concerning the new 'native states', as the areas under the control of a head chief were called, alternated with complaints about the head chiefs' limited authority. For example, after his tour of inspection, Watherston pronounced himself satisfied that all the important chiefs in Lobi-Dagarti had 'agreed to re-organise themselves under their old paramount chiefs, instead of living, as they were, in independence and constant warfare with one another'.[34] Read, too, reported having made great strides in establishing the 'boundaries of head chiefs'.[35] Yet, a short while later, he received a disappointing report regarding the inability of the 'King of Lambussie' to get things done.[36] Reports concerning Kyiir, the head chief of Nandom, were also contra-dictory. He was reported to be a 'chief of intelligence', a 'strong man' and a 'popular chief who has complete control over some 34 towns of various sizes'.[37] However, only a few months later Read had to intervene in order to secure the 'King' of Nandom's authority. When he wanted to know why the road between Lambussie and Tuopare had not been cleared of grass, the inhabitants of Tuopare replied

> that they had no chief and the chief denied himself though pointed out to me as such by the King of Nandom. They denied having received summons to Nandom, or any orders to clear the road. ... I told them to nominate a chief, [but] they were unwilling to do so. I then asked the King of Nandom to select one of the inhabitants whom he could vouch for as likely to make a strong and intelligent chief. He selected one Doyaga whom, none dissenting, I appointed chief, instructing him in his duties, and warning the people that punishment would follow disobedience of his orders.[38]

In other settlements too, Read had to install new chiefs, as in Gegenkpe, whose chief 'had trouble with his people and then crossed into French [territory]'. In some places, Read was faced with obstruction from 'fetish priests', as well as with 'witchcraft', as was the case in Guo, on the road to Tuopare, where by chance he surprised the 'fetish priest and his satellites' preparing a 'fetish' in order to prevent him entering the village. With the aid of the new chief of Tuopare, Read managed to arrest the 'fetish priest' and

> after holding up the Fetish Priest to ridicule I told the people he could no longer be allowed to act as chief and told them to appoint another man. I again had to resort to the King of Nandom who selected one Gado ... The two new chiefs [of Tuopare and Guo] are sensible, well dressed and intelligent men, both speak Hausa. I informed the two villages that for their former disobedience and stupidity they must pay a fine of ten pounds.[39]

Summing up Read's and other commissioners' reports, Watherston complained about the lack of 'any really big chiefs' and the 'absolute imbecility of 60 per cent of the present elected chiefs', who had been

> selected as a rule for their incapacity to make anyone obey them. Partial blindness, paralysis, and often idiocy appear to have been the qualifications in many parts of the country, the only *sine qua non* being that the chief should have plenty of cattle, as on him falls the privilege of paying any fines that the Commissioner might impose on the town.[40]

Even in the years that followed, it was repeatedly made apparent that the head chiefs' authority was not as uncontested as colonial officers would have liked to believe. For one, the variable assessments of the new chiefs were indicative of local differences in the pre-colonial political situation and of the different strategies of coping with colonial innovations. 'Strongmen' like Kyiir were not to be found everywhere, or else they demonstrated little skill in using their influence, provoking instead local opposition. For another, the British refused to acknowledge local political institutions. For example, the 'fetish priests' and 'foolish old men' whom Read had arrested in Lambussie and Guo were far from being powerless, having successfully opposed the orders of the new head chiefs and sent the young men into the bush, so that the British could not enslave them.[41] Yet this was not the sort of power the British were prepared to take seriously. Their ideas regarding chiefs were shaped on the one hand by the neo-traditionalism of the British royal family, and on the other by the manner in which political rule manifested itself in West African savannah states. Thus, individuals who could produce some of the insignia of power typical to the area, such as a horse and clothes, and maybe even spoke Hausa – like Kyiir and the new chiefs of Tuopare and Guo who probably had been connected in one way or the other with Babatu or Samori – had a better chance of being recognised by the British as chiefs than, for example, the earth priests, those derided 'old fetish priests', who for their part tended to avoid the Britsh anyway.

Yet over the years, the combination of coercion and inducement imposed the *pax Britannica*. Attacks on merchants and armed conflicts between villages became increasingly rare.[42] Although, as Chief Commissioner Watherston noted, there was still a certain tendency 'to fly to the bow and arrow on the least provocation', the chiefs were 'beginning to realize how trade is affected by the danger of being shot at and how little of it comes to these districts in consequence'. They would, therefore, support the British policy of pacification in their own interests, 'for though they do not want to buy anything, they make money out of providing the caravans with food'.[43] The fact that the 'coming of the white man' brought an end to slave-raiding and village feuding was also acknowledged, and welcomed without exception, by my interlocutors. Hardly anyone could or wanted to recall a British punitive expedition or the ritual humiliation of those who resisted. It is possible that when recalling those times, people today prefer to associate themselves with those who had welcomed the new order. However, it is just as possible that the costs of pacification might have been regarded as relatively modest in light of the attacks and the insecurity that had prevailed during the last decades of the nineteenth century.

THE LOCAL APPROPRIATION OF THE CHIEFTAINCY

Colonial sources emphasise the British initiative involved in the pacification of the area and in the installation of head chiefs. Although Berthon's report does not make it clear whether and how a chief was installed in Nandom (one ought to assume that he can hardly have had time to do this, being so preoccupied with his pursuit), District Commissioner Read was convinced that it was thanks to Berthon that there was now a chief in Nandom exercising his office.[44] Benedict Der (2001: 41–5) rightly draws attention to this contradiction and ascertains that early British reports generally write about meetings with chiefs, but not about the installment of chiefs where none had existed before. However, to conclude from this, as Der does, that during the pre-colonial period the institution of the chieftaincy already existed throughout the North-West, and that only paramount chiefs were an institution of colonial origin, seems to me problematic. British complaints concerning the lack of clout on the part of these new village authorities cast doubt over the real identity of those the British described as 'chiefs'. My thesis of the colonial introduction of the chieftaincy (Lentz 1993), which Der has sharply criticised, certainly does not imply that the British appointed all the chiefs in one decisive act. Rather, the new political office emerged out of a series of 'working misunderstandings' (Dorward 1974) between local actors and colonial administrators. The British asked for chiefs, and the local population, the earth priests or individual strongmen, who hoped to benefit from co-operating with the colonial authorities, presented them with chiefs.

This is also clear from the oral traditions relating the history of the chieftaincy. Although the British were only too glad to take credit for the success of the new political order in the North-West, my interlocutors viewed the initiative in shaping the chieftaincy to have come unmistakably from local actors. The general view was that, although the *nasa naalʋ*, the 'white man's chieftaincy', was a British innovation, it only formalised the existing local relations of power. However, opinions differed considerably as to whose power and which pre-colonial political order the colonial masters had recognised.

Accounts relating the installation of the first chiefs can be classified into two basic types. The first is usually told in the house and patriclan of the earth priest and runs roughly as follows. In the pre-colonial period there were no chiefs, and the earth priest was the actual head of the village. Whenever the white man asked for the chief, the earth priest would send a messenger to him from his own or from an allied lineage. For one thing, it was beneath the wise old earth priest's dignity to deal with the colonial officer directly, and for another, the messenger had the linguistic ability and a certain knowledge of the ways of the world in order to carry out his task, which the earth priest usually lacked. In addition, encounters with the white man involved certain risks to which the earth priest had best not expose himself, given that he was indispensable for religious rituals. So, a slave was sometimes sent first. Finally, the earth priest wanted to avoid any accumulation of offices: it was even feared that combining the offices of chief and earth priest might cause the imminent death of the incumbent. At first, the messenger consulted with the earth priest on all decisions. In time, however, he became more and more independent, last but not least because the white man erroneously regarded him as the real chief, making him the official chief accordingly. Nevertheless, in this version, the chief drew and still draws his legitimacy solely from the fact that it had been the earth priest who entrusted him with this office; and he could take it away again if the chief did not act in accordance with his wishes.

The second type of account concerning the origins of the chieftaincy predominates in the house and patriclan of the chiefs themselves, especially in settlements where the earth priest and the chief belong to different clans. In this case, it is stressed that the new chief had already been in a position of power prior to the arrival of the British and that he was a strongman – a wealthy farmer, a widely travelled merchant or an experienced soldier who had fought in Babatu's armies. He had more cattle than the other villagers, a larger following, was sometimes proficient in several languages, and could afford clothes and a horse. In short, he had the qualifications necessary for the office of chief. In this version, the earth priest plays no significant role in either choosing or installing the chief.

To some extent these contradictory versions, which may refer to one and the same settlement, spring from present and past conflicts over the chieftaincy. Yet they also reflect differences in historical development of the chieftaincy in different villages. Drawing on the example of Nandom, I will illustrate a typical case of such competing accounts regarding the choice and legitimation of the first head chief, and then go on to explain how this chief was able to extend his rule over previously independent settlements.[45]

The first Nandom Naa

My interlocutors in Nandom all stressed that Nandom Naa Kyiir, a member of the Bekuone patriclan, was rich, widely travelled and powerful. His recently deceased son, whom I was able to interview in 1989, left no doubt that his father

> was very strong before the white man came. He used to get a lot of food from his farm and he could feed plenty of people with what he harvested. So they were calling him *tuor-naa* [chief of the mortar]. He also bought people and horses. ... It is not that he just sat down and was made chief [by the British] all of a sudden. ... He was very wealthy [*térásòb*] and very powerful [*fàŋsòb*] before the white man came to make him chief. ... He was also a trader and used to go to places like Diébougou to buy cloth to come and sew and then sell. He could also sew. It was all these things that made him rich and famous.[46]

Kyiir is said to have acquired the Dyula nickname 'Chemogoh', which his own descendants have since adopted as a family name, on a journey to Bobo-Dioulasso. His safe return from such a long journey also convinced many of those who had stayed behind that he must possess magical powers.[47] However, in reply to District Commissioner Read's question, Kyiir described himself as a Muslim.[48] Informants outside Nandom saw Kyiir above all as a strongman 'who was fond of harassing people very much' and who had acquired at least some of his wealth through highway robbery, marauding, slave raids, and slave-trading. Yet whatever the sources of Kyiir's power, there is no doubt that he exercised some influence before the British arrived.

All the Bekuone accounts link the British acknowledgement of Kyiir as chief with the conflict between Lambussie and Nandom that had triggered Captain Berthon's intervention in December 1903. Although Kyiir is said not to have even been involved in the confrontation between the Sisala and the Dagara, the district commissioner held him responsible for the escalation of the conflict, because as a 'strongman' it was up to him to keep the peace. The officer is said to have arrested Kyiir, had him sent off towards Wa, and finally released him again either in Gegenkpe or Wa (depending on the version), from where he returned (or was even escorted back) to Nandom, now as a chief officially recognised by the British. The Nandom earth priest did not play any role in this and therefore had no right to interfere in matters of the succession – an argument that was first vehemently asserted in the 1958 dispute over succession. My interviews took place at a time when the bitter contention over succession to the chieftaincy, which had been going on since 1985, enflamed anew, laying bare the essence of the narrative controversy over the relationship between earth priest and chief (Lentz 2000b).

The house of the Nandom earth priest, which is of the Dikpiele patriclan, has long been divided into two factions, which give different accounts of the details pertaining to the history of how the office of chief originated. However, all agreed that the British first offered it to the *tèŋgánsòb*, who then transferred it voluntarily to his friend Kyiir, 'so that he [the earth priest] could concentrate his attention on the *tèŋgán yele* [earth-shrine matters] for it would have been difficult to combine the two, *naalv* and *tèŋgán yele*'.[49] One member of the earth priest's family described the installation of the first Nandom Naa as follows:

> At that time people were fighting and killing one another. Then one day, the white man came to know the owner of this area [*tèŋsòb*] and traced him to this house ... Daga [the narrator's grandfather] said that he was the one. So the white man told him to take care of the place and to make sure that nobody kills another person. ... So Naajie [Daga's senior brother] was the *tèŋgánsòb* and Daga was the chief [*naa*]; it was the white man who gave him the chieftaincy... When Naajie died, Daga was the *naa* and the *tèŋgánsòb* as well. So when these people [Kyiir's family] were moving towards French territory and arrived here, he asked them to stay here for some time until the place was peaceful. ... They agreed, and when there was no more fighting, they said they would like to continue their journey. Then Daga said that he

would like them to stay so that they will be together. So that is how these people have come to be chiefs. It was Daga who gave them his throne and told them that if they did anything to abuse the throne, he would come back for his throne.[50]

The last sentence has a strategic meaning in the recent succession conflicts: it seeks to justify the earth priest's attempts to influence the selection of a chiefly successor. Yet the Nandom earth-priestly family is divided over the matter, one faction insisting 'that the chieftaincy belongs to our grandfather and we know that it will come back to us one day',[51] the other regarding the transfer of the chiefly office to the Bekuone clan as irreversible: 'the chieftaincy is theirs, and we don't have to meddle in it'.[52]

The claim that the earth-priestly family were the first in Nandom to hold the office of chief implies that the British had already visited Nandom before Berthon's punitive expedition of 1903, which is referred to by the Bekuone. In fact, the Anglo-French Boundary Commission mapped and demarcated the border along the 11th degree of latitude in 1900 and did the same along the Black Volta in 1902, thus coming into contact with many of the inhabitants of settlements near the border.[53] It is quite probable that the British commissioners handed out flags in these villages, as I was told in many interviews. Daga is also said to have received such a flag, though it was burnt in the course of Berthon's punitive expedition. Presumably the British flag was intended to symbolise coming under the dominion of the British Empire, but the Nandom earth priests interpreted it as evidence that the chiefly office had been granted to Daga.

The Dikpiele who tell the story used terms like *tèŋsòb*, 'owner of the earth' (i.e. settlement), and *tèŋgánsòb*, 'owner of the earth shrine', as synonyms, and occasionally also described the pre-colonial office of Daga as *tèŋ-naa*, 'village chief'. Similarly, Bekuone story-tellers see the new *naa* as emerging from the *tuor-naa* or *kúórbɛ-naa*. Such terminological shifts are typical of the accounts concerning the chieftaincy that I recorded in the Dagara language. These legitimise the new political order by anchoring the terminology in indigenous political traditions.

The creation of native states

The Dikpiele versions of the installation of the first Nandom Naa may be characterised as traditionalising, since they draw on the pre-existing legitimacy of the earth priest to bolster the new office of chief. The Bekuone, on the other hand, tell the 'climber's' version of the story. Traditionalising narrative types predominate in Lambussie, Lawra and Jirapa, the three neighbouring native states, not least because here, unlike in Nandom, the chief and earth priest come from the same patriclan.[54] However, as far as the identity of the first chief is concerned, it is said that 'strongmen' were the first to step in to fill the office of chief, much as was claimed to be the case in

Nandom. The first Lawra Naa Nale (or Lala) from Lawra-Yirkpee was a great warrior; Gbeliñu of Lambussie had fought in Babatu's armies and protected his home town from them by cutting a deal with the latter; Ganaa of Jirapa was described sometimes as a warrior and other times as marauder.[55] Yet in the eyes of my interlocutors, these early chiefs did not establish their office on the grounds of their ability or wealth, but through appointment by the earth priest and his elders.

However successful the traditionalising strategy of legitimation may have been in supporting the choice of chief, it still does not explain how he was able to extend his rule over previously independent settlements; for neither in Nandom nor in Lawra, Jirapa or Lambussie did the boundaries of the new native states conform with those of the earth-shrine parishes. The new chief therefore had to extend his influence beyond his own earth-shrine area. In this respect, many informants attributed some importance to the interventions of the British, especially in explaining why a particular village did not become the capital of a given paramountcy. It is hardly surprising that accounts differ, depending on whether the speaker be positioned at the 'centre' or at the 'periphery' of the new political structure. This point can best be illustrated by turning once again to the case of Nandom.

Interlocutors from the 'centre' stress Kyiir's active role – a combination of strategic presents and skilful rhetoric – in incorporating villages that declared their subordination to Nandom in 1905:

> The white man gave Kyiir sugar and told him that if he would be able to handle the place well, it will be as sweet as sugar. Kyiir took the sugar and went about telling people that the white man was a sweet, good man, ... and said that if they handle the place well, it will be like that sugar ... and that made the people stop fighting.[56]

Other informants emphasised Kyiir's diplomatic recognition of the existing structures of authority, asking the earth priests and elders of the surrounding villages for support. The earth priests promised this and recognised him as chief, 'since the white man was only a visitor [sáán], and since Kyiir himself ... was a stranger [because he was not one of the founders of Nandom] and a trader, he knew best how to handle strangers and visitors'.[57] Kyiir's son Fatchu stressed the importance of Kyiir's friendships and alliances with other strongmen, which he probably established through his involvement in slave-raiding and slave trade networks:

> You see, at that time Kandeme [in Kokoligu] was strong, Doyaga [in Tuopare] was strong, Bapure [in Gegenkpe] was strong, but then my father was stronger than all of them. So they all made friends with my father and he was 'commanding' all of them. ... Somebody might be in his own village ... and may be having some problem with his neighbours and decide to join this man [Kyiir] so that he can get help

in times of difficulties. So a lot of people came to join him. ... That is how he was able to control all these areas.[58]

Kokoligu, Tuopare and Gegenkpe – the settlements listed by Fatchu – together with Guo, Tantuo and Panyaan (in colonial sources 'Panyati'), comprised the six 'traditional' Nandom sub-divisions, each controlling a number of village chiefs and headmen. In the course of the 1952 local government reforms, Varpuo and Zimuopere were added as the seventh and eighth sub-divisions. More recently, party-political struggles for power in the 1960s led to what can best be described as an inflation of sub-divisional chiefs.[59] However, the first six settlements were and still are accorded special status. Except for in Panyaan,[60] these sub-divisional chiefs generally were not installed by the Nandom Naa, but directly by the British – at least, this is what my village informants claimed. This 'installation' appears to have taken place as early as 1902 in Gegenkpe, Tantuo and Kokoligu, in the course of the demarcation of the boundary along the Black Volta mentioned above.[61] Matters are not so clear in the case of Guo or Tuopare, but here too oral traditions stress that the British recognised local strongmen as chiefs, who then, for various reasons, accepted, or were forced to accept, their own subordination to Nandom.[62] In Gegenkpe, for example, people related that Bapure, the first Gegenkpe Naa, had provided the animals with which Kyiir's release from British custody had been secured and out of friendship later agreed that Kyiir should become head chief. In Kokoligu and Tuopari, my informants pointed out that the local chiefs accepted Kyiir's elevation to head chief because they all belonged to the same matriclan. In addition, Doyaga, the first Tuopari Naa, was said to be obliged to Kyiir, because the latter had once helped him to raise the brideprice for his wife.

The Tuopari case is especially interesting, because oral traditions can be compared with British material. Captain Read reported that he only installed Doyaga as chief, after the Nandom Naa had named him as a suitable candidate.[63] However, my informants in Tuopare did not mention the presence of the Nandom Naa at all, but merely referred to the fact that the British wanted an influential chief, because Tuopare had a large (slave) market and therefore played an important role in the pacification of the whole region. The fact that here, as elsewhere on the 'periphery' of the new Nandom chiefdom, the conferment of the chiefly office by the British is presented as a source of power independent of Nandom is indicative of the role these oral traditions play in recent power struggles between the Nandom Naa and his sub-divisional chiefs. Conversely, granting high status in the Nandom native state may have been a strategy deployed by Kyiir and his successors intended to convert potential rivals into powerful allies.

Less problematic was the incorporation of villages in which the Nandom Naa himself, not the British, had installed a chief. A typical example is Ko, to which a colonial official came as late as 1917.[64] According to the first Ko Naa's son, his father Gmiri was 'a strongman and could harass people in Ko, just as Kyiir did in Nandom. ... So when Kyiir was tamed as a result of the appointment as chief, he also appointed Gmiri in order to tame him too'. It was obvious that Ko would recognise the Nandom Naa as paramount: 'once Kyiir installed the Ko Naa, we had to follow the Nandom Naa'.[65] Others saw the reason for Nandom's predominance as lying in a type of political agreement between the village chiefs to facilitate communication, both with the British and with one another. The choice thus ultimately fell on Nandom, because it was located in the 'middle' of the new chiefdom.

In villages of the Lawra and Lambussie divisions, I frequently encountered the speculation that one's own village might have become the centre of the new native state, or even the district headquarters, if only one's forefathers had not chased away the British or had not fled from them. For example in Dikpe, near the Lawra district station, the inhabitants are said to have implored the earth shrine to expel the British who were camping there; and so the latter moved on to on Lawra.[66] In Meto, south of Lawra, I was told that, at the request of the villagers, the earth god sent a swarm of bees, which scared the horses of the British.[67] The chief of Nabaala mused over the consequences, unforeseen at the time, of some villages' refusal to house the British:

> When the white man ... came to Bangwon, he made an attempt to settle. But the Bangwon people didn't take it lightly, so he continued and ... ultimately settled at Lawra. The present Lawra should have been at Bangwon if they had allowed him to stay. But because they rejected him, Lawra was fortunate and has attained its present heights.[68]

The chief of Happa, on the other hand, explained that the British made Lambussie rather than Bangwon the seat of a head chief (and Lawra the seat of the district commissioner), because the aged chief of Bangwon knew no Hausa, while Gbeliñu of Lambussie knew it well.[69] The chief of Billaw also explained Lambussie's paramountcy status in terms of both historical chance and administrative routine. Both Billaw and Lambussie had built rest houses. Yet because the British came from Lawra, they arrived first at Lambussie and spent the night there, summoning the chiefs of the other villages to where they lodged .[70] The Lambussie Kuoro himself stressed that in the pre-colonial period 'there were no paramountcies in the whole of the Lawra area': these had been an innovation of the British, 'the white man's administration', based on administrative convenience, not traditional hierarchies.[71] Yet this innovation has since taken hold, mobilising considerable political energies as well as inspiring the narrative imagination.

THE BRITISH MODEL OF THE NATIVE STATE

The pre-colonial landscape of the North-West was marked by networks of clans and neighbourhoods, by personal forms of power (the strongmen), by shifting alliances, by mobility and by multiple group membership, not by clear spatial or linear boundaries. In contrast, the British model of political order, the native states model, was based on a territorial understanding of rule and social belonging that tolerated neither overlapping, multi-faceted loyalties nor mobility. From the perspective of this model, every compound in a settlement was clearly subject to one, and only one, chief or headman, who for his part was subordinate to a single head chief. In order to effect this model, the district commissioners, in co-operation with the chiefs, pursued what was basically terminological deceit: they redefined the personal networks of the strongmen, their kin and client relationships, as territorial spheres of authority.

District Commissioner Read reported that he had demarcated twenty-five native states in the North-West and even mapped them.[72] Yet in fact, the maps at that time only show the boundaries of the administrative districts, not the chiefdoms. In practice, the British had to rely on a network model of power. In collecting the maintenance tax, chiefs were supposed to deliver a particular sum total, but the details of where and from whom they levied it were left to them. Later, colonial officers were only interested in whether the roads had actually been cleaned, not where the chief recruited road labour, or how he actually controlled the settlements under his authority. Initially, the boundaries between the native states were not territorially linear, but rather determined by personal hierarchies and affiliations. Often they were only defined when conflict arose, such as when village inhabitants complained that two different chiefs were claiming their labour or levying fines, or when a village sought to evade its obligations by repeatedly changing its affiliation to different chiefs. Yet whenever a chief asked for it, his power to rule was buttressed by the district commissioner and his constabulary in ways that went far beyond the usual sanctions that could have been imposed by pre-colonial strongmen, whose *modus operandi* had consisted of a combination of raids and generosity. Thus, the new territorial order was paradoxically enforced by strengthening personal rule.

For the British, the natural political community, which fell under the rule of a paramount chief, was the tribe. This entity was seen as having the same significance for the native state as the nation, in the tradition of natural-law legitimations of sovereignty, had for the modern European state: a natural legal subject which gave birth to its own political constitution. The legitimacy of the chiefs, through whom the British wanted to administer the Protectorate, was to be based on the ethnic identification that they shared with their subjects, an identification represented as 'natural', and therefore pre-political. However, alongside this model of legitimate rule, was another model, applied in areas where 'foreign' rule was a reality before the British arrived, a situation imagined to be akin to the Norman conquest of the Anglo-Saxons, an analogy colonial officials often cited in this context.

The political ideas held by British colonial officials in the Northern Territories took up both evolutionist and diffusionist arguments of the late nineteenth century.[73] Tribes were ascribed a fixed place in the natural evolution of political communities: families joined together as clans, clans as tribes, and finally tribes as nations. In the eyes of the British, the Northern Territories still found themselves at a relatively early stage of development historically, a stage through which Great Britain and the other European nations had passed long ago. However, colonial officials though they perceived a cline of development within the Protectorate itself, the Lobi being at the lowest level, the Dagomba at the highest, a level that still had to be reached by the other groups. Natural political evolution could be accelerated at certain moments, namely through the conquest of a 'primitive' tribe by a more developed one (or the peaceful immigration of the latter and the former's voluntary recognition of it as ruler), as was the case with the founding of the Mamprussi, Dagomba, Gonja and Wala kingdoms. However, evolution might also be interrupted or endangered, as it was by the political disorder that was triggered by the military campaigns of Babatu and Sarankye Mori. British colonial rule was regarded as legitimate, because it subdued the marauding and village feuds that were inimical to further political development. By bringing politically still fragmented tribes under the aegis of powerful native states, the British were merely accelerating the natural, and therefore also desirable, course of political evolution.

In the eyes of the British, rule was legitimate if it was able to protect subjects from outside attack. In this respect, according to Chief Commissioner Armitage, the kingdoms of the Northern Territories had failed: 'The waning powers of the Mamprussis, Walas and Gonjas, who found themselves unable to protect the aboriginal pagans from the attacks of slave raiders, left the country ... in the state of anarchy from which we rescued it.'[74] Whether, however, the 'Dagarti', 'Lobi' and 'Grunshi' had ever been subject to the pre-colonial kingdoms was a matter of dispute. Chief Commissioners Watherston and Armitage regarded the extreme political fractionalism of the Lobi and Dagarti to be a consequence of the destructive campaigns launched by the Zaberma and Sofa. Watherston therefore believed it was up to the British 'to divide these people up into their original divisions, so as to come under the paramount Chiefs they were in the habit of obeying before Samory and Babatu overran the country' (1907–8: 357). Chief Commissioner Northcott, for his part, was convinced that the Mamprussi had once ruled the whole of the Northern Protectorate, from the Ivory Coast to Sansanne-Mango. Only in the last third of the nineteenth century had slave-raiders brought an end to the peaceful relations between the Mamprussi king and his subjects and undermined his authority (ibid.: 349–50).[75] However, Northcott and his successors were pragmatic enough to cease trying to assert the Mamprussi's claims to sovereignty, at least in the North-West. At the end of the 1920s, in the course of the indirect-rule reforms, it was conceded 'that it is now too late to think of making the Na of Mamprusi the head of practically all the Northern Province even if it had ever been practical politics'.[76]

Other officers were convinced that the Dagarti, Lobi and Issala had never belonged to Mamprussi, Wa or any other kingdom, and that in Lawra District, the institution of the chieftaincy had been an entirely colonial innovation. Yet even these colonial officers believed the North-West to be populated by tribes, even though these had not yet joined to form a single political community. The views of a Read or a Duncan-Johnstone on the one hand, and a Northcott, a Watherston or an Armitage on the other, thus ultimately differed only with respect to the question of whether the political future represented a particular stage of development that the 'lawless tribes' once had already reached, only to lose it again during the period of political turmoil of the late nineteenth century; or whether the step towards the development of a chiefdom was about to be taken for the very first time. Yet, both sides were in basic agreement over the objectives of British intervention in the Northern Territories, to unite the tribes and create strong native states. The administrative boundaries between provinces and districts, too, should follow 'existing racial boundaries' as closely as possible, as Northcott asserted.[77]

In practice, however, it quickly became clear that not only the culturally and linguistically variegated map, with its countless multi-ethnic settlements, but also the administrative technicalities – territorial size and number of inhabitants, as well as the availability of British personnel – were at odds with the vision of shaping the districts and chiefdoms to conform with ethnic boundaries. There were cases in which a chief's rule over a particular village was retracted on the grounds that it belonged to a different ethnic group.[78] Yet in general, the head chiefs were assigned villages on grounds having nothing to do with ethnicity; and each native state was only allocated a given ethnic label retroactively.[79] Thus, the 'tribe' was, and remains, a normative, not a descriptive category.

CONSOLIDATING THE CHIEFDOMS

An important step towards shaping local political realities to fit the native-state model somewhat more closely was the opening of a district station in Lawra in 1907. From the local perspective, the first British tours of inspection and punitive expeditions must have been hardly distinguishable from the Muslim warlords' attacks. However, the 'objectification of the

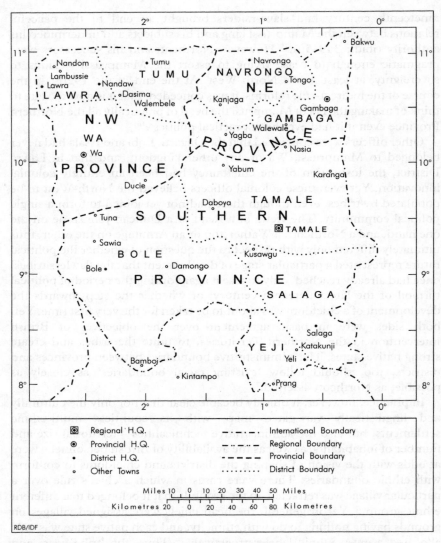

Map 3 Northern Territories of the Gold Coast, Provinces and Districts 1907
Source: Bening 1975a

central power' manifest in the station (Trotha 1994) as well as the physical
presence of the district commissioner and the mounted police represented a
stark contrast between the periodic incursions by slave-raiders and the
continuous exercise of power by the British. Fleeing and waiting were now
at most individual tactics, and could no longer serve as collective strategies

to provide effective protection from the demands of the new power-holders. People now had to come to terms with a type of rule that was designed to be permanent.

Stations, rest houses and roads: the material framework of the native states
Until 1907, the setting up of a station was tied to the availability of troops, a situation that kept the number of stations in the Northern Territories low. District commissioners were responsible, not only for the administration of extensive territories, but also for the supervision and training of the troops there stationed. This left little time for regular tours of inspection. Then, in 1907, since co-ordinated armed uprisings were no longer a concern, the military administration was substituted by a civilian one, the troops of the Gold Coast Regiment were replaced by the smaller Northern Territories Constabulary, and a number of new districts were created.[80] Black Volta District became North-Western Province, incorporating the districts of Wa, Lawra and Tumu. From 1921 to 1946, Lawra and Tumu were joined together as one district to save costs, and North-Western and North-Eastern Provinces were combined to form Northern Province.[81]

The spatial proximity of colonial officials increased the chiefs' ability to assert themselves, which is why some of them wished to see stations established at their places of residence. Thus, Kyiir, the Nandom Naa, strove to have the district station brought to Nandom by promising to provide all the assistance required for the construction.[82] However, the decision still fell in favour of Lawra, which in British eyes had a more favourable strategic location, being on the trade route between Wa and Diébougou, near a ferry and two fords across the Black Volta, and not too far from the French station at Gaoua.

Yet the new district station was not welcomed by everybody. When in January 1907 Captain Read came to Lawra with the new district commissioner and some constables, he was neither greeted by the head chief, nor did he find that sufficient building materials had been provided, and 'the people were undecided whether to bolt or not', because 'two French Lobi fetish priests had ... found a strong fetish that ordered them not to pay hut tax and fight the white man.'[83] Despite this, construction on the station began the following day, and at a palaver the representatives of the villages under Lawra promised 'to help loyally in building and when I asked if there was anything they wanted to say they replied: "If your father tells you to make a farm you do not ask what a farm is made for".'[84] Admittedly, this response was more an expression of defensive rhetoric than conviction, since in April 1907 the Chief Commissioner still reported that numerous villages along the Volta were following the 'Tenga fetish' and refusing to recognise the authority of the district commissioner.[85] Presumably this was a reference to the earth shrine (*tèŋgán*) being invoked in order to prevent the British (and French) from settling in the area, as was reported to me in a number of interviews. Orders from the British officials and the newly established chiefs were obviously far from receiving automatic recognition.

The concern that individual acts of recalcitrance in Lawra District might lead to collective rebellion, as had been the case in Bongo and Bole,[86] was voiced only once, when in 1919–21 the French sought to end Lobi resistance to paying taxes and to submitting to *corvée* labour. For this purpose, all available troops were assembled in the Gaoua area, encouraging the Dagara and Birifor living to the north, up near Lawra and Birifu, to take up arms again and resume their old inter-clan and inter-village feuds – at least according to what was reported by a concerned Duncan-Johnstone, the Lawra District Commissioner. To him, it was 'a wonder' that the 'Lobi-Wiilis on the British side' were not following 'the bad example ... of the apparently unchecked lawlessness of their French cousins.'[87] Only the news that the British Lobi were not going to sympathise with the French Lobi, because the latter had stolen cattle and other riches from them when they had sought refuge from Babatu's warriors on the opposite bank of the Volta, soothed British fears. A relieved Duncan-Johnstone noted: 'The people are not out against us but against each other, and of course resist arrest by the French authorities.'[88] Nevertheless, to counter any possible eventuality, an additional border patrol consisting of a fifty-man troop of the Northern Territories Constabulary was dispatched.[89] What the border controls could not prevent was the spread of seditious stories and songs from across the river. Duncan-Johnstone reported a song 'with a catchy tune' that became popular in the autumn of 1920 during the Kobine dances in Lawra 'and runs to the effect that the white man called the Lobis to Gaoua but that he could go on calling, his voice would go before they went.' Duncan-Johnstone's counter-measure: 'Told Binney [the Government interpreter] to set new and better words to it, as it is no use forbidding a popular tune.'[90] Only in mid-1921 did the British feel safe enough to withdraw the extra troops.

The stability of British rule in Lawra District was not only due to the station and the presence of the district commissioner and his constables – it was also achieved through the successful piecemeal co-optation of chiefs as administrative assistants. One of the chiefs' most important duties was the recruitment of labour required to construct roads and rest houses, that is, precisely the material framework that buttressed the new territorial and political order. The purpose that the stations fulfilled on a grand scale, the rest houses did so on a smaller one, as corporeal assertion of the new power. By 1913, there were already sixty-five rest houses in North-Western Province, almost half of them in Lawra District. Most of these houses were used rarely, if at all, and often fell victim to the termites. Yet, the district commissioner was not alone in ordering their construction, a number of chiefs did so as well, competing with each other 'as to which of them has the best built European rest house', in hopes that such rest houses would encourage visits by colonial officials, and thus strengthen their own position.[91]

In a similar fashion, British talk of 'opening up ... the country' was put into action in matters concerning road construction. In Lawra District, which measured barely forty miles from north to south, there were 109 miles of drained roads in 1913 – not a particularly impressive sum. But by 1918, Duncan-Johnstone could proudly point to 250 miles of made-up roads.[92] In 1926, two years after the first cars and lorries had reached the North-West, there were 370 miles of passable routes, enough to put Lawra-Tumu ahead of all other districts in the Northern Territories. Finally, it was decided not to extend the existing road network any further, since it had become almost impossible to maintain it.[93]

Early on, it was decided that each village had to create a path leading to its head chief's residence that measured at least two-and-a-half metres wide.[94] Lawra, Nandom, Lambussie, Jirapa and the residences of other head chiefs thus became central places. This, in turn, enabled the head chiefs to gradually increase their control over their own native states. The presence of the district commissioner, the police force and the chiefs created spaces that were relatively free from violence, thus allowing greater mobility. To some extent, pre-colonial trade networks influenced the colonial topography, because in places where there were flourishing markets – the hubs of communication between villages – strongmen stood a fairly good chance of becoming influential head chiefs or sub-chiefs. Conversely, the colonial administration to some extent also shaped the topography by creating new markets and bringing in merchants in villages in which a head chief resided.

The construction of roads, markets, rest houses and buildings for the native courts not only constituted the material framework of the new territorial order: at the same time, it functioned as an instrument in defining and asserting it. Head chiefs and sub-chiefs had to decide which villages were subject to them and could therefore be recruited for *corvée* labour. Neighbouring chiefs had to agree who was responsible for the maintenance of link roads and up to which point. The points at which such areas of responsibility met came to be considered a particular chiefdom's boundaries. In short, the new hierarchy of the native states was put to a practical test, even though especially in the early years the district commissioner was called in repeatedly to hold up the chiefs' authority.

'Not yet ripe to be made into Kingdoms'

The British ideal of placing each tribe under the leadership of a single chief was not even remotely feasible. As Captain Read put it, after receiving disappointing reports that chiefs were unable to assert themselves: 'This [Lobi] country is not yet ripe to be made into Kingdoms.'[95] When Duncan-Johnstone summoned all the district chiefs and headmen to a meeting at Lawra, a good 180 office-holders turned up.[96] According to the 1921 Census, in a population of 57,708 there was one chief for every 320 inhabitants,[97] and in Nandom Division one chief for every 245 inhabitants.[98] It was obviously not difficult to install chiefs at the village level, even if finding someone actually respected by a majority of the villagers involved a lengthy process of trial and error. The problem was rather integrating these chiefs into a hierarchical structure with as few rulers at the top as possible.

In Lawra District from 1905 to 1907 the British installed a total of ten paramount chiefs or head chiefs, as the upper chiefs were alternately known, in Lawra, Nandom, Lissa, Jirapa, Ulu, Sabuli, Nandaw, Lambussie, Samoa and Zini. At the time, the main concern was the pacification of what was regarded as a rebellious region. In some cases, therefore, men, who hardly controlled more than their own village, were appointed head chiefs, simply for agreeing to co-operate with the British. When the desire later arose to simplify the administration, this state of affairs seemed untenable, in part because each appointment of a paramount chief required confirmation by the governor. Read therefore requested 'a ruling as to the qualification of a Chief to be Paramount'. '[T]hat the King of Wa with 15,558 people should be on the same footing as [the chief of] Tumu with 2,464 is in my opinion ridiculous', Read argued. For years he had sought in vain 'to get the tribes to combine and elect a really Paramount Chief'. So long as this was wanting, the title of 'Paramount Chief' should be reserved for the 'King of Wa' alone.[99] However, even attempts to limit the inflationary proliferation of claims to the title 'paramount chief' met with no success prior to the 1930s. The confusion in the titles used by the district commissioners reflected both the inconsistency of the British policy of centralisation as well as the successful strategy of the new chiefs in maintaining, and even enhancing, the positions they had secured for themselves.[100]

In Lawra District, the British first wanted to make the Lawra Naa, then the Jirapa Naa, 'Paramount chief over the whole District'. However, this failed because of the lack of influence on the part of the chiefs who were chosen for this role and the 'jealousies' and 'frictions' among the other chiefs and head chiefs. The district commissioner had instructed the chiefs 'that they must always salute Gari when they come into Lawra', but Lawra Naa Gari was 'not a strongman and has no presence'.[101] The paramount chiefs of Nandom and Jirapa put themselves forward as loyal supporters of the British government and suitable paramount chiefs of Lawra District, without much success. Even though the district commissioners' attempts to install a paramount chief for all of Lawra were frustrated, at least the number of head chiefs was not to increase any further, and sub-chiefs and headmen were to be forced by all means, from persuasion to arrests, heavy fines and threats of removal from office, to recognise their paramount. As was to be expected, this policy encountered resistance. Typical of early forms of non-compliance was the explanation of some village chiefs, officially under Lambussie, that they did not follow their head chief, because 'they never really understood they had to'. The district commissioner then made these chiefs drink sorghum beer together as a sign of their friendship and promise that they would obey the chief of Lambussie in future,[102] but complaints concerning the lack of authority of the Lambussie Kuoro (and the other head chiefs) did not cease until well into the 1930s.[103] Later, rebellious sub-chiefs no longer claimed ignorance to be the reason for their non-compliance, but rather cited the head chiefs' unfair demands, old pre-colonial rights or the promises of earlier colonial officers. For example, the chief of Gegenkpe, who 'ignored' the paramount rule of the Nandom Naa, explained that his grandfather had once been promised the paramountcy over the surrounding villages, because he was the only one in the village who had not run away when the British first arrived there.[104]

Regardless of how valid such historical arguments and complaints concerning the arbitrariness of a head chief might have seemed to them, the British hardly ever yielded to desires for independence or reassignment to another chief. Whoever voiced complaints against head chiefs was dismissed as being a notorious 'trouble-maker', as District Commissioner Eyre-Smith later explained self-critically.[105] The suspicion on the part of the British that those who complained wanted above all else to promote the interests of their own faction was not invariably unfounded.[106] Yet even if colonial officials had better understood the maze of local power struggles, they still would not have been able implement their policy of centralisation any more effectively or, from the local perspective, more justly. Redefining the chiefdoms would have provoked just as many protests as the British preference for maintaining the native states once they had been set up.

Only two changes were made before the Lawra Confederacy was introduced. In 1918 the chief of Tugu became independent, 'being at the head of a Wilo population of 4530 people, quite distinct from the Lobi Dagarti who make up the rest of the population of Girapa'.[107] Until then, he had been subject to the Jirapa Naa, who, however, had rarely succeeded in conscripting him for road work. In exchange, the chief of Lissa was to come under the Nandom Naa, because he supposedly had been subject to him earlier and because the mere 486 inhabitants of Lissa were 'exactly the same people as the Toparo people who are under Nandom'.[108] A little later, however, Lissa fell to Lawra, to whom the chief of Lissa and his people were accustomed to turning for quite some time already.[109] Thus, the number of divisions remained at ten, which Duncan-Johnstone listed in the District Record Book as follows:[110]

Division	Race	Population	Head Chief	Remarks
Lorha	Lobi Burifon	15,670	Nanweni	3" Medallion
Nandom	Lobi Dagarti	9,807	Bora	3" Medallion
Girapa	Lobi Dagarti	9,067	Gana	4" Medallion
Tugu	Lobo Wili	3,647	Kayani	3" Medallion
Lamboussie	Sissalla	4,231	Kantombie	3" Medallion
Samoa	Sissalla	1,730	Pora	–
Zini	Sissalla	2,826	Nivia	3" Medallion
Nandaw	Dagarti	2,160	Dakora	–
Ulu[111]	Dagarti	3,666	Lunko	2" Medallion
Sabule	Dagarti	1,830	Gariba	–

Disciplining the chiefs

Not only were the chiefs reluctant to accept the authority of the head chiefs, ordinary people, too, were 'still very independent' and unwilling to 'recognize the authority of their chiefs', as Read expressed it.[112] The chiefs could impose monetary fines, which were mostly levied in cattle, on insubordinate sub-chiefs and villagers, and also have constables arrest anyone who refused to work.[113] Yet few managed to discipline their subjects with any kind of lasting effect, as can be seen from the numerous complaints over people refusing to work, transferring their place of residence,[114] migrating in search of work without the chief's permission,[115] and failing to report the outbreak of epidemics.[116]

In British eyes, the key to solving all such problems of insubordination was simply the correct choice of chiefs. During these years, the reports are full of praise and criticism regarding individual chiefs and of thoughts concerning who might replace incapable office-holders at the next opportunity. In the district record book, we find entries such as the following:

Confidential Record of Chiefs. Paramount Chiefs 1918.

Girapa: Chief Ganaa easily the best, most intelligent and strongest chief in the District. A good man, requires checking occasionally, however.

Lawra: Has not been chief for very long, but is handicapped by his relations, the old chief, his brother Polli and Basala. Every innovation is upheld by these for fear of witchcraft, in reality laziness is at the bottom of it. Lawra is a fool, wants a lot of pushing.

Nandom: Denye is a useless old drunkard whose hand is always inside a pito-pot. The work in this division is done by Bora, son of the late

Paramount Chief and nephew of Denye. Bora is a very capable man with a large following and is the heir to the Division. Bora, the heir, is the real chief.
Lamboussie: Tries hard, but is so afraid of witchcraft that he has not much power over his people, rather weak. ...
Samoa: Has been a slave, a non-entity.[117]

In the eyes of the district commissioner, a successful chief distinguished himself by his readiness to co-operate with the British and by 'a decided tendency for progress and development'.[118] A good chief should also enjoy the respect of the people placed under him, be thoroughly familiar with their demographic circumstances, and be well-informed concerning all relevant events in the village so that he may either take measures himself or inform the district commissioner. Finally, the chief should belong to the 'correct' family, because the British believed that, even in formerly chiefless societies, the legitimacy of the office-holder was a product of the correct line of descent and that the office of chief was heritable. The British, then, regarded descent, effectiveness and popularity as the three pillars of legitimation. However, these three criteria not only originated from competing political projects, but also often ended up contradicting one another in practice. As such, they presented local actors with room to manoeuvre.

Chiefs who failed to comply effectively with British orders, or, conversely, carried them out so enthusiastically that villagers repeatedly complained about them to the district commissioner were warned, in case of gross violations imprisoned in Lawra or Tamale for some months, and ultimately even removed from office.[119] New chiefs were generally 'elected' at an assembly of headmen and villagers under the district commissioner's supervision. The selection was made mostly from among a pool of candidates belonging to the kin of the previous chief and had to be confirmed by the Chief Commissioner after a year's trial period. The election was supposed to ensure the chief's popularity, but usually boiled down to simple acclamation. In Lawra, for instance, District Commissioner Eyre-Smith had the aged Nanweni, whom he had pressured into resigning, name candidates to succeed him and then asked any others there assembled who were interested in the office to stand up. Only Binni Lobi, the district commissioner's interpreter, whom Nanweni had nominated, responded. The sub-chiefs and headmen who were prepared to follow him were then asked to stand, which they did.[120] In a similar fashion Nandom Naa Boro's successor, Konkuu, was 'elected' unanimously by the elders of Nandom, the Nandom earth priest, and the village headmen and chiefs.[121] Sometimes, however, real competitors presented themselves, the election then becoming a public demonstration of who had the greater following. This was to be the case in Nandom in 1940, after Konkuu's death.[122]

Imprisonment, removal from office and the re-appointment of chiefs were all part of the process of trial and error in the mutual adaptation of British demands and local power interests. A striking example of this is the story of Kantonbie, the head chief of Lambussie, who was installed in 1915. Kantonbie complained repeatedly about an opponent called Kanton, who was said to be a 'powerful wizard' with his ambitions of becoming chief. When Kanton incited young villagers to refuse labour duties, he was warned several times by the district commissioner and finally imprisoned in Lawra for several months.[123] However, when chief Kantonbie's headmen threatened Kanton's men with heavy fines for refusing to do road work and the latter fled into French territory, the native tribunal in Lawra, with the district commissioner's approval, sentenced the headmen to one month 'political detention' and removed them from office, because they had provoked the flight.[124] After this incident, Kantonbie's support began to erode, with most Lambussie Division chiefs refusing to accompany him to meetings in Lawra.[125] Thereafter, Kanton's followers complained to District Commissioner Eyre-Smith that a man had died following a beating ordered by Kantonbie. Although initial investigations proved inconclusive, Eyre-Smith banished Kanton to Navrongo for disregarding Kantonbie's authority.[126] Eventually, however, the district commissioner turned against the head chief, accusing him of, among other things, failing to provide porters and to maintain a rest house.[127] Finally, Eyre-Smith removed Kantonbie from office and sentenced him to a fine of £25 and four months' imprisonment with hard labour for concealing an outbreak of cattle fever in his division.[128] Meanwhile, the village headmen and compound owners 'elected' a new chief, Yesibie, 'unanimously' – a man who, although from the same house as his predecessor, was accepted by Kantonbie's opponents.[129]

The case of Lambussie shows that, in course of time, the initially unconditional support of the district commissioner for a particular chief could waver and change to criticism, punishment, and ultimately removal from office. Goody rightly refers to the fact that, unlike in pre-colonial kingdoms, the new chiefs in acephalous societies were not controlled by institutionalised 'checks and balances' (1975: 98). However, even the informal, 'passive' resistance on the part of subjects could be effective, because it demonstrated to the British that a particular chief was of no use for their purposes. Neither wholly powerless chiefs, nor those who were too despotic, were able to hold on to their office for long periods. The 'silent violence of colonial tyranny', which Hawkins (1996: 206) believes dominated Lawra District generally, certainly had its limits. To be a successful chief meant performing a balancing act between British demands and the people's expectations. This required both modern administrative skills as well as tried-and-true strongman strategies that entailed a minimum of redistribution – including taking over fines that had been imposed on subordinates and caring for villagers in times of need. In addition, the chiefs sacrificed at ancestral shrines and at powerful hills and streams, relied on local healers as well as Islamic marabouts, and themselves set up powerful shrines so that they would be equipped with spiritual powers to counter attacks by critics or rivals.[130]

Chiefs did not draw a regular salary until the start of the 1930s, profiting instead from irregular sources of income, such as presents and fees for acting as magistrates, fines in the form of cattle from those who refused labour conscription,[131] and gifts from sub-chiefs and headmen upon their appointment, as well as from the district commissioner or other colonial officers when they came by on tour.[132] In addition, the chiefs could demand from their subjects five days' work a year to do agricultural work on chiefly lands, and they usually diverted a number of road workers for this purpose too. However, the complaints recorded show that the obligation to do agricultural work in the chief's fields encountered resistance, when the sorghum beer that was customarily distributed among those assisting each other was not provided.[133] The reply of one individual who appeared before Eyre-Smith armed with bow and arrows, clearly refers to this norm of reciprocity: 'When I asked him why he did no work on the road, he replied that I did not come and work on his farm.'[134]

The questions of how much chiefs were able to enrich themselves and the extent of their 'tyranny' warrant different answers for different native states and different periods. Nandom Naa Kyiir and his successor Danye, for instance, were typical wealthy strongmen who had become chiefs, in part because they could entertain colonial officials and pay any fines imposed on their subjects. Kyiir died in 1908, before road work was routinely demanded to the extent that Danye had to organise it later. Although Danye made himself unpopular by arbitrarily levying fines and stealing wives from other men, he did not force the people of Nandom to work in his fields.[135] This practice was introduced by Boro, who was installed as Nandom Naa in 1919 and only began to accumulate wealth once he had become chief. In each of the villages under his jurisdiction, he had his followers supervise the clearing of a farm. The harvest then had to be brought by the villagers to his stores in Nandom. Eyre-Smith estimated Boro's farms at a good 500 acres.[136] Despite this, there is no record of complaints against Boro, either because no one dared to bring the matter forward, or because he himself was always ready to help in turn, as his son emphasised.[137]

Whether with more or less redistribution, some head chiefs and sub-chiefs accumulated considerable wealth. In the early 1920s, one colonial officer remarked, after his first tour through Lawra District, that some chiefs were living like 'robber barons' in 'a distinctly medieval life-style'.[138] Boro, for example, is said to have had 50 wives and over 100 children. At his death in 1950, Birifu Naa Gandah left behind 35 widows and over 100 descendants, as well as nearly 20 horses and more than 500 cows. Over time, Lawra Naa J. A. Karbo managed to acquire 65 wives and innumerable descendants.[139] The large number of wives also testifies to the fact that head chiefs sought to bolster their power over villages under their jurisdiction through marriage alliances.

Colonial officers disagreed about whether the power of the chiefs was too great, as well as about how to discipline them. Captain Eyre-Smith, for example, who at the age of 32, full of reformist zeal, entered his first period of colonial service in Lawra, where he would spend a total of four-and-a-half years between 1921 and 1929, developed a better grasp of indigenous political organisation, with its earth priests and lineage elders, and was particularly critical of the chiefs. When his investigations into the abuses of power alleged against the chiefs of Tizza, Tugu and Jirapa merely ended in a thicket of interest-led misinformation on the part of the chiefs and their interpreters, he began to wonder who was actually controlling whom:

> We, that is to say the District Commissioner, does not in fact guide the administration of the District, we have in this District as Chiefs nothing better than tax collectors whom we unwittingly assist in many ways to oppress their people.[140]

For Eyre-Smith, the reasons for the abuses lay in the unconditional support given to chiefs by his predecessors, especially Duncan-Johnstone, who understood nothing of the traditional political organisation and who instead introduced native tribunals headed by the chiefs, in which the village elders had no say.[141] However, Eyre-Smith's superior, Whittall, saw the problem as being not the native tribunals, but the people's low level of development. Whittall believed the tribunals to be 'an excellent system amongst a sophisticated people, but, shown wanting, when dealing with a very primitive people.'[142] Chief Commissioner Walker Leigh, a committed opponent of the plans for indirect rule that were debated since the mid-1920s, commented laconically on Eyre-Smith's scolding of the chiefs and his reform proposals:[143]

> the more power a Chief is given, the more he will abuse it … it is a question of having Chiefs whose people obey and fear them, or Chiefs who have no power at all, and whose people neither obey nor fear them.[144]

Walker Leigh's sympathies were clearly in favour of a policy that supported strong chiefs, who, however, should be supervised as closely as possible by the British.

Native courts, medallions and durbars: rituals of incorporation
Although colonial rule was formally bureaucratic, in practice, it was personalised, and at the local level heavily influenced by the personal convictions, abilities and decisions of the various district commissioners. The influence of the 'man on the spot' was particularly great where he was assigned to the same station over a long period of time.[145] Duncan-Johnstone was the first officer in Lawra District to be stationed for such an extended period, from 1917 to 1921 with intermittent interruptions.[146]

Later, as Commissioner of Southern Province and Chief Commissioner of the Northern Territories, Duncan-Johnstone became an ardent supporter of the policy of indirect rule. Yet he hardly bothered to study the indigenous political institutions, and instead reserved all his efforts for instituting new traditions – honours, medals, uniforms, flags, agricultural exhibitions, royal visits and Empire Day, to mention just a few. These traditions were invariably framed by the inevitable 'durbar', a courtly ritual borrowed from eighteenth-century Mughal India that the British first adopted in colonial India before introducing it into Africa. The durbar was a ceremonial gathering of colonial officials and chiefs together with their followers, which in its seating and standing arrangement served to vividly display the colonial hierarchy, and strikingly enacted the incorporation of key actors into the hierarchy of authority through the bestowal of insignia and presents.[147] Duncan-Johnstone's professed aim was to instruct the chiefs in the 'art of self-government'; and he was convinced of the success of his innovations: 'A new spirit of progress and efficiency is manifesting itself amongst the chiefs who now really form what one might term as an "imperium in imperio".'[148] In fact, the rituals and symbols he introduced continue to shape the politics of the chieftaincy in Lawra District today.

Duncan-Johnstone's time in Lawra, towards the end of the First World War, corresponded to the period when colonial pacification was nearing an end and the new order was being consolidated. The former strongman strategies of power – patronage, predation and redistribution – no longer sufficed to assert chiefly rule effectively nor to legitimise it. Moreover, with the *pax Britannica* now ensconced, the inhabitants of the North-West enjoyed unparalleled mobility. The first labour migrants travelled to Tarkwa in 1906 and soon afterwards sought out many other parts of Asante and the Gold Coast. Such early contacts with the outside world are one reason why the colonial invention of traditions fell on such fertile soil in Lawra District. These neo-traditions presented the people with an opportunity to free themselves from the stigma of being uncivilised, heathen savages and to become the equals of the people of the neighbouring kingdoms.

As his first official act, Duncan-Johnstone introduced a three-level system of native courts – at the levels of headmen, sub-chiefs and head chiefs – with the district commissioner as the final court of appeal, 'the etiquette ... [being] modelled on that of the District Commissioner's court'.[149] Just one year later, he declared with satisfaction that eleven chiefs had already built court houses at their residences.[150] While earlier every 'petty complaint' would have been brought to the district commissioner, most complaints now came before the new native courts,[151] though Eyre-Smith was later to interpret this as an expression of the natives' fear of their chiefs. In order to put an end to the rivalry between the various head chiefs, which he explained in terms of ethnic difference, Duncan-Johnstone came up with a solution that anticipated the model of the Lawra Confederacy that was introduced in the 1930s. As already mentioned, the head chiefs of Lawra District did not recognise the Lawra Naa as the district paramount chief. Moreover, 'people did not like to bring their cases to the Chief of Lorha ... for as Lobi he knew nothing about the Sissallas and Dagartis, who at that time looked down on the Lobis.' Therefore, Duncan-Johnstone created a 'district native tribunal of which every paramount chief was ex officio a member, with the Chief of Lorha as president', which should then deal with 'appeal cases' from the divisional native courts.[152]

At his first attempt to summon an assembly of all chiefs to Lawra, Duncan-Johnstone was confronted by the limits of the method used by his predecessors, who had messages conveyed by a messenger carrying a 'message stick'. Some chiefs claimed that they never received the invitation, and the message stick was finally found somewhere in Tumu District. Duncan-Johnstone therefore suggested that every important chief should station one of his relatives in Lawra to serve as his representative and messenger. The latter had to inform his chief promptly of all important decrees – a suggestion which, according to Duncan-Johnstone, was taken up with some enthusiasm. The messengers, known by the Hausa word *dogari*, were remunerated by their chiefs, and could supplement their income with tips paid by the district commissioner for special errands. They were housed in Lawra in barracks, provided with a uniform consisting of a 'blue shirt or tunic, red sash, blue cap and brass medallion', put through military drills, taught Hausa and English, and gradually assumed the duties of an unarmed native police.[153]

One of the most important symbols of incorporation was the chief's medallion, which symbolised the new hierarchy and the membership of the native states in the British Empire. Worn around the neck on a chain, this displayed on the front a portrait of the King with the inscription 'Georgius Rex et Imp', while on the back was minted the seal of the Gold Coast, the elephant and coconut palm, framed by the words 'Northern Territories of the Gold Coast'.[154] These silver medallions measured two, three or four inches in diameter to symbolise the chief's relative degree of importance, and they were numbered. When a chief died, or was removed from office, the medallion was usually returned to the district commissioner, who then handed it over to the successor, thereby formally confirming the appointment. By the end of the 1920s, no additional medallions were put into circulation, thus making them a scarce prestige object, which could only be redistributed. Awarding one chief a larger medallion therefore required that this medallion first be 'freed' through the death or demotion of another chief.

In Lawra District, the first chief's medallions were presented by the Chief Commissioner in 1918. The one and only four-inch medallion was given to the Jirapa Naa, as the head chief with the longest period of service in the district at that time. Nandom Naa Danye, Lawra Naa Nanweni, Lambussie Kuoro Kantonbie and the Zini Kuoro all received three-inch medallions, while two chiefs from Ulu Division, the Gegenkpe Naa and the chiefs of Tugu and Tizza, each received two-inch ones.[155] Initially, the medallions were awarded on the basis of rank as well as in recognition of special services. While some of the ten head chiefs had no medallion at all, such as Samoa and Nandaw, a number of other sub-chiefs, like Birifu and Gegenkpe, were honoured with three-inch medallions for the effectiveness of their co-operation with the British. This combination of status and service-related criteria created confusion and provided material for conflict. At any rate, in the chiefs' view whoever had the larger medallion was higher in rank.

In 1929, therefore, the British finally decided that rank should be the sole criterion for giving out medallions – four-inch ones for 'Paramount Chiefs', three-inch ones for 'Tribal and Divisional Chiefs' and two-inch ones for 'other genuine Chiefs'.[156] However, when the Lawra Confederacy was established in 1934, and Lawra, Jirapa, Nandom and Lambussie were made divisional chiefs of equal rank (though in 1935 Lambussie was placed under Nandom), this hierarchy was not accurately reflected in the distribution of the symbols of power. While Jirapa had the four-inch medallion, Lawra and Nandom had only three-inch ones. Birifu, which came under Lawra, and Sabuli, under Jirapa, also had three-inch medallions, leading the Birifu Naa to assert his equality with respect to Lawra.[157] The district commissioner therefore suggested that the chiefs of Lawra and Nandom also be given four-inch medallions to underscore their pre-eminence over the sub-divisional chiefs and the parity of their rank to the Jirapa Naa, whose service record had been sufficiently commended by the 'King's Medal for African Chiefs for long and loyal service to the Government' granted to him in 1926.[158] The Chief Commissioner replied that there were no four-inch medallions available, nor were there plans to have any more made. Instead, the four-inch medallion was to rotate with the presidency of the Lawra Confederacy, a solution that remained effective until the end of the 1980s.

In addition to the medallions, which gained great significance for local power politics, the chiefs also appropriated as their insignia of office local symbols from the realm of the earth priests, the hunters and the warriors. Like earth priests, they sat on cow hides – a symbol of wealth – and prestigious hunters also were known to place the hide of their kill underneath them. On festive occasions, many donned a war-smock decorated with magical mirrors,[159] and the Lawra Naa held a horse-tail fly whisk in his hand in commemoration of his victories over the mounted Muslim warlords. Yet the medallion awarded by the British was decisive in marking the official recognition of chiefly office. For example, the Sabuli Naa feared for his authority when his medallion had to be sent to Navrongo for repair: 'his people think that his medallion has been taken from him as a result of misconduct'.[160] The large Mary medallions, which the White Fathers later distributed to their converts, were interpreted as an attack on the chieftaincy. Whether or not the chiefs' medallions were ascribed magical powers remains unclear. However, it is clear that today they continue to be regarded as essential evidence in proving claims to chiefly office.

It was not just the festive bestowal of chiefs' medallions that ceremonially underscored membership in the British Empire, but also events such as Empire Day, celebrated every year on 24 May in all the district towns of the Northern Territories with parades, the hoisting of flags, speeches, sports, plays put on by children, songs and dances. Since the 1930s, Empire Day centred on His Royal Majesty's speech heard over the radio and then translated into Dagara by the Lawra Naa.[161] The Prince of Wales's visits to Accra and Kumasi in April 1925 were magnificently staged, with delegations of chiefs from all over the country; the North-West being represented by the Wa Na and the Jirapa Naa.[162] An event vividly remembered in Lawra District was the subsequent visit of Princess Marie Louise, who came to Lawra and Birifu with the Governor of the Gold Coast and the Chief Commissioner, stayed the night and then went hunting hippopotamus with District Commissioner Eyre-Smith.[163] In honour of the coronation of George VI, all the divisional chiefs of Lawra-Tumu District, together with their sub-chiefs and a large entourage of messengers, dancers, drummers and xylophone-players, assembled in Lawra for a whole week. With standards and large umbrellas, they rode on horse-back to the ceremonial and drill grounds in front of the Lawra Naa's compound, where they attended sports competitions, marches, songs, and plays put on by pupils of the Lawra Confederacy Native Authority Primary School, opened in 1935. The high point of the festivities was a firework display, during which a rocket illuminated a portrait of the new king and queen in the night sky. The district commissioner gave every pupil in the district a coronation cup as a memento of this august event.[164]

What also appealed to the chiefs' pride in contributing to the glory of the great British Empire were the not entirely voluntary 'donations' of a shilling per compound to the Imperial War Fund and Red Cross Fund during the

First World War, as well the campaign to recruit soldiers, in response to which 790 young men actually reported, even though not all of them were deemed to be fit.[165] During the Second World War, at least 1,600 men from the Lawra Confederacy, some 2 per cent of the population, served in the army.[166] The Lawra-Tumu District Commissioner was himself astonished by how many volunteers signed up,[167] and even with the later compulsory conscription, there were hardly any problems in filling the necessary quotas.[168] However, it was probably less love of the Empire than pragmatic considerations that played a role, for during the war £41,000 in remittances and family support flowed into Lawra,[169] and the district commissioner compared the army with the long familiar practice of migrating to the South 'as a way of seeing the world'.[170] However, on the 'home front', things tended to be more patriotic. Regular speeches informed chiefs and pupils of world events. The Home Guard staged regular paramilitary exercises and paraded on Empire Day.[171] Pupils were instructed in Morse Code and made toothpicks to send to the soldiers at the front in East Africa and Burma.[172] A Victory Club, founded by the district commissioner with the first school graduates, organised monthly discussion groups, as well as horse-races and football matches with the aim of collecting donations for the war effort and organised the victory celebrations of 9 May 1945.[173]

Such rituals of incorporation in times of both war and peace evinced the imperial hierarchy and made the 'Dagarti', 'Lobi', 'Lobi-Dagarti' and 'Issala' a part of the great community of subjects under the British king. Duncan-Johnstone introduced annual conferences of chiefs held at rotating venues, at which the host chiefs competed with one another as to who could be the most generous host and had the best rest houses and roads.[174] Visits by the Provincial or Chief Commissioner became occasions for large meetings of chiefs, an exercise in unity. By holding a magnificent durbar (not to mention showing off well-maintained roads and rest houses), a district commissioner could not only shine in front of his superiors, he could at the same time use their presence to stress to the chiefs the importance of the honours that had been conferred on them. Thus Duncan-Johnstone, for example, waited for a visit by the Provincial Commissioner to have flags festively bestowed on the paramount chiefs, a device he thought up as a way of celebrating the tribal membership of the native states. The chiefs' gunmen fired a salute, and '[t]hey all seemed delighted with the flags, the Lobi standard consisting of different patterns of red white and blue, the Dagarti of yellow and red, and the Sissalla of black and yellow.'[175] In this way, the earlier inter-village feuds were to be transformed into constructive competition. All in all, Duncan-Johnstone praised the fact that the head chiefs and sub-chiefs had now become 'quite a happy family'.[176]

The new collective identities would also reach beyond Lawra District. As early as 1908, 88 chiefs from the Northern Territories, with an entourage of over 1,000 people were sent with their local agricultural products to the agricultural show in Kumasi. From the North-West alone at least 160 people went, all of whom must have been considerably impressed by the sight of a town like Kumasi.[177] Excursions like this brought such chiefs into contact with one another who had either never met at all, or at least not managed to do so in peacetime. For the chiefs of the Lawra Confederacy, the first conference of all the native authorities of the Northern Territories in Tamale, December 1938, must have been especially impressive. This gathering was intended to further the wider sense of belonging to the Northern Territories as a whole, 'breaking down the narrow inter-tribal parochial spirit which was so marked a feature formerly'.[178] The extensive 'entertainment programme' included a large durbar, horse-racing, a football competition between state and mission schools, theatrical performances by pupils, and various military displays.[179] It was pupils from Lawra who won the first prize in the theatrical competition, contributing to a great sense of pride among Lawra Confederacy chiefs. The prize-winning play was about Wussilewura, a Kusiele warrior from Lawra, who, armed with bows and arrows, is said to have led the resistance to Babatu's mounted troops. At the Senior School in Tamale too, youths from Lawra were often cast as archers in school plays.[180] The symbolic incorporation of the Lobi and Dagarti into the community of the Northern Territories was thus accompanied by an emphasis on, and re-evaluation of, their ascribed propensity for feuding and resistance to authority: what had once been regarded as rebelliousness and a dangerous, unpredictable aggressiveness gradually came to be admired – at least by the district commissioners, the chiefs, and the early educated elite – as manly pride and military skill.

One mediating factor between the feuding and attacks during the first decade of the twentieth century and the sublimated displays of violence in school plays, war dances and archery competitions[181] was the warlike reception that some chiefs gave Duncan-Johnstone and his successors. These were staged rituals of rebellion, as Duncan-Johnstone vividly described them:

> The paramount Chiefs and a mounted following together with an N.T.C. escort met us two miles out of Lorha and at one mile out, the bush became alive with people. There must have been between six and seven thousand. The young men of Burifo, easily distinguishable by head-dresses of whitened calabashes and white clay smeared on their bodies, who had come in with us, dashed forward and engaged in mimic conflict with the Lorha young men with their equally distinctive uniform of red Fez, long red tail and red clay smeared on them. From the first mile just almost into the Station the road was lined each side by the gunmen, who made deafening noise.[182]

That the admiration was also coupled by fear is revealed by Duncan-Johnstone's commentary regarding a reception in Lambussie: 'The Lambussie gun men are positively dangerous not caring where they fire. I think that they would be secretly overjoyed to see one of us fall off.'[183] In Birifu, and later also in other places, Duncan-Johnstone was nicknamed 'Muryi' or 'sudden appearance', allegedly because he would do his best to evade warlike receptions and reach the local rest house unnoticed, thus popping up unexpectedly.[184] When Duncan-Johnstone returned to Lawra once more in 1932, he stated with satisfaction that the Lobi were now conducting their large-scale greeting offensive armed only with bows, no longer with arrows, as had previously been the case.[185] Duncan-Johnstone and his successors saw the increasing domestication of such rituals of rebellion as a sign of advancing civilisation, a process in which not only the new institution of the chieftaincy, but also labour migration played a considerable part.

3

THE DISCURSIVE CREATION
OF ETHNICITY

'Could not obtain any information about the Lobi as a tribe, and could not find out what tribe Kontol [the founding ancestor of Lawra] belonged to', complained Jackson, the new Lawra District Commissioner, when he set out on the task of writing the first report on the 'laws and customs' of the 'native communities' in his district in 1907. However, he added that 'they think he was a Lobi, hence they call themselves Lobi', apparently after some leading questions to Issa, a Wangara Muslim who worked for the Lawra Naa as an interpreter.[1] When, some forty years later, the native authorities were about to be replaced by local councils, the Birifu Naa insisted that the area under his rule must be independent of Lawra, because 'Burifo is an entirely different tribe to that of Lawra and our customs are not the same'.[2] By this time, local actors had thoroughly adopted the tribalistic discourse as their own and were using it to pursue their own political interests. Ironically, this came right at the moment when the British model of the tribe as a natural political community was gradually being replaced by the new post-war discourse of community development.

In this chapter,[3] I discuss the British production of an ethnic map of the North-West and of a corpus of 'tribal laws and customs'. However, I am also concerned with the adoption and, at the same time, transformation of tribalistic discourse by African chiefs and interpreters. From the start, the intellectual colonisation of the North-West by the British was not a one-sided hegemonic imposition of a new discursive order, but a process of communication marked by many (interest-led) misunderstandings and mutual manipulations. In the course of time, a growing number of Africans began more forcefully to make themselves heard, and it became increasingly obvious that neither they nor the British spoke with one voice. Colonial ethnography and historiography were not a monolithic block of 'invented traditions' that had successfully, and irreversibly, reified what had once been flexible, authentic African 'customs' (Ranger 1983), but were rather the result of 'creative negotiation between agents of both discursive communities, the British and the African' (Pels 1996: 740), marked by unexpected and often also undiscerned moments of mutual instrumentalisation.[4]

The tour of inspection, with 'palavers' in every village visited, was the most important instrument in the British production of ethnographic knowledge. While the 'palaver', typically an assembly attended by the chief and his elders, was used by the British to dispense instructions and news, it could on occasion become something like a British interrogation of local agents. Especially in the early years, the interpreter played a decisive role in these assemblies by mediating linguistically as well as conceptually between questions as posed by the British and local political idioms. Even after the district station was opened in Lawra, the tour remained an important means of gathering information. However, this was now complemented by permanent contact with African assistants working in the station and by conversations with local chiefs, who gradually came to pursue a more active policy of providing information and making visits to the district commissioner.

Yet the British could not further their knowledge of local reality without creating certain conditions conducive to doing so. After the First World War, the military men who had predominated during the first two decades of the colonial regime were gradually replaced by a new type of political officer who tended to be more highly educated than his predecessors and committed to a civilian career. While employment prior to the change in policy only required a secondary-school certificate and a successful job interview, in 1924 a one-year preparatory course at Oxford or Cambridge became obligatory for all colonial officers heading out to Africa, and included instruction in anthropology, languages, law, hygiene, accounting and surveying.[5]

Only after the First World War was there any systematic attempt to have district commissioners serve at the same station continuously for an extended period of time. Only thus, argued the Chief Commissioner, could the trust necessary for the effective administration of the natives be established.[6] In contrast to the period from 1907 to 1917, when fourteen different officers served at the Lawra district station in succession, most for only a few months each, during the inter-war period several district commissioners served for relatively long periods of time: Duncan-Johnstone (1917–21), Eyre-Smith (1921–9), Dasent (1923–5), Armstrong (1929–35), Ellison (1934–8) and Amherst (1939–45) all stayed in Lawra for three years or even longer.

Serving longer at a particular station made the commissioners more familiar with their districts, and they also came to identify with them more. As a result, many of the negative stereotypes formed earlier about the 'Lobi' were revised. Beginning in the mid-1920s, colonial officers were required to pass an examination in native languages, before their appointments could be confirmed, or before they could be promoted.[7] Although none of the Lawra district commissioners spoke fluent Dagara or Sisala, their knowledge of Hausa and Dagbani enabled them to communicate with the local population more directly than their predecessors had been able to do.[8] At the same time, more and more of the local population also learned Hausa, Twi or some English in the course of their military service or labour migration. Since 1918, some chiefs' sons were sent to colonial schools so that afterwards they might work as clerks or court interpreters. This development certainly benefited the chiefs, who eventually felt that it could only be to their advantage to play a more active part in shaping the British view of their society.

In this chapter three main themes will concern us. The first is the manner in which colonial officers came to terms with the contradiction between the British tribal model and complex local realities. The expectations that the British brought with them shaped how they would come to map out the ethnic landscape, but their ethnic categories would also be partly defined by African informants, first Muslims in Wa, and later the chiefs in Lawra and the surrounding area. As British administrators came to know more and more, the tribal model was transformed and modified.[9] Even if their perceptions were strongly influenced by European models, many British administrators knew an astonishing amount about the social and political particularities of their African districts. Moreover, colonial knowledge was varied, heterogeneous and internally disputed.

However, a gap did exist between ethnographic knowledge and colonial practice – the second theme addressed by this chapter. By the early 1930s, the old concept of the 'tribe' as a descent-based community with a common language and culture was already being fundamentally revised. However, when, in the course of the introduction of indirect rule, new territorial arrangements were being considered, they were discussed in terms of tribal concepts, as if this critical debate had never taken place. The 'ignorance' that can be discerned here was not a question of not knowing, but of the almost inevitable need to reduce complexity in administrative decision-making, especially in a multi-faceted political landscape like that of the North-West. At any rate, until the 1950s the united tribe headed by a strong chief remained the dominant British model which should govern political reform.

The third theme is the link between political objectives and ethnographic discourse. Often the ethnographic and historical projects of the district commissioners can only be properly understood against the backdrop of their political visions. An exponent of *realpolitik*, such as Guinness (a Lawra district commissionor serving in the 1930s), might refer to the 'tradition' of African big-men strategies, while Eyre-Smith, who was inspired by Catholic corporatist ideas of democracy, pleaded for a return to the 'traditional' earth-shrine parishes. In such debates, African actors intervened by deploying strategies that alternately provided or refused information, depending on what most effectively furthered their own political interests. The historical development of this unequal dialogue between Africans and the British is reflected in the structure of this chapter. It begins with the almost 'voiceless' mapping of ethnic identities by the British and then turns to the process by which the resulting blueprints of ethnic stereotypes were gradually refined. This is followed by historical speculations regarding the origin of ethnic differences, and concludes by recording in detail local discourses, in the form of patrilineage accounts of migration and settlement, that legitimate power and territorial claims.

MAPPING ETHNIC IDENTITIES

Ethnicity, says Worby, writing about colonial mapping projects, 'is fundamentally about the power to name others [and is] increasingly bound up with an imaginary knowledge of the relationship between ethnic identities and socio-geographic space' (1994: 371). British notions held that every African belonged from birth to death to a particular tribe that was clearly distinct from neighbouring tribes in its physiological, linguistic and cultural features. What is revealing, however, are the ambiguities that vexed colonial ethnic mapping in an area like the Black Volta region, with its overlapping identities and fuzzy boundaries, a region lying 'between' more centralised polities. Toponyms were redefined as ethnonyms and vice versa. The tremendous mobility of the population was disregarded or conceptually watered-down as 'intermingling', because the ethnic maps as imagined by the British required that people be allocated to clear territorial entities. Moreover, the ethnic identities that were then recorded during population censuses or military conscription show that the self-designations of African subjects often defied and limited the colonial power to name. Yet the terms the British used in drafting their ethnic maps were not entirely products of the European imagination: they also employed African names, such as those used by Muslim state-builders to designate the heathen 'others'. Once established, however, the ethnic nomenclature of the British proved quite enduring. This resulted partly from the self-referentiality of colonial reporting, and partly from the central significance accorded to the tribe as a model of political order. Yet despite the rigidity of the taxonomic terms, their geographic location, as well as their specific content (i.e. the attributes and value judgement ascribed to them) changed as the British were confronted with new realities – which is precisely what permitted these categories to be retained, once they had been constructed. This was particularly so in the case of the category 'Lobi', as we will see.

The first maps of the hinterland of the Gold Coast
One of the first Europeans to map the region of present-day North-West Ghana was Captain Louis Binger, who in 1888–9 travelled from Senegal via Kong and Bobo-Dioulasso to Ouagadougou on behalf of the French

government, returning to the Atlantic coast via Salaga and Kintampo. Yet the names of the places and populations along the Black Volta his two Dagomba informants in Wale-Wale had proposed for inclusion on his map could not be verified by his further enquiries. Nor was Binger able to verify them on the spot since his route did not lead him through this region, which his two informants had called 'Gourounsi'. This was no accident, however. According to Binger, the Africans only spoke of 'Gourounsi' as a group of territories that filled them with a certain apprehension. Gourounsi was a rugged back region into which various groups from the neighbouring kingdoms fled and whose linguistically and culturally heterogeneous peoples were constantly feuding among themselves (1892, II: 34–5). Among the 'tribes' of Gourounsi west of the Black Volta, Binger listed the 'Dagari' and 'Dagabakha', who seemed to him to be 'one and the same people'; north of them the 'Oulé'; and to the east, on what was later to become Lawra District, the 'Lama', 'Lakhama' or 'Nokhodosi' (Map 4).[10]

The map drawn up by George Ekem Ferguson (Map 5), who was to conclude treaties of friendship and free commerce with Dagomba, Gonja, Gourounsi and Mossi,[11] included no cartographic specifics, but only provided a general indication that 'Dagarti', 'Kaparasi' and 'Ule' were vaguely associated with the vicinity later to be known as Lawra District. The map had already been drafted after Ferguson's first mission in 1892, which only took him as far as the regions of Gonja and Dagomba via Bole. Only on his second mission in 1894 did he conclude a Treaty of Friendship and Trade with Wa Na Seidu Takora, thus bringing the 'Country of Dagarti, otherwise known as Dagaba' under the British sphere of influence.[12]

Ferguson complained that political boundaries throughout the hinterland of the Gold Coast were imprecisely defined, because the political relations between the larger 'states' and the 'weaker tribes' were in a constant state of flux (in Arhin 1974: 74). Boundaries were not permanently fixed, but shaped by temporary, reversible alliances between local rulers and by relations defined in terms of power and tribute. Because the domain in which friendship treaties applied depended on the extent of the networks that the local treaty partners controlled, Ferguson paid special attention to their 'various degrees of capacity for political negotiations' (ibid.: 116). He regarded 'countries with organized government', like Mamprussi, Dagomba, Gonja, Mossi and Wa, as reliable partners. In contrast, 'barbarous tribes', which lived in autonomous, small 'family communities' and were continually feuding among themselves, were incapable of negotiating with Europeans (ibid.: 99–100). Among the latter, Ferguson included the 'Lobi' to the west of the Black Volta and the inhabitants of 'Gurunshi' to the east, that 'belt of inhospitable barbarous tribes, through which caravans often have to fight their way', living between the Mossi and Dagbon states (ibid.: 74). Following Binger, Ferguson initially included the 'Dagari' and

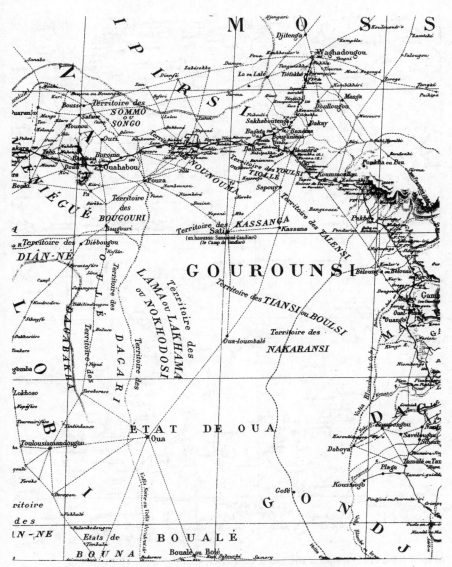

Map 4 Haut-Niger au Golfe de Guinée, L. H. Binger, 1887–9 (detail)
Source: Binger 1892

'Dagabaka' under 'Gurunshi', but later drew a distinction between the 'country of Dagarti', which the Wa Na claimed to rule, and 'Grunshi', whose 'sub-tribes' (Talensi, Bulsi, Isale, Lama etc.) could only be 'civilized' by means of armed force (ibid.: 100, 117).

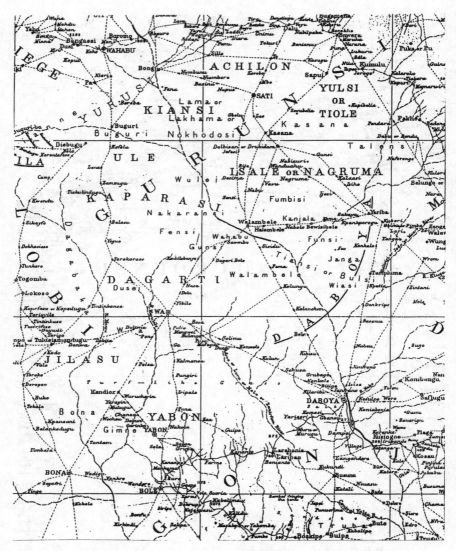

Map 5 The Hinterland of the Gold Coast, G. E. Ferguson, 1893 (detail)
Source: PRO, CO 700, Gold Coast 29

One might be tempted to read Ferguson's distinction between 'countries with organized government' and 'barbarous tribes', or Binger's opposition between 'states' and 'territories', as early versions of the dichotomy between states and segmentary societies later posited by Fortes and Evans-Pritchard (1940). However, Binger and Ferguson were not describing an isolated juxtaposition of acephalous and centralised societies, but a complex network of alliances and enmities between political units of differing ranges and various degrees of internal empowerment. The polysemic nature of Ferguson's terminology alone, with names usually being used simultaneously as toponyms and ethnonyms, resists simple dichotomies. Thus, Dagomba, Gonja, Mamprussi and Mossi are described alternately as 'powerful states' or 'warlike tribes'; 'Grunshi' and 'Lobi' sometimes as 'territories', sometimes as 'savage tribes'. Ferguson's sketch of the hinterland of the Gold Coast showed states torn apart by internal factionalism, which exercised only weak control over their peripheries. Between these were stateless areas, whose territory flowed in seamless transition into that of the states and whose settlements united under 'strongmen' when it was necessary for ensuring the common defence or for launching attacks on merchants. Finally, there were extremely mobile groups who secured their livelihoods by participating in slave raids and offering their services as mercenaries, like Babatu's Zaberma, which many villagers joined and which were on the verge of founding new states.

Ferguson's perspective was coloured by his task of widening the British crown's sphere of influence through the signing of treaties of friendship with local rulers. In order to do this, he had to be able to assess the alliance policies of his treaty partners and know which territory and which populations they claimed to control. More precise knowledge of the Gold Coast hinterland only became indispensable once it became a British protectorate. The Northern Territories were then surveyed from the newly established military and administrative posts, mapped both literally and metaphorically, in the sense that political, economic, linguistic and cultural structures were classified more precisely.

'Scattered compounds' and 'mixed races'

Despite all evidence to the contrary, the British held fast to their conviction that every African belonged to one, and only one, tribe. In their eyes, ethnic boundaries were natural: one only needed to discover them in order to be able to transform them into the bases for boundaries of the native states. However, the precise mapping of the tribes created problems, for cultural and linguistic differences in the North-West did not correlate, but rather formed a complex web of differences and similarities, rather than a mosaic of individual tribes. As Captain Read, a perceptive observer, averred on his first tour of inspection through 'Lobi' and 'Dagarti' country, not only were the villages 'greatly intermixed, making sketching very difficult', but the precise ethnic boundaries were also difficult to ascertain.[13] Nonetheless, he was convinced that mapping them was not wholly impossible, and the legend of the map he drafted indicates that he intended to record linear tribal boundaries. However, in actual fact Read's map, as the ones prepared by Binger and Ferguson, only vaguely ascribed the different tribes to particular areas (see Maps 2 and 6). In the case of the Wala, Read equated tribe and kingdom without much ado and declared the boundaries of the area ruled by the Wa Na to be ethnic boundaries.[14] Defining the boundaries of the territories of the stateless 'Dagarti' and 'Lobi', on the other hand, posed far greater difficulties:

> English Lobi lies along the eastbank [sic] of the Black Volta, between the 10th and the 11th parallels of latitude and extends only 10 to 20 miles east of the river.[15]
>
> The Dagarti country extends from the north of the Wala country to almost as far as the 11th parallel, on the west the tribe is so intermingled with the Lobi that it is not yet possible to give the delimitation but it may be roughly stated to follow a line about six to eight miles from the Black Volta River. On the east there is a well defined boundary in the Kulpawn river.[16]

Assuming that they were dealing in the North-West with primitive, small-scale societies that were isolated from one another, the British interpreted river courses as barriers to communication, along which ethnic boundaries must also run. In the open savannah, on the other hand, the transition was more fluid. Here, notions like 'intermingling' and 'intermixing' allowed the ambiguity of ethnic boundaries to be taken into account, without, however, giving up the idea that a boundary existed. Because the border between Lobi and Dagarti was so difficult to determine precisely, the British invented a new ethnic category here, namely 'Lobi-Dagarti'.

The ethnic map of the North-West that the British had drawn up by 1907 was drafted from a political and military perspective influenced by the fact that the station was located in Wa. As a result, this map adopted the nomenclature used by the local Wala Muslims and former Zabarima and Sofa fighters, who had now entered British service. In their eyes, the 'Dagaba' (or, in British terminology, the 'Dagarti') were infidels over whom the Wa Na claimed the right of sovereignty. For Captain Berthon too, therefore, 'Dagarti' was the better known, apparently less hostile area, and initially, he referred to the less peaceful area of what would later become Lawra District as 'outlying districts of Dagarti'. Like 'Dagaba', for the Dyula traders and Muslim warlords west of the Volta, 'Lobi' was a synonym for heathenism, primitiveness, nakedness, political fragmentation and bitter resistance to all forms of foreign rule.[17] We do not know whether Berthon himself, while on his tour of inspection in December 1903, introduced the name 'Lobi', because he had heard of Lobi attacks on the trade route between Buna and Diébougou, or because his interpreter, Mama Dagarti, had coined the term by deriving it from the local nomenclature.[18] In any event, Berthon associated the term 'Lobi' with hostility, so that anyone who

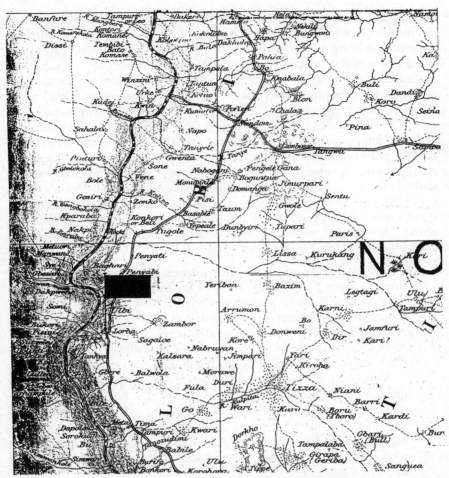

Map 6 North-Western District of the Northern Territories of the Gold Coast, 1905 (detail)
Source: PRO, CO 1047, Gold Coast 425

attacked the troops had to be Lobi. This meant that, in the minds of the British, the Lobi, who for Binger and Ferguson only lived west of the Black Volta, had now 'migrated' to the east. The 'outlying district of Dagarti' now became 'Lobi-Dagarti', an as yet unknown 'wild country' where attacks by robbers, murders and feuds were daily events, though it also promised a wealth of untapped resources (supposedly rubber and gold), just like the Lobi area west of the Black Volta.[19]

Berthon considered the hostility of the Lobi and Lobi-Dagarti to be a permanent characteristic anchored in the physiognomy of a 'very big and strongly built race'. What were originally politically and religiously inspired appellations were thus changed into quasi-biological ethnic categories. Read in particular continued to naturalise social categories. Expectations regarding the intensity of resistance to the British presence were similarly oriented along the lines of Berthon's Lobi/Dagarti framework. Thus, on his journey through Black Volta District in early 1905, he sent some of his armed escort ahead to Wa as soon as he left 'Lobi country' and had only 'Dagarti' left to cross, since he regarded the latter to be pacified. In Read's report, therefore, the different stages of pacification were recast as characteristics inherent to the various tribes or, more precisely, to the individual native, who, like a specimen taken of the local flora or fauna, could be nothing more than an exact replica of his particular species. In Read's report it also becomes clear how ethnic categories were imagined as plural from the start, embedded in a system of similarities and contrasts that corresponded to the degree of civilisation:

> The Lobi native is of an extremely independent nature and will owe no other authority beyond the head of his own family. ... They are ... always ready to resort to their poisoned arrows on the least provocation. Fighting between compounds have been frequent occurrences ... Neither men nor women wear any clothes, but the men sometimes carry sheep skin tied over their shoulders and falling down their backs. They are generally of good physique though not tall. ...
>
> Along the Lobi or western boundary the Dagarba or Dagarti as he is generally miscalled are intermixed with the Lobi and the same description applies equally to both of them. ... They are uncivilised and turbulent in the extreme on the West, but an improvement is made towards the centre and East where there are many Mohamedan settlements. Except in the latter places the men are generally naked and invariably armed with bows and arrows. ...
>
> As compared to the other tribes described in this report, the [Isala] inhabitants are peaceful and quiet except where the towns are adjacent to Lobi and Dagarti where they copy the habits of their neighbours.[20]

Ascriptions such as these were included by Read, and by the authors of other reports written in these early years, along with information on the physiognomy and natural environment of each tribe, resources, architecture, types of settlement, agriculture and pastoralism. The alternating use of tribal names as toponyms and ethnonyms reinforced the idea of tribes as territorially anchored, natural communities. Thus arose the image of an ethnic landscape in which groups, clearly distinguishable from one another by nature of their biology, character, language, culture, political organisation and economic activities, lived on their ancestral lands. This image was further the product of representations found in travel literature and popular anthropological writings of the time, with which colonial officers were familiar.[21]

However, the reports also reveal that Read and his colleagues were aware that reality did not fit their taxonomies all that well. This was especially apparent in their search for unequivocal markers of difference in house-building styles and human physiognomy. In particular 'tribal marks', if they existed, would certainly have made it easier for any outsider who had no knowledge of the local language and no recourse to an interpreter to orient himself in a world that seemed threateningly alien and chaotic, and would have enabled him to gauge immediately any new 'Other' he might encounter. However, types of compound were not sufficiently different from one another to allow someone to ascertain whether he was approaching a Dagarti, Issala or Lobi settlement, nor could a coherent system of facial marks be discerned. As far as the Dagarti were concerned, Read reckoned that there were no signs of any 'common facial mark'.[22] Among the Lobi, District Commissioner Jackson certainly discovered decorative scars, but had to admit that the 'marks are very seldom used as they [the Lobi] prefer having a plain face'.[23]

It was because the boundaries between Lobi and Dagarti could not be outlined clearly on a map, and because they could also not be read off the bodies or houses, that the category of 'mixed Lobi-Dagarti' became so important. The British never made clear whether they saw the Lobi-Dagarti to represent a single tribe or merely a residual category that was the product of the 'mixing' effected by intermarriage and neighbourly relations. In his annual report for 1905, for example, Chief Commissioner Watherston stated that the North-West was peopled by the tribes of the Wala, Lobi, Dagarti, mixed Lobi-Dagarti and Issala Grunshi.[24] However, in a lecture to the London African Society, he only spoke of the Wala, Lobi, Dagarti and Grunshi (1907–8: 351). Where exactly the Lobi-Dagarti lived was also an open question: the territory ascribed to them by the British changed several times in the course of time. While for Berthon the whole of what was to become Lawra District was 'Lobi Dagarti country', Read only classified certain settlements like Tizza, Duori and Eremon as Lobi-Dagarti: in his view, Nandom and Lawra were Lobi, while Jirapa was Dagarti.[25] Read's successors, on the other hand, classified Jirapa as Lobi-Dagarti.[26] In 1918, Jirapa was then classified, together with Nandom and Lawra, as the 'Lobi Division',[27] but afterwards regarded as Lobi-Dagarti once again, and from the mid-1930s finally as Dagarti, while Nandom now counted as Lobi-Dagarti. Only Lawra was consistently classified as Lobi.[28]

This flexibility in classifying individual entities contributed to the stability of the ethnic model as a whole. In fact, in their reports on their earliest journeys, Read and his colleagues laid down ethnic categories that were to survive the entire colonial period and are still in use today, though the assessments of them changed. Thus, Read no longer considered the Lobi to be particularly warlike and even to be 'more truthful than any [other] natives', while his colleague Taylor took the Dagarti to task that it was not they but the Lobi who were proving 'sensible and going ahead'.[29] Nonetheless, the classificatory model endured. And, despite all the problems in drawing boundaries, Read did not hesitate to calculate the 'fighting force' of the various tribes at exactly 8,689 Wala, 15,474 Dagarti, 19,493 Grunshi and 17,175 Lobi.[30]

Censuses and names

Population censuses and the recording of names in recruiting for the military service or for work in the mines were moments at which British categorisations of ethnicity and local self-ascriptions had to be 'translated' into one another.[31] In this respect, the British alone did not simply impose their classificatory scheme on chiefs and interpreters: the local population also shaped the contours of the British ethnic map. This is especially clear from the striking differences in the number of 'Lobi' recorded in the censuses of 1921 and 1931.

How Duncan-Johnstone, who was charged with carrying out the 1921 census, went about the count we do not know, but presumably his methods corresponded to those used elsewhere in the Northern Territories. Each head of family had to place an ear of maize for each male and a cowry for each female into a calabash, which was then taken to the chief or native clerk, who entered the figures in special tables, which the District Commissioner then collected.[32] However, it is unclear who decided the ethnic ascriptions – the responsible village chief, the head chief, Duncan-Johnstone, his interpreter Binni Lobi or all four – and what happened when they did not agree. In any case, the inhabitants of a village were usually assigned as a whole to one of the ethnic categories, which Duncan-Johnstone adopted from his predecessors and refined further by creating the sub-categories Lobi Burifo, Lobi Dagarti, Lobi Wili, Dagarti and Issalla Grunshi.[33] Only in the larger settlements like Nandom, Hamile and Lawra did he register an ethnically mixed population, including Mossi, Wala, Hausa and other 'strangers'. With the exception of Lawra, which counted as 'purely' Lobi Burifo, the native states were ethnically mixed: Nandom Division consisting of Lobi Burifo and Lobi Dagarti settlements, Lambussie Division of Issalla and Lobi Burifo, and Jirapa Division of Lobi Dagarti and Dagarti. This bewildering variety of tribes led the Chief Commissioner to remark that the boundaries between them were very unclear: 'Lobis, Dagartis, Issalas and Grunshis are very much mixed up and the inhabitants of many compounds might with propriety be counted under either head or as a combination of both.'[34] Nonetheless Duncan-Johnstone did not hesitate to divide the population of Lawra District up into precisely 64 per cent Lobi (Lobi Dagarti and Lobi Burifo), 17 per cent Dagarti and 19 per cent Sissalla.[35]

What is especially striking here is the extension of the category 'Lobi'. While Read had once restricted the category 'English Lobi' to those living on a ten-mile-wide strip along the east bank of the Black Volta, now two-thirds of the population of Lawra District were being classified as Lobi. Perhaps Duncan-Johnstone's positive view of the Lobi may be have had something to do with this. In any case, he assumed Lobi origins at many places which Read and others had found to be 'purely Dagarti'. Seeking to establish the most comprehensive ethnic categories possible, which might allow the administration to reduce the number of native states in Lawra-Tumu District, Duncan-Johnstone's successor, Dasent, took these matters still further. According to him, only Sabuli was a 'pure [sic] Dagati division', while 70 per cent of the natives of Jirapa, Ulu and Nandaw, who had hitherto been classified as 'Dagati', were 'of Lobi stock'.[36]

Although colonial officials had come to view the Lobi character positively, exactly the opposite developed among the natives themselves, as can be seen from their resistance to the name 'Lobi'. While censuses were instances of collective ethnic classification, the recording of names in recruitment for the army or for mine labour was a moment of individual self-ascription. A common practice was to add the tribal designation to the forename as a 'family name'. Already in 1918, Duncan-Johnstone noted that it was 'curious that so many Lobi ... enlisted as Dagarti as if ashamed of the name Lobi'. His attempts to increase pride in the Lobi identity and the name led nowhere, and there were increasing numbers of cases like the recruit 'who left Lorha in the spring of this year as Mora Lobi' and came 'back with his discharge certificate as Mora Dagarti'.[37] The migrants wished to avoid the stigma of primitivism that was associated with the name 'Lobi'. Lawra Naa J. A. Karbo ardently refused to sign documents 'Karbo Lobi', as the district commissioner expected from the head chief of a 'Lobi division'.[38] Much to Karbo's indignation, the chief of the 'Lobi Dagarti division' of Nandom, Naa Konkuu, was allowed to sign himself 'Kumkun Dagarti'.[39]

The obstinacy with which military recruits and labour migrants designated themselves as Dagarti probably contributed to the shift in ethnic classification that once again favoured the Dagarti at the next census of 1931. The Commissioner of Northern Province complained at the lack of consistency in the ethnic appellations that the district commissioners were using and thus decreed that the only 'recognised tribes' in Lawra-Tumu District would be the Dagati, Lobi, Issala and Kassena (previously Grunshi).[40] Now District Commissioner Ellison estimated the number of Lobi in the Lawra Confederacy (the area of the former Lawra District, but excluding Zini) at around 40,000, the Dagarti at 17,000 and the Issala at

6,000.[41] Compared to 1921 the number of Lobi had stagnated, while the number of Dagarti had practically doubled, because many of the villages classified as Lobi in 1921 were now classified as Dagarti. It was not only the unpopularity of the ethnic label that contributed to this shift, but also the in-migration of 'proper Lobi' from the neighbouring French colony into the area south of Wa. Chief Commissioner Jones argued that, of all the tribes in the Protectorate, these Lobi were actually at the lowest level of social development and that they should not be confused with the relatively cultivated Lobi-Dagarti in Lawra District.[42] The popular trend towards the supercession of the Lobi category in Lawra District continued: in 1960 only 5,430 Lobi were registered there, 4.8 per cent of the entire population, compared to 81.4 per cent Dagaba.[43]

THE PRODUCTION OF COLONIAL ETHNOGRAPHY

Having completed their rough sketch of the ethnic map, the British took to the task of fleshing out this framework with information about the history, political organisation and customs of the various tribes. The first comprehensive ethnographic report on the Wala, Dagarti, Grunshi and Lobi was written in 1907–8 by Commissioner Read in Wa and Commissioner Jackson in Lawra, in response to a questionnaire from the Colonial Ministry on the 'laws and customs of West African native communities'.[44] Here, and in later ethnographies, it became clear that the British realised that realities on the ground did not correspond to the landscape of primitive tribes ruled by chiefs that they expected. Nonetheless, they held fast to this idea. Some accounted for the fragmentation they encountered by referring to the political upheaval of the late nineteenth century, which had divided the once united tribes; others referred to the image of a family tree and sought to explain the undeniable similarities between tribes they considered distinct by pointing to the long history of conquest, intermarriage and co-residence. From the very beginning, however, it was not only European views that fed into this discourse about tribal characteristics, history and ethnicity; African knowledge and ideas, introduced by the new chiefs, also played their part.

'There is no tribal organisation'

Read's report from 1907–8 presented information on the history and political organisation of the Dagarti, Lobi, Grunshi and Wala separately, but listed under one heading information on the civil and criminal law of all groups 'who have not come under the influence of Mahommedanism'. Although customs and traditions were certainly tribe-specific, in Read's view, the religious boundary between the Muslim Wala and the heathen Dagarti, Lobi and Grunshi seemed more important to him in many respects. This was already true when it came to acquiring information. 'Mallams Izaka and Abdulai', Read's co-operative primary informants in

Wa matters, could read and write (Arabic) and had helped pacify the neighbouring Dagaba villages around the turn of the century. Izaka was installed by the British as 'Mohamedan Chief', while Abdulai was employed as a court interpreter.[45] Among the Dagarti and Lobi, on the other hand, hardly any competent informants could be found that were willing to give information:

> Many Dagarti have been enlisted as soldiers and I have interrogated many on the subject [of their own customs and fetish laws], but they never give me any information beyond that of their own families and others profess total ignorance, saying, that they have been out of their country so long that they have forgotten them. The natives themselves are extremely reticent and suspicious of giving any information about their customs.[46]

Regarding to the history of the Dagarti, he merely stated: 'Dagarti has never been a kingdom and the natives know little or nothing of their past history.'[47] '[T]he lack of discipline and combination' had turned them, like the Grunshi, into the defenceless prey of slave-raiders. According to Read, the Dagarti lacked anything resembling a 'tribal organisation' or 'ceremonies of initiation to the tribe'. Membership was determined by place of birth and residence, not by descent: 'A man that was born in the country and had never seen his father country would be considered to be a Dagarti.'[48] Lawra District Commissioner Jackson also noted that the Lobi had 'nothing common to the whole tribe except the earth which they all swear by'.[49] Read concluded that nowhere in the North-West was the 'tribe' or the 'village or local community' a legal entity which, for example, held property in common or could inherit from deceased members.[50]

Generally among the 'Dagarti, Lobi, Issala and Grunshi Pagans', Read asserted, 'fetishes' and 'fetish priests' were the most important institution:

> The Fetish is omnipotent and is to them as a Diety [sic]. Fetishes are so numerous that to describe them all would be an impossibility ... Belief in the fetish is absolute throughout the country and for any dispute ... and ... everything that is not in the ordinary smooth course of events, fetish is made. ... The power held by many priests is therefore very great and it is no uncommon thing for a man to gain reputation for a fetish and make large sums of money from it as well as collect a large following for any enterprise he may desire.[51]

Read obviously subsumed the *tèngándèm*, as well as the diviners, healers and owners of special forms of magic, under the category 'fetish priests', implying that the transitions between these functions were fluid ones. He also emphasised time and again the flexibility and interest-relatedness of all rules and institutions. Thus, the family was seen as an extraordinarily flexible concept: 'The family includes all blood relations and may also include wives' relations should they desire it, or more correctly should they think it to their advantage.'[52] The norm of paternal authority only counted as long as the father was able to impose his authority physically. 'To sum up the civil and criminal laws of these Pagans', Read concluded,

> there are none beyond those of the fetish, and no ruling authority beyond the head of the family whose power is confined only to those who wish to obey him, and ... both these authorities can be avoided either by payments to the fetish or by a declaration of independence against the head of the family.[53]

On the one hand, such statements belonged to the standard repertoire of contemporary descriptions of 'primitive' societies that was inspired by evolutionist ideas. The assumption was that where no kingdoms had as yet developed, feud and the rule of force, or to put it pointedly: lawlessness, prevailed. On the other hand, Read's reference to mobility, flexibility and lack of hierarchies indicates that he certainly grasped the rudiments of political realities at that time. Nonetheless, neither Read nor his colleagues fundamentally called into question the tribal model. That every native belonged to a tribe and that the North-West consisted of Wala, Dagarti, Lobi and Grunshi was to remain a indubitable fact.

History/ies as a co-production of chiefs and colonial officers

Among Dagara and Sisala villagers, 'history' exists in the plural, in the form of the various migration narratives of different patrilineages explaining who among one's ancestors set out from where, and how he came to settle in the present abode. When Lawra District Commissioner Jackson asked about the historical origins of the Lobi, his informants most likely offered him just such a patrilineage narrative, namely that of the hunter Kontol, who settled down in Lawra with his brothers. This account is exemplary of how lineage myths were re-interpreted as historical narratives relating the establishment of a chieftaincy. Lawra Naa Gari, who apparently told this story, was interested in legitimising his new position as the head chief of Lawra District. His claim happened to concur with colonial officials' search for information corroborating their own ideas of African tribal histories.

> History of tribe.
> Hundreds of years ago a hunter named KANTOL[54] came to this country shooting from a French town called BECHE (location unknown)[55] and finding game plentiful including elephant he returned and brought his family including his brother and some other settlers. They made LORHA their headquarters and started building compounds. Gradually others followed, with the result that KANTOL was

made their chief. He introduced certain laws one being that on death the deceased's brother should be heir, should a brother not exist, his nephew. KANTOL's brother would not agree to this. He said the deceased's son should be the heir, they fell out over this and his brother treked [sic] East with his followers and formed DAGARTI, hence the Lobi customs of brother succeeding and Dagarti son succeeding.

Another man named ULLIAMAE[56] settled in NANDOM and his people and KANTOL'S intermarried and all agreed to follow the latter.

It would appear that the people South of BABILE are not descended from KANTOL. ... [T]hey think [Kantol] was a Lobi, hence they call themselves Lobis.[57]

Kontol's migration to Lawra forms part of the *bàgr* myth as recited in Lawra by members of the Kusiele patriclan at initiation rituals. However, the *bàgr* elders make absolutely no reference to questions of the chieftaincy. They tell solely of Kontol's migration from Babile to Lawra via a number of stopovers, at which sacrifices are still made today.[58] Yobo Kiebang, an aged Kusiele elder whom I was able to interview, has the migration of his forefathers begin with Kontol's grandfather Gangnaa in what is the present-day Ivory Coast, well 'before' the Batié noted by Jackson.[59] According to Kiebang, Gangnaa and his family repeatedly had to flee from enemies, finally crossing the Black Volta and founding Kuselbe, which is still seen as the cradle of the Kusiele in Ghana. From there, one of Gangnaa's sons migrated to the south and founded Nadawli, while another went east into the Jirapa region, and a third finally went north to Babile, from which Kontol later started out for Lawra. A number of Kontol's brothers and sons later migrated even further north, founding, among others, Piiri and Kokoligu. Being the first-comer, Kontol became earth priest of Lawra, and because it had been a woman who had given him the earth shrine, this office came to be inherited matrilineally. However, Kiebang mentioned no conflicts over this rule of inheritance nor that one of Kontol's brothers left because of it. According to Kiebang, the chieftaincy was only introduced by the British, who made the officiating earth priest, Kuuzaa, the first Lawra Naa. Kuuzaa transferred the office to his son Nale, who, in turn, passed it on to Gari, Jackson's informant.

It is now hardly possible to reconstruct which narrative elements in the recorded text are to be traced back to Gari's interest-led manipulations and which to Jackson's misunderstandings. That in Jackson's report Kontol was made chief by the late-comers could well be the product of a 'mistranslation' of *tèngánsòb* as chief (*tènnaa*). More likely, however, is that Gari was seeking to use genealogical links to the first settler to legitimise his claim to the office of chief. He therefore had allowed the offices of earth priest and chief to coalesce in his account. That the Nandome were said to have willingly recognised Kontol's rule because of affinal links was apparently a fabrication perpetuated by the ambitious Lawra Naa; although Jackson, who wanted to subordinate all the chiefs in his district to the Lawra Naa, had some influence in privileging this version. The claim that the Dagarti were constituted when one of Kontol's brothers seceded was also supposed to justify Lawra's paramountcy, this time over Jirapa, Gari being able to link himself genealogically with the Kusiele living there. On the other hand, the fact that ties to the Kusiele in Nadawli and Wa were not mobilised probably has something to do with the fact that Jackson did not want to extend the supremacy of the Lawra Naa beyond Lawra District.

The story of Kontol is the earliest 'tribal history' from Lawra District that is documented in writing and, unlike the later historical speculations posited by Duncan-Johnstone and Eyre-Smith, it remained true to the narrative structure typical of the patrilineage accounts. Explaining political division with reference to a quarrel between two brothers is also a traditional indigenous narrative strategy. Yet Jackson understood references to such quarrels as implying the birth of a new tribe. So, while African informants translated the British concept of 'tribe' into kinship terms, conversely the British extrapolated tribal histories from local patriclan narratives. In doing so, British colonial officers and the new chiefs were working hand in hand. In the story of Kontol, for example, the meaning of Lawra was tacitly extended so that as many villages and groups as possible could be traced from one of Kontol's forefathers. In this way, the founder of a patriclan segment became the great ancestor of the whole of Lawra District.[60]

The fact that the district commissioner tended to be interested only in the versions told by the chiefs privileged the latter in many respects. By being recorded in the District Record Book, these versions came to be regarded as binding by later colonial officials, and acquired great publicity when they were published by anthropologists like Rattray or recited in schools. For example, the story of Kontol, in a version that cast him as the founding father of the 'Lobi tribe' and of all its 'traditions and customs', became part of a collection of legends from Northern Ghana that was widely read in schools in the 1950s.[61] Of course, competing versions of local histories continued and continue to exist, as has become apparent time and again in conflicts over the succession to the chieftaincy or the possession of land (Lentz 2000a, 2000b, 2001a). However, the example of the Kontol narrative makes it clear that, right from the start, the new chiefs participated in the production of new historical and cultural discourses, translating the British model of tribes into local concepts of social belonging in a manner intended to strengthen their own positions.

'Bluff, manly Lobi', 'sullen Dagarti' and 'lazy Sissalla'

Some fifteen years after Jackson, Duncan-Johnstone was still trying to explain ethnic characteristics by means of the tribal migration histories. His report[62] marks a point of transition between the cruder ethnic stereotypes held by early British administrators and the more nuanced views of a Rattray, an Eyre-Smith or a Guinness. Duncan-Johnstone's point of departure was the British classification of the inhabitants of Nandom and Lawra as 'Lobi' which French colonial officials had criticised, insisting that these 'Lobi' were actually 'Dagari'.[63] The French commissioner even brought his Lobi interpreter from Gaoua with him on a visit to Lawra, and found that this 'French Lobi' man and the 'English Lobi' from Lawra could not understand one another, 'the language being not only a different dialect, but a totally different language'.[64] Duncan-Johnstone accepted the linguistic arguments of his French colleague, but insisted that the British Lobi and Dagarti were nonetheless different tribes because of their different characteristics. But what could explain the fact that the British Lobi were so similar to the French 'Lobi proper', yet spoke a different language? Only history could provide the answer. Chief Commissioner Armitage had already conjectured that the Lobi had been one of the 'aboriginal tribes' while the Dagarti had immigrated later, but, through intermarriage, had become so mixed with the Lobi that the two groups could scarcely be distinguished from one another.[65] This became the standard explanation for the ethnic landscape of the North-West. It was assumed that while the 'Lobi' of Lawra and Nandom owed their anti-authoritarianism, matrilineal inheritance of moveable property, women's lip-plugs and other shared traits and customs to the Lobi aborigines, their language had been adopted from Dagarti immigrants.

The basic elements of this history of migration and conquest were borrowed from the French, particularly from Delafosse's articles and books on the region.[66] Delafosse assumed that the Dagomba, coming from the east, had invaded the Black Volta region and crossed the river, where they mixed with the Lobi, from which the Birifo emerged. Some Birifo had settled on the east bank of the Black Volta and mixed with the Dagari, giving rise to the 'Lobi-Dagarti', as the British would call them. The Dagari, on the other hand, were supposed to have their origins in Gonja migrations (1912: 312–13).[67] Duncan-Johnstone explicitly drew on Delafosse, but also relied on information provided by the chiefs of Lawra and Jirapa and his interpreter Binni Lobi.[68] He was convinced that the Lobi were refugees who had not wanted to be incorporated into the Mossi empire. They had expelled the indigenous Dian, Gan, Pougouli and Bougowriba, and finally settled down in the region of Gaoua, later spreading out across the Black Volta, where they successfully defended themselves against all Muslim warlords.[69] Duncan-Johnstone drew a tumultuous picture of conquerors founding kingdoms, from whom tribes not wishing to submit fled, and of refugees who became conquerors themselves in their adopted homelands – a picture inspired by the historical writings of classical antiquity and Great Britain. 'The parallel to the present state of the French Lobi country', noted Duncan-Johnstone, 'is that of Scotland in the 16th and 17th centuries or that of Corsica to the middle of the 19th century.'[70]

Unlike his French sources, Duncan-Johnstone sketched an idealised picture of the Lobi as 'lovers of liberty independence' [sic] and praised their 'warlike qualities'. The last punitive expedition had taken place more than ten years before, and a certain admiration for the fighting spirit of the natives, characterised earlier as 'truculent' and 'uncivilised', was now permissible. It is possible that Duncan-Johnstone even sympathised with the Lobi's resistance to the French.[71] In one of the sections rounding off his historical explanations, he wrote with the pride of a military officer who believes he has welded his men together into an outstandingly disciplined team:

> There was little or no war organization amongst the Tribes owing to the fact that prior to the advent of British rule there was absolutely no cohesion amongst them. Formerly when war came to a compound ... it was customary for the compound adjoining, bound either by ties of blood or friendship, to rally round the compound attacked. There was apparently no leadership and no storategy [sic] but each man plunged in where the fight was thickest ...
>
> It was this inability to unite ... that enabled the Lobi to be overrun first by Dagombas and afterwards by Samory and Barbatu. ... It is certain that were we now to vacate the Country an invader would no longer find a weak disintegrated people, but would probably encounter a formidable resistance from the united Lobi Country led by Chiefs who have learnt the value of cooperation and unity.[72]

Like his predecessors, Duncan-Johnstone was convinced that the modes of behaviour of the Issalla, Dagarti and Lobi were clearly different from one another and that every individual replicated the personality of the tribe – or more precisely every man, for these ethnic typologies were applied almost exclusively to men. However, with the changing priorities of colonial policy, from pacification to the recruitment of manpower for the mines and the army, these stereotypes changed. The unpredictable, hostile, unruly Lobi, encountered during the first tours of inspection, turned into Duncan-Johnstone's home-loving, hard-working Lobi Burifon. What had earlier been stigmatised negatively as savagery and primitiveness was now honest conservatism and welcome directness:

> The Lobi Burifons are a bluff manly jovial people, very friendly and hospitable and extremely hard working as a glance at their farms will

testify, they are easy to manage when taken the right way, and enjoy a joke even against themselves. They are [a] very conservative and home loving people. ...

[T]he Lobi Dagarti ... perhaps are not quite so wild and show a tendency to cloth[e] themselves.

The Lobi Wili ... are easily distinguishable by the fashion of their men, who wear their hair in little plaits. They are still rather wild, intractable and intolerant of any authority and have the reputation of being extremely ready to settle their affairs with bows and arrows.

The Dagarti ... are a curiously reserved and some what sullen people, very hard to know. ... [The Dagarti man] is an artist in passive resistance ...

The Sissalla or Issalla Grunshi ... are slightly less primitive than their neighbours of Lobi and Dagarti whom they wrongly affect to despise. The majority of them wear clothes, trousers and shirts or riga of native cloth, although the women are mostly naked except for [an] apron of leaves. The Sissalla is lazy, but intelligent or amenable. Many go South trading and a large number find their way into the Regiment, N. T. C. [Northern Territories Constabulary] and Police.[73]

Duncan-Johnstone developed his ethnic map by working from Lawra, and like his predecessors he translated the various reactions the 'natives' demonstrated towards the British administration into enduring tribal characteristics. It is therefore not surprising that he characterised the Lobi Burifon of Lawra, whom he quite obviously favoured, as hard-working and hospitable, while to him the Dagarti, who lived further away and were visited less frequently, were 'sullen' and obstinate.

Certainly, Duncan-Johnstone was no ethnographer. He was so absorbed by the introduction of new traditions that he scarcely interested himself in older indigenous ones. He was the last Lawra district commissioner to draw up a tribal typology that was obviously derived from the perspective of practical administration. In later documents, one rarely finds such sweeping assessments of 'the' Lobi or 'the' Dagarti. Rather, on the one hand, reference was made to the growing corpus of ethnographic knowledge, while on the other hand value judgements were expressed with regards to named individuals, mainly chiefs or native clerks, who showed themselves to be particularly capable or particularly incompetent administrators, as the case may have been. However, many of the old stereotypes lived on, outside the files, in the daily discourse by colonial officials about, and with, local people.

COLONIAL HISTORIOGRAPHY AND POLITICAL REFORM

The inter-war period, when British administrators attempted to centralise the chiefdoms and sought to increase the administrative role of the chiefs, also saw the production of new discourses on local history and culture. As can be seen from the quantity of paperwork, district commissioners particularly turned to anthropology and history whenever reforms in the local administration were to be justified in terms of 'traditional structures.' Thus, Duncan-Johnstone made the observations summarised above while he was preparing to institute the native tribunals and other chiefly rituals around 1918; and the texts of Rattray, Eyre-Smith and Guinness, which I shall discuss below, arose out of preparations for the introduction of indirect rule in the early 1930s.

The discovery of the tendana

On 12 January 1929, Captain R. S. Rattray landed at Tamale in a Cirrus Moth airplane which he had flown himself from England to Africa – a 'notable incident,' as Chief Commissioner Walker Leigh noted in his annual report.[74] In fact, it marked the beginning of the academic ethnography of the Northern Territories, for Rattray was the first author to write on *The Tribes of the Ashanti Hinterland* – the result of his fieldwork, published in 1932 – with the authority of a university-trained anthropologist. Born in 1881, the son of a colonial officer in India with a public-school and university education in England, he fought in the cavalry in the Boer War. Later, he entered the colonial service as a customs officer, subsequently acting as district commissioner in Togoland, and, after the First World War, as Assistant Colonial Secretary and Clerk to the Legislative Council of the Gold Coast. Finally, in 1920, he was appointed Director of the Gold Coast Anthropology Department. On study leave from 1909 to 1911, he studied anthropology at Oxford under Marett, who familiarised Rattray with, among others, the works of Morgan, Frazer, Tylor and especially Durkheim. Apart from anthropology, Rattray also studied law and was a member of the bar.

Rattray made much of being the first professionally trained observer to apply himself to the Northern Territories, 'a rich, almost unploughed anthropological field.'[75] None of the many 'tribes' of the North, he explained, had as yet been researched, and hardly anything was available on their relations with one another, their religion or political constitutions.[76] It is not surprising that Duncan-Johnstone was annoyed by this claim, accusing Rattray of simply ignoring previous ethnographic studies undertaken by colonial officers.[77] However, even though Rattray claimed that colonial officers had simply reproduced the ideology of the local 'ruling class', while he interviewed mainly the 'plain-folk', his methods of interrogating chosen informants were not fundamentally different.[78] Yet Rattray's work did differ in that it was not determined from the outset by administrative interests, and it produced a wealth of data which appeared utterly superfluous to a practical man like Duncan-Johnstone. Rattray himself saw the practical relevance of his research in his discovery of an astonishing 'uniformity' among the traditional institutions of the tribes of the Northern Territories. This uniformity would be very useful, he believed, in introducing a unitary system of native administration.[79]

The 'uniformity' that Rattray discovered was, of course, in the first instance the uniformity of his Oxford-anthropology model of a primitive society. He then explained variations in terms of the different stages of evolution at which the various 'tribes' found themselves. All groups had once shared 'a practically uniform religion, a uniform tribal and totemic organization, and, originally, an identical constitution or system of tribal government', living under the rule of 'priestly kings' or earth priests (*tendana*).[80] In this primitive, egalitarian society, all power and authority was rooted in the clan structure and based on moral and spiritual sanctions, not physical ones, Rattray claimed. Without the disruption caused by the invasion of 'bands of strangers', 'who had passed from the very primitive to the barbaric state', the institution of the *tendana* would itself have developed in the direction of the type of territorial rule that characterised the Akan.[81] Obviously Rattray saw the constitution of Akan society, 'with its wonderful system of decentralization', as the prototype for the planned reform of native administration. This was why it was so important for him to discover the 'germs' of Akan institutions among the Northern Territories peoples.[82]

Vestiges of these original institutions were particularly noticeable in the North-West and North-East of the Protectorate, into which the African state-founders had never penetrated. Here, the rule of the *tendana* continued undisturbed until a new, far ruder invasion broke in, namely that of the European colonial rulers.[83] Rattray accused the British of having completely ignored the local traditions and imposed their own concept of territorial rule by appointing the earth priests' messengers as chiefs and thus vesting them with a power that often degenerated into 'despotism'.[84] Thus, restoring the 'democratic' principles of the pre-colonial order was the most important task of administrative reform. At every succession to office, the 'petty unconstitutional European-made chiefs' should be replaced by the legitimate rulers, the *tendana*. Instead of equating the absence of chiefs with anarchy, as Duncan-Johnstone and others had done, Rattray painted an idealised picture of chiefless societies as strongholds of democracy.

For most of his fifteen-month stay in the Northern Territories, Rattray had his headquarters in Tumu, among the Sisala. His accounts of the Dagaba are based on a stay of about a week in Han in 1929, where he interviewed the chiefs and some elders. His material on the 'Lober', as he called the British Lobi, was collected during a short stay in Tiole, near Wa, 'among "wild" Lobi', and during a one-week visit to Lawra, where he worked with Lawra Naa Lobi Binni and his school-educated brother and interpreter, J. A. Karbo.[85] As the Lawra District Commissioner noted, Rattray was especially enthusiastic about his encounter with the Lobi, because he hoped to find in them 'the key to many puzzles in Ashanti and elsewhere'.[86] For as he put it, the Lobi, with their intermediate position between matrilineal and patrilineal forms of social organisation, 'represent the most primitive stage in evolution found among the whole of the tribes [of the Northern Territories] ... a stage ... through which all the other tribes have probably passed' (1932: 425).

The Dagaba, Isala and 'Lober' were, in Rattray's eyes, prime examples of the 'old régime' of the *tendana*. However, in order to uphold his view of the *tendana* as the central institution of a society based on kinship, as opposed to chiefly societies based on territoriality, Rattray constantly had to re-interpret ethnographic information that did not fit his model. He met few problems with respect to the Dagaba, among whom members of a single large patriclan usually resided together in a single settlement. Here, the *tendana* was indeed the 'head of the clan' and, at the same time, 'lord of the earth' (1932: 408). Among the 'Lober', however, most patriclans had sub-divided in the course of time, and many individuals had migrated and gone to live with a maternal uncle, resulting in settlements comprised of different patriclans (ibid.: 428). These might well be regarded as territorial associations under the leadership of an earth priest. But Rattray avoided this conclusion by simply claiming that, for the 'Lober' too, their earth priest was merely a 'trustee for the land of the clan' (ibid.: 429).

The concepts of 'clan,' 'totem' and 'taboo' had been developed by Morgan, Tylor, Frazer and others with the aid of material from Australia and North America. Rattray's application of these concepts to the Northern Territories found support in the existence of local institutions like the *yir*, which could be assimilated to the 'exogamous patriclans' that he was looking for. At any rate, the clans were more strongly rooted in local discourse than the colonial 'tribes'. In fact, Rattray found that drawing clear boundaries between the 'tribes' was nearly impossible, because they usually consisted of clans of different geographical origin (1932: 404, 465). For Rattray, the Northern Territories tribes were not communities of descent, but of (in-)migration and co-residence. Interestingly, however, he did not go to the trouble of demonstrating the heterogeneous origins of the tribes among the 'Lober', probably because that would have interfered with their interpretation as the original tribe.

More generally, Rattray did not explain his idea of the tribes as communities of (in-)migrants further, because this would have ruptured the dichotomy between the 'primitive' community based only on kinship ties and the 'barbarian' society constituted through territorial rule. Instead, he employed all his energy in proving that the exogamous, totemic clans were the original descent-based communities, and held to this model in spite of all the evidence to the contrary.[87] Nor did his critical view of the tribe prevent him from retaining the tribe as a unit of analysis. He accepted the census categories and figures, assumed that these corresponded to self-designations and linguistic boundaries, and then wrote in a generalising manner of 'the' Dagaba, 'Lober' or Isala on the basis of work he carried out in just one or two villages. Not even the earlier ethnic ranking was questioned – it was just placed on a different footing. The 'Lober' no longer owed their classification as an especially primitive tribe to their warlike character or their nakedness, but to their matrilineality.

'The hopeless tangle of sectional migrations'

When, in 1932, the young Assistant District Commissioner John Guinness asked earth priests and lineage elders in Lawra District about their family origins, he compared his own 'small collection of family stories' to the 'firm body of tradition as is found to this day in the Dagbon kingdom, stretching back over five hundred years'.[88] He apologised for the fact that the migration accounts of the Dagarti, Lobi and Issala lineages (which he described as sections, not as clans, like Rattray had done) were 'beheaded traditions' and went 'no further in memory than villages near the north border of the present Wa district'.[89] But, in opposition to Duncan-Johnstone and others, Guinness firmly declined to engage in historical speculations that went beyond local oral traditions. These traditions, he insisted, did not confirm the current view of a history of invasions and conquest, but pointed to the peaceful immigration of small groups into unoccupied land – 'virgin bush-country' – from different directions.[90]

In a good dozen villages of Lambussie and Nandom Divisions, and in Lawra itself, Guinness wrote down migration and settlement narratives, apparently in translations by J. A. Karbo, who had already accompanied Eyre-Smith on his surveys and who was to become Lawra Naa himself in 1935. We do not know what informants were told about the purpose of the enquiry, but it is conceivable that Karbo made them aware of the planned administrative reforms. At any rate, the Sisala elders referred to their 'Dagarti' origins with noticeable frequency. At that time, they (or Karbo) intended to use their histories to justify their Lambussie chiefdom remaining in the Dagara-dominated Lawra Confederacy, instead of joining an all-Sisala native authority, as planned by the British.[91] Settlement histories were as politically significant, and as potentially explosive, for the local population as for the British, even if Guinness concealed the sensitivity of the subject behind his apparently innocent project of documentation.

Guinness's report recorded a selection of 'section histories', each under headings that supplemented patriclan names with remarks on their tribal identity and – probably inspired by Rattray – their 'totem', for example:

'Dikpielle Dagarti, totem: monkey', 'Kushiele Lobi, totem: python', 'Shentuo Issalas, totem: crocodile'. Guinness adopted the ethnic classification of the clans used by his informants and his interpreter; and because of the popular preference for a Dagarti over a Lobi identity, most of the groups on which Guinness reported belonged to the Dagarti.[92] District Commissioner Eyre-Smith attacked Guinness heavily for his lack of judgement in this regard, and pointed out 'objective' differences in house forms, dialects, inheritance rules, agricultural methods, xylophones, food and not least 'temperament', insisting that the Lobi and Dagarti were 'to all intents and purposes totally different people'.[93]

In general, Eyre-Smith accused Guinness of naively accepting the statements of his informants 'at face value'.[94] In fact, Guinness's report did follow closely the local narratives, including the vivid description of the hunter wandering around and his claim that he came 'first'. Guinness believed that the fragmented lineage traditions summarised three great streams of migration: first Dagarti from the south, then the Lobi from the south-west, and finally the Issala from the north-east and east.[95] Yet, in the end Guinness capitulated, for ultimately, despite all his analysis, the local histories dissolved into a 'hopeless tangle of sectional migrations and settlements'.[96]

That Guinness withstood the temptations of historical speculation may also have had a quite pragmatic reason. As a young officer, Guinness was writing against the authority of his predecessor Eyre-Smith, who had made the first historical sketch of Lawra-Tumu District, as well as written a memorandum on the reform of the native administration.[97] Guinness excused himself in advance for conclusions that partially deviated from those of his predecessor, explaining that all his information had been 'carefully written down from testimony, talked over, and where possible corroborated', and that he had worked 'with a mind free and unbiased [sic] by any pre-conceived theory'.[98] Yet nothing could hold back Eyre-Smith's criticism. Family histories he generally regarded to be only of secondary importance, and they should be seen as part of a supra-regional historical landscape shaped by the upheavals of migration, conquests, and expulsion. His main attack concerned 'Mr. Guinness's theory of the peaceful penetration of "virgin bush country"', which he regarded as 'obviously absurd'.[99] Before the arrival of the Issala, Lobi and Dagarti, Eyre-Smith believed, the district had not been uninhabited, nor had the new immigrants gone there willingly and peacefully. Rather, their desire to escape Dagomba invaders had forced them to leave their old homeland in search of safety; and in the process of settling their new home, they drove out the territory's original inhabitants. The search for these original inhabitants had already been preoccupying Eyre-Smith's thoughts for quite some time, when he finally hit upon what he thought was definitive evidence 'in the shape of pottery' made by the 'Janni people', who had been driven out of the area around Lawra in the seventeenth century and come to settle west of the Black Volta in Diébougou.[100] Like the 'Soro',[101] their counterparts in the area of Zini and Lambussie, the Janni were central to Eyre-Smith's vision of history, on the one hand because they were connected to the supra-regional history of conquests and expulsions, and on the other because they were an element in his theory of an ancient complex of earth-shrine parishes that had survived in spite of all the in-migrations that took place in subsequent centuries.

Clearly Eyre-Smith saw the history of Lawra District in the light of the 'Hamitic hypothesis' and was proud of Seligman's endorsement of his account.[102] Eyre-Smith sought vestiges of the influence of higher cultures 'from the north', ultimately from the Mediterranean world, to which alone the development of higher civilisation or attempts at state organisation were to be attributed (1933: 2). Where no evidence was to be found in the oral traditions, amateur archaeology and imaginative etymology had to provide the material that would fill the gaps. Thus, Eyre-Smith speculated that the Janni were the 'Jenné or Janni people from the important Songhois [sic] town, Jenné', and that the 'ancient slag heaps to be found in the North-West ... would seem to be indications of the impress of superior cultures', namely the Berbers (ibid.: 8). Eyre-Smith admitted that these early movements could no longer be reconstructed in detail, but he was certain that the population of the Northern Territories consisted of those descended from refugees and from men of the conquering tribes who had formed unions with women of the conquered ones. He identified 'five or six main invasions' that had had an impact on the North-West, including Lawra District, 'causing decimations, scattering and fusions of peoples' (ibid.: 10). In contrast to Guinness, Eyre-Smith maintained that, without invasions, neither clan migrations nor the composite of cultural and linguistic traits found among the present-day population could be explained. The reason that the oral traditions of the inhabitants of the Nandom Division contained no references to such wars was simply that they had only immigrated to the area around the beginning of the nineteenth century, in the course of a peaceful expansion from one of their first refuges in Babile or Tie.[103]

Few of Eyre-Smith's colleagues were speculatively as he was, yet his enthusiasm for the Hamitic thesis was typical of colonial historiography. Authors such as Guinness remained in the minority. Most others also tried to incorporate the history of acephalous groups into a larger West African and trans-Saharan context history of tribal wars which was inspired not by local lineage accounts, but by the myths of the savannah states and by the historiography of classical antiquity and Great Britain. Some authors favoured less martial metaphors and described the migrations as 'successive waves of the sea, following one another and sometimes falling upon one another'.[104] But the desire to legitimise colonial rule as the continuation of a long tradition of indigenous expansionism was a strong motive for insisting on a history of conquest and migration.[105]

Chiefs or earth priests as the basis of a 'model state'?
The historical model preferred by a district commissioner did not determine his view of European colonialism in any straightforward manner. For Eyre-Smith, as much as for Guinness, the idea that the further development of 'primitive tribes' required colonial intervention was beyond question. Yet with regards to the methods used by the colonial regime up until then, Eyre-Smith had a much more critical attitude than Guinness. The latter was convinced that since no 'political authority' had existed before the arrival of the British, 'some kind of order had [had] to be made, and thus it was that Chiefs were imposed on the people'[106] – a system that 'has worked very well'. Eyre-Smith, on the other hand, had come to conclude that the unconditional support of the chiefs by the British was the main cause of the former's unscrupulous exploitation of their subjects.[107] His first suggestion for reform was that the chiefs be obliged to consult the village 'elders' regularly, that a tax in money should be substituted for unpaid road labour and work on the chiefs' farms, and that the chiefs should be paid a salary from it.[108] Rattray's 'discovery' of the earth priest enabled Eyre-Smith some years later to sharpen his criticism of the administration and accuse the British of having undermined 'the very democratic land and religious organisation vested in the Tengansobe and council of elders which had existed for centuries'.[109]

In contrast to Rattray, Eyre-Smith placed the *tendana* at the centre of what had fundamentally been a territorial organisation. The earth-shrine parishes, whose boundaries had supposedly remained unaltered for centuries, were the cornerstone of stability in that primitive society, which had occasionally been shaken by periodic invasions and migrations (1933: 26). This is why Eyre-Smith had felt it necessary to criticise Guinness's 'virgin-bush' thesis so vehemently and to search for 'aboriginal' inhabitants. The earth-shrine parishes had arisen in the course of the first human settlement of the territory, and the earth priests mediated between the 'primitive people' and the earth deity (ibid.: 18). New immigrants too 'would journey till they found someone who could propitiate or depute to them the knowledge of how to propitiate the spirits and Earth God of the area'.[110] Eyre-Smith was well aware that his thesis of the stability of the original 'tengani areas' was difficult to reconcile with the mobility and population growth that undeniably had shaped the region. But he insisted that the 'tengani-le', the dependent shrines of later settlers, would always unquestioningly recognise the 'Chief Priest' of the ancient earth shrine, which remained the decisive religious-territorial unit (1933: 22f.).

The assumption that the existence of earth-shrine parishes went back centuries was intimately bound up with Eyre-Smith's search for a traditional form of legitimation for future political centralisation. Paradoxically, although he professed the need to return to the old 'democracy', at the same time he developed plans to introduce a central native authority in Wa that would administer all the *tengani* areas of the North-West.[111] Here the political interests that both African informants and British district commissioners invested in the reconstruction of the history of settlement became particularly apparent. To Eyre-Smith it was clear, for example, that the Lobi-Dagarti of Nandom had once acquired their earth shrine from the Sisala of Lambussie, as Guinness's informants in Lambussie and Nandom had also confirmed. But he went on to insist that Nandom had always remained ritually subordinate to Lambussie and that politically, too, Nandom should be brought under Lambussie – a conclusion that Guinness's informants vehemently opposed.[112]

Like Rattray, Eyre-Smith wanted to see the Northern Territories turned into a 'model state' linking the democratic achievements and high moral standards of the past with political centralisation, economic progress and secularisation (1933: 42–5). Ever threatened by crop failures, unknown diseases and attacks from slave raiders, farmers' lives had formerly been regulated entirely by religious sanctions. In the present 'transitional period' the old religious taboos had to be replaced by a secularised native law uniting the best of the pre-colonial tradition with the highest ethical standards of the West (ibid.: 16–21, 41–2). In the pre-colonial period, Eyre-Smith explained further, the power of the chiefs – where it existed – had been religiously based and circumscribed. However, the arrival of the Europeans and their attractive goods had created a stimulus to produce for the market and had turned land into a valuable resource. It had spurred the chiefs to abuse their power, an abuse exacerbated by the British practice of drawing the boundaries of the new chiefdoms right across those of the earth-shrine parishes. Since people were subject to the taboos and sanctions of their own earth god, not those of neighbouring ones, the chiefs in many places were effectively given free licence to behave like real tyrants (ibid.: 27, 37–41). The old *tengani* boundaries therefore had to be reinstated.

Guinness, on the other hand, campaigned for the continuance of the existing native states and stressed the pre-colonial roots of the chiefly office in the prosperous, influential 'self-made men' who had existed in many places.[113] The *tingdana*, the earth priest, was also a type of 'self-made man', the difference simply being that the title of *tingdana* was inherited, 'and the Tingdanas would therefore tend to become keepers of the traditions, and gather to themselves all the spiritual power that attaches to secret knowledge'.[114] Nowhere did Guinness claim explicitly that the earth priests had been rich men, but he listed their revenues quite meticulously, including their rights to stray cattle, homeless children, lost objects and fines for breaking a taboo of the earth god. Eyre-Smith, for his part, was appalled at the insinuation that the earth priests were interested in wealth and worldly power, and he accused Guinness of being 'singularly unobservant'. If Guinness had ever visited 'the abode of a Tengansobe and observe[d] his character which is that of a recluse', he would have known that the earth priest sacrificed all the gifts he received for the good of the community.[115] Strongmen played no part in Eyre-Smith's reconstruction of the traditional political order.

Although Guinness certainly recognised that conflicts of authority could arise in situations where the boundaries of the chiefdoms and 'tengani areas' did not coincide, he noted that the population had come up with pragmatic solutions to this problem. In Gegenkpe, for instance, the chief obeyed the Nandom Naa but lived on a farm in the earth-shrine parish of Lawra, while most of his villagers had settled on Nandom land. In Guinness's eyes, the chief and the earth priest had come to represent two institutions that were more or less independent of one another, one worldly and political, the other religious; and they would work well together if their spheres of influence did not overlap. Any re-organisation along *tengani* boundaries would create new problems, particularly if, as was sometimes the case, they ran through the middle of a settlement.[116] And finally, he was convinced that 'the people themselves are markedly unwilling to have any further change'.[117]

Eyre-Smith, on the other hand, accused Guinness of being uncritical and pandering to the interests of the chiefs. Out of fear of the chief and the district commissioner, no one would dare criticise the chiefs openly, even though 'the people would more than welcome a return to their existing Tengani organisation'.[118] As an indication of the widespread opposition to the existing order, he cited the recent mass conversions to Catholicism, a true 'revolution' that had supposedly even led many earth priests to place their hopes in the White Fathers' support of their struggles against the arbitrary rule of the chiefs.[119]

Politically, the romanticised picture that Rattray and Eyre-Smith painted of the North-West's past had little effect on the shape of the new native authorities. Here what carried the day was the position of Guinness and many of his colleagues, who wanted to stabilise the system of chiefdoms introduced thirty years earlier and who assumed that the earth-shrine organisation was too complex and controversial to serve as the basis for an effective administrative order. Intellectually, however, the utopia that Rattray and Eyre-Smith projected onto the pre-colonial history of the North-West, namely that of an egalitarian, spiritually legitimated, democratic and decentralised society retained an extraordinary appeal. These images live on in Goody's (1956, 1962) ethnographies of the 'LoDagaa' and can also be found in more recent studies of North-West Ghana, like those of

Sabelli (1986) and Hawkins (2002). Many Dagara intellectuals, who have produced a wealth of texts on the history and ethnography of their society since the 1970s, also owe a great deal to this idealised picture of a harmonious, deeply religious, segmentary society. Other Dagara authors, however, have drawn on Guinness's 'strongman' type by projecting the origins of hereditary chieftaincy back into the pre-colonial past.[120]

This controversy between Eyre-Smith and Guinness also involved local struggles for power, between the various chiefs in Lawra District, and between chiefs and earth priests who competed to steer the reform of the native administration towards their own interests. In their discussions with district commissioners, they deployed the various registers of legitimation that I sketched out in Chapter 2 in order to bolster the new institution of chieftaincy. Guinness's and Eyre-Smith's view of the pre-colonial landscape of Lawra District were therefore also shaped by the on-going political struggles that took place in the context of the introduction of the Lawra Confederacy.

4

THE LAWRA CONFEDERACY
NATIVE AUTHORITY

Limited self-government under strong chiefs: this basic tenet of indirect rule was recommended for the Northern Territories as early as 1921 by Governor Guggisberg.[1] However, Chief Commissioner Walker Leigh regarded any reform that granted the chiefs more responsibility to be premature. It was only in the late 1920s that a number of younger officials – foremost among them Duncan-Johnstone, now stationed in Tamale as the Commissioner of the Southern Province – began to push for changes in the native administration. In the wake of the world economic crisis, expenditures on colonial administration were to be cut, and the introduction of direct taxes – to be administered by native authorities – were to replace the forced labour which had been common practice in the Northern Territories but was now prohibited by the Geneva Convention. Yet for Duncan-Johnstone and others, indirect rule was not merely a cost-effective administrative instrument, but a philosophy of development. The path to reform was finally cleared when Walker Leigh was pensioned off in 1930.[2]

Duncan-Johnstone looked in particular to Governor Cameron of Tanganyika as a role-model,[3] probably because Cameron also confronted the consequences of a long tradition of direct rule and the problems of organising traditionally stateless societies. Like Cameron, Duncan-Johnstone supported a policy of 'progressive traditionalism':

> [I]t is our duty to do everything in our power to develop the native on lines which will not westernise him and turn him into a bad imitation of a European ... We want to make him a good African and we shall not achieve this goal if we destroy all institutions, all the traditions, all the habits of the people.[4]

However, stubbornly clinging to old 'tribal institutions' was not what was required, but rather the introduction of European 'standards and methods', wherever necessary, 'grafted on to the existing stock'. For Duncan-Johnstone it was a matter of 'gradual nation-building' via the creation of the largest native states possible and the education of chiefs to become effective administrators. When, at a meeting in Tamale, a teacher from Cape Coast publicly accused him of pursuing a policy of 'divide and rule', 'splitting the country up in Native States so that the Gold Coast would never become a nation', he invoked the example of Great Britain:

> First the little autonomous Saxon and Danish States, then Saxon England, then Norman Saxon England with independent Wales, Scotland and Ireland and gradually we became a nation. So it will be one day, little local languages will die out and there will be one or two main languages, with intermarriage, education and the intercourse made possible by modern transport conditions the tribal jealousies and differences will gradually disappear and the little states will come together and form one or two big kingdoms.[5]

The reforms were to be linked to the traditional 'native institutions'. In Lawra-Tumu, however, as the investigations of Rattray, Eyre-Smith and Guinness showed, the native states were an innovation of purely colonial provenance. Nevertheless, Eyre-Smith's proposal that the chiefs be replaced by the traditionally legitimated *tendana*s and that the administrative districts be created in accordance with the boundaries of earth-shrine parishes, were not adopted. Rather, officials opted for a policy that had been tried out in Tanganyika, namely that of merging small chiefdoms, equal in rank, into federations.[6]

No one ever denied that it was nearly impossible to ascertain clearly along which lines ethnic boundaries could be drawn, and that therefore tribal belonging would not be an effective means of creating a sense of community. In fact, the tribes in the North-West, as defined by the British, never developed into political communities, and all attempts to make chiefdoms and 'tribes' coincide had failed. The native states were not an agglomeration of tribes, but rather entities, whose borders were determined by factors quite different from ethnic ones, the ethnic labels being attached *ex post-facto*. Yet British political philosophy continued to rely on the concept of 'tribes'. Cardinall sought the root of the difficulties in the history of the tribes:

> Ordinarily it [the tribe] might be defined as a social group comprising a number of families descended from a common ancestor; in the course of time slaves and others seeking protection or adoption are included until, although the idea of consanguinity persists, the tribe becomes based more and more on common social and political institutions rather than kinship. (1931: 8–9)

Although this was not in keeping with the author's intention, this definition may be interpreted as the British programme for the Lawra Confederacy as it was created in 1934 to bring together native states that had allegedly been set up on the basis of tribal membership. They only became an effective framework for collective identification and self-understanding by means of

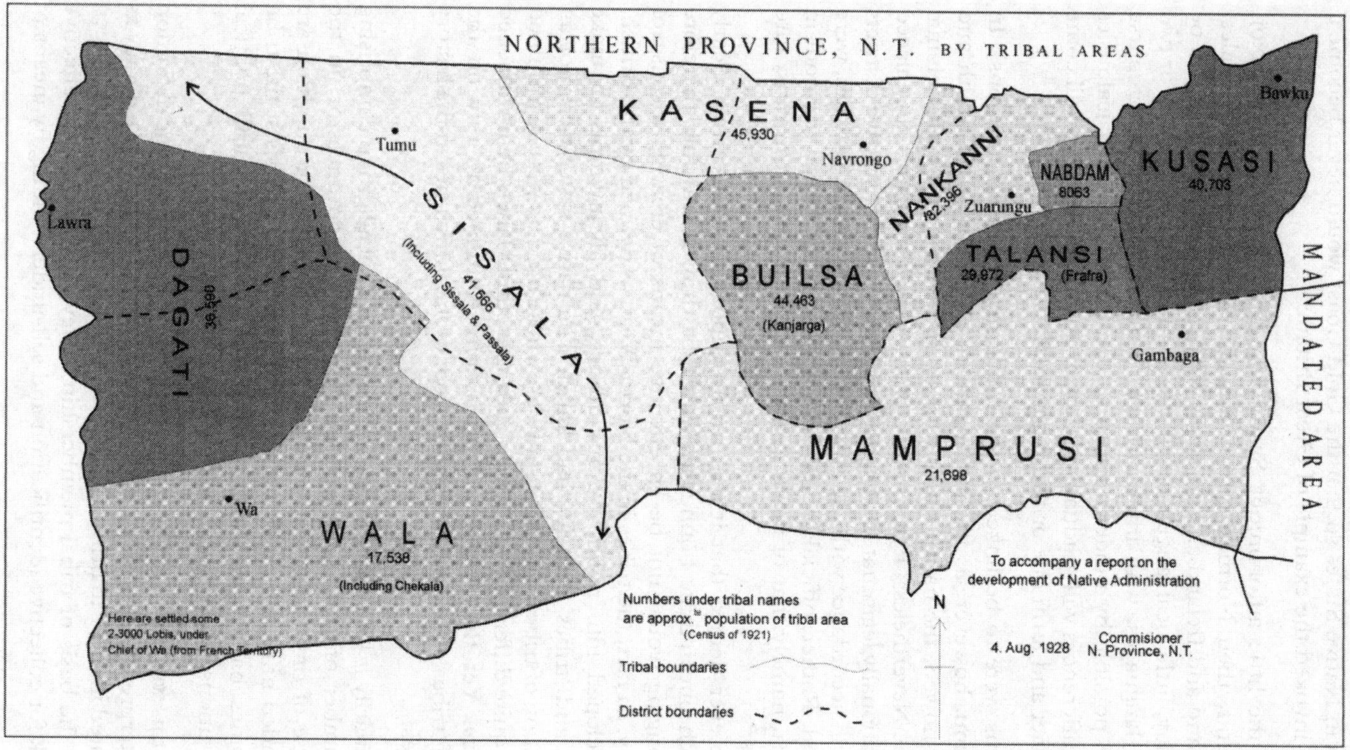
NORTHERN PROVINCE, N.T. BY TRIBAL AREAS
MANDATED AREA
KASENA
45,930
Navrongo
Tumu
SISALA
41,666
(Including Sissala & Passala)
NANKANNI
82,396
Zuarungu
NABDAM
8063
KUSASI
40,703
Bawku
TALANSI
29,972
(Frafra)
BUILSA
44,463
(Kanjarga)
MAMPRUSI
21,698
Gambaga
Lawra
DAGATI
Wa
WALA
17,538
(Including Chekala)
Here are settled some
2-3000 Lobis, under
Chief of Wa (from French Territory)
Numbers under tribal names
are approx.ly population of tribal area
(Census of 1921)
Tribal boundaries
District boundaries
N
To accompany a report on the
development of Native Administration
4. Aug. 1928
Commisioner
N. Province, N.T.

Map 7 Northern Province by tribal areas, 1928
Source: NAG, MP 38

such new 'common social and political institutions' as taxation, the codification of native law, and the tribalistic education of the chiefs' sons. Thus, administrative practice gradually imparted the 'invented' tribes a tangible reality.

Once the poll tax was introduced, local revenue, investments, services and the legitimacy of the native authorities became much more closely linked, promoting a new sense of 'local patriotism', as District Commissioner Mead termed it.[7] At the same time, however, this development harboured new potential for conflict, since the model of unambiguous territorial-political ties ran counter to local practices of mobility and multi-locality. In border zones especially, conflicts were sparked off by the question of which particular compounds belonged to which chiefdom, and to whom farmers owed their taxes if they resided in one division but worked their farms elsewhere. Basically, however, these conflicts strengthened rather than weakened 'local patriotism', and anchored the new structures all the deeper in the minds of the local political elite. Of course, the cohesion of the Lawra Confederacy was promoted not only through conflicts, but also through the friendships and marriage alliances between the chiefly houses. Important, too, was the role of the Lawra Confederacy Native Authority School, which opened in 1935, and which above all trained the sons of chiefs, who would later work as teachers, council clerks, and ultimately as new divisional chiefs, and who would also represent the Lawra Confederacy politically in the Northern Territories Council and in the Legislative Assembly in Accra. In any case, the Lawra Confederacy survived the administrative reforms of the 1950s, and the alliances and enmities that were created during the 1930s and 1940s continue to shape local politics today.

(DE)CENTRALISATION, POLL TAXES AND THE TERRITORIALISATION OF THE CHIEFS' RULE

Faced with Guggisberg's plea for indirect rule, Lawra District Commissioner Dasent asked himself how the twenty-one small chiefdoms of Lawra and Tumu could be centralised. He suggested uniting all 'Issala' chiefdoms under a single paramount chief, preferably the chief of Tumu or Zini, and placing the 'Lobi', 'Lobi-Dagarti' and 'Dagati' divisions under the chief of Jirapa, who was already 'more or less accepted as the senior chief'. Only the two 'Grunshi' divisions should remain autonomous.[8] For Dasent the existence of a shared Issala identity was without question, and uniting all Lobi and Dagati was perfectly justified, since even supposedly 'pure Dagarti' were actually 'of Lobi stock' – a Lobification of the ethnic map that I discussed in the previous chapter. Not only Dasent but the traditionalist Eyre-Smith too wanted centralisation and recommended strengthening the chief of Jirapa, who was to rule over all 'Dagarti'-speaking villages.[9] The Commissioner of Northern Province, P. F. Whittall, went even further and hoped for the unification of all 'Dagati' and 'Issala' under their respective chiefs, who would then, for their part, pay tribute to the Wa Na.[10] Whittall demanded that the district boundaries be redrawn 'so that each tribe is brought complete into one District. Two Tribes in one District can be dealt with but one tribe divided between two Districts is not sound'.[11] In the North-West he wanted to create a new Issala district with headquarters in Walembele, and a Wala-Dagarti district with headquarters in Lawra.[12] In the interests of 'amalgamation', he evidently even subsumed the 'Lobi' – numbering 32,140 according to the 1921 Census, but conspicuously absent from Whittall's map (Map 7) – under the Dagarti.

Whittall's plans were not feasible. The Dagarti and Lobi chiefs vehemently refused to subordinate themselves to the Wa Na.[13] The fifteen Sisala chiefs, up until then independent of one another and scattered across two districts, were summoned to a 'unification' conference in Kunchuggo, but could not be persuaded to recognise the chief of Tumu or anyone else as a common tribal chief. '[H]aving sprung up from the outcasts of at least three other tribes [the Sisala] have no "pride of race" to urge them to amalgamate,' Lawra-Tumu District Commissioner Olivier explained the failure of the conference.[14] Duncan-Johnstone, on the other hand, stressed that given the alliances and enmities between the various Sisala chiefs formed since the period of Babatu's attacks, Whittall's plans were 'radically unsound at this stage of affairs'. Duncan-Johnstone therefore recommended the intro-duction of 'Tribal Councils' which would 'give the Chiefs time to get used to the idea of meeting and working together before getting them to elect any particular member as their Tribal Chief'.[15] In fact, Whittall ultimately had to retain the two former districts, Wa and Lawra-Tumu. However, the smaller divisions of Lawra District were to be persuaded to join with the larger native states of Jirapa, Nandom, Lawra and Lambussie,[16] and indeed, under some pressure from District Commissioner Armstrong, Sabuli, Han, Ulu and Karni eventually agreed to join Jirapa, while Samoa joined Lambussie.[17]

In 1934 the Lawra Confederacy Native Authority was officially estab-lished, entirely in keeping with the Cameronian model of a federation comprised of four equal divisions: Lawra, Jirapa, Nandom and Lambussie.[18] The chairmanship of the Lawra Confederacy was supposed to rotate automatically every six months among the divisions, but was then held for life by the divisional chief who had served the longest. Thus the first Confederacy president was Jirapa Naa Ganaa, followed in 1938 by Nandom Naa Konkuu, and in 1940 by Lawra Naa J. A. Karbo, who officiated until the Confederacy was temporarily dissolved in the 1960s. Each division had its own native court C; the Federal Court A was only responsible for difficult cases, appeals, and conflicts between sub-divisional and divisional chiefs. The common native treasury was located in Lawra and operated under the supervision of the district commissioner, though, like the

Plate 1 Lawra Confederacty divisional chiefs, *c.* 1939
Front row, from the left (sitting): Lawra Naa J. A. Karbo, Nandom Naa Konkuu,
Jirapa Naa Yelpoe, Kofi Dagarti (Dagaba chief of Kumasi), unknown (squatting on
the floor); back row, from the right (standing): Imoru, Nitori (Lawra Confederacy
N. A. clerk), elder of the Jirapa Naa, native police (with caps), wives of chiefs (with
kind permission of Nandom Naa Dr Charles Imoro)

assembly of the Federal Court, the annual budgetary meetings rotated
between Jirapa, Lawra and Nandom.[19] Eyre-Smith's and Rattray's high-
flown suggestions for reform were never implemented. Neither did earth-
shrine boundaries play a role in bringing together the chiefdoms, nor was
the position of the earth priests strengthened. On the contrary, because all
markets were now controlled by the native authorities, the earth priests lost
an important source of income and only received what the chiefs granted
them.

Duncan-Johnstone hoped that, through patient training, the divisional
chiefs would one day willingly submit to complete unification into one large
kingdom, but this never became a reality – for quite tangible reasons.
Instead of receiving their income from court fees, fines and unpaid farm
work, as had formerly been the case, the chiefs now received a fixed monthly
salary.[20] Further 'amalgamation' of the chiefdoms would, as a matter of
course, lead to some chiefs' demotion within the chiefly hierarchy. The
divisional chiefs, complained District Commissioner Blair, were like

children 'struggling for the sugariest bits of a cake ... They seemed interested only in items which make for their own profit and aggrandisement.'[21]

However, linking the chiefs' income to the revenue raised in the Confederacy also led to the chiefs' growing interest in infrastructural investments that might increase their division's income. Thus in Lawra, Nandom and Jirapa caravanserais, markets and courthouses were expanded in order to attract more clients and therefore more income. The nexus between local revenue, investment and the legitimacy of the native authorities became even closer through the introduction of a poll tax in 1936. The British regarded this tax, which was to replace the people's tributes, gifts and labour offered to their chiefs, as the *sine qua non* for local development and progress, 'not a tax to Government but ... for the good of the tribe or [Native] State.'[22] Nevertheless, they feared that the tax might destabilise the native authorities they had worked so hard to create, and were surprised by the general willingness to pay the tax.[23] The rate of tax amounted to merely one shilling per year per adult male, a symbolic rather than substantial sum. Only about half the native authorities' total expenditure could be covered by local sources of income, the other half coming from grants-in-aid paid by the colonial government.[24] What was decisive in the eyes of the British, however, was the fact that taxation established a link between local efforts and development. The taxpayer expected that the native authority provide a certain level of infrastructure throughout the district, and District Commissioner Ellison assured that 'efforts have been made to try and give the people "in the bush" something for their money.'[25] Competition for scarce tax revenues strengthened the Lawra Confederacy because the latter was the arena in which the divisions competed for their shares of the common native treasury and compared each other with respect to tax revenues and subsidies from the central budget.

Furthermore, the introduction of the poll tax was a major step towards a modern territorial conception of rule and political community. Tax collection was the responsibility of the chiefs, initially only the divisional chiefs and their clerks, but later also the village headmen.[26] The drawing up of tax lists required for the first time that the membership of all men in a compound, of all compounds in a village, and of all villages in a division be clearly defined and recorded in writing. District Commissioner Ellison remarked that the introduction of taxation 'continues to strengthen the family tie and has given a definite status to the compound owner and the family council.'[27] Above all, however, residency, farmland and political loyalty (and therefore tax payments) were now all to be brought into accordance.

The model that assigned all compounds, including their respective farmlands, to specific territorial-political units – a model which colonial officials and chiefs jointly sought to implement – ran counter to local practices of mobility and multi-locality. It assumed the concurrence of landownership with political control and unambiguous linear boundaries between the chiefdoms. Just how problematic these assumptions were is evident in the fact that these boundaries were conspicuously absent from all British (and subsequent Ghanaian) maps. Instead, the colonial officials drew up lists containing the names of the villages and village headmen who were subordinate to a given native authority. Lawra District Commissioner Armstrong had initially suggested that the territory of the Lawra Confederacy be defined tribally, as including

> all those lands occupied by the Lobi, Dagarti and Issalla Grunshi tribes (exclusive of the Zini Division) North of the 10.30 parallel, together with that portion of those lands occupied by the Lobi and Dagarti tribes which are subject to the Chief of Jirapa.[28]

However, the relevant decree of 1934 defined the 'limits of area' of the (subordinate) native authorities not in terms of ethnicity, but solely in terms of the range of the chiefs' authority, as 'all lands subject to the Chief of Nandom', Jirapa, Lambussie or Lawra.[29] This wording was a product of the native-area definitions in Dagbon and Gonja, where the paramount chiefs claimed allodial landownership. However, in the North-West chiefs controlled not the land but rather the people living on it, and the boundaries of earth-shrine parishes and chiefdoms did not coincide. The new decree thus treated rule that was determined by personal networks as if it were determined territorially, without, however, clarifying the precise nature of the authority exercised by the divisional chiefs with respect to land rights.

One instructive example of the conflicts that developed in the course of the territorialisation of political loyalties is Samoa, a Sisala settlement in the Lawra Confederacy, bordering the Tumu Native Authority. The compounds in the sections of Sino, Kongo and Dende refused to pay taxes to Lawra via Nandom – which had been in control of the Lambussie division since 1935 – an offence for which the Nandom Naa imposed a rather severe penalty of ten shillings each (ten times the tax due) or alternatively ten days' hard labour. 'They are the people who have been wishing to go over to Tumu', explained the Lawra District Commissioner. 'They have been told that they may follow Tumu, if they move on to Tumu land. Meanwhile they are doing their best to pay tax to neither.'[30] A year later, the families affected had indeed resettled in the chiefdom of Zini, which belonged to Tumu, but the Nandom Naa complained that they were still farming on 'his land'.[31] In the following year, the 'mischievous sections' continued to cultivate their old fields in Samoa. 'They have successively and successfully humbugged me, Prendergast and Blair', complained District Commissioner Amherst, threatening that 'this time there will be no leniency': the wrong-doers were to be punished severely by the Federal Court.[32]

It is not unlikely that the Samoa compounds had in fact sought to evade all taxes. However, the fact that people farmed outside their place of residence in areas falling within the bounds of a neighbouring village, even building a hut on the farm when the field was far away from the compound, was and is not 'humbuggery' but standard local practice. With its ambiguous wording of 'lands subject to ...', the native-authority model gave the chiefs the opportunity to demand that not only people living in their divisions, but also anyone wanting to farm 'their' land pay taxes and accept political subordination. The flipside of the new 'local patriotism' was therefore the stricture of mobility and multi-locality. Time and again in the course of the history of the Lawra Confederacy the definition of the relationship between control over land and political authority, and the question of how to deal with mobile farmers, provoked massive conflicts. Even the assumption held by the British, one which the chiefs themselves adopted in part, that organised political communities in the native states were defined tribally, provided sufficient material to ignite conflict in the multi-ethnic reality of the chiefdoms. It is particularly in the history of the conflict-ridden relationship between Nandom and Lambussie, to which I now wish to turn, that the contradictions inherent in the native-authority model become apparent.

LAMBUSSIE AND NANDOM: NEIGHBOURS IN CONFLICT

To this very day relations between the divisions of Nandom and Lambussie continue to be tense. The idea that the Dagara of Nandom allegedly dominate the Sisala of Lambussie politically and want to 'snatch' their land from them is anchored firmly in the minds of the local Lambussie political elite. Conversely, many Dagara accuse the Sisala of using their status as 'first-comers' to secure for themselves political privileges at the expense of the Dagara 'late-comers', in spite of having lived together for so many generations. The roots of these mutual accusations may be found primarily in developments that occurred in the 1930s, which will be discussed below. However, in order to legitimise their political projects, British district commissioners and local actors time and again presented arguments that rested on prior settlement histories, which I shall presently sketch out. Afterwards I shall turn to the political and legal dynamics of the process by which Dagara farmers in the 1920s began settling on Sisala land.

The controversial settlement history
In the context of his study of native institutions, John Guinness interviewed the Nandom earth priest, 'a descendant of Zenoo [Zenuo], the Dagara hunter of the Dikpiele clan, who is said to have founded Nandom'.[33] Although Guinness claimed that his enquiries when addressed to the Sisala earth priest of Lambussie brought to light the same story, the version he

recorded in writing was unmistakably biased in favour of the Dagara in that it emphasised the early autonomy of Nandom from Lambussie and the equality between the two divisions. According to this version, Zenuo encountered the Sisala of Lambussie on his first hunting expedition into the area that would become Nandom, but could not communicate with them and therefore built a hut without asking the Sisala for permission. Only when the people of Lambussie 'kidnapped' his family and took them to their village while he was out hunting did he accept the Sisala's invitation to settle in Lambussie. However, because of constant squabbles over the theft of his goats, he soon reasserted his autonomy. For this, he was granted land by the Sisala, with their permission built a house near his first hut, and, in return for 60,000 cowries and several animals, was even given his own earth shrine, with which he became earth priest of Nandom and rightful owner of Nandom land.[34] This version of the settlement history concedes that Nandom acquired its earth shrine from the Sisala, but at the same time emphasises Nandom's autonomy. This contradiction is bridged in the episode where Zenuo first settled independently of the Sisala, although only temporarily, as well as in the theme of reciprocal exchange of Zenuo's hunting spoils for Sisala domestic animals, an agreement which the Sisala violated by stealing Zenuo's goats.

All versions that my Sisala informants related to me had Zenuo come directly to Lambussie on his hunting expedition, where he settled down at the invitation of the earth priest. The kidnapping episode was absent, and only the theft of the goats as the motive for the subsequent founding of Nandom with the permission of the Lambussie earth priest was told in a fashion similar to the version recounted by the Nandom earth priest. However, the Sisala insisted that the people of Nandom received their own shrine stones only long after they left Lambussie. Furthermore, they were said not to have paid for these, since the 'sale' of an earth shrine was strictly forbidden. Even today, my Sisala informants insisted, the Nandom earth priests must consult the Lambussie earth priests when faced with serious matters. In fact, Lambussie and Nandom sacrifice to the same earth god, Kabir, but in the eyes of the Lambussiele their shrine to Kabir is not only older, but also more significant than that of Nandom.[35]

We do not know exactly what the Sisala earth priest Nansie told Guinness and whether his version resembled that related to me a good fifty years later by his son Nansie Issifu Tomo. The fact that Guinness claimed that the Lambussie version was the same, word for word, as the Nandom version may well have been due to his aversion to recording variants that seemed similar to him. However, it is also possible that the identical semantics were produced by the interpreter, from the Lawra Naa's house, or else it suited the interests of the Sisala earth priest, who at this stage was not yet wanting to distance himself from his Nandom neighbours. However,

Eyre-Smith's severe criticism of Guinness's report indicates that even back then different interpretations of the ties between Nandom and Lambussie resulting from the historical circumstances of settlement may have been in circulation.

Eyre-Smith's main criticism concerned the alleged payment of 60,000 cowries for the Nandom earth shrine. '[T]his cannot be accepted at its face value and ... such a procedure was unknown and is not supported by the facts', he insisted, stressing his theory of the stability of the original 'tengani areas' to support this view.[36] Guinness emphasised that it was not the land itself, but 'the privilege of the tingdanaship' that had been paid for.[37] Central to the dispute over the purchase of the shrine stones was the question as to the status of Lambussie's and Nandom's earth shrines. Guinness postulated their independence and emphasised that the earth priests of Nandom and Lambussie would rarely visit one another. Only in the event of a drought would they meet near Lambussie in order to consult the earth deity and make offerings to it. 'Apart from this the Tingdanaships have no other than a historical connexion, and the people of Nandom do not look to a spiritual authority beyond their own home.'[38] Eyre-Smith, on the other hand, was convinced that Nandom, as well as Lambussie, continued to be *tengani-le* (small earth-shrine areas) that had to consult the superior shrine in many matters. If Guinness had only further investigated the references to joint consultations by the 'old men', Eyre-Smith insisted, he would have discovered the large earth shrine in Katu, some three miles from Lambussie. He claimed to have obtained confirmation from both the Nandom Naa and the Lambussie Kuoro that 'if any "bad thing" happened to this country they would have to go to the Tengansobe of the Tengani of Katu'.[39] The fact that the earth priests of Nandom and Lambussie had obviously concealed this truth from Guinness was possibly due to the fact that their chiefs had forbidden them to speak about it for fear that the reference to their belonging to a single large *tengani* area would lead to curtailment of their own power.[40] And indeed, Eyre-Smith did suggest that Nandom Division be abolished and placed under Lambussie.[41]

So who was this earth priest of Katu, of which my informants had never heard? The Lambussie Kuoro speculated that 'Katu' might refer to Keltu, an area in Lambussie. There resides a family that plays a central role in the installation of a new earth priest and which exercises the earth priest's duties during an interregnum.[42] Thus, Eyre-Smith's large original earth shrine might be explained by the fact that he had interviewed this Keltu family during such an interregnum, before the new Lambussie earth priest, Nansie, had assumed office, the very earth priest that Guinness questioned subsequently.[43] Furthermore, Guinness and Eyre-Smith may have been drawn into a power struggle over the chieftaincy in Lambussie, which mobilised local factions in light of their settlement histories. The chiefs and earth priests of Lambussie trace themselves back to Dagaba immigrants from Sankana who converted to Sisala and live in the Panna section. They were and are opposed by the families of the Challa section, who are said to have migrated into the area from a place called 'Char' in present-day Burkina Faso. My Challa informants even claimed that the Lambussie earth shrine originally belonged to their side, and that their forefathers had only later given it to the late-comers from Sankana.[44] When Eyre-Smith conducted his interviews, Lambussie Kuoro Kantonbie from the Panna section was struggling with the embittered opposition of some Challa men[45] who may have supported their claims to power with the idea of the earth shrine originating in their section. Eyre-Smith probably had dealings mainly with informants from the Challa side, while Guinness, some years later, only questioned the Panna side.

In 1932, at the time of Guinness's enquiry, the new Lambussie Kuoro Yesibie, from the Panna section, had long since succeeded Kantonbie, and Nansie's instalment had ended the earth priest interregnum. In Nandom meanwhile, Konkuu had succeeded to the chieftaincy of Boro. In both Lambussie and Nandom I was repeatedly told how well Konkuu and Yesibie got along. Whether the Nandom Naa ever came to hear about Eyre-Smith's plans to incorporate his sub-division into Lambussie is unclear. However, that administrative changes were forthcoming was fairly obvious to all the chiefs in Lawra District, and most of them, especially the Nandom Naa, were interested in maintaining the status quo – as, incidentally, was Guinness, who accordingly was only too willing to adopt Nandom's historical arguments for autonomy from Lambussie.

Yesibie too wanted to maintain the status quo of Lambussie's incorporation into Lawra District and presented the settlement history as an argument when District Commissioner Armstrong asked him whether or not he wanted to join an all-Sisala native authority:

> neither he nor his people wished to follow Tumu, the reason being that they were not really Issallas and did not speak the proper Issalla language. ... The Lambussie people originally came from around Lawra. Kantombie's ... grandfather came from Lawra itself. ... The Nandom people came from round about Babile, Burifoo, Lawra etc. and were given land by the Lambussie people (at that time Dagarti). Lambussie people intermarried with Issalla women and eventually came to speak a kind of bastard Issalla, though they nearly all can still speak Dagarti. Lambussie therefore wishes to be incorporated with the Lobi-Dagarti district rather than with the Issalla district.[46]

Assuming that Armstrong was not just putting his own ideas into Yesibie's mouth, these statements show that the chiefs had begun to deploy the colonial discourse concerning tribal origins, language and culture in pursuit

of their own interests, coupling it with older local arguments which linked
political authority to land ownership. Whether Yesibie actually believed that
the Lambussiele were more 'Dagarti' than 'Issalla', or whether this was
merely a part of a strategy designed to avoid being attached to Tumu, must
remain an open question. Yesibie's successor, at any rate, was to claim
precisely the opposite fifteen years later, stressing the differences between
Sisala and Dagara.

The most important argument for why Lambussie wanted to remain with
Lawra was not, however, cultural propinquity to the 'Dagarti', but the land
question. As Yesibie's son Baloro explained, 'Yesibie felt that ... the
Nandom people have settled on his land. So if we were to go with Tumu, he
would risk losing this land'.[47] Yesibie's claims to control over 'Lambussie
lands', which Armstrong disseminated, encompassed Nandom, Samoa,
and even the area to the north of Lambussie in the neighbouring French
colony. They thus went well beyond those stipulated by traditional land
rights, for all Sisala settlements actually have independent earth shrines and
thus do not belong to the territory of Lambussie. For Yesibie, however, the
main issue was probably not economic or ritual control over these
'Lambussie lands', but rather the desire to strengthen political rule over the
villages in his division – as well as to bolster in a traditionalising fashion his
prospects to secure political claims on still independent Samoa, which only
fell to Lambussie in 1934. In any case, Yesibie had nothing to gain by being
separated from the Lawra Confederacy and joining Tumu, but he certainly
stood to lose a good deal.

Dagara settlers on Sisala land

Nandom Naa Konkuu's concern that Lambussie remain with Lawra also
had to do with land issues, though recent ones. Since the 1920s, an
increasing number of Dagara farmers from Nandom Division and from
villages in the neighbouring colony of Upper Volta had settled on Sisala land
in the Lambussie, Billaw, Nabaala areas as well as in various places along
the Franco-British border. Konkuu wanted to retain some form of control
over these Dagara farmers as subjects and taxpayers, and this would have
become much more difficult with the separation of Lambussie from the
Lawra Confederacy.

Land scarcity is what mostly drove farmers from villages in Nandom
Division to seek out new livelihoods among their Sisala neighbours.
Immigrants from the French colony usually came in order to escape the
more onerous demands of forced labour, taxes and the high-handedness of
the chiefs there. Once a Dagara pioneer had obtained permission to settle
and farm from a Sisala earth priest, other relatives soon followed. In this
way, settlements that were exclusively Dagara gradually arose in the Sisala
area, such as Fielmuo, Kyetuu, Koro, Piina, Cheboggo and Kulkya.[48]

Goody (1954: 4) estimated the number of Dagara settlers in Lambussie Division to have been at least 4,000 in the early 1950s, a third of the total population of the division, and 1,600 in the Fielmuo area, which belongs to Zini Division in Tumu District.

The new settlers claimed links of friendship with the Sisala, or appealed to customary rights, which did not permit the refusal of requests for land put forward by someone who needed it to feed his family if one had enough land oneself. The flow of gifts from Dagara settlers to Sisala landowners depended on the quality of their relationship. The possibilities here ran from the one-time gift of a few chickens and a goat to the bestowal of small portions of the annual harvest, such regular gifts being more symbolic in nature than actually serving to enrich the landowners. However, the gifts acted as a reminder that the land ultimately did not belong to the settlers, and after the death of the original landholder, his heirs could only continue to work the fields with the express permission of the Sisala landowners.[49]

Here the decisive difference from the pre-colonial practice of the appropriation of land becomes apparent. It is difficult to ascertain exactly when small groups of Sisala-speaking farmers first settled in what came to be Lawra District. There is agreement, however, that in many parts of the district the expansionist Dagara-speaking agriculturalists were forced to come to terms with Sisala first-comers. They did so through ethnic assimilation, the purchase of land and earth shrines from the Sisala, or their forcible expulsion. In any case the Dagara transformed themselves into allodial landowners, in full control of the land and the earth shrines.[50] Probably under the influence of informants who wished to stress their ancient status, District Commissioner Dasent defined the boundary between 'native community' and 'tenants' according to length of settlement: 'By native community I mean inhabitants who have been located on the same land for six or more generations.'[51] However, most of the region's settlement histories indicate that newcomers integrated considerably more rapidly, either by becoming part of an existing settlement, or by securing permission to found their own small earth shrine.

This process of autochthonisation, however, came to a halt with colonial pacification, when property rights and ethnic boundaries were 'frozen'. The Dagara continued to establish new settlements on Sisala land, but were no longer given earth shrines and were thus unable to become allodial landowners. Though the Sisala earth priests finally granted Christian newcomers their own cemetery, so that they could bury their own dead, the carrying out sacrifices to the earth deity remained the preserve of the Sisala earth priest. The Dagara settlers' non-integration into the Sisala village order was also manifest in their spatial separation from the Sisala and in the place names that the Sisala gave these new settlements, which were conceived from a Sisala-centred perspective, such as 'Behind the hill'

(Palaharra) – designations against which the Dagara then usually posited their own place names.

In the eyes of the British, local land rights only conceived of two paradigms that legitimated land acquisition and ownership: first-comer status and conquest. This excluded the manifold intermediate flexible arrangements common in the pre-colonial period, whereby land was acquired and property relations negotiated. Since pacification by the British ruled out further conquest, the distribution of ownership rights prevailing at the time of colonisation was petrified. The distinction between first-comers and late-comers, which in the pre-colonial period was relative, reversible and negotiable, was transformed into a much more rigid dichotomy that set natives off against tenants/settlers. Furthermore, the boundary between landowners and land users was now defined ethnically. If a newcomer to a village happened to belong to the same ethnic group as the landowners, he was integrated into the native community, while ethnic strangers continued to be regarded as non-natives, even after residing there for more than a generation.

So the spatial and politico-ritual exclusion of ethnically alien settlers prevented the cultural and linguistic process of assimilation that had prevailed earlier. Dagara could no longer become Sisala, regardless of whether they or their children learned to speak Sisala. One-sided marriage patterns also contributed to this situation. Although Sisala men married and continue to marry Dagara women, the reverse is rarely the case. It is not clear whether this was the result of a deliberate collective strategy, or simply the outcome of numerous individual decisions, but the tendency is undisputed. The strategic effect was and still is that the children of mixed marriages are Sisala, meaning that they produce no Dagara offspring who could articulate claims to their Sisala mothers' brothers, claims pertaining to land or the participation in earth-shrine rituals, for example.[52]

Many of the new Dagara settlers need not have experienced their lack of participation in the politico-religious organisation of the Sisala villages as problematic. They probably rather welcomed it, since, as converts to Catholicism, they rejected the traditional rituals of sacrifice. Moreover, ties of friendship and kinship, ritual taboos connected with the earth shrine and customary norms hindered the commercialisation of land allocation. Thus, as far as specific use rights were concerned, the ethnicisation of land rights was probably hardly noticed, at least initially. Only in the 1980s did many Sisala landowners begin to draw material advantage from the Dagara settlers' dependent status. Right from the start, however, the ethnicisation of land ownership had political consequences. The British model of indirect rule made allodial land ownership the cornerstone of defining the 'native community' that was to be governed by an indigenous chief. Only natives were entitled to local citizenship; strangers, such as the Dagara on Sisala land, had no right to furnish the village chief. Usually Dagara settlers chose only their own headmen, typically the earliest migrant, who represented their concerns to the Sisala chief in charge, but were not granted the right to have any further say in matters that pertained to the affairs of the entire village.

As Yesibie's discussion with District Commissioner Armstrong shows, chiefs exploited the British discourse on native land tenure in order to stabilise their rule. Though Yesibie's attempt (if that is what it was) to translate the argument of ancient status vis-à-vis Nandom into political control failed, the impending land shortage in the neighbouring chiefdom meant that control over 'Lambussie lands' could potentially be transformed into control over the labour and tax revenues of more subjects. For his part, Nandom Naa Konkuu tried to prevent his people from being drawn into the Lambussie Division. As one old Dagara farmer from Kulkya, near Lambussie, whose father had moved from Nandom into Sisala territory in the 1930s, emphatically described,

> at that time our fathers used to work for the colonial masters, pay tax and also farm for the chief. So if he [Konkuu] allowed the people to move over here, then he will be losing all this. ... If you had many people in your area you get plenty tax and that will also increase your pay.[53]

Though Konkuu could not prevent increasing numbers of Dagara from settling on Sisala land, Lambussie's remaining in the Lawra Confederacy at least allowed him to exert some influence.

'These Lobi-Dagarti, they know politics': Lambussie under Nandom

In October 1935, District Commissioner Armstrong and Nandom Naa Konkuu visited Lambussie Kuoro Yesibie, who was terminally ill. Yesibie refused medical help, but asked that the chief of Nandom 'should be allowed to look after his division while he is ill'.[54] Not quite one week later, Yesibie died, and Armstrong noted: 'At Ysibie's request the Chief of Nandom will look after the Division until an election is held'.[55] Some years before, Yesibie had complained about the lack of support he received from his own family and apparently thought his interests would be better served if placed in the hands of his friend Konkuu than in those of his own house.[56] Six months after Yesibie's death, the election of a new Lambussie Kuoro took place. Konkuu summoned the Lambussie headmen to Nandom in order to demonstrate his newly won sovereignty over Lambussie. They wanted to make Hilla, 'son of the late Chief of Lambussie', the new chief but also requested, at least according to Armstrong's report, 'that the Chief of Nandom should continue to be their divisional Chief'. Armstrong's comment on this was: 'As these people are settlers on Nandom land I agreed. It also makes the Lawra Confederacy more compact'.[57]

It remains unclear why Armstrong actually thought the Lambussiele had settled on Nandom land and therefore should follow the Nandom Naa. Only two years earlier he had claimed the exact opposite, namely that Nandom had acquired its land from Lambussie.[58] Had Konkuu convinced him of a new version of the settlement history? Did this perhaps have something to do with the new Lawra District interpreter, Dasoberi, one of Nandom Naa Boro's sons, who managed to use his position to further the interests of Nandom? In any case, Armstrong considered Konkuu to be 'young, energetic and progressive', and thus supported his claims to rule.[59] Many of my interlocutors agreed that Konkuu was a well-liked chief, and that the Lambussie headmen may therefore have been quite willing to continue to recognise him as divisional chief.

Several months after Hilla's election, Konkuu complained to Armstrong that the new Lambussie Kuoro was acting on his own account, calling his own court to session instead of transferring the cases to the Nandom court.[60] Armstrong warned Hilla by reminding him that his trial period had not yet ended. Hilla, said Armstrong, rationalising this behaviour, 'has spent most of his life on the Coast and has brought his Coast habits up here'.[61] The next entry in the station book notes: 'The Chief of Lambussie now wishes to follow Tumu, but the people wish to remain under Nandom. Hilla has therefore resigned and states he will go to live at Tumu.'[62] Lambussie Division therefore remained subordinate to the Nandom Naa, and Hilla was replaced by Bombieh, a man from the Challa faction that had long vied for power against Yesibie's and Hilla's family. However, the 1934 decree, declaring Lambussie to be one of the four Sub-ordinate Native Authorities of the Lawra Confederacy, was not amended, and the Lambussie native court was formally dissolved only in 1943.[63]

Armstrong's successor had problems reconstructing the reasons for which Lambussie had been subordinated to Nandom. After viewing the files, District Commissioner Mead, who later pleaded for the restoration of Lambussie's autonomy, wrote:

> I make two guesses; first that some of the Issallas once expressed a desire to join Tumu and that this was done to 'discipline' them; and secondly that when Native Authorities were established we simply had not the trained staff to allow all of them to operate. It is still a fact that it is even more difficult to find competent literates among the Issallas than it is among the Lobis and Dagarti. ... But all of these are mere guesses on my part. The people I have talked to are unable to suggest any reason whatever.[64]

As early as a year after Hilla's replacement, however, Hilla's 'brother' Tekowah Grunshie had brought his version of events to the attention of the British and demanded redress:

That the Nandowa [Nandom] chief pressing the chief of Bosie [Lambussie] to be his follower and the latter refusing the proposals resulted in his destoolment. That I shall be greatly thankful if the learned chief commisioner may kindly investigate this with a view of restoring peace in the country.[65]

In a second communiqué, Tekowah Grunshie added that Hilla was Yesibie's son and his only legitimate successor. Furthermore, he insisted that Yesibie was 'superior' to the Nandom Naa, since 'the whole land belongs to the chief of Bosie'.[66] The Chief Commissioner countered that Hilla had voluntarily relinquished the office of chief after a majority of Lambussiele refused to support his decision to follow Tumu instead of Nandom. Thus 'the peace of the country' had not been disturbed at all, and there was no need for action.[67]

Some of my Sisala informants shared Tekowa Grunshie's view that these events were determined above all by the Nandom Naa's power interests. 'These Lobi-Dagartis, they know politics', commented Happa Kuoro Babrimatoh, who saw in Konkuu's strategy of alliance with the 'white man' the central building block of Nandom's hegemony.[68] Lambussie Kuoro Baloro, Yesibie's son, was convinced that the population of Lambussie had indeed wanted to follow Hilla's wish to join Tumu, but the chiefs of Nandom, Jirapa and Lawra had protested against this and managed to bring the district commissioner over to their side.[69] Bombieh's relatives, on the other hand, placed more emphasis on the internal conflicts over the office of chief within Lambussie. According to their version, Hilla, from Lambussie-Panna, had wanted to join the Tumu Kuoro against the wishes of most Lambussiele, and behind Konkuu's back. As a result, Konkuu had no other choice but to pass on the office of chief to a member of Lambussie's Challa section loyal to him, namely Bombieh, who, as a sister's son of Yesibie's house, also had a certain right to the office.[70] Informants from the Panna section, however, countered that Bombieh rather usurped the chiefly office and that this was what made it possible for Konkuu to incorporate Lambussie into the Nandom Division for more than ten years.

Regardless of which version corresponds more closely to actual historical events, in all of them it is clear how the internal conflicts surrounding the Lambussie chieftaincy met with the power interests of neighbouring divisions and British administrative concerns to coalesce into the complex dynamics that arose out of Nandom–Lambussie relations.

Playing the ethnic card: the restoration of Lambussie's autonomy
The chiefly family of the Panna section wanted to accept neither Challa political hegemony nor Lambussie's subordination to Nandom. The driving force behind attempts to return the chiefly honour to the 'proper'

house was Salifu Teñe Bisse, who returned to Lambussie in 1943, after
many years of having lived as a trader in Wenchi. Salifu's first attempt to
replace Bombieh failed, not least because, according to District
Commissioner Amherst's view of the matter, Nandom Naa Imoru, who in
the meantime had succeeded to Nandom Naa Konkuu, used his influence
to hinder this. Imoru must have urgently warned Amherst of Salifu's
ambitions, which might have endangered his own interests in maintaining
control over Lambussie. After conducting an inquiry into the matter,
Amherst was conviced that Salifu's complaints 'were without real
foundation but had been fostered by the Tingansob's [namely Salifu's]
family, chiefly I think from jealousy of the powers now vested in the Chiefs
and N.A. [Native Authority] but which formerly belonged to them'. Salifu
'had come back to fish in troubled waters', Amherst concluded, but 'the
stories he has put up have been shown up and effectively discredited'.[71]
Until Bombieh's death in 1948, Salifu did cease to pursue openly his goal to
win back the chieftaincy, and instead allowed himself to be made one of
Bombieh's elders. As his son Dy-Yakah explained, he 'thus linked up with
the district commissioner and got to know the other traditional rulers ... and
when Bombieh's life passed off, then asserted himself'.[72]

With Salifu's return, the struggle to restore Lambussie's autonomy
began. Lambussie Kuoro K. Y. Baloro, who, after graduating from the
teacher training college in Tamale, opened Lambussie's first primary
school in 1947 and played a central role in the quest for independence,
related the nature of the obstacles that had to be overcome. The Nandom
Naa could rely not only on Bombieh for support, but also on several
Lambussie sub-chiefs, particularly the chief of Samoa, who had only
unwillingly subordinated himself to Lambussie in 1934, and now hoped
that Nandom would once again recognise his status as being equal to
Lambussie. Besides, Nandom's claims to rule were supported by the district
commissioner and tolerated by the chiefs of Jirapa and Lawra. These
alliances all had to be undermined. Salifu first tried to win Bombieh for the
project of seceding from Nandom. Then, together with Baloro, he contacted
Mead, the new Lawra District Commissioner, and convinced him of the
need to reinstate Lambussie's autonomy. With Mead's help, Samoa's initial
resistance to secession from Nandom was overcome. The chiefs of Lawra
and Jirapa eventually shifted their support in favour of Lambussie because,
as Baloro explained, they were ever more concerned that Nandom might
obtain too great an influence in the Confederacy and receive too large a
share of the common funds. When drawing estimates, the Nandom Naa
would argue

> that his division was larger than Lawra and larger than Jirapa, so he
> should take a lion's share. ... So the Lawra Naa and the Jirapa Naa
> became angry: 'We have helped you to get the Lambussie people

added to you and now you want to use that to say that you should get more than us. Well, in this case the paramountcy better go back!' [laughs] … So when we started to fight for our separation they were then on our side and we were able to go through with that.[73]

The increasing urgency with which Lambussie attempted to restore its autonomy from Nandom was also due to the leadership style of the newly elected Nandom Naa Imoru. Lawra Naa Abeyifaa Karbo, son of J. A. Karbo, who was then in office as Chief of Lawra, even saw this 'question of personalities' to be one of the most important reasons for the secession:

> Konkuu was very kind to the Sisala, he treated them as his own people. He was a very good ruler, so the Sisala liked him. And that was the time they allowed a lot of Nandom people to have settlements within Lambussie … But Imoru would call the Sisala to come and they would sit in front of his palace from morning till evening, he didn't talk to them. And when he went to talk to them, he started insulting them, 'Langme', you know, it is derogatory, it means you are sub-standard … So they started actually fighting, petitioning, coming to the district commissioners.[74]

Finally, the secession project was buttressed by the fact that Lambussie Division, like Nandom, Lawra and Jirapa previously, now also had its own first generation of school graduates – a fact that facilitated direct communication with the British, without the intervention of interpreters from Lawra, Nandom or Tumu. K. Y. Baloro accompanied District Commissioner Mead on all his inspection trips in matters concerning Lambussie and Nandom, Salifu himself spoke some English, and several sub-divisional chiefs were assisted by their educated sons.

District Commissioner Mead's memorandum, which Chief Commissioner Ingrams endorsed, recapitulated the arguments in favour of secession, ones that my Sisala informants also presented: the Nandom Naa's discriminatory behaviour and Nandom's monopolisation of tax revenues, from which Lambussie scarcely profited. In addition, Mead's interlocutors emphasised the cultural differences between the Sisala and Dagara. Summing up, Mead did not believe

> that local government is likely to flourish unless the system we set up makes some appeal to the natural loyalties the people possess. … [The Sisala] point out that after eight years of taxation they have had very little value for their money. … They also point out that they speak their own language and that their customs, though similar in general, are quite distinct in detail from those of the Lobis and the Dagarti; and they add that they would have more confidence in the quality of the justice dispensed to them if they had a Court of their own.[75]

Plate 2 Nandom Naa Imoru and chiefs, 1940s
Front row, from the left: Puffien Naa, Kontiere-mà (Imoru's first wife), Nandom
Naa Imoru, Dagaba chief of Prestea; back row, from the left: K. P. Polkuu, Dienon
Dery (Imoro's brother), Kobina Dagarti (Dagaba chief of Kumasi), Neotig
(Konkuu's daughter), a clerk of Jirapa Naa, Naawerepuor (Polkuu's brother),
unknown (with kind permission of Nandon Naa Dr Charles Imoro

After the Second World War, the British remained as convinced as they had
been in the early 1930s that the foundations of political community must
rest upon the 'natural loyalties' that stemmed from shared ethnicity. Local
actors too adopted this discourse. While Yesibie had stressed that he should
remain in the Lawra Confederacy, because the Lambussiele were 'not really
Issallas' but 'Dagartis', the Sisala chiefs now claimed the opposite. Internal
differences, like those between the chiefs of Samoa and Lambussie, had to
stand aside in the face of a common adversary, namely Nandom Division.
As one of Mead's informants in Koro emphasised, 'all the Issalla were the
same, they were unhappy under Nandom, they had their own language and
customs, and they thought they would make much better progress if they
had their own subordinate Native Authority too.'[76]

However, the argument that 'all the Issalla were the same' drew the
cultural and linguistic boundaries not only externally, in opposition to
Nandom, but also within Lambussie Division: it was precisely in the Koro
area, where Mead's informant had claimed Sisala ethnic solidarity, that

many Dagara migrants from Nandom, who had not been incorporated into the Sisala community, had come to settle down. We cannot say for certain whether at that time the Sisala chief of Koro experienced the presence of numerous Dagara farmers as a threat to his political sovereignty. However, ten years later, a Dagara and a Sisala were competing for the chiefly office in Piina, a village subject to Koro. The Dagara candidate justified his claim to office by pointing out that the Dagara made up a majority of the population in Piina.[77] To this the chief of Koro, who wanted to make a Sisala headman of Piina, countered that no one had the right 'to replace the sub-chief with a non-native of the area according to our customary right of the area'.[78] In Lambussie Division, therefore, the discourse concerning the cultural difference between Sisala and Dagara was and still is a discourse concerning the different political rights of natives and settlers.

That such 'natural loyalties' could also justify a discourse of exclusion did not, however, feature in Mead's considerations. Presumably his Sisala informants did not mention, or at least downplayed, the settlement of numerous Dagara farmers, for Mead nowhere refers to the multi-ethnic make-up of Lambussie Division. He supported Lambussie's demand for autonomy without reservation and justified his position by invoking the same theory of political evolution that Duncan-Johnstone had formulated in 1930:

> The loyalties of the people are still extremely local, and granted that ... we must always guard against disintegration, I still think that local patriotism can be applied to promote the people's political develop-ment and that we ought to use it rather than suppress it. If the Lawra Confederacy is on the whole a healthy institution, it is because it recognizes this principle; and in my experience the slighter the bonds that bind the members of a Confederacy the greater will be the sympathy that will exist between them and their ability to work together. ... [T]he more decentralization we introduce into local government the more interest will be taken in by the mass of the people and the more efficient it will become.[79]

In November 1947, therefore, Lambussie Division once again became an autonomous native authority, within the Lawra Confederacy.[80] Mead suggested marking the distinction from the old 'Lambussie Native Authority' by giving it a new, more expressive name. The old-new native authority was now to be called 'Issalla Tuntumer', literally 'Issalla Affairs', a name that involved shifting the emphasis from locality to ethnicity while calling for active participation.

The Issalla Tuntumer Native Authority started work at the beginning of 1948, but Bombieh was at this time already terminally ill. As had been the case with Yesibie, the district commissioner asked Bombieh who should manage the affairs of office, and he is supposed to have named Salifu.[81] In

December 1948, after Bombieh's death, three candidates stood for election: Namuka from the house of Buratoo on the Challa side (Bombieh's sons were still too young), Zowina from Happa, and finally Salifu, who, according to statements made by his family, won with an overwhelming majority, though Bombieh's supporters only conceded him a slight edge.[82] As a result, the chieftaincy returned to the Panna side.

'A BENEVOLENT, PROGRESSIVE DESPOT': A NEW GENERATION OF DIVISIONAL CHIEFS

Indirect rule demanded a new type of chief, not the rich, warlike strongman of the first generation of chiefs, who knew how to manipulate power networks through gifts and violence, but rather the capable and at the same time obedient administrator, who allowed himself to be incorporated in the bureaucratic hierarchy. In the eyes of the British, the chief should be a civil servant, who received a salary for his service to his community's benefit, collected taxes instead of tribute, and neatly separated personal wealth from the native treasury. The absence of such office-holders was one of the reasons for Commissioner Whittall's objections to the introduction of the native authorities: 'Our chief difficulties are illiteracy ... and the two great flaws in the equipment of the average African (to quote Temple) the inherent lack of honesty and lack of mental initiative.'[83] Until capable administrator-chiefs came along, 'careful supervision' by the British was regarded as imperative.

In order to make the effectiveness of the native authorities more independent of the person currently serving as divisional chief, district commissioners in the Lawra Confederacy tried to introduce councils to advise them, to which were to belong the sub-divisional chiefs, important elders and the earth priests.[84] However, these efforts were largely unsuccessful. The stability of the territorial order and the implementation of British ideas for development continued to depend on the personalities, strategic skills and networks of the serving divisional chiefs. For this reason, chiefly succession was a matter of great importance. For the neighbouring and subordinate chiefs, the death of an office-holder presented an opportunity to settle old scores or to effect new territorial claims, as we saw was the case in the relationship between Nandom and Lambussie. The British, for their part, hoped that a capable administrator would take over the office – once again or finally, according to the case.

In the Lawra Confederacy, the district commissioners had no less than four opportunities to exert their influence in the matter of the succession to the divisional chieftaincy: in Lawra in 1935, Lambussie in 1936, Jirapa in 1938, and Nandom in 1940. However, their principles of selection were riddled with contradictions which to this day provide the leeway for a myriad of political machinations at the local level. First, in the eyes of the

British, the chieftaincy was a hereditary office, and legitimate successors were only those who came from the 'right' family. Second, the new office-holder should be a true civil servant, intelligent, open-minded, experienced, co-operative, incorruptible, a guarantor of good governance – criteria that were not necessarily fulfilled by the person who was the most legitimate candidate in the genealogical sense. Third and finally, the chief should be popular and recognised not only by his own family, but also by the sub-chiefs under him, by neighbouring divisional chiefs, and by the population of his division in general. Only when the new chief was 'congenial to the other chiefs and people, trustworthy by Government and as far as possible of unblemished character' could a successful discharge of office be ensured.[85]

The British regarded elections as the best means of finding successors suitable in this respect. Thus when Jirapa Naa Ganaa died in 1938, District Commissioner Blair first carried out a 'genealogical enquiry' in order to ascertain the genealogical closeness of three candidates to the deceased chief. Some of the candidates who were 'eligible by birth' he considered 'too old, too young or too characterless'.[86] One additional criterion of legitimacy, which Yelpoe, the candidate that ultimately succeeded, cited, namely that Ganaa himself had nominated him to be his successor, was rejected by Blair.[87] That the chiefs of Nandom and Lawra supported Yelpoe did not impress him either: 'I suppose they are afraid to oppose him.'[88] To settle the matter, Blair insisted on a vote by secret ballot, from which, against his expectations, Yelpoe emerged the winner with 171 votes for and only two against. Yelpoe, every bit the statesman, made his opposition candidates 'personal advisors'.[89]

The public acclamation of the new chief had already played some part in the 1920s. In the new Lawra Confederacy, elections confirmed J. A. Karbo as Lawra Naa, and Hilla as Lambussie Kuoro.[90] Yet it was only with the Jirapa Naa's successor that the British introduced this refined process, which then became fixed as 'native custom' and was later used in Nandom (1940) and Lambussie (1948). The divisional chiefs of Nandom and Lawra had 10 votes each, the sub-divisional chiefs of Jirapa 5 each, the section headmen from Jirapa 3 each, the 'head tendanas' 2 each, and the local earth priest of Jirapa along with the 'compound owners' of Jirapa town one vote each.[91] For each vote, the voter was handed a stone, the candidates being symbolised by three differently-coloured boxes. Each voter was summoned individually, one after the other, to a room in which only the district commissioner was present to monitor that the votes were correctly cast. The counting was then done publicly. Blair was fully aware that this was a British innovation: 'My own prejudices are all in favour of leaving these matters to native custom', he commented, 'but in this district where no chiefs existed before our arrival, there can be no question of consulting any custom, except our own.'[92]

The trial period of a year, during which the British could replace an unpopular or inept chief, ensured that winning an election alone could not keep a chief in office. However, administrative competence was a criterion that chiefly families probably already considered when choosing the candidates they would nominate. At any rate, it happened that the new divisional chiefs of the 1930s and 1940s tended to demonstrate some formal education, or at least experience with the chiefly office. The new chiefs of Jirapa and Nandom, for example, had served as confidantes and messengers to their predecessors. Nandom Naa Imoru was widely travelled and spoke many languages. Lawra Naa J. A. Karbo had for some years attended school in Wa, could read and write, and had long worked as an interpreter for the various district commissioners before being named chief. District Commissioner Amherst even wrote enthusiastically about what a pleasure it was to work with the Lawra Naa, who was a 'benevolent, progressive despot', had 'great authority with his people', 'progressive ideas' and took 'a definite executive part of the administration of the District'.[93] Above all, so District Commissioner Ellison's praises, Karbo was of great assistance to the British administrator because of his ability to mediate between the British and local perspectives: 'He is able to give immensely valuable advice in carrying out any new proposal and realizes both European and native outlook on such proposals.'[94]

Under British guidance, the chiefs were to modernise their divisions cautiously but comprehensively by, for example, setting up demonstration farms and cattle kraals, digging water wells, supporting campaigns for the eradication of sleeping sickness, and reforming customary law regarding child betrothal and divorce. The district record books and informal diaries from the 1930s and 1940s read for long stretches like progress reports written by development aid workers, characterised by a mixture of conservatism and enthusiasm for education, a tone that still pervades the development discourse of the educated local elite and the Ghanaian bureaucracy today.[95] The governor of the Gold Coast even pointed out, on the occasion of the successful introduction of the poll tax, that the Northern Territories had given the 'more advanced and sophisticated peoples of the Colony and Ashanti' a shining example in matters of 'self-help'.[96] Since, however, the majority of the population in the North evidenced little noticeable improvement in their day-to-day standard of living, moral progress was declared to be the native authorities' greatest achievement:

> Native rulers have to be taught that the success of native administration ultimately depends not ... on the erection of a record number of market sheds, latrines etc. but on the strength of their own characters, and their ability ... to govern their subjects wisely and impartially under modern conditions.[97]

However, such populism was always closely tied to bureaucratic paternalism and the claim to control. The chief commissioner saw his role and that of his officials vis-à-vis the native authorities as being one of 'professional parent' with the well-being of his 'offspring' at heart.[98] For all the encouragement to effect the 'necessary progress', it was also important to protect the natives 'from the evils of civilization which we represent'.[99] Despite occasional enthusiasm for progressive chiefs, the district commissioner stated with resignation that

> [t]he salient feature of object lessons in this country ... appears to be that they are never learnt, except bad ones such as English legal procedure, tin roof architecture and Christian intolerance. I'm not at all sure that the French method of forced agricultural improvement isn't the best.[100]

The district diary and annual reports repeatedly complain that chiefs were not ruling wisely or unselfishly at all. For example, the Han Naa had to be removed from office for embezzling taxes.[101] The Jirapa Naa and other chiefs were accused of using communal farms which were ostensibly intended to produce food for the native authority school as a pretext to appropriate labour for their own farms.[102] District Commissioner Amherst from time to time felt obliged to engage the chiefs in a 'heart-to-heart talk', telling them that in no way could they continue to force people to work their fields in the name of the colonial government.[103] And, on the occasion of one of the innumerable debates over the distribution of tax revenues, he noted:

> Personal jealousies are rampant. One is apt to forget that their view of government and a governor is fundamentally different from ours. No ethical idea of duty exists. Dog eats dog while the sun shines was the outlook in these Men's formative years.[104]

And so even greater hopes were placed in the next generation of chiefs who were to have gone through the native authority school system, where they could be trained for their future roles starting in early youth.

'NATIVE LAWS AND CUSTOMS'

Indirect rule not only predicated a new type of administrator-chief, but also the codification of customary law, according to which the chiefs were to govern and pass judgement. Although Read complained in 1908 that among the Dagarti and Lobi there were no 'laws' outside the family or the 'fetish', the British had since then become convinced that an unwritten legal code existed. Thus, with the help of knowledgeable informants, they intended to learn all they could about it and set its rules down in writing.[105] Here we must distinguish between two interrelated processes: on the one hand the production of descriptions of native customs as ideal types that covered, for example, kinship, the *bàgr* initiation or burial rituals, as authored by certain district commissioners and Rattray, the government anthropologist;[106] and on the other hand, the negotiation and recording of native law in order to formulate guidelines for the functioning of the native authority courts. Both processes underscored the idea that each tribe was a natural, historically constituted community with shared customs and practices, distinct from those of other tribes.

The primary concern here is the second process, the codification of native law. Since the establishment of the Lawra Confederacy, the divisional chiefs and their advisers held conferences regularly, not only to lay down numerous regulations concerning revenue,[107] but also to discuss matters such as chiefly succession, the inheritance of property, marriage, divorce, and land rights. The results of these discussions were recorded in English by the district commissioner and his native clerk, and then, following oral translation back into Dagara, were signed by the divisional chiefs. Attempts to encourage the earth priests' participation in these conferences and the activities of the native courts failed because of resistance from the earth priests themselves, at least according to District Commissioner Amherst.[108] Despite an offer to pay them an attendance fee, they were not prepared to partake in the chiefs' discussions, not even in debates on traditional land rights.[109] Amherst regarded this resistance as primarily due to their 'jealousy'. Although cases involving spiritual matters like death in the bush, murder and suicide could not be settled without earth priests' intervention, other issues that were usually their prerogative, such as decisions concerning construction, land and market places, were now handled by the chiefs. 'They [the *tendanas*] are still jealous of the Chiefs, and also, I think, prefer to remain in the background and let the Chiefs take any kicks that are going.'[110]

At these native authority conferences, therefore, neo-traditional rulers created new traditions to serve their own interests and recorded what had in the previous twenty years become standard practice in the native tribunals. However, one must not overlook important variations. In the case of land rights and matters regarding marriage and inheritance, district commissioners and chiefs were convinced that they were merely recording existing 'ancient customs'.[111] The innovations produced by their being written down and standardised remained hidden behind a traditionalistic façade. With regard to the chieftaincy, on the other hand, everyone was aware that new customs were in the making. In the following I shall comment on such consciously 'invented traditions' pertaining to the chieftaincy, and include some observations concerning marriage and divorce law.

'The Lawra area is a tangle of Lobi-Dagarti and Issala custom which is changing continuously', complained District Commissioner Ellison, observing time and again that succession to the office of village headman did not follow any 'definite custom', but was decided arbitrarily by the divisional chiefs. In the latter case, however, continued Ellison, a 'tradition' had since evolved, namely elections, which he now wished to introduce for the village headmanship too.[112] When the divisional chiefs discussed the 'rules of succession to chieftainships' at their first conference in January 1935, they drew on what was familiar, basing these rules on the same norms that governed the inheritance of moveable property, namely 'matrilineal succession' among the Lobi and 'patrilineal succession' among the Dagarti.[113] However, the set of rules that the chief commissioner desired and that the chiefs' conference produced were never implemented. The chiefs knew that they themselves had not attained office in accordance with these rules. Lawra Naa Karbo, a Lobi according to British understanding, belonged to a different matriclan than his predecessor Binni. Konkuu, a Dagarti, was neither the younger brother nor the son of his predecessor Boro. Even in determining later successors the rules were not strictly followed. The chiefs therefore added a 'disabilities' clause, which could exclude a genealogically legitimate candidate from chiefly office by reason of 'blindness, leprosy, unpopularity'.[114] In the case of the succession to the Jirapa Naa, the limited practical relevance of these rules as initially laid down became quite apparent, given that not even District Commissioner Blair referred back to them, to say nothing of the local actors.

The matter of chiefly succession was therefore debated again at a native authority conference in 1940, which was now to codify the 'secret ballot' first tested in Jirapa. Especially interesting are the Lawra Naa's introductory remarks on the innovative nature of the chieftaincy and the deliberate creation of procedures that henceforth would be regarded as 'customary':

> The Lawra Na related, and the meeting agreed, that before the advent of Europeans, the head of each family was the ruler of each family, that leaders in war would be regarded as men whose opinion must be listened to (for obvious reasons), and that the Tingansobs, as descendants of the first settlers, held power in the adjudication of land and imposed sanctions in matters where the land had been defiled i.e. in criminal acts where blood had been spilt, etc. It was recognised that chiefship was a modern innovation, and that very little custom attached to rules of succession. ... It transpired that the first chiefs appointed on the European arrival were nominated to the first Commissioners by the Tingansobs, and that in this action lay the only 'Custom' that could be said to pertain. It was agreed that in all future appointments the following principles and procedures should be carried out, and should be regarded as 'customary':
> a) that a candidate for chiefship must be a member of the patrilineal family of a former chief;

  b) that a candidature must be approved by the Tingansob of the area
  concerned;
  c) that election of a candidate to the chiefship shall be by secret
  ballot.[115]

These stipulations restricted the circle of potential successors, while at the
same time defining it more flexibly than had been the case in 1935. There
was no more talk of matrilinearity, and who exactly belonged to the
'patrilineal family of a former chief' could be highly controversial matter. A
few months before the chiefs' conference Nandom Naa Boro's successor
Konkuu had died, and the discussions were overshadowed by the rivalry
between Yuori, Boro's son, and Imoru, descended from Konkuu. It is likely
that this struggle over succession was the reason why the conference
participants were so vague in formulating their agreement; moreover, the
officiating interpreter, Dasoberi, was Yuori's brother. Also new was that the
chiefs at the conference granted the earth priest a sort of veto power, which
may also have been a concession to Dasoberi, since the Nandom earth
priests supported Boro's claims over Imoru's. Finally, also new was that the
'secret ballot' first tested in Jirapa was now to be conducted regularly.
However, this innovation was rather short-lived, since in 1954 the assembled
chiefs of the Lawra Confederacy decided that '[t]here is no balloting for
chiefship when there are capable sons of the deceased chief', unless two
members of the 'Royal family' were competing with one another for the
office.[116]

    When the next Jirapa Naa was to be installed in June 1955, there was
neither an election, nor was the Lawra Confederacy State Council (the
successor of the chiefs' conferences) consulted. Government Agent Venables
expressed his surprise at this 'modernisation' of 'customary rites': 'It has
been possible to considerably modernise custom without objection being
raised, and possibly a more suitable title to this letter might have been
"*tempora mutantur, nos et mutamur in illis*"!'[117] Apparently, he was not aware
that these same reformed 'customary rights' had only fifteen years earlier
been introduced by one of his predecessors in co-operation with the chiefs.
And, just like his predecessors, Venables did not understand that these
'customs' were not rooted in sacred cultural traditions, but were in fact the
product of secular local power politics. The chiefs quickly learned to
disguise political intrigues under the cloak of 'customary law', so that
behind what seemed like stable native political institutions local struggles
for power continued.[118]

    Conflicts over bridewealth payments, adultery and divorce were among
the disputes most frequently brought before the chiefs' courts. For this
reason, the chief commissioner ordered that the customary rules be written
down, District Commissioner Blair doing his best to obtain from the chiefs
the requisite information. On the other hand, the administration had little

interest in detail.[119] The 'Marriage laws of the Lobi and Dagarti tribes', a 'true account of Lobi and Dagarti Customary Law', were codified in 1938.[120] Among the Lobi in Lawra and Nandom, it was reported to be customary for the groom and his friends to work in his father-in-law's fields and pay 13,000 cowries before the wedding, as well as three cows, by the birth of the second child at the latest. Among the Dagarti in Jirapa and in some villages in Nandom and Lawra,[121] the payment was fixed at a maximum of 50,000 cowries payable before the wedding, as well as 19,500 cowries or a cow 'on the betrothal of the first born girl' (a sheep in the case of a boy). In addition, the procedures for courting of a bride and for 'divorce' were laid down. If the amount of the bridewealth stated is compared with the information given by Read and Jackson in their first ethnographic report of 1908, one cannot help suspect that the chiefs were trying to increase the payments required of the groom and strengthen the rights of husbands over their wives.[122] Even more importantly, it was only now, with written codification, that the various forms of cohabitation were defined as 'marriage' at all. There was and still is no Dagara word that translates as 'marriage'. 'Woman' and 'wife' are designated with the same word. In the non-Christian context, there was no ceremony and no point in time from which a 'marriage' was regarded as official. Women could leave their men to live with new partners, so long as the latter reimbursed any bridewealth that had already been paid by their predecessors. Even District Commissioner Amherst noticed that a European concept of 'marriage' was not entirely useful,[123] and conceded 'that there is no definite "divorce"'.[124] Hence the 'divorce laws' were revised to state: 'No act, rite or form of words ... is necessary to effect a divorce.'[125]

In case rulings chiefs followed codified native law only partially, and the courts' power of sanction was limited.[126] However, the codification of the native law did standardise the myriad of commonly held ideas regarding Dagara and Dagaba 'traditions'. Time and again in interviews with labour migrants, in conversations with local intellectuals and in their writings,[127] as well as in many petitions concerning conflicts over succession to chiefly office, I encountered 'traditional' regulations and procedures cited almost word for word as first codified in the 1930s and 1940s.

EDUCATING FUTURE CHIEFS AND POLITICIANS

Decisive in anchoring the new ethno-political order in the minds of local actors was the Native Authority Primary School, which the Lawra Confederacy opened in 1935. Here, the British intended to raise a new generation of educated chiefs and native authority clerks, who were not only literate and had practical knowledge of agriculture and hygiene, but who were also qualified to carry out their future roles as political authorities in the spirit of a 'progressive traditionalism'.

In Lawra a primary school had already been opened in 1919, with a good forty pupils, and two teachers from the Gold Coast Colony who could speak neither Dagara nor Sisala. The number of pupils dropped from year to year, and finally in 1927 the school was closed, either because of a lack of resources and insufficient demand for education, as the colonial government argued, or, as local rumours had it, because a pupil had been beaten to death.[128] A number of the Lawra pupils continued their education at the primary school in Wa, others at the commercial school in Yendi. Most of those in this first generation of educated locals were subsequently employed as interpreters, native clerks and assistants to the British medical officer, like J. A. Karbo, the later Lawra Naa, or Nandom Naa Boro's son Dasoberi, who succeeded Karbo as the district commissioner's interpreter. With the establishment of the native authorities, the demand for educated administrative employees, who would ideally work in their home divisions, became more pressing. After some initial misgivings, the chiefs finally agreed to the re-opening of a primary school in Lawra, a school of which in course of time they were to become extraordinarily proud, because it was regarded as one of the best ones in the Northern Territories.[129]

While the cost of constructing buildings and paying teachers' salaries was met by the colonial government, the maintenance of the buildings, the purchase of teaching materials and the pupils' living expenses had to be financed by the parents and by the native treasury. In addition, the divisional chiefs set up school farms in various villages which served to feed the students. To begin with, tuition was set at 10 shillings per pupil per annum, or alternatively at 5 shillings and a sheep. In 1943 tuition was increased to 30 shillings, against which the chiefs vehemently protested, not least because they themselves had sent many of their own children to receive schooling.[130] Of the 86 boys and 4 girls who in 1938–9 were enrolled at school in Lawra, over two-thirds were the children of chiefs and sub-chiefs, and a further 20 the children of headmen.[131] In 1936 the Lawra Confederacy chiefs decided to finance 24 scholarships from the resources of the native treasury, 12 for 'heirs to chieftainships' and 12 for children who performed well in school, though again it was mostly chiefs' sons who profited.[132] The weight that education was accorded in the native authority budget did in fact reflect the great significance the chiefs attached to it.[133] In the Lawra Confederacy formal education was to be the most important means of upward social mobility; at the same time, it played an important role in socialising the next generation into the new ethnic order.

With the opening of Lawra's first school in 1919 began the practice of organising the boarding school along tribal principles. In order 'to promote a healthy spirit of rivalry and competition', Duncan-Johnstone had the boys divided into two 'houses', one for the Lobi and one for the Grunshi and Dagarti.[134] Similarly, the school that was opened in 1935 deliberately reproduced the structure of the Lawra Confederacy Native Authority. In recruiting pupils, care was taken that each division, being identified with a particular tribe, was equally represented. The annual report for 1938–9 listed 23 Dagarti from Jirapa, 20 Lobi-Dagarti from Nandom (under which category the few Sisala pupils from Lambussie were subsumed), 22 Lobi from Lawra, and 23 Sisala from Tumu.[135] Headmaster William Henkel – born out of a liaison between a German colonial officer formerly stationed in Togo and a Wangara woman – housed the pupils by division, in different compounds on the school grounds. Thus, there was a Nandom compound, in which pupils from Lambussie also lived, a Jirapa compound, a Lawra compound, and later also a Tumu compound. Each of these compounds was headed by a 'chief' and his assistant, who was subordinate to a 'paramount chief' that represented the whole school. Other positions in the school hierarchy, including the dining-hall chairman, office boy, dispensary orderly and school prefects, were inspired by the English boarding school system. At morning assembly pupils marched to xylophone music under the Union Jack; and in addition to the regularly scheduled football matches, they also had to attend tribal dancing every Saturday afternoon. The lower forms were taught in Dagara, which was also obligatory for Sisala pupils.[136] School plays, which were performed at the chiefs' conferences, were devoted to local history; and occasionally elderly earth priests and chiefs were invited to come and share with pupils the history of their villages.[137]

District commissioners and divisional chiefs did not always agree on how much modernisation the schools should propagate. The Lawra Naa, for example, wished to see the school equipped with a musical band that included brass instruments and a percussion section, while the district commissioner, who ultimately got his way, insisted on xylophones and local drums, citing financial reasons as well as the desire to preserve local traditions.[138] In another case, the Lawra Naa ordered schoolgirls' skirts be part of the uniform in spite of opposition from Commissioner Amherst, who felt compelled to hold a 'sermon' on the meaning and purpose of the native authority schools and to warn against a 'coat and collar *ersatz* Western outlook'.[139] The boys, for their part, were required always to wear the local smock, not the uniform with khaki shorts usually worn in the South. Until the late 1940s, this rule also applied to student teachers in Tamale, who were to wear a smock not only at college, but also during their free time when on excursions into the city. It was only after the students went on strike to protest against such 'discrimination' compared to their colleagues from the South – which is how they perceived the smock-based dress code – that the uniform issue was handled more liberally.[140]

Amherst appreciated that older pupils, who transferred to the middle school in Tamale, 'want to see LIFE [*sic*] at Achimota, Kumasi etc. and want work that will take them there for training'.[141] However, such a commendable interest in 'progress' should not be allowed to endanger the primary goal of the native authority schools: developing respect for 'tradition', and preparing to enter positions of responsibility in the local native administration. Headmaster Henkel's regime could certainly help to attain this goal, as District Commissioner Blair stated with satisfaction: 'The children return home in their holidays, not (as formerly) a set of conceited and detribalised imps, but still proud of their Lobi and Dagati [sic] blood, and taught to reverence the traditions of their fathers.'[142] Unlike the French, as Duncan-Johnstone had put it in his memorandum on indirect rule, the British did not wish to integrate the educated 'intelligentsia' into European society.[143]

Whether British educational policy in the Northern Territories really created a tradition-conscious elite that refused any and all forms of 'westernisation' is rather questionable. However, there is no doubt that the further careers of almost all the Lawra Confederacy Native Authority School graduates were linked very closely with their home divisions and with the institution of the chieftaincy. Of the twenty pupils who first reached Standard III in 1939, twelve qualified to attend the middle school in Tamale. The rest were employed by the native authority, either immediately or following further training in crafts or agriculture, as market supervisors, tax collectors, assistants to the medical officer, on the trial farms, in construction, or as office or court assistants.[144] Many of the pupils sent from Lawra to the middle school at Tamale went on to graduate from the new teachers training college there, and subsequently returned to their home district to teach at one of the newly opened village schools. There were few other career opportunities open to them, but many felt morally obliged to do so, to some extent because their studies had been financed with local taxes. Almost all these early teachers and native clerks became involved in local politics in the early 1950s.

Over the years quite a few of this first generation of pupils from the Lawra Native Authority Primary School also went on to take over prominent chiefly offices. The sub-divisional chiefs of Birifu, Eremon, Sabuli, Tizza and Duori, as well as three of the four divisional chiefs of the Lawra Confederacy, who held office in the 1960s, belonged to this first generation of graduates from the Lawra Confederacy Primary School. The fourth divisional chief, Jirapa Naa Bapenyiri Yelpoe, attended the primary school in Wa, but then, together with the other divisional chiefs, went on to attend the middle school and teaching seminary in Tamale.

And so it was, much as the British had hoped, that the Native Authority Primary School, and the schools in Tamale produced a generation of educated chiefs, who until very recently exerted great influence on local politics in the North-West. Despite the political differences that later developed along party lines, these men were closely bound to one another by old school friendships, which were often reinforced by intermarriage between their families. At the same time, the middle school in Tamale became a place at which they met pupils from other native authorities of the Northern Territories, often forming lifelong friendships. These young men were thoroughly socialised into the colonial ethnic categories and into that hierarchically arranged sense of belonging propagated by the British model of the native states – from local patriotism for one's home division and the pride in being part of the Lawra Confederacy, to a distinct sense of a Northern identity, to the feeling of belonging to the civilised world of the British Empire.

5

LABOUR MIGRATION, HOME-TIES AND ETHNICITY

Civilization advances apace, if the standard of progress can be judged by the number of natives who now wear clothes and carry walking sticks or spears, in preference to the old order of perhaps nothing or at best a sheep or goat skin hung over the back, the bow in the hand and the quiver under the arm. The people of bow and arrow used to meet the Commissioner on his arrival perhaps two miles from the rest house, and would ... leap out with twanging bows and bloodcurling yells ... Now they are a much more sedate crowd, 75 per cent at least being clothed, many of them in European clothes, all wearing some kind of headgear, who meet the Commissioner a few hundred yards from the rest house.[1]

For the British, 'nakedness' was an indicator of native primitiveness; and if, as was almost always the case, men carried bows and arrows, it was a sign of dangerous aggressiveness. By as early as the 1920s this nakedness was largely covered up and the aggressiveness disciplined, a development that the Lawra District Commissioner Eyre-Smith, the author of the above remarks, attributed to the impact of labour migration. Through work in the mines, in railway construction and on cocoa plantations, an increasing number of young men were not only earning the money required to buy clothing, but also adopting new ideas of what was considered beautiful and what constituted desirable consumer goods. They were becoming familiar with the world that extended beyond their village and experiencing a certain degree of autonomy from their fathers and ancestors. In short, they were 'civilising' themselves, and, by sharing their experiences and views, they were also civilising their brothers back home. As Eyre-Smith reflected, '[t]hese boys return with a wider outlook and new ideas; they have discovered that they can live for twelve months without frequently consulting the family fetish; all these facts are imparted ... to their less civilized brothers.'[2]

Labour migration linked virtually every compound in Lawra District with the wider world of the Gold Coast and the Ashanti Protectorate, ensuring the tangible economic integration of Lawra District into the colony and into the empire. At the same time, it brought with it a sort of socialisation of the migrant into his own 'tribe'. In the migration context, ethnic stereotypes were developed on all sides – by the migrants themselves, by local or British employers, and by local traders, householders and chiefs – which aided orientation. Here, the domestic groups of clan and neighbourhood were extended not only cognitively, but also through practical activities. For labour migrants, ethnicity became an idiom of solidarity and of the organisation of home-ties. Ethnicity was therefore constructed not only from 'above', by colonial officials and chiefs, but also from below, by labour migrants themselves.

Migrants defined the boundaries of their ethnic communities along the lines of common language and origin. Such ethnic categories were defined more narrowly or widely depending on the context, be it living together and finding help in obtaining work, providing mutual aid in cases of illness or death, and affiliating oneself with a tribal headman who was to represent the migrants to outsiders. However, these categories almost always cross-cut the smaller-scale ethnic boundaries that the native states sought to draw in their home districts.

THE 'LABOUR CRUSADE'

In his 1905 report on the Northern Territories Chief Commissioner Watherston concluded that the 'peaceful state of the country' had freed the natives from the need 'to keep up large armed forces to preserve their own existence'.[3] Many young men therefore now led an 'idle life' for half the year, during the dry season, and Watherston had great hopes that he could win their services as workers in the mines of Tarkwa and Ashanti. Since South African gold production stagnated because of the Boer War, the gold mines of the Gold Coast Colony and the Ashanti Protectorate had been experiencing a real boom since the turn of the century. However, they had massive problems in recruiting sufficient labour, especially for work underground.[4] In 1905, the managers of the mine in Tarkwa directed the first enquiry to the colonial government regarding the possibility of recruiting labour from the recently accessed Northern Territories. Chief Commissioner Watherston was not against the idea, but insisted on certain conditions: men from the same village should work in the same mine, they should be able to contact their chief at any time, and a colonial official should accompany them at least to Kumasi. He also stressed that the chiefs were not terribly willing to let the young men go – especially in the rainy season, the main season for cultivation – for fear that they would not return.[5] Despite this, Watherston opened the 'labour crusade' in 1906 with a speech before several hundred chiefs in Wa, which was to serve district officials as a model for future recruitment campaigns. Appealing to the pride of his audience, he declared that in 'the Whiteman's country all young men work, only old men sit down', and painted a shining picture of the future: in one year a group of twenty-five mine workers could save up to £250, which could then be invested profitably in cattle farming.[6]

Lawra District was densely settled, and Watherston was highly impressed by the striking physique and intelligence of Lobi men, 'strongly resembling the Zulu'.[7] He therefore took advantage of every opportunity to convey to the chiefs the educational and economic benefits of work in the mines. For their part, the chiefs of Nandom and Lawra were prepared to send a number of men on a preliminary reconnaissance trip to the mines. Thirty 'intelligent men', chosen by colonial officials in Wa and Navrongo, were then brought to the mines at the end of 1906, so that they could inform themselves of the type of work, payment and living conditions they could expect there.[8] However, it was fairly obvious that not all of these 'labour representatives' had reported of their own volition, and that their prevailing concern was not so much the prospect of future wealth, but rather the fear of being enslaved. Even the Lawra Naa himself, of all people, refused to join the delegation: as Black Volta District Commissioner Read reported, 'in spite of all my assurances ... he thought it was a device to obtain slaves'.[9] However, the other chiefs did return safe, sound and full of new impressions, and were now seen by their neighbours, to put it in Read's words, as 'quite important people'. In any case, the journey helped overcome people's initial apprehension.[10]

In February 1907, the first 26 workers were recruited for the mines in Tarkwa, 17 Sisala from Tumu, who stayed for a year or more, and 9 'Dagarti', who returned to the North-West after only two months.[11] Then, an epidemic of meningitis, which caused at least 2,000 deaths in the Northern Territories, led to the suspension of recruitment for some months.[12] The fact that despite this another 170 workers could in September 1907 be sent to Tarkwa, Abbontiakoon and Aboso, followed by a further 75 in November, was probably due to the subsidy of five shillings per recruit that the chiefs were paid from that time on.[13] At the same time, the district commissioner also threatened to impose penalties on chiefs who failed to send enough workers.[14] Yet whether voluntarily or by compulsion, in October 1908 another 47 mine workers from the North-West arrived in Tarkwa, half of them Lobi and the other half Dagarti. In July 1909 they already numbered 444, including 104 Wala, 135 Dagarti, 164 Isala and 41 Grunshi, followed by another 382 in December.[15]

Workers recruited in the North-Eastern part of the Northern Territories 'deserted' en masse, as the colonial officials expressed it, while still on the way to Kumasi and Tarkwa. By contrast, most of the migrants from the North-West remained in the mines as expected, between six months and a year, or even longer. Provincial Commissioner Read ascribed the resounding response with which the recruitment campaign was received in 1909 to the patent success of the first young men who returned home in 1908. After deduction of all living expenses, the 134 migrants had altogether earned £900 and brought home 'clothes, boxes and some savings', many up to £12.[16] Yet recruitment also had a dark side: although in July 1909 a total of 444 migrants arrived in Tarkwa, only 363 migrants returned to Wa a year later, 16 having remained in Tarkwa, 22 having 'deserted', almost 30 not yet having reported to the District Commissioner, and 15 having died.[17]

Similarly disturbing in the eyes of some British were the noticeable changes in life-style and political attitude, namely 'that among the returned labourers there are men who have contracted drinking habits and other vices, who have been infected with venereal and other diseases, and who have become insubordinate to their tribal chiefs'.[18] These observations were part of a report that the colonial government had prepared in response to the mines' petition for an even larger labour contingent. The chief commissioner argued that the maintenance of political and social stability in the Northern Territories and the mines' growing demand for labour were hardly reconcilable. He negotiated a series of agreements with the mine managers that called for increased security and control, as well as improvements in the living conditions of workers from the North. Yet doubts about the usefulness of work in the mines prevailed, and the colonial government stopped recruiting efforts until further notice. Despite this mine officials themselves continued to be allowed to recruit labour, even in the North, at least until soldiers were needed for the First World War.[19]

After the war, the boom in cocoa production, the further expansion of the mining industry and Governor Guggisberg's ambitious development programme all tremendously increased the demand for labour from the North, at a time when not all former soldiers had as yet returned, and when at least 28,000 people in the Northern Territories alone had fallen victim to the influenza epidemic that ravaged the region in 1918–19.[20] When the mines complained repeatedly about the lack of support from the colonial administration, the governor pointed out that the government itself was finding it difficult to compete with the cocoa industry for labour, where a porter could earn three to five times the wage paid by the colonial administration or the mines. 'Government work' in the overflowing towns, with their high cost of living, was just as unattractive to migrants from the North as the dangerous and insalubrious work underground in the gold mines. While ten years earlier the natives still more or less blindly trusted their district commissioner and could be satisfied with a daily wage of a shilling, the governor wrote, they had since then learnt to assess the value of their work themselves. Under these circumstances, the only possible course of action, according to the governor, was to introduce a system of voluntary recruitment. Thus, the district commissioner was to inform the chiefs of how many workers were required for railway construction or in the mines, and to have workers recruited without compulsion in groups of twenty-five, 'including a headman and a musician'. Colonial officials were then to record the migrants' names and hand them metal tags carrying identification numbers, which were supposed to ease registration upon return.[21]

The new recruitment offensive was launched in 1920 when Lawra District Commissioner Shields called upon each of the ten native states to provide at least ten migrants to work in railway construction. Shields' successor Duncan-Johnstone had much higher expectations. When Nandom Naa Boro sent him 81 labour recruits, he asked some of these men to recruit some of their friends, so that by means of the 'snowball effect' there would be enough workers to send four complete groups from Nandom to Kumasi. From Nandom alone, 132 men went to Kumasi, another 129 from Lawra and an additional 117 from Jirapa. At first the other chiefs provided at the most 20 workers each, even though Duncan-Johnstone put them under a good deal of pressure to provide more.[22] Altogether 721 men were recruited from Lawra District alone to work for six months in railway construction, almost half the contingent provided by the entire North-Western Province.[23]

However, the volume of such 'voluntary' recruitment declined in the years to follow. In the first half of 1921, only 274 men were sent to work the mines and 47 to construct railways.[24] In November 1921 District Commissioner Eyre-Smith managed to recruit another 131 men for the mines, but had to admit that underground work had become a virtual 'taboo'. Bad food, poor accommodation, and harsh treatment by overseers did not make for easy working conditions, and the negative experiences suffered by the first groups of migrants to the mines had left a lasting impact.[25] The statistics concerning illness and mortality rates in the mines justified these misgivings: more than half of the Lawra mine migrants fell ill from tuberculosis, pneumonia, ulcers, dysentery, diarrhoea, malaria or syphilis, and nearly 7 per cent died of these illnesses or in accidents.[26]

The shockingly high death rate for underground work stimulated renewed debate between the colonial government and mine management. The managers attributed the large number of fatalities to the fact that many of the recruits were already ill upon their arrival at the mines. The colonial officials, on the other hand, insisted quite the contrary, that the poor working conditions and high mortality rates were the reason that not enough workers could be recruited.[27] Miserable working conditions in the mines were certainly responsible for the illnesses and fatalities. However, it is also likely that the chiefs actually sent off less robust men to work in the mines, because they wished to keep the stronger men in the villages. Moreover, the latter had long since already opted for the much more attractive work on the cocoa plantations. When in 1925 the colonial government finally refused to recruit for the mines (or for railway construction), the mine agents in Lawra managed to recruit a mere 65 workers.[28] In 1927, the mines gave up recruiting in the Northern Territories altogether, since the return on the recruitment campaign no longer bore any relation to the cost and effort involved.[29]

'A PRAISEWORTHY DESIRE TO BETTER THEIR FORTUNES'?[30]

The end of recruitment in no way implied that migration to the gold mines ceased. On the contrary, labour recruits had merely paved the way for a route that was then taken by an increasing number of North-Westerners on their own initiative. Since the late 1920s, some migrants also took their wives with them if they were planning a longer stay, and small communities of Northerners were springing up in all mining towns.[31] In 1914, according to official estimates, a total of 3,800 migrants from the Northern Territories were employed in the mines, a quarter of the entire mine work force. In 1920, Northerners counted for 19 per cent of the total work force and 27 per cent of those working underground;[32] and the number of mine migrants from the North-West, particularly from Nandom and Lawra, continued to grow. In the 1950s and 1960s the 'Dagarti' probably constituted a good quarter of the underground work force.[33]

Seasonal labour migration to the cocoa-growing areas was probably even more extensive than migration to the mines.[34] In the dry season, from late October to April or May, many small groups of friends and relatives, usually headed by an experienced migrant, sought out the cocoa plantations on their own initiative, often against the wishes of the chiefs and the district commissioner. As early as 1908 the Lawra District Commissioner reported many young men going to work on the cocoa plantations in Ashanti and earning good money there.[35] Initially those in search of work must have imagined 'Kumasi' to be a land of promise, but only in a very vague sense. Later, however, migrants knew very well what to expect on their journey and the work that would be involved, and took with them sufficient food stocks or a few animal skins to exchange along the way.[36] Even into the late 1930s, most travelled south on foot, partly because they had no money for transport, but also because trucks did not take passengers.

As to the total extent of labour migration from the North-West, the documented figures only allow an estimate. From mid-September to mid-November 1915, 1,231 Lobi and Dagarti came through Wa on their way to Kumasi; altogether 2,000 to 3,000 men are said to have migrated from North-Western Province.[37] Later, migrants were counted crossing the Volta on the ferries at Yeji, Bamboi, Buipe and Krachi. Whether these migrants were coming from French colonies or the Northern Territories is not easy to determine, though the British annual report for 1925–6 gave figures of over 6,000 'British' and over 30,000 'French' migrants. Most crossed the Volta by the ferry at Bamboi, suggesting that they came from the North-West. In 1929–30 more than 55,000 migrants were counted, and the reference in the annual reports to the yearly 'exodus to the South of young men in search of work' had by then become an established convention.[38] In the 1930s too, apart from a short-term decline due to the cocoa hold-ups, some 40,000 to 50,000 migrants from the Northern Territories were counted using the ferries. At the end of the 1940s the figure even exceeded 130,000.[39]

Half-way reliable assessments as to the demographic importance of migration for Lawra District can only be gleaned from figures dating from the 1940s. The census carried out by the Lawra-Tumu District Commissioner in August 1943 – that is, still during the rainy season – showed that of the 33,074 inhabitants of Nandom Division (which at that time included Lambussie), 1,376 men were currently working in the South, a mere 4 per cent of the total population, but nevertheless 18 per cent of all men over sixteen. In the dry season, the proportion of migrants was probably much higher still.[40] In 1948, 10 per cent of the Dagarti and 6.2 per cent of the Lobi were counted as being away from their home region, while in 1960 this was as many as 17.4 per cent of Dagarti and 14 per cent of Lobi.[41] Taking sex and age into account, almost half the adult male population was living outside Lawra District in March 1960 (that is, during the dry season),[42] and most of the others had at least worked earlier in their lives in the South for some period of time. During my research, I met in the villages of Nandom and Lawra literally not a single man who had not on occasion migrated south during the dry season, and many had worked for ten, twenty or even thirty years in the mines, on the yam farms or on the cocoa plantations. In most compounds only one man spent the entire year in the North, all the others migrating seasonally or spending longer periods of time outside their home region.[43] Even in the 1930s, half the adult men in Lawra District had apparently already acquired migration experience.[44]

As the number of migrants increased, so too did the number of complaints from the chiefs over the 'continual drain on the population', which they regarded as detrimental to agriculture and road maintenance.[45] Many chiefs believed that the colonial authorities should bring the migration of young men under control, if not prohibit it entirely.[46] Yet even when district commissioners concurred with the complaints of the chiefs they believed the effective control of migration to be impossible.

Typical of this state of affairs is the exchange of letters in response to a complaint lodged by the Jirapa Naa, to the effect 'that many of his young men were leaving their homes to go to Coomassie and the Colony and were staying there permanently'.[47] The district commissioner took no practical measures whatsoever, for which reason the Jirapa Naa, who was probably also concerned about the work of his subjects on his own farms, repeated his complaint that '[a]ll the youths of one household will go away leaving only the old people to work the farms and do Government work'.[48] The Jirapa Naa thus demanded that the district commissioner ensure the return of all migrants after seven or eight months, at the very latest. The colonial officer objected that 'forcible measures are practically impossible', and advised the Jirapa Naa to urge his subjects to allow only one or two sons per compound to go south,[49] a practice that was probably already the rule. The Jirapa Naa decided to put the matter before the provincial commissioner who wrote to Chief Commissioner Armitage that although it was necessary to consider the labour demands of Ashanti and the colony, 'some check should be put on the young men leaving their villages in large numbers'.[50] Armitage replied that it would be impossible to regulate migration administratively, and, besides, the migrants and their villages of origin had ultimately only benefited from it. The young Dagarti men could not be reproached

> for a praiseworthy desire to better their fortunes or work for money. ... Those that I have seen who returned were better clothed than their neighbours and satisfied with their sojourn in Ashanti or elsewhere. ... the movement is on the whole for the benefit of the community and therefore one that is to be encouraged.[51]

Initial attempts by colonial officials to ensure the thrift and safe return of the labour migrants by having part of their wages paid out by the district commissioner only upon their return to the North were soon abandoned.[52] The administrative effort was far too great, and the migrants preferred to use their wages in Kumasi to buy consumer goods for themselves and their families before returning back home.[53] But even so, a fair sum of money did reach the North with the migrants, and even made it into the hands of the chiefs.

Armitage stressed not only the benefits of migration for the migrants and their communities of origin, but also their contribution to the economy of the entire colony. He cited with satisfaction Governor Clifford, who defended the Northern Territories against the accusation that they represented a financial burden for the colony, and stressed that, quite the contrary, it was only the export of labour from the North to the mines and cocoa plantations that made the wealth of the South at all possible.[54] Clifford's successor Guggisberg also referred to the indispensable contribution that labour migrants and soldiers from the Northern Territories made towards the development of the Gold Coast and promised a swift end to the North's Cinderella existence, a promise which was never fulfilled, however.[55] Thus, ten years later, Chief Commissioner Jones adopted a more aggressive tone, railing against the neglect of the Northern Territories. The degree of condescension with which the inhabitants of the Protectorate were treated was unacceptable, 'an amiable but backward people, useful as soldiers, policemen and labourers in the mines and cocoa farms, in short fit only to be hewers of wood and drawers of water for their brothers in the Colony and Ashanti'.[56] This discourse was later adopted by the educated elite of the North; and Marxist-inspired authors spoke not only of neglect, but of a deliberate policy of protracted 'under-development', pursued by the colonial government for the express purpose of sustaining in the North a reservoir of labour.[57]

Although the colonial officials in the Northern Territories may have been in agreement regarding the significant contribution of labour migration to the economic development of the South, their assessment as to its consequences for the North remained in doubt. Yet initial fears of social destabilisation quickly abated, as it became clear that no permanent migration was likely to arise out of the yearly 'exodus'.[58] However, not all district commissioners welcomed the new consumer goods that migrants introduced. For many the adoption of European clothes was 'a bad habit',[59] while others feared that the introduction of corrugated-iron roofs would transform Lawra into the 'usual colonial tin horror'.[60] Some were convinced that seasonal labour migration would ultimately prove detrimental to local agriculture.[61] And finally, not a few complained about the negative role of the migrants, as well as soldiers returning from the First World War, in conflicts over the chieftaincy, exhibiting behaviour that included insulting the chiefs, calling them as 'bushmen', and 'flouting' their authority.[62]

THE MIGRANT'S PERSPECTIVE: HOME-TIES, SOCIAL CONTROL AND ETHNIC SOLIDARITY

Despite criticism from colonial officials and chiefs, the young men of Lawra District voted with their feet and during the dry season went south in ever-increasing numbers. Acquiring clothes was for the first migrants the most important motive for migrating to 'Kumasi'. Clothes must have sparked the imagination of whole generations of young men in the villages, not the locally manufactured 'Mossi cloth' of woven strips of cotton, but clothes that could only be bought in Kumasi, such as white and printed fabrics, shorts, long trousers and shirts. Such clothes were undeniable proof of having been 'there', a symbol of participation in a strange, alluring, civilised world.[63] The Commissioner of North-Western Province was not exaggerating when in 1914 he wrote:

> In parts of Lobi there are still many natives to whom cloth is unknown and the arrival of a boy at one such village in a white coat who had been working in Ashanti was the signal of some 30 to 40 youths from the village starting empty-handed to go to the country where such marvels can be obtained.[64]

However, the point of labour migration was not just to acquire clothes and other consumer goods like salt, buckets and axes, but also to take an important step towards adulthood, 'to open one's eyes', as many people still put it. For even after paid work and many of the desired goods became available in Lawra District itself, labour migration remained attractive. As the Lawra District Commissioner put it, the 'spirit of adventure is very strong amongst all the people in the district and a young man is of no importance till he is able to spin fabulous yarns of his adventures in the Colony'.[65]

Old men in Nandom told me of their first migration experiences, representing the motives and dynamics of labour migration in a manner similar to this, though without the paternalistic undertone of the colonial reports. The old Tantuoyir of Tantuo, for example, who made his way to the South with some relatives in the late 1920s, reported:

> People went before us but many of them are dead now. Some of them went on the 'girmati' [recruited labour].[66] It was when they came back that we knew there was a place like Kumasi. ... At that time we were just here [in the village] and when people came from Kumasi with soap, pomade and towels, we used to wonder at these things. It was these things that I used to see that also enticed me to go to Kumasi. When they come home with the soap and pomade that smell so nicely, and even the salt and other things that they brought home, I used to become so excited and I also decided that I will go and get these things. Even at that time we never imagined that when you go to Kumasi you will have to work! ... That time we had no other clothes apart from these, the woven cloth. If you wanted any different dress, then you had to buy it from Kumasi. ... Those who went to Kumasi used to buy these 'singlets' and sweaters and also coats and very nice soap. So when you see these things you become eager and also want to go to Kumasi.[67]

The more young men went to the South, the greater became the desire of those remaining behind to be able to emulate them. According to my informants, migrants not only came back from 'Kumasi' physically changed, 'looking nice and having many clothes to wear', they also knew how to behave in a more sophisticated manner: 'they play "life" ... so I was happy that I was also going down and one day I will return home and bluff others'.[68] For Naamwin-ire Der, being able to join the discussion was the driving motivation for his first journey to Tarkwa: 'The way they used to talk about the place, it was necessary for everyone to go there and see things for himself.'[69] When, however, Naamwin-ire Dir made his way south in the early 1950s, his initial enthusiasm was dampened when confronted with migrants' suffering, and ultimately gave way to a realism that he expressed laconically as follows:

> We came to see the good things that were down South. When you come down South and you get work you enjoy, but when you don't get work, then you suffer. It is just like up North: When you are there and you don't farm then you will have to go hungry.

Plate 3 Gratiano Naabesog and his wife in Tarkwa, 1950s (with kind permission of Gratiano Naabesog, Dondometeng)

A critical view of labour migration is also provided by the innumerable women's songs that express the fears and mockery of those remaining at home. The song 'Going to Kumasi and never coming back, it is a stick they bring home, yeeee, just remove it from the pocket and they start mourning', for example, alludes to the way in which news of a migrant who has died in the South was brought home, that is, by means of a stick or piece of clothing once belonging to the deceased. Similarly, the popular song about the *Kumasi-kpékvra-sòb* mocks the migrant who remains too long in the South, only returning home once he has become a useless cripple. Additionally, many songs take up the theme of clothing, criticising 'Kumasi cloth' as thin and of poor quality, and migrants for bringing back home with them either not enough, or only clothing of poor quality. Especially popular is the following song, which pokes fun by inverting the above-mentioned aspiration for clothing:

> Ghana young boys (girls), don't make fun of your parents!
> At the beginning of the dry season the father (mother) allows them to go,
> they will come back one day with one cloth and one shirt,
> then wash them and dry them,
> as soon as they are dry wear them 'gubogubo'.
> *Chorus:*
> In the morning they wear them 'gubogubo',
> in the evening they wear them 'gubogubo',
> every Sunday they wear the same thing,
> every feast they wear the same thing,
> every market day they wear the same thing 'gubogubo'.[70]

All these songs are still sung and danced today, though many of the lyrics are several decades old, probably as old as labour migration itself, and were subject to continual variation. They make it clear that, besides the 'fabulous yarns', ridiculed by the Lawra District Commissioner, spun by migrants to extol their adventures, there was also a discourse of social control to which migrant labourers were themselves subject.

Social control and home-based networks extended all the way into the mining areas and cocoa plantations, although there they were subject to processes of change and expansion. Thus, Tantuoyir described how one would only travel south together with relatives or friends already experienced in migration, since if one was among strangers one had to fear 'being sold' by them en route. In the cocoa-cultivating areas these groups of migrants usually stayed together the whole time, hiring themselves out as a group to the same Ashanti farmer. But in the mining areas too, workers from the North-West generally lived segregated from other ethnic groups, most often in clusters of men from neighbouring villages, depending on whether the mine had built accommodation for them, as was the case in Tarkwa, or whether the workers had to find rooms for themselves, as in Obuasi.[71]

In order to extend the social networks beyond direct kinship relations and the home village, migrants drew on both of the basic indigenous principles of organisation, discussed in Chapter 1: the patriclan and the neighbourhood. For Dagara migrants, belonging to the same patriclan already offered in itself a supra-local network of great geographical reach, because in the home region too members of the same patriclan often lived and still live scattered among many villages. Along with this came the concept of closely related patriclans that traced themselves back to a shared origin, as well as the principle of joking relationships between specific patriclans. Finally, the patriclan also served as the foundation for asserting kinship between groups that were linguistically and culturally remote. When dealing with other groups, the kinship groups that 'corresponded' to one's own patriclan were sought out (a correlation usually determined on the basis of shared clan taboos), or else the whole of the other group was declared to be joking relations (*lonluore*), such as the Frafra from the North-Eastern part of the Protectorate. To effect immediate solidarity even in unfamiliar territory, particularly when it came to making the preparations necessary for conducting burial rituals, it was important to extend kinship networks into linguistic and cultural groups similar to one's 'own'. Thus, ethnicity developed here as a sort of extension to kinship; and the first informal organisations the migrants founded away from home were usually patriclan associations whose aim was to ensure a respectable burial.

Parallel to this, however, ethnicity also developed as an extension of the spatial neighbourhood going beyond specific patriclan links. Here the starting point for a sense of solidarity was a common origin in a particular village or micro-region. Expansion was then achieved on the basis of a shared language, initially in the context of a common dialect, though subsequently also transcending dialect boundaries. If there were not enough migrants from one's own linguistic group available in a particular locale or occupational sector, then the neighbourhood could also serve as a basis of co-operation, one that transcended ethnic identification. Hence, as North-Westerners, Dagara and Sisala felt themselves to be more closely related than, for example, the Dagara and Dagomba, who are linguistically much closer.

However, social control and ethnic belonging were not entirely spontaneous and self-organised, but were also imposed by the mine management and the colonial regime. From the very beginning the mine workers from the North were subordinated to the control of 'tribal heads', who were supposed to function as intermediaries between the migrants and the local chiefs, as well as the mine management and the district commissioner. For example, these headmen were supposed to act as justices of the peace in conflicts arising within their own group or with members of other ethnic groups. They were also charged with collecting occasional taxes on behalf of local chiefs and, if their fellow tribesmen walked out, with ordering them back to work. Conversely, the tribal headmen were frequently the first to be sought out by new migrants upon their arrival, provided bail in the event a labourer was arrested, helped inform relatives back home in case of death, and buried the deceased. Since the 1970s, this role of the tribal headmen has often been fulfilled by associations with formal statutes and elected boards, in which migrants from a common home region come together for the purpose of offering mutual help, as well as for contributing to the development of their home region. Outside of such formalised associations, however, there also existed (and continue to exist to this day) patriclan-specific associations set up to organise burials and provide other immediate mutual aid.[72]

Whether self-organised or imposed from above, when one examines more closely who unites with whom when away from home over a longer period, it becomes clear that the ethnic boundaries forming the basis of these associations are fluid. In the mining towns, for example, all migrants from the Northern Territories initially came together under a single tribal headman, who was almost always recruited from the ranks of the first Northern migrants to arrive in any considerable numbers at the migration destination. Sometimes this was a Dagomba, a member of one of the pre-colonial kingdoms of the North. However, according to my sources the first tribal headman of the Northerners in Tarkwa was a Sisala, and in Obuasi a Grunshi. In any case, the migrants behaved as if they all belonged to a single 'tribe', namely that of the 'Northerners', and their employers and fellow workers hardly differentiated between the different groups of Northerners, but referred to them all by the same nickname, for example *NTfos* (people from the Northern Territories) or *pepeni* (etymology unclear).

With the increase in the number of migrants coming from the North came the need for further sub-division, and additional tribal headmanships were established for smaller groups. Such designation of new 'tribes' was frequently provoked by conflict. The seceding group would generally accuse the old headman of not being properly concerned with their customs and practices, particularly in cases where Muslims and non-Muslims comprised part of the old headman's constituency. This was why, in Obuasi in the 1950s, one 'Dagarti chief' and his group split from the other Northerners, something that had already occurred in Tarkwa in the mid-1930s.[73] Things were similar in Kumasi, where, however, Kofi Dagarti, whom most Dagarti regarded as their spokesman, was not officially recognised as tribal headman by the Sarkin Zongo, the Hausa chief representing all migrants from the North.[74] Similar processes of secession were at play later in the ethnic associations: as soon as the number of members rose, so too did a tendency towards further fragmentation. Thus, one can sometimes hear mine workers from the North-West saying today that migrants from Jirapa belong to a different 'tribe' than those from Nandom. Yet for many decades all 'Dagarti' (and the same goes for the Sisala), regardless of the district or native state in the North-West from which they came, belonged to the same community under the authority of a single tribal head. Even today, in particular situations, the categories 'North-Westerners' and 'Northerners' continue to have meaning for more widely defined communities, such as the 'Dagaba' (or 'Dagara'). In sum, we can observe among migrants a complex layer of potential ethnic communities, with differing degrees of inclusion, defined by stressing different components of commonality (language or dialect, descent, territorial origin, etc.), which can be activated according to context. The categories Lobi and Lobi-Dagarti, which the British had carefully distinguished in the North, were meaningless in the South, or had only very slight relevance to migrants' social networks and political associations.

Unlike the mines in Southern Africa, the Gold Coast (and Ghanaian) mining industry never introduced pass laws, and all attempts to control labour migrants more rigidly failed. Migrants could therefore return to their homes fairly easily and at their own initiative travel between their village and the mine (or cocoa plantation or yam farm). 'Home' and 'town' were closely linked, and the ethnic categories created away from home fed back into rural discourses on social belonging and vice versa.[75] With the returning migrants, the all-embracing ethnic category 'Dagarti' became popular even in Lawra itself. That this more inclusive understanding of ethnic belonging could to some extent conflict with the administratively imposed tribes has already been discussed in Chapter 3 by drawing on examples from the population census and the naming of people. The returning migrants and their families saw themselves as Dagarti, not Lobi, and were in the long run responsible for the 'Dagabafication' of the ethnic map. Labour migrants, then, have been important makers of ethnicity in their own right. Not only did they subvert the colonial ethnic terminology, they also created a community potentially much wider than that envisaged by the colonial authorities' native states model.

6

'LIGHT OVER THE VOLTA': THE MISSION OF THE WHITE FATHERS

In 1985, together with hundreds of believers, the bishop of Wa, the archbishop of Tamale and more than fifty priests celebrated a festive mass in the large brick church of Jirapa. For the first time, a young Dagara, Alphonsus Bakyil, from Jirapa, was entering the order of the White Fathers, which since 1929 had converted thousands of men and women from the North-West and the neighbouring French colony to Catholicism. At the same time, Father Remigius McCoy from Canada, at that time Father-Superior in Jirapa, was celebrating the jubilee of his ordination. In his commemoratory sermon, Bishop Kpiebaya, a Dagao from Kaleo, reflected on the history of the mission in North-West Ghana:

> What we are really celebrating here today is God's love for the Dagaabas. We are among those fortunate people of the world whom He has chosen to bless again and again. Christianity came to us nearly fifty-six years ago, but little more than twenty of those had passed before the first Dagati [sic] priest in Ghana was ordained [in 1951]. And less than nine years later ... the first diocese in the Northwest was established with a Dagati bishop at its head. Great things were happening in our small corner of the Lord's vineyard. ... The first place in the Northwest to receive the Word of God now sends forth the first missionary priest of the Northwest ... This day the Church in Jirapa and the Church of Wa diocese have truly come of age! (quoted in McCoy 1988: 238–9)

Bishop Kpiebaya's words bespoke gratitude that God had chosen the Dagaba/Dagara as his people, pride in the successful Africanisation of the Catholic Church in the North-West, and ethnic self-confidence. Today Dagara and Dagaba bishops officiate in three of the four dioceses in Northern Ghana, and the majority of the faculty of the theological seminary in Tamale comes from the North-West – facts that irritate many non-Dagara. For Bishop Kpiebaya and many others, being Dagara/Dagaba and being Catholic are intimately linked to one another, although in the region around Wa and Kaleo especially there were and are numerous Muslim Dagaba, in addition to families that were formerly Christians, but have since returned to their traditional practices. Catholic Dagara/Dagaba, however, have in the course of several decades developed an ethnic sense of community, which has interacted with the new ethnic networks of labour migrants and affected the self-understanding of the non-Catholic Dagara as well – a sense of community which transcends the small-scale colonial ethnic categories and the local patriotism of the native states.[1]

The Catholic church thus created a different, but no less powerful geography which was just as effective as the political geography of the native states in shaping social location and self-understanding. The 'pays Dagari' (Paternot 1949) of the White Fathers transcended all colonial borders, in its early years even including the neighbouring French colony. This great community of Catholic Dagara/Dagaare-speakers became a lived reality not only through the material infrastructure provided by the Church but also through new social networks, for instance through Christian marriages that often crossed the boundaries of dialect and chiefdoms, and through educational institutions which brought together Dagara and Dagaba from across the entire North-West. If the colonial introduction of chiefdoms was successful because it mediated the incorporation of local societies into a larger political and economic context, so was the Catholic mission because it made accessible a world religion and modern education, thus promising both individual and collective advancement. It was particularly attractive to those who were marginal in the chieftaincy – women, younger men and 'late-comers', without allodial land rights.

MASS CONVERSION AND CONFLICTS
WITH THE COLONIAL REGIME

Until 1929, the British would not permit any Christian mission to establish a presence in the North-West. When in 1905 the White Fathers first expressed an interest in opening a mission station in the Northern Territories, the chief commissioner suggested Navrongo in the Protectorate's North-East as a suitable site, where a district station had just been opened. However, the White Fathers, who had learned Mooré in Ouagadougou, preferred to work among the linguistically related Dagara rather than the Kassena. In the spring of 1906 the first group of missionaries, including porters and all the requisite household supplies, was sent to Wa, believing that the Governor of the Gold Coast had permitted the founding of a mission station there. However, Chief Commissioner Watherston prohibited the unexpected visitors from settling permanently in Wa, because his most important allies, the Wala Muslims, feared their influence, and because the presence of French missionaries was giving rise to rumours that the British had 'sold' the North-West to the French. Because of these political reservations vis-à-vis the White Fathers and the concern that religious competition with Islam might make the pacification of the Lobi and Dagarti more difficult, the North-West was to remain off-limits to the White Fathers.[2]

In 1906 the White Fathers opened a mission station at Navrongo, where, however, they were only able to win relatively few converts.[3] Nonetheless, the presence of the missionaries changed the British view of the White Fathers. Despite some tensions between converts and chiefs, missionary work struck them as politically relatively harmless and Catholic education as useful.[4] Yet the White Fathers' renewed attempts to extend their radius of activity to the North-West in order to forestall the expansion of North-American and British Protestants met initially with resistance. Lawra District Commissioner Eyre-Smith, himself an Irish Catholic, was generally well-disposed to the White Fathers and recommended the Dagaba to them as a hard-working, honest, peaceable and gracious tribe, open to innovation, who one day might make good Catholics. However, the chief commissioner and the governor continued to have political reservations regarding the 'French' White Fathers. Only via the intervention of the apostolic delegate, who turned to the governor in Accra for help, was permission attained to open a mission station in Jirapa in 1929.[5]

The White Fathers thus began their work in the North-West at a time when the colonial geography of administrative districts and native states had long since become fact, and the chiefs, at least, had become familiar with the new political order. It was also a time of intense debate over political reform. Eyre-Smith's critical reports on abuses of the chiefly office had sensitised the district commissioners and their superiors to the potential for conflict that was brewing in some areas due to the arbitrariness of the chiefs. Colonial officials therefore observed the work of the White Fathers with even greater mistrust and soon saw confirmed their fears that the mission might very well destabilise the political order they had so carefully built.

In the first year after the mission station was opened, the three White Fathers who had been delegated to Jirapa from Navrongo, with Father McCoy as their superior, learned the local language in accordance with the methods of their order. At the bidding of the district commissioner, Jirapa Naa Ganaa allotted the new settlers a plot of land and provided labour to build the station. Otherwise Ganaa and most of the other inhabitants of Jirapa kept their distance. In March 1930, the missionaries, with the support of the British medical officer stationed in Lawra, set up a medical post. Since their modern medicine cured many illnesses like yaws, dysentery and sleeping sickness, something traditional diviners and medicines failed to do, trust in the White Fathers gradually increased. According to the mission's statistics, over 16,000 patients sought treatment at the station in 1931–2.[6] The reputation of the White Fathers as powerful healers, as Father McCoy recalled (1988: 55–61), was furthered particularly by the 'miracle' healing of a headman, whose relatives had long given up hope for recovery.

Medical treatment was always accompanied by prayer and religious instruction. However, the missionaries also used modern, worldly methods of winning devotees, such as records, films and football, which soon became a favourite sport among village youths.[7] Already by the end of 1931 the White Fathers counted 68 baptised Christians and 432 catechumens, while the number of those who sojourned to Jirapa Sunday after Sunday, or who stayed there several weeks on end for catechism instruction, finally obtaining a Mary medal, went into the thousands.[8]

Among the primary factors contributing to the exponential spread of the new belief were return migrants, who, driven by curiosity, stopped over in Jirapa and then spread word of the new powerful cult in their home villages. The new faith was especially attractive to those young migrants who may already have been introduced to the Christian religion in Ashanti and the colony. On the one hand, it allowed them to overcome the stigma of 'primitiveness' and of being 'uncivilised', with which they were confronted when away from home. On the other hand, with its emphasis on the individual and its criticism of unquestioned subordination to one's elders, it offered potential backing in family conflicts over decisions to migrate, the distribution of income from migration, and marriage preferences. Conversely, their experience of having survived apart from the extended family and their ancestral cult back home contributed to their receptiveness for the new religion.[9]

Isolated conflicts between converts and chiefs already seem to have arisen at the start of 1932, as some headmen later reported to Lawra District Commissioner Guinness. Many converts met in their villages to pray daily and refused to take part in sacrifices at the earth shrine or to work for their chief on Sundays. The only 'Whites' whom they would still recognise, according to Guinness, were the 'White Fathers':

> [C]ertain men, notably Dapila of Bazin, have been going about making wild statements such as that 'there were no more Chiefs now and no white men any longer but the White Fathers' and 'they should not obey their Headmen any more.' Jirapa has become a convenient excuse for avoiding work ... The headman of Bazin further states that 'a certain gang' has walked about the country carrying a red cloth on a stick, and giving out that the authority of the Chiefs was at an end.[10]

The headman of Bazin admitted that he did not know the significance of the red flag. However, he and other chiefs saw another Christian symbol as a direct attack on the dignity of the chiefs, namely the Mary medals that converts wore proudly around their necks, which bore a certain similarity to the chiefs' medals.[11] Looking back, Archbishop Peter Dery remarked that the chiefs saw the Christians to be potential rivals.[12]

In summer 1932, the flow of converts to Jirapa and the conflicts with the chiefs reached a peak in connection with an occurrence that Catholic chroniclers later came to call the 'rain event', raising it to the status of the single most important event that paved the way for a Christian mass movement. As Chief Commissioner Duncan-Johnstone noted in his diary, 1932 was a year of 'food shortages'. In Tamale, there was less rainfall than had been in any of the previous twenty-three years.[13] Despite all the offerings at the earth shrines and rainmakers' supplications, no rain fell in Lawra District either. Only in Jirapa, noted Guinness, did any rain fall, and '[t]he White Fathers are making a lot of converts in consequence'.[14] As Father McCoy writes in his memoirs, one village headman is supposed to have gone to the White Fathers with his elders and promised to take up the new faith, even destroying all 'fetishes', if only rain could be summoned. And in fact, on that very day, it is said to have rained heavily in that village, a sign sent by God, as Father McCoy believed, which was to aid Christianity achieve a breakthrough.[15] In any case, an increasing number of delegations came to Jirapa to pray for rain. As Guinness reported, the missionaries emphatically preached to them,

> [t]hat they could not expect rain if they prayed to God and to their old Fetishes as well. Those of them who were doing so therefore went home and destroyed their own Fetishes. But the rain still held up, and on the 24th July five men ... followed by twenty-nine other converts went in a body to the villages of Gengempe [sic], Kushele and Piiri, entered the compounds, broke into the Fetish-rooms and smashed the Fetishes [...]. The rioters appear to have met with little or no resistance ... until they reached the house of the headman of Piiri, who refused them entry, and a brawl took place.[16]

Guinness accused the White Fathers of inciting their converts to religious fanaticism. Archbishop Dery, invoking the eyewitness reports of his father Porekuu, an early convert and charismatic preacher, countered that the less active converts had invited courageous young Christians into their houses to do what they themselves dared not do, namely destroy their shrines. Only where influential heads of family did not want to convert were there conflicts.[17] Guinness's remark, that on the whole converts encountered little opposition, fits this interpretation well. The White Fathers distanced themselves from such actions undertaken by their followers. Father Paquet assured Guinness 'that he has never instructed his people to force their neighbour's consciences', and Father McCoy delivered 'a strong moral lecture' to the 'iconoclasts' before the district commissioner sentenced them to prison. Whether this measure was really in line with his own convictions, or an attempt to avoid the escalation of conflicts with the colonial government remains uncertain.[18]

In the eyes of the missionaries and, later, Catholic historians, neither the mass conversions nor the conflicts with the chiefs were politically motivated. The converts were merely opposing restrictions on the exercise of their new belief, which inevitably ended in conflicts with many chiefs and lineage elders.[19] By contrast, colonial officials tended to read these events politically, though in two contrasting manners. Eyre-Smith regarded the mass conversion to be a true 'revolution' that expressed the people's aversion to the 'tyranny' of the chiefs imposed upon them.[20] For Guinness and most other administrators, on the other hand, the popularity of the White Fathers was 'merely the result of a fortunate and apparently miraculous answer to a prayer for rain',[21] after which the missionaries had begun to incite those in their flock to resist the chiefs. Chief Commissioner Duncan-Johnstone saw parallels with the Watchtower Movement, which in the 1920s had challenged the colonial hierarchy in Northern Rhodesia. He doubted whether a 'fanatic' like McCoy was the right man for an area like Lawra District, 'among such a high spirited and excited people'.[22]

The district commissioners on the spot reacted to the conflicts of 1932 and 1933 with a combination of tough intervention in support of the chiefs and readiness to compromise. Guinness, for example, sentenced the 'iconoclasts' of Piiri and Bazin and other active Christians like Archbishop Dery's father Porekuu to several months' imprisonment with hard labour. However, he also ordered that a weekday be designated on which converts might attend mass in Jirapa, undisturbed by their chiefs.[23] Underlying conflicts between Christians and chiefs over the attendance of mass was the issue of 'Sunday work'. This stemmed from the fact that local time-reckoning did not recognise Sunday as a day of the week, since the local calendar was based on a six-day week structured in accordance with regularly occurring markets. As a result, the missionaries, in their work outside Jirapa, initially declared that day on which they visited a particular area to be Sunday. Only in the course of 1932 did a uniform Sunday gradually become part of the local calendar.[24] In May 1935, District Commissioner Armstrong finally called a meeting of missionaries and chiefs in Lawra, at which the latter were obliged to cease exacting Sunday work, while the former promised to enjoin their followers to fulfil their other obligations to their chiefs.[25] The introduction of taxation one year later, which did away with obligatory road work, further de-escalated the conflicts between chiefs and converts.

'The history of the relations between the native authorities and the Mission have passed from outright antagonism to compromise and then more compromise': in these words District Commissioner Ellison summed matters in 1939.[26] One contributing factor was certainly that the White Fathers themselves had no interest whatsoever in being at odds with the colonial government. Father Barsalou from Navrongo assured the chief commissioner that the missionaries entirely supported the aims pursued by the colonial government through the introduction of the native authorities. At the same time, however, he expressed his own ideas concerning the characteristics of a good chief:

> Like you we are desirous of seeing ... real chiefs who thoroughly understand the meaning of authority and who have always in their mind the good of their subjects; that they may know that authority does not merely consist in getting rich by all possible means and to increase their family without seeing to the advancement of their people. ... From what I have learned, the Kasenas, Nankanni and also Dagari chiefs had never been real Chiefs with great authority before the occupation of the country by Europeans. Their subjects have never learned to obey ... We are therefore very pleased indeed to learn that little by little more authority will be given to the Chiefs, as in this way the people will learn to obey.[27]

Although on the one hand, Barsalou's letter was certainly inspired by tactical considerations seeking to contain the conflict, on the other hand, he and his fellows also shared the colonial aim of disciplining ('learning to obey') the Africans. They were themselves surprised by the success of their mission and were genuinely concerned about how the new Christian movement was to be controlled. Following the 'rain event' the number of converts rapidly increased, and by December 1932 mission reports already recorded over 20,000 believers in the North-West.[28] However, within a few short years, the systematic training of catechists made it possible to transform what had once been a radical 'sect' into a well-organised church. Since the catechists, initially trained for three and then for four years in Jirapa, were sent back to serve the new congregations in the villages, and since more mission stations were set up – at Kaleo in 1932 and Nandom in 1933, as well as at Dissin and Dano on French territory – the weekly stream of pilgrims to Jirapa also gradually abated.[29] In the three mission stations of Jirapa, Kaleo and Nandom the numbers of baptised Christians increased from a good 500 in 1933–4 to just under 10,000 in 1937–8.[30] District Commissioner Ellison estimated that by now a quarter of the population of the Lawra Confederacy 'followed' the White Fathers. In Nandom alone the congregation had grown to some 8,000 adherents trained in the catechism and baptised, who were served by four missionaries and thirty catechists.[31] A mere ten years later the White Fathers counted in Nandom over 15,000 baptised Catholics, more than two-thirds of the population.[32]

Although the anti-authoritarian impulse had been harnessed, the new religious community in many respects continued to present a challenge to the power of the elders supported by the ancestors, and to the colonial political order. It offered a different framework of collective identification than the native states, produced a different infrastructure, drew ethnic boundaries differently than did the colonial government, and contended with the chiefs over the definition of customary law.

PAYS DAGARI: A CATHOLIC TRANS-BORDER COMMUNITY

The mission principle of the White Fathers was 'one post, one language' (Lesourd 1938). Differences in dialect or culture and political boundaries were not terribly important in evangelisation, so long as the people could only understand the missionaries' message. As a result, the *pays dagari*, as the White Fathers, who spoke French among themselves, called their new mission area, transcended all colonial boundaries and existing ethnographic conventions. Lesourd (1938) and Paternot (1949: 23) even have the *territoire dagari* stretching from 10° to 12° latitude, from Wa to Boromo. The area shown in Paternot's cartographic sketch (Map 8) still forms the basis for many Dagara intellectuals' idea of 'Dagaraland'.

Despite more widely drawn ethnic boundaries, the view of the White Fathers was based on notions of the 'Dagari' (in the French-speaking context) or 'Dagaaba' (in the English-speaking context), which by no means gainsaid colonial ethnography. The missionaries not only shared colonial officials' essentialist understanding of ethnicity, they also adopted the current colonial ethnic stereotypes and, if only partly, the colonial nomenclature. The 'tribe of the Dagaris' was seen as a hard-working, modest and hospitable tribe, 'with rather docile customs and quite open to European penetration' (Lesourd 1938), unlike the still 'untamed' Lobi. Like French colonial officials, Paternot stressed the close relationship of the 'Dagari' with the 'Ouilé'. He even obtained his initial information on the Dagari from the *commandant de cercle* in Diébougou.[33] Father McCoy, working in British territory, spoke of the Dagaaba, Wala, LoWilli and Lobi, though he probably only later adopted the term 'Lowilli' [*sic*] from Goody (1956), meaning by 'Lobi' not the Lobi-Dagarti of the colonial officials, but the recently in-migrated Birifor south of Wa.[34]

Alongside language, religious aspects also influenced how Christians defined ethnic boundaries, much as colonial officials had created ethnic categories from the administrative point of view. The extraordinary success of the White Fathers among the Dagara/Dagaba presented missionaries, and later the local priesthood, with the question as to what distinguished them from other groups. In the first instance, of course, they referred to God's ineffable will, but also sought and continue to seek a psychology, traditional religion and social organisation peculiar to the Dagaba that were supposed to have favoured conversion:

> Their naturally religious background and incorporeal concept of God which, together with a rather high moral code and a value system similar to that of Christianity, made it relatively easy for them to accept the Ngwinsore ['God's way', i.e. the Christian faith]; their

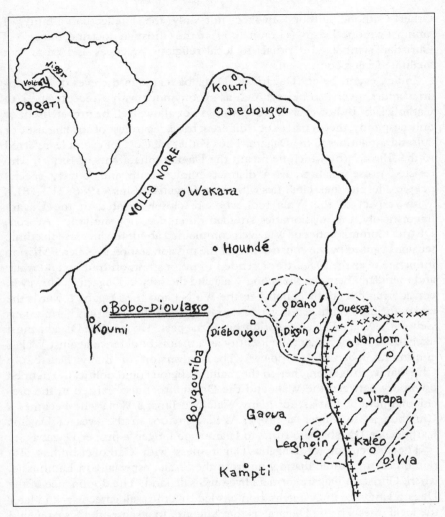

+ + + + + : Boundary Côte d'Ivoire – Gold Coast
- - - - - - - - : Territory occupied by the Dagari

Map 8 'Territoire dagari'
Source: Paternot 1949

gradual dissatisfaction with the fruits of spirit worship; the relative tolerance of personal choice and alternative lifestyle among the Dagaabas, abetted by a remarkably unservile attitude towards their chiefs. ... It *was* grace in any event, regardless of what components God used to bring it about. (McCoy 1988: 229–30)

Other Catholic authors invoked not only the intellectual affinity of 'animistic monotheism' (Girault 1959) to the Christian doctrine, but also of Christian symbols and rituals to local religious practices as factors that facilitated mass conversion.[35]

In any event, being 'Dagari' or 'Dagaaba' came in the eyes of missionaries and converts to be regarded as synonymous with a receptiveness to Catholicism. If, however, a group would not allow itself be proselytised, or only hesitantly, then it had to be a different tribe, regardless of any linguistic or cultural similarities to the Dagara. Thus Father McCoy, for example, referred to the 'Birofo' (by which he meant the Dagara inhabitants of Birifu), who resisted proselytisation, as a distinct ethnic group and 'a very special people', despite their close ties with their 'Dagati cousins' (1988: 217–18).[36] With respect to the Wala too, who are closely related to the Dagara linguistically, the missionaries stressed difference, not similarity. Ardron, District Commissioner of Wa, even complained about the increase in ethnic tensions caused by the construction of the mission station in Kaleo: 'Mission influence over the Dagarti has tended to put a strain on traditional loyalty and friendship between the ruling Wala and the subject Dagarti.'[37] However, considering the conflicts between the Wa Na and the Dagaba towards the end of the nineteenth century, one cannot but question Ardron's harmonious view of the Wala–Dagaba relationship of the past.[38] In fact, the Dagaba most likely used the new Catholic identity as a means of defence against Wala's continuing assertion of power. The conversion of many Dagaba to Christianity thus strengthened the mainly religious (and politically) defined boundary between the Wala and the Dagaba that also existed in the pre-colonial period. Just as, for many Wala Muslims, a Wala who becomes a Christian is no longer 'a proper Wala', so too, in the eyes of Dagaba Catholics, a Dagaba who turns to Islam is no longer 'a proper Dagaba'.

The association of Dagaba-/Dagara-ness with Catholicism has also reinforced the ethnic distinction from the Sisala, especially in Lambussie, where Christian Dagara farmers live on Sisala land. The dominance of the Dagara language in evangelisation has led to almost all catechists and later the local priests being Dagara, as they still are. In a sense, the Sisala would have been required to undergo a double conversion, to Christianity and to Dagara speech. Few were prepared to do this, particularly since the material advantages of belonging to the new religion, schools, medical posts and other development projects, had scarcely reached Sisala villages. Only Peter Dery, who refers to himself as 'of mixed Sisala–Dagaba origin', and who became Bishop of the new Diocese of Wa in 1960, ensured that all catechists and priests who were active in Sisala areas, whether Dagara or not, learnt and used Sisala.[39]

While ethnic boundaries 'to the outside', to the Sisala and Wala, were stressed, the small-scale ethnic differences between the Dagarti, Lobi and

Lobi-Dagarti, which had been emphasised by the British, generally lost their significance. Whereas the British had pursued the 'Lobification' of the ethnic map in the 1920s, the missionaries supported the popular trend towards 'Dagabafication'. This was possible because the missionaries transferred the French nomenclature onto British territory. Whereas the British distinguished between the Lobi and Lobi-Dagarti, both the French colonial authorities and the missionaries regarded them all in truth as 'Dagari', or, in the dialect prevailing in Jirapa, 'Dagaaba'. In the eyes of the White Fathers, therefore, they were dealing with one large people living on both sides of the international border.[40]

This unity also began to take shape in practice through the masses of Dagaba/Dagara who sojourned to Jirapa from all over, including villages in French territory, in order to take part in the catechism.[41] In the summer of 1932, more than 10,000 followers and onlookers frequently gathered together in Jirapa, and the flood of Dagara from Upper Volta took on such proportions that French colonial authorities became concerned that some of the many pilgrims might become emigrants, resulting in a drain of taxpayers and labour power. In 1933, therefore, the responsible French *commandant de cercle* called a meeting with representatives of the White Fathers from Ouagadougou, Bobo Dioulasso, Navrongo and Jirapa. After the proposal to close the border was rejected, the commandant finally suggested that the missionaries open new stations on French territory too, thus making the pilgrims' journey to Jirapa unnecessary. The choice fell on Dano and Dissin, places that had the most Dagara converts up to that point. In turn, the White Fathers had to promise to send all Upper Volta converts in Jirapa back to the stations on French territory.[42] The brief period of a large, trans-border religious community thus gave way to a separate development of Catholicism. From teaching the catechists to training the local clergy, to the production of written material, the 'British' and 'French' vicariates reproduced certain colonial idiosyncrasies. However, in neither local community did the awareness of belonging to a trans-border, pan-Dagara community ever disappear.

A NEW INFRASTRUCTURE

Although the mission had to recognise the international border, the territorial organisation of the Catholic Church within the North-West stood and continues to stand in a tense relationship to the colonial political geography of the native states. Neither in the early years of the mission nor today, in a time when the Diocese of Wa is divided into many parishes, do parish and chiefdom boundaries coincide. This has provided material for conflict, especially in Nandom and Jirapa, where Catholicism has taken root more firmly than in Lambussie and Lawra, and where most of the educated elite is a product of the mission schools.

Jirapa was recommended to the White Fathers as 'the most central of the Dagati villages' (McCoy 1988: 34, 48), and their evangelical work benefited from the colonial infrastructure, but, in the course of time, also altered it in a way that was to have secular political consequences. Colonial officials probably also recommended Jirapa, because it kept the mission at a distance from the district station. When, in 1932–3, additional mission stations were to be built, and the White Fathers considered Lawra as a potential site, Lawra Naa Lobi Binni, together with District Commissioner Armstrong, rejected any such idea.[43] Nandom Naa Konkuu, however, thought otherwise. True, he had imprisoned those responsible for the destruction of the ancestral shrines of Piiri and Gegenkpe, and jailed Porekuu for incitement against the chiefs, who had built a chapel in Zimuopere that attracted a thousand converts. Yet at the same time, he offered to let the White Fathers build a church in Nandom, hoping this move would pull the rug from under Zimuopere's unwanted rivalry, as Father McCoy reckoned in hindsight (1988: 78–82, 250–1). This coincided with the tactical considerations of the White Fathers, who did not want to further heighten anxieties among the divisional chiefs that their power was threatened. Moreover, Konkuu is said to have acted exactly as the Jirapa Naa had done some years earlier, in that he allotted the missionaries a barren piece of land allegedly haunted by spirits, and waited to see whether they would drive out the White Fathers or the White Fathers drive them out.[44] Later, colonial officials heaped praise on the Nandom Naa for having successfully managed 'to steer his course between the diametrically opposed creeds of his people, keep on good terms with the mission, and with a purely pagan belief adjudicate impartially'.[45]

The location of new mission stations thus had to take local power relations into account. Nevertheless the parish boundaries cross-cut those of the divisions, a situation that time and again gave rise to conflicts. District Commissioner Ellison, for example, reported that the converts of Lissa were not prepared to recognise the Lawra Naa's authority in settling a dispute over the creation of a Christian cemetery, but instead turned to Nandom. Lissa was only made subject to Lawra Division in 1918, and Ellison suspected that affiliation with the Nandom parish might actually lead to political secession. In response, Ellison advised: 'I feel sure it would be preferable if the Mission would agree to confine their activities and conform to Administrative areas.'[46] However, the missionaries were not able to follow this advice, nor did they want to. Lissa remained in the parish of Nandom, later becoming part of Ko, which became an independent parish in 1952.

Similarly, the Tumu Kuoro tried to prevent the White Fathers from constructing a chapel in Fielmuo, which belonged to Tumu, but the colonial authorities rejected his complaint, and he had to accept that the many Dagara settlers in and around Fielmuo would in matters of faith remain bound to the mission in Nandom.[47] In Tumu, a mission was only opened in 1960, and Fielmuo only became a parish in its own right in the 1970s. Before 1960, therefore, the spiritual needs of Dagara converts living on Sisala land in Tumu and Lambussie were served by the Nandom parish. This happened also to correspond perfectly to their social ties, given that many of them had only recently migrated into the Sisala area from villages in Nandom Division. And although parts of the old Nandom parish have long since been split up, Catholic 'greater Nandom' still lives on in the minds of many Dagara. It is present as an ethnic rather than a territorial community and includes Dagara who, because of land shortage, have settled on Sisala land. As long as this notion of a 'greater Nandom' only manifests itself in feelings of religious and cultural solidarity, it is not conflict-laden. However, the Nandom Youth and Development Association's recent push for the establishment of a common Nandom-Lambussie District raised fears among Sisala politicians that such an entity would relegate them to a marginal position and that the Dagara might perhaps even dispute their land rights in the longer term.[48]

The material infrastructure created by the White Fathers also tended to compete with that of the native authorities, or at least had different geographical foci. The settlement of the mission in Jirapa, for example, involved building a church and a catechism school, followed by the opening of a girls' school, a hospital and a credit union, which boosted the local economy and increased the population of Jirapa so that it exceeded Lawra's. Since the 1970s, therefore, the Jirapa Naa and the Jirapa Youth Association have been petitioning for a district of their own, which was finally granted in the late 1980s, though jointly with Lambussie.[49] Like Jirapa, Nandom also grew in importance, which it might not have done had it not been for the White Fathers. Initially opposed by the Nandom Naa, but later coming under his protection, a lively Sunday market developed here; and after 1940, a daily market in the street leading to the mission followed.[50] In 1937 the region's first Catholic primary school for boys opened, followed in 1950 by a middle school, then in 1958 a primary school and a middle school for girls, and finally, in 1968, a secondary school, as well as a hospital, two technical craft schools and various agricultural development projects. Yet apart from a brief period in the 1960s, Nandom never succeed in achieving the rank of district headquarters.

The Church also created new social networks, which cut across the ties of the patriclan and the earth shrine, as well as the 'local patriotism' of the chiefdoms. The masses held in Jirapa, particularly in the early years, which attracted thousands of believers of all persuasions, clearly manifested the existence of a large community of Dagara speakers. No political occasion could bring together in Lawra District so many people who could communicate in a single language.[51] The central catechism school and the mobility of its graduates, who were normally not assigned to their own villages; the need to transcend the boundaries of culture and dialect in search of a Christian spouse; the Christian schools, whose pupils and teachers were recruited almost exclusively from among the Dagaba/Dagara; the rise of a local clergy; new associations, courses and festivals, which mobilised Dagaba/Dagara believers from across the North-West: all of this helped make a living reality a language area and a new, broadly inclusive definition of a great Dagaba/Dagara community, at least for Catholics.

However, the fact that the expansion of this language area progressed from Jirapa had consequences that were later to give rise to conflicts. The first Dagaare catechism was printed in 1931, soon followed by a two-volume comprehensive version for catechism training, numerous prayer books, school primers and a dictionary, all texts translated by the White Fathers, in consultation with their catechists, into the dialect most familiar to them, namely that used in Jirapa and its environs.[52] Because it was the first to be put into writing, the Jirapa dialect was predominant in the training of catechists and priests, as well as in religious services and schools. Even if other dialects could be used in sermons and oral explications, the Dagaare of Jirapa became a sort of standard speech, with its written form, even adopted by native authority schools.[53] Speakers of other dialects thus were, and to some extent continue to be, at a disadvantage – at least, this is the current view of many educated Dagara from Nandom, where the dialect spoken is the one that predominates among the Dagara congregations of Upper Volta, having there been given a written form by the White Fathers.[54] As with the chiefs of the various divisions in the native administration, the educated of the various dialect groups competed with one another over scarce resources and influence. Nevertheless, Christians shared the conviction that Dagara or Dagaare constituted a large trans-border language area, a more inclusive principle of community creation than the narrower concepts of colonial ethnicity.

'CHRISTIAN LAW' VERSUS 'NATIVE CUSTOM'

The Catholic Church prescribed and still prescribes norms that collided with local values and practices. Conflicts, between converts on the one hand and chiefs, earth priests and non-Christian elders on the other, flared up particularly when converts refused to participate in sacrifices to the ancestors or the earth deity, or any other 'pagan' rituals. Furthermore, there were disputes over particular burial ceremonies and the regulation of marriage and divorce, questions touching on relationships between young and old, and between men and women. However, despite their deep-seated differences of opinion, the adversaries were genuinely interested in negotiating compromises so that they could, more or less, live together in peace. The district commissioners, according to a tenet expressed by Chief Commissioner Jones in 1937, were charged '[t]o ensure for the individual complete liberty of conscience and worship'. On the other had, however, they should not let missionaries and converts forget 'that Christians remained under the authority of the chiefs'.[55]

One example of a practical compromise involved the sacrifices that the earth priest made prior to the construction of a new house, a practice Christians rejected. The Lawra District Commissioner laid down that '[c]onverts wishing to build new compounds will in future give the Tengdana a "dash" and a paper from the Fathers.'[56] The former ritual of sacrifice was therefore divided into a voluntary, religious part and a secular, political component, obligatory for everyone, including Christians, a move that protected one of the earth priests' sources of income. Similar compromises were reached for 'funeral customs'. When Father McCoy complained that 'pagan' relatives were refusing to bury deceased Christians without the usual rituals of sacrifice, District Commissioner Ellison suggested that chiefs and earth priests permit the establishment of Christian cemeteries.[57]

Yet these and other compromises were just a sort of framework agreement; the details continued to be a matter of dispute. Disagreements ensued not only over the actual allotment of Christian cemeteries,[58] but also over the question of whether Christians might be permitted to absent themselves when the sacrifice was made at the earth shrine, but still be obligated to provide material contributions. For example, one missionary advocated the abolition of the native custom 'by which stray sheep, goats or anything else found on the land had to be taken to the Tindana who then makes the owner make a small sacrifice to the land god'. In this matter, District Commissioner Armstrong sided with the earth priests and saw no reason why this 'age-old custom' should be changed.[59] Because of the district commissioners' refusal to budge on this and other matters, Bishop Morin finally demanded that the colonial government endeavour to clarify the fundamental principles according to which conflicts between 'native custom' and 'Christian law' could be reconciled.[60]

Morin persuaded the Catholic bishops of the Gold Coast to hand over his memorandum as a joint petition to the governor, which Chief Commissioner Jones took greatly amiss. Nevertheless, all political officers were now instructed to report on the state of relations between Christians and non-Christians in their districts. All of them, even Ellison in Lawra and Ardron in Wa, disputed Morin's claim that Christians were being hindered in the practice of their faith. Ardron asserted quite the contrary, that the converts caused divisiveness in the village communities with their 'attitude of superiority over their own kith and kin' and further complained they were provoking 'tribal friction'.[61] Ellison was concerned that freedom of conscience might turn into a pretext for the preferential treatment of Christians, 'thereby disrupting the authority of the family or family groups'.[62] The governor ultimately rejected Morin's demand for a new arrangement between the mission and the native authorities. '[T]he relations existing at present between Christians and pagans in the Gold Coast are generally satisfactory', wrote the colonial secretary to the bishops' conference; 'in the rare cases of conflict ... a reference to the District Commissioner is all that is required to effect a settlement.'[63]

Thus all conflicts were referred back to the local actors. In 1937, therefore, the Lawra-Tumu District Commissioner summoned a public meeting, at which the chiefs and the White Fathers were supposed to agree on a mode of compromise.[64] Thus it was now decided that Christians need not provide any material contributions for sacrifices at the earth shrine. When a Christian died, believers should allow their non-Christian relatives to carry out the rituals they thought necessary and then be allowed to lay the body to rest in their consecrated cemetery. When a non-Christian died, the Christians must be allowed to pray briefly for the deceased. As for the matter of marriage, Christians agreed they should pay the bridewealth in full as a precondition for proceeding with the church ceremony. In return, the chiefs were to respect the Christian dictate of monogamy, recognise the indissolubility of Christian marriage, and ensure that Christian girls were not married to non-Christian partners against their will (Hawkins 2002: 249–51).

In practice, conflicts continued to break out, which then had to be brought before the native courts or the district commissioners, launching renewed debate over contradictions between customary law and Christian ethics, the authority of the elders and chiefs, the rights of women, and the leeway granted for the exercise of individual liberty.[65] To Morin, conversion to Christianity represented a transition to the new order of 'Christian law', and he impressed on the colonial government that to enable Christians to live in accordance with this 'Christian law', would be 'a further step in the splendid work of civilization undertaken by the Government in these districts.'[66] Chief Commissioner Jones, on the other hand, only granted the status of legal code to 'native law' (and naturally also British civil law), while he regarded 'Christian law', to which Morin referred, to be nothing more than a 'Christian code of ethics'.[67] 'Pagan law', wrote Wa District Commissioner Ardron, was 'highly developed and contains little that is repugnant to understanding minds', a view with which Jones concurred.[68] Jones pleaded for the preservation of everything he regarded as a pillar of the local social order and was sympathetic to chiefs, who regarded Christian activities to be detrimental,

> in that the adoption of Christianity by a minority means a break in the
> administrative control of the Chiefs and in the magical authority of

family heads and tindana which, in common with the great majority of the people, they believe to be essential for the maintenance of peace and good order in the community.[69]

At the heart of the debate stood the authority of family heads and the rights of husbands. The missionaries demanded freedom of conscience for their often young converts, and also that the district commissioners should support their right to this freedom, if necessary even against the wishes of lineage elders. Colonial officials, by contrast, defended the authority of the old men, which should under no circumstances be challenged lest the social order should break:

> In Victorian England the house owner was in most cases the autocrat over its inhabitants including servants and others – why that privilege cannot be extended to the compound owner in Africa I fail to understand. The Christian can always go away from the compound.[70]

Two things become clear here. First is the colonial projection of a model of domesticity and paternal authority that had long ceased to be the reality even in England.[71] Second is the challenge this new religious mass movement represented for the colonial authorities, since, despite all the civilising rhetoric, the colonial state's project was a minimalist one, at least until the Second World War.[72] So long as public order was not dramatically threatened, the aim was to interfere as little as possible in domestic matters. Yet the missionaries forced the colonial authorities to take a firmer stand on matters which they would have preferred to leave to the neo-traditional control of the chiefs. Thus, for example, the persecution and even killing of 'witches' was tacitly tolerated, becoming a target for administrative action only when the White Fathers began hiding women who were being persecuted as witches.[73] And it was only when the White Fathers began protecting Christian girls who were to be married against their will from the attacks of their fathers and husbands that an intense debate was set off regarding the 'marriage custom'.[74]

Here Lawra District Commissioner Ellison and his colleagues defended the soundness and humaneness of local marriage customs against the Christian norm of indissoluble church marriages. Ellison even found the relevant practices of the Lobi and Dagarti 'far in advance of European custom less than a century ago'.[75] 'It is totally untrue', he explained, 'to imagine that any woman by native custom is bound in marriage any further than the dictates of her own heart.'[76] Child betrothal was not at all as inhuman as the missionaries claimed, because young women could always run away and remarry later if their husbands did not please them. Here Ellison drew support from a report by Meyer Fortes on 'Marriage customs among the Tallensi' describing the traditional practices as a functional system.[77]

The White Fathers never directly responded to the assertion by colonial authorities that the Catholic rule of the indissolubility of marriage robbed women of one of the most important means of exerting pressure on their husbands. They did, however, insist that the traditional 'marriage customs', namely bridewealth, polygamy and 'forced marriage', were aimed at the unrestricted control of women by men, making them the property of their husbands and the latter's clans, 'just as purchased cattle' (McCoy 1988: 154). In their eyes, Christian marriage decidedly raised a woman's status. At the same time, however, missionaries sought to draw on the local concept of the 'ideal wife'.[78] In general, they sought elements in the local culture that resembled Catholic belief. For example, they emphasised the Dagara's supposedly distinctive moral code and the traditionally high value placed on individual freedom, quite unlike colonial officers, who considered the unrestricted authority of the elders and clan solidarity to be the most important characteristics of the indigenous society.[79]

The chiefs used the conflicts between the colonial authorities and the missionaries to strengthen their own position wherever they could. Hardly any chiefs converted, mainly because they would then have to give up polygamy, one of the pillars of chiefly power. For many chiefs, converts and catechists provided welcome scapegoats who could be blamed for all problems relating to the enforcement of road work and other colonial decrees. However, whether a chief chose confrontation or co-operation with the Christians depended ultimately on local power relations. Thus while the Lawra Naa is said to have forbidden his subjects to join the new religion,[80] the Nandom Naa ensured that the mission station was built not in Zimuopere, but in Nandom itself. The rest of the population too, apart from a core group of devoted Christians, soon adopted a rather pragmatic attitude to the opportunities presented by the new faith, as the missionaries themselves fully admitted.[81] The healing of many hitherto incurable illnesses, rain, and a degree of protection against attacks by chiefs were some of the definite advantages of associating with the White Fathers.[82] Later came further benefits, such as participation in development projects and credit unions, access to formal education, and with it new opportunities for social advancement. In negotiating everyday conflicts, one could play off against each other customary law, Christian norms and, under certain circumstances, even British civil law in order to further one's interests. Among young labour migrants from Nandom, for example, it became customary to get married in church before going off to the mines, 'so that the Roman Catholic rules of divorce shall keep the girl on ice for him', a strategy that District Commissioner Amherst found extraordinarily unfair to the young women, who were then frequently accused of marital infidelity.[83] Conversely, many men suspected that women only became Catholics in order to escape their unwanted 'pagan' husbands, or because they could no longer be repudiated by their Christian spouses, even if the former failed to be faithful.

In spite of the prevailing pragmatism, the new religion forced all the affected parties to elucidate local norms in a manner that had not been necessary earlier. The colonial codification of customary law took place in this context. It may, therefore, have tacitly incorporated a number of Christian norms and declared them to be integral to local tradition. Conversely, the missionaries were continually forced to integrate local practices into Christian rules of behaviour and ritual.[84]

EDUCATING THE 'LOWER ORDERS'

For British colonial authorities the stabilisation of chieftaincy was accorded a higher priority than modernisation or 'development' of the Protectorate, including formal education. The first petition from the White Fathers to open a school in Nandom was therefore rejected. First, there was ostensibly not enough qualified teaching staff available;[85] second, the colonial government asserted that it needed educated native clerks, not catechists or priests; and third, Chief Commissioner Jones feared, educated Christians might undermine the authority of the native chiefs. He regarded 'semi-literate catechists', who believed themselves to be superior leaders to the chiefs, as the main culprits in conflicts between the latter and converts.[86] Power, the director of education, did not support the opening of Catholic schools either, not until native authority schools were firmly established for the education of the chiefs' sons. He argued that 'the chiefs and ruling classes, conservative in view and often polygamous in habit, will be usually the last to send their children to a Christian mission school'. Mission schools therefore entailed 'a danger of setting up an educated class among the lower orders before the ruling classes become literate'.[87] Nevertheless, a second petition to set up a mission school in Nandom was accepted and approved. In the meantime, mission school graduates from Navrongo and Bolgatanga had proved their worth as native clerks, and it had also become increasingly clear that the native authority schools could not produce enough graduates on their own to cover the demand for administrative personnel. In 1937 St Paul's Primary School opened its doors in Nandom, first as an infants' school, and from 1939 as a fully accredited primary boarding school, with seventy pupils, who were taught by a missionary and two graduates of the senior school in Navrongo.

Apart from the Catholic primary school for girls opened in Jirapa in 1940, St Paul's Primary School for boys was until the early 1950s the only mission school in the entire North-West. Unlike the Lawra Confederacy Native Authority School, therefore, it recruited its pupils not only in parishes belonging to Lawra-Tumu District, but also in Kaleo and adjacent areas. In the school, the Sisala constituted a negligible minority. Most of the boys were Dagara and Dagaba, and, as one of the first pupils recalled, they were initially astonished at the differences in the dialects they spoke, but soon made friends with boys from all over the North-West and thus became aware of the size of their own ethnic and linguistic community.[88] However, this new sense of community appears to have come about 'incidentally' since, unlike in the native authority schools, the White Fathers did not teach the basics of local culture and history, nor did they wish their pupils to become socialised into any sort of ethnic pride. At the newly founded St Andrew's Middle School in Nandom, it was only in the 1950s that 'tribal dances' began to be performed occasionally alongside English folk dances – in which case everybody then had to learn the dances of fellow pupils from other regions – while in 'dramatization', scenes with local themes and stories told in Dagara were sometimes staged alongside English plays.[89] The missionaries firmly sought to avoid the formation of groups along the lines of shared origin and dialect, and the boys had to speak English as much as possible. The community towards which pupils were to develop their sense of responsibility and of which they were to become productive members was not the tribe or the chiefdom, but the Catholic Church.

In a sense, Power's expectation that the mission school would produce an 'educated class' that did not stem from the chieftaincy proved well-founded. Only Catholic children were accepted into St Paul's, chiefs' sons being among them only in the rarest of cases. Whoever had not yet converted by the late 1930s had more or less explicitly decided against Christianity. Such families therefore usually did not permit their children to go to the mission school. Conversely, Catholic parents did not wish to send their children to the native authority school, and even after the Second World War when native authority day schools were opened in many villages, most Catholics hesitated to expose their offspring to the moral and spiritual dangers of a lay school. Consequently, school attendance split the population into two camps: Catholics on the one hand and the non-Catholic chiefs' sons and relatives on the other, each side mostly keeping to themselves.

Whether educated Catholics really belonged to the 'lower orders' of local society, as Power expected, is, however, questionable. Until 1946 no school fees were levied,[90] and thereafter fees only amounted to five shillings, half the sum charged by the native authority school. However, from my interviews it became apparent that the privilege of formal education was mostly a matter for the sons of catechists. The latter did not exactly belong to the poorest in the village, since they received a fixed salary from the mission and often worked relatively large farms, aided energetically by some of their congregation. At the catechism school in Jirapa they not only acquired religious instruction, but also learnt reading, writing and arithmetic.[91] They therefore wanted their own children to have access to higher education, so that these might enter higher social positions as priests or teachers. Evarist

Kuuwulong, one of the first Dagara priests, vividly described how the catechist in his village campaigned for his religion by asserting that the priesthood was not the preserve of whites, and that any Catholic could become a priest if only he went to school.[92] To become like the White Fathers represented greater social advancement than the district commissioner could offer pupils in the native authority schools. Because catechists usually lived separated from their families in other villages, their children's school attendance met with less resistance from relatives, who regarded school children as 'lost' to the family. Finally, because of their close relationship with the missionaries, catechists had better opportunities than other parents to secure for their children a spot at school when the capacity of the educational system to take on pupils was limited.[93]

At St Paul's, teaching only went as far as the third standard. Only in 1950 did the White Fathers open a middle school in Nandom, the first in the North-West. Until then Catholic pupils could only obtain further education in Navrongo or Bolgatanga, to which the missionaries had sent a few young graduates of the Jirapa catechist school even before St Paul's had been opened. Archbishop Peter Dery was one of the first educated Catholics from the North-West. Apart from him, another four graduates of the catechist school became priests, while five boys underwent teacher training and then worked in the mission schools in the North-West.[94] The first graduates of St Paul's, who continued their education at the senior school in Navrongo, also mostly became priests or teachers. Future priests were sent to the theological seminary that was first opened in Wiagha in 1946 and subsequently moved to Tamale in 1953. Student teachers mainly worked for the first two or three years as 'pupil teachers', graduating from the St John Bosco Training College in Navrongo, and then teaching in the Catholic schools at Nandom and Jirapa.[95]

Yet by no means did all mission pupils remain loyal to the White Fathers. Some were frightened off by the missionaries' authoritarian and paternalistic teaching style and their treatment of employees, or they were simply attracted by the promise of better pay in other types of employment.[96] The boundary between mission school pupils and native authority school graduates therefore cannot be drawn too rigidly: especially in later years there were always pupils who changed between the two educational systems, as well as mission pupils who subsequently worked in occupational fields not affiliated with the church. Nonetheless, the mission schools and the native authority schools did exist separately, being mostly self-reproducing institutions each with their own educational goals in which pupils had different experiences, created different friendship networks, and normally also pursued different careers. The rise of party politics in the 1950s in particular intensified the competition between teachers at state and mission schools, which partly carried over on to the pupils.

The central point in all this is that the mission of the White Fathers not only drew the boundaries of the 'Dagaaba' community and defined its culture differently from the colonial authorities and the chiefs, it also promoted the formation of a separate educated elite, which was later to participate actively in the debates concerning ethnic politics and cultural practice. Mission schools also provided social groups with access to education who would otherwise not have been educated at all, or at least not at such an early stage, by the native authority schools, due to their remoteness from the chiefs. In the regional context, the great success of the mission and the educational efforts of the White Fathers in the North-West not only led to the Dagaba dominating the ranks of Catholic priesthood and other Catholic institutions in Northern Ghana today, but also to their disproportional predominance in many higher-level positions in the North's regional administration – a situation that has by no means won them only friends.

DECOLONISATION AND LOCAL GOVERNMENT REFORM

'Social democracy', 'self-government' and the 'partnership of free peoples' – these should be the new goals of post-war British politics, both in the Gold Coast and in its marginalised, underdeveloped hinterland, wrote Harold Ingrams, reflecting on his brief experience as Chief Commissioner of the Northern Territories (1949: 193–5). In Ingrams' view it was high time to propagate the idea of a 'common citizenship throughout the Gold Coast' and to grant the Northern Territories appropriate political representation in colonial institutions. Moreover, the chieftaincy should be transformed into a kind of 'constitutional monarchy' (ibid.: 210). Ingrams' time in office, from 1947 to 1948, ushered in the end of indirect rule and of what one colonial officer called the 'national park approach' to politics in the North during the inter-war period.[1]

The discussion in this and the following chapter[2] will focus on how local and national politics intertwined during the decolonisation period, and on the complex interplay between elements of continuity and change resulting from new linkages with national power blocks. Local politics did not, as Mamdani (1996) suggests, play out as largely unbroken continuation of the colonial configuration of 'decentralised despotism' (or its substitution by 'centralised despotism'). Instead, the release from the iron brace of the British district commissioner permitted greater local political initiative. If the territorial administrative units and the institution of chieftaincy were retained in the North-West, then it was the outcome of controversy, debate and negotiation, not of automatism.

Conflicts over landownership, political authority, local citizenship and taxes, which had first become manifest upon the introduction of indirect rule, set in anew under local government reform. At the heart of these debates were three controversial issues. The first concerned the relationship between earth-shrine parishes and chiefdoms. The introduction of local councils revived the dispute over whether political authority should rest with allodial landowners, or whether the structures of chiefly authority created by local strongmen and colonial intervention should be retained. The second issue was closely linked with the first, namely, what role should the distinctions between first-comers and late-comers, between landowners and settlers, play in the new political order? Were there first- and second-class citizens, with different rights of political participation? This question became particularly critical with the introduction of elections (for local and district councils in 1952, and for parliament in 1954), since in many Sisala villages, Dagara immigrants had come to constitute a majority of the inhabitants and a majority of the voters. Should they not only be allowed to vote, but also to represent their new settlements politically? Third, as in the 1930s, disputes arose over the political authority to which farmers who continued to farm in more than one locality should pay their taxes. Should this be the local council of the area in which they farmed, or the council that governed their home compound? In all these debates, ethnicity continued to serve as a basis for legitimating administrative boundaries and political rights, though ethnic identities were (re-)defined more narrowly or widely by local actors according to their political interests.

THE NORTH IN THE NATIONAL ARENA

For the North, decolonisation was a period of negotiation regarding how it would be integrated into the new state of Ghana created out of the Gold Coast Colony and the protectorates of Ashanti and the Northern Territories. Economically, mass labour migration had long closely linked the Northern Territories with the rest of the colony. Politically, however, the British regarded the Northern Territories as a hinterland, requiring protection and careful modernisation along the lines of 'progressive traditionalism'. The Northern Territories were therefore represented in political institutions at the colony level only by the Chief Commissioner, not by African representatives.

The first step in granting the Northern Territories more weight in the Gold Coast legislature was the 1946 creation of the Northern Territories Council (NTC), in which representatives from all Northern native authorities were to discuss 'matters of common interest' and to learn 'to think further than purely local affairs'.[3] With five of forty members appointed by the NTC, Northerners too were to participate in the Coussey Committee, set up in December 1948 to prepare drafts for a new constitution.[4] Lawra Naa J. A. Karbo, one of the few chiefs with a formal education, represented the North-West. The resulting report of August 1949 recommended the abolition of the native authorities and the separation of chieftaincy from local government. Most NTC members considered these proposals too far-reaching, fearing that early independence and the rapid Africanisation of the civil service would lead to 'Black imperialism from the south', since not enough Northern staff was available to occupy the relevant posts, and that the North would remain 'nothing other than a labour camp'.[5] The NTC also felt that restricting chiefly influence presented considerable risks, because the chief's authority was respected, and his

Plate 4 Lawra J. A. Karbo, with the King George Medal for Chiefs (4"), 1949 (with kind permission of Ghana Information Services, Accra)

paternalistic rule 'suited ... a people whose needs are simple'. Democracy and 'modern electoral procedure' would be hampered, the NTC members cautioned, by 'the ignorance, inexperience and apathy of Northerners' of which political parties in the South could take undue advantage.[6]

Indeed, the educational gap between the North and the Gold Coast was vast, and the NTC's fears regarding the lack of qualified Northern personnel were not altogether unwarranted.[7] But the NTC's arguments also indicate the degree to which chiefs and their educated sons had imbibed the British philosophy of indirect rule. Yet the image of a politically ignorant people in need of paternalistic leadership was outdated by the 1950s. Mass labour migration, the expansion of primary school education and the influence of the Catholic mission had created new realities, and in 1948 'a small faction with a dynamic political creed', a group of teachers and businessmen, founded a local branch of the United Gold Coast Convention (UGCC) in Tamale that later joined the CPP.[8] However, at this time neither these Northern CPP pioneers nor the more critical labour migrants and Catholic converts who were potentially at odds with the chieftaincy as yet played a visible role.

The 1951 Local Government Act mostly ignored the NTC's reservations, stipulating that two-thirds of the local government and district council members were to be elected directly, instead of a maximum of half, as the NTC demanded. Only the scepticism regarding the direct election of parliamentarians was heeded. An NTC-organised electoral college selected 19 Northern parliamentarians, charged with representing the Northern Territories in the 75-member legislature in Accra. Of the Lawra Confederacy's five nominees, only one received the necessary votes, namely S. D. Dombo, the son of a chief, a graduate of the Tamale Teacher Training College, and himself a chief in Jirapa Division since 1949, who was later to become leader of the parliamentary opposition to Nkrumah's CPP government. But in 1951 Dombo, like other Northern parliamentarians, was concerned with the 'upliftment of the whole country', not party politics.[9] Such corporatist concepts of political representation ultimately reflected the Northern parliamentarians' origins. Like most of the educated Northern elite, they were the sons or close relatives of chiefs who had attended native authority schools and who knew one another very well, because almost all of them had continued their education at the same boarding school in Tamale.

The Northern politicians' common front in the CPP-dominated Legislative Assembly quickly encountered its limits when the general interest in better infrastructure needed to be addressed in terms of specific projects. Some younger parliamentarians were successfully recruited by the CPP, siding with the governing party in hopes of being better able to serve their constituency's interests. By the end of the legislative session, Northern MPs were divided into a minority CPP faction and a majority that held firm to the corporatist model of representation thereby becoming a government opposition without so intending.

In the 1954 parliamentary elections, the representatives from the North too were elected directly, the CPP presenting candidates in almost all constituencies. As a result CPP opponents such as S. D. Dombo and others founded their own party in the spring of 1954, the Northern People's Party (NPP). Its official logo displayed a clenched fist, symbolising unity, and the platform claimed among its central objectives 'respect for the culture of the people of the Northern Territories', 'political and social advancement', and 'a progressively increasing share [of Northerners] in the administrative and other services of the country'.[10] The NPP was largely supported by chiefs, particularly in the North-West. It won 12 of the 26 Northern parliamentary seats; later, when independent parliamentarians joined the party, the number increased to 17. Of the successful Northern CPP candidates, two became ministers in Nkrumah's cabinet, and two others permanent secretaries. Thus, representatives from the Northern Territories now sat both in government and on the opposition bench.[11] This ended the NPP's self-appointed role as a neutral, regional representative. In the 1956 elections, the NPP ran as the opposition to the CPP from the outset and won 49.6 per cent of the votes. Independent candidates no longer played a significant role – an indication that the Northern electorate too had become split along party lines.[12]

The regionalist representation finally came to an end in 1957, when, in order to forestall the Avoidance of Discrimination Act that prohibited regional, ethnic and religious political organisations, the NPP united with other regional opposition parties from the South under the United Party.[13] With the end of the Northern Territories' special status in independent Ghana, the NTC became obsolete, meeting for the last time in January 1958. Although the former Protectorate still formally existed as an administrative unit (the Northern Region, later divided into the Northern and Upper Regions), there was no corresponding government institution under which Northerners could discuss their specific interests. However, political activists still viewed themselves as Northerners and remained convinced it was up to them to promote this disadvantaged region's interests.

For regional and local politics, decolonisation had two important consequences. First, the removal of British colonial officials from local government opened the arena for local political initiatives. Although British government agents were still stationed in many districts, after the war staff changed so frequently that few colonial officials were as well acquainted with local conditions as their colleagues during the inter-war period. In addition, most post-war British administrators now saw their role as that of administrative co-ordinator and adviser to local elites on their way to independence. But with the gradual withdrawal of colonial officials from the mid-1950s onward, the fetters that had buttressed local hierarchies and boundaries also gave way. Nkrumah's Ghanaian district commissioners were CPP party members, who, at least initially, were often recruited from among local teachers and so directly involved in local conflicts. As a result, divisive tendencies became more pervasive: conflicts and competition erupted between villages, among chiefs, and, to some extent, along ethnic lines.

The second consequence was the multiplication of possible alliances and political arenas. Whereas before there had been one 'external' ally, the district commissioner, capable of supporting local actors in pursuit of their own interests, now different levels of the administrative hierarchy – local council, district council, regional and central government – were played off against one another. Yet despite these new developments chiefdoms continued to comprise the framework within which local political alliances were forged and the establishment of districts and constituencies contested.

THE LOCAL POLITICAL ELITE

Although Northern representatives could not prevent the constitutional separation of chieftaincy affairs from local government, until 1960 the chiefs were allocated a third of the seats on the new local and district councils *ex officio*. In the North, the CPP's earlier anti-chief rhetoric was largely ignored, and no one demanded the chieftaincy's abolition.[14] However, Nkrumah's later policy of stabilising CPP rule by supporting certain factions in local chieftaincy succession conflicts significantly affected Northern politics. Some villages used populist CPP ideology to demand their own chiefdom or local council, accusing the paramount chief of 'exploitation'. Those competing for chiefly office stressed that a successor should not be chosen by the chiefly family alone, but be democratically elected by all the inhabitants of the chiefdom.[15]

Since the late 1940s, it had been almost exclusively educated family members who succeeded to the paramount and important divisional chieftaincies of the Lawra Confederacy. Neo-traditional thus fused with modern political offices and elites, making chiefly office convertible into positions within the modern political system, a practice of 'reciprocal assimilation of elites' (Bayart 1993) that continues to this day. The mission-educated elite acted as a counterweight only to a limited extent. More often, mission education became an alternative route to joining supra-regional religious and administrative elites, which did not yet pose a serious challenge to local and regional political elites.

On the Lawra Confederacy State Council, which the new constitution had charged with all chieftaincy matters, sat 4 divisional chiefs (Lawra, Nandom, Jirapa and Lambussie) and 8 sub-divisional chiefs from each division, 36 chiefs altogether. Its president, Lawra Naa Karbo, also presided over the District Council until Nandom Naa Polkuu and Lambussie Kuoro Salifu took over the District Council presidency in 1958 and 1961 respectively.[16] Until 1958, divisional chiefs also served as local council chairmen, and they selected from among their chiefs and closest relatives the 'traditional members' for the local and the district council. In practice this resulted in an overlap of personnel, so that the four divisional chiefs and a small group of sub-divisional chiefs dominated all three institutions, the local, district and state councils. Also quite common was that certain families had several members sitting on these councils. In 1955, for instance, Lawra Naa Karbo was President of the Lawra Confederacy District Council, his son Abayifaa was a traditional member, and C. K. Binni, a cousin, was the Council's Lawra representative. The Gandah family from Birifu also had two brothers sitting on the District Council, Birifu Naa Nonatuo as a traditional member and his brother Biz as a representative.

The fact that the chiefs were now outnumbered by a two-thirds majority of popularly elected members in the local and district councils mattered little, because until the end of the 1950s even these elected members were usually members of chiefly families.[17] Even with the 1960 local government reforms, which replaced the old district council and four local councils with the Lawra Confederacy Local Council that consisted of elected members only, of the 20 elected councillors, 4 were chiefs and at least 5 the sons or brothers of chiefs.[18] A person's chances of becoming councillor and gaining political influence still increased considerably if he was both educated and either a chief himself or a close relative. The chiefs' dominance, however, did not preclude political disputes – quite the contrary – but the lines of conflict ran between the various chiefs and their followers, not between chiefs and commoners.

A vital issue for local and state councils was the budget. Chiefs were still expected to assist tax collection, in turn receiving a certain share of the revenue.[19] What once constituted the chiefs' primary income – corvée labour, gifts and court fees – was rendered only voluntarily. As a result, demands that local councils pay a salary to the chiefs increased. In one of the Lawra Confederacy State Council's first sessions, the chiefs proposed an appropriate salary structure, which would correspond to that of teachers – £240 p.a. for each divisional chief (the salary of a middle-aged middle school teacher), £120 for a sub-divisional chief and another £30 for a village chief – unrealistic expectations given that the sum would exceed the head tax collected by the Lawra Confederacy District Council for the entire 1953–4 fiscal year.[20] Beyond a salary and various allowances, some chiefs tried to tap local council finances in other ways, often co-operating closely with local council clerks. The British Government Agent's complaint about Nandom Naa Imoru is typical of this period: despite various warnings, he repeatedly helped himself to the Nandom Local Council Treasury as if it were his 'Privy Purse'.[21]

That the chieftaincy and local government were supposed to be separate entities may not have been quite obvious to the electorate either. In any case, acting on both levels was generally deemed advantageous. As a rule, therefore, petitions regarding village matters, whether chieftaincy-related or otherwise, were copied and sent to numerous addressees – to the divisional chief, the local and district councils, the district commissioner, and later also the local CPP chairman. Moreover the demands made were often unclear. The Birifu Naa, for instance, initially petitioned for an independent division, that is, for an upgrading of his chiefdom. Later, he demanded his own local council, that is, a change in secular local government structures. The addressees for their part pushed petitions back and forth between administrative levels, often avoiding having to deal with these demands at all.

The chiefs remained influential in local council affairs throughout the Nkrumah regime. Very soon the CPP-appointed district commissioners realised that they could do very little without the chiefs' co-operation. A. P. S. Termaghre, member of the chiefly family of Tom, a village in Nandom Division, one of the region's first CPP members and the first African District Commissioner in Lawra (and later Nandom), recommended to his successors the following:

> [D]o not forgo to reconcile with the chiefs. ... [C]hieftaincy is a very sensitive institution and [chiefs] wish to remain above the ordinary member of the masses. ... The Traditional Council arrogates strong feelings to dominate both the Party and the [Local] Council and their activities. With careful education this tendancy [sic] can be uprooted.[22]

But before this 'careful education' could take root, the CPP government was toppled. What chiefs did learn from the Nkrumah regime was less to limit their own quest for power than to recognise the political signs of the times as soon as possible, and always to garner the support of relevant regional and national political power-brokers.

Interestingly, the chieftaincy among the Dagara and the Sisala in neighbouring Upper Volta was much more unstable than in Ghana, and today is all but meaningless. This seems to be due in part to the fact that the French only implemented the chieftaincy slowly after much experimentation and did so with much more *dirigisme* than the British. For another, they did not institute chiefs' conferences or institutions that were comparable to those established in the Lawra Confederacy, nor did they involve chiefs in co-ordinating the affairs of neighbouring *chefferies de canton*. And finally, unlike the British, the French did not raise a sufficiently large and politically experienced educated elite of chiefly sons, which would have ensured the chieftaincy's continuation and promoted the amalgamation of modern and neo-traditional institutions during decolonisation.

INTEGRATIONISTS AND SECESSIONISTS: THE LAWRA CONFEDERACY IN CONTEST

When the new local and district council boundaries were to be determined, Lawra Naa J. A. Karbo pleaded for the Lawra Confederacy's retention as an administrative unit, arguing that the shared history and cultural affinity which had once guaranteed peace and co-operation could also foster progress in the future.[23] Not all political actors, however, shared Karbo's view. Some aimed at incorporating Lawra Confederacy into a larger administrative unit, while others sought a secession.

Controversies over the North-West District

In 1948 the British once again considered consolidating the native authorities of Lawra, Tumu and Wa into a single administrative unit under the North-Western District Council, but it soon became clear that the 'long standing jealousy between Lawra and Wa' would hinder this.[24] When a Wala representative reasserted the claim to regional hegemony – '"Before the White man came" the people of Lawra had no chiefs and had made their submission to the Wala hierarchy'[25] – Lawra Confederacy chiefs protested vehemently. Nandom Naa Imoru argued for two districts, Lawra-Tumu und Wa. The Tumu Native Authority representatives wanted either a North-West District or a Wa-Tumu District, but under no circumstances a Lawra-Tumu District. Wa District Commissioner Amherst convened an extraordinary meeting of representatives from the three native authorities, hoping to win their support for the proposed consolidation. But the meeting achieved just the opposite, and after many hours of bitter debate, the Lawra Confederacy was eventually granted its own district.

This debate is a powerful example of the intertwining of various discourses that shape local politics up to the present. Pragmatic arguments for efficient administration mixed with legitimating references to history, and underlying political interests were formulated in ethnic terms. Commoners were played off against chiefs, and structural conflicts were re-framed as personal enmities between chiefs. Colonial officers now found it increasingly difficult to exert influence over local politics, because the political initiative had largely passed into the hands of the chiefs.

The debate opened with District Commissioner Amherst's passionate plea for a single North-West District. Only Lawra, Tumu and Wa together, Amherst explained, were populous enough to form a district council as recommended by the Coussey Committee. He insisted that the expansion of road networks to the 'centres of wealth in the South' would be more economical and that minor differences in political traditions could be easily overcome by instituting a co-presidency in the district council.[26] Later, C. K. Binni of the Lawra chiefly family voiced his interpretation of Amherst's recommendations: 'the British Government is to give us help and then to leave us to rule ourselves and only guide us when we make a mistake. We should not be forced against our wishes.'[27]

Luri Kanton, son of the Tumu Kuoro, supported consolidation, referring to experiences from the time of Babatu, when the destructive consequences of disunity first became manifest. The Wa Na emphasised the ties of 'friendship' and 'affinity' between the three native authorities.[28] But Lawra Naa J. A. Karbo, a staunch opponent of consolidation, insisted that he had already explained to the Chief Commissioner 'why we never wanted to follow Wala: because their ways are different from ours.'[29] Karbo was particularly worried that the Wa Na would involve himself in local conflicts with Wala traders living in the Lawra Confederacy.[30] However, in order not to forestall future political alliances with Wa or Tumu, Karbo maintained it was the 'people's wish' he adopt this stance:

> The Wa-na is my close friend; if the matter lies between him and me, I agree to follow, but what about our people? Tumu-koro is my father … I grew up in Tumu. If my people agree there should be one District Council, I also agree.[31]

Seidu Wala, member of the Wala Native Authority, asked the Lawra Naa to forget former wrongs: 'I think this is a tribal prejudice that should have been forgotten long ago'. Imoro Egala, a Sisala teacher, who was to become a minister in Nkrumah's cabinet, assured that the forthcoming democratic constitution would certainly forestall attempts to secure further hegemony. He appealed to the solidarity of the North-Western elite during their schooldays: 'I agree that our customs are different – but in the old days Sissala boys [from Tumu] went to Lawra to school, and Dagarti boys [from Lawra] to Wa, and were happy there.'[32] Furthermore, he argued, Tumu had plenty of good land, and, in a common district, the 'Dagarti' from the densely populated Lawra area could settle there without the re-emergence of old tax disputes.

The Dorimon Naa from Wa Native Authority stressed the necessity of unity vis-à-vis the more developed South: 'We are looking forward to self-government, and if we in the North cannot agree with our brothers, how much less can we agree with others from far away'?[33] But the debate went nowhere. Lawra Naa Karbo hid behind his subjects' reservations. C. K. Binni argued that the 'religion and customs' of the Wala on the one hand and the Lobi and Dagarti on the other were incompatible.[34] Amherst countered that district councils were not going to be concerned with 'religion and customs'. Imoro Egala, annoyed with Lawra's general accusations of 'one tribe troubling another', warned: 'If we do not agree, we are giving the people from the South an opportunity to trouble us'.[35] Duori Naa S. D. Dombo shifted the discussion to the often debated question of the administrative centre's location: 'There is no fear in joining Wala, but there is fear in building the chief station in Wa'.[36] Amherst commented, quite unnerved, that 'the people in the bush [do not] really care if the Senior D.C. lives in Wa, Lawra or Timbuktu. They want to get on with their farms'.[37] Would the Lawra Naa actually agree to a common district if headquarters were moved to a 'neutral place'? The Lawra Naa replied 'no', the concession being too little too late, and insisted: 'We wish Lawra to be alone.'

The Tumu and Wala representatives agreed to a consolidated Wala-Tumu District, but the Wa Na immediately made it clear that its headquarters had to remain in Wa.[38] Although Amherst continued to hope that Lawra might one day join a common district, the only realistic solution at the time was the establishment of two districts, Lawra and Wala-Tumu. A subsequent NTC report concluded that 'historical difficulties' had prevented the Lawra Confederacy's consolidation with Wa.[39]

Secessionist endeavours

When the new districts were eventually announced in spring 1952, a common Wala-Tumu District Council was not mentioned. With three district councils – Wa, Lawra and Tumu – the old native authority boundaries had prevailed, despite reservations regarding low population and financial viability.[40] Also, the sub-division of the Lawra Confederacy District Council into four local councils was based on the former subordinate native authorities (divisions) of Lawra, Jirapa, Nandom and Lambussie. All the old boundaries were retained, with the exception of Hamile, a case I shall discuss below.

Orientation along chiefdom boundaries was to ensure the local councils indeed constituted 'units of co-operation and common interest'.[41] But some local actors hoped to finally correct what they felt to be an injustice, namely the 1930s rescission of their autonomy as separate native states. Two settlements in particular lobbied for a return to the *status quo ante*: Samoa, which was subordinated to Lambussie only in 1932,[42] and Birifu, subordinated to Lawra, whose chief claimed his rank to have formerly been on par with the Lawra Naa. Birifu's attempts at secession demonstrate how historical and ethnic arguments first produced by colonial officers and a new political discourse of democracy and development mingled to produce a highly explosive combination that still resonates in local political conflicts today.[43]

That Birifu's discontent regarding its subordination to Lawra turned into demands for an independent local council was closely connected to the death of the old Birifu Naa Gandah in 1950. Lawra Naa Karbo and the old Gandah were good friends – Karbo had married several of Gandah's daughters – having long ago laid to rest the 'very old quarrel' between Lawra and Birifu. '[B]ut the sons of the Birifu Na', wrote the Lawra District Commissioner, 'decided they could get something out of claiming equality with Lawra and proceeded to make themselves very unpleasant'.[44] In fact, Chief Gandah's sons were annoyed that, immediately after the burial, they had to turn in for a two-inch medal the three-inch chief's medal their father had been awarded for his services as chief in 1921. This three-inch medal was needed for the Lambussie Kuoro, who, upon re-establishment of his autonomy from Nandom, had been elevated to divisional chief.[45] In the eyes of Gandah's sons, this three-inch medal was proof of Birifu's former status as an independent division. Nonatuo Gandah, the new Birifu Naa, presented his first demand 'to break off from the Lawra Division' to the Lawra Confederacy chiefs' conference. He argued that Lawra and Birifu were separate 'tribes' hostile to each other, further pointing out that Birifu had so far received nothing for the taxes it had paid to Lawra:

> Burifo [sic] was placed under Lawra not by her own will but through political force. This means that ... it could also break away from Lawra by means of [because of] political maltreatment. ... For many years Burifo has not been in a good turn with Lawra because of tribal discrimination and hereditary hatred ... As we were not fairly represented, nothing practical has been done in Burifo ... This means we started paying head tax in 1935 up till now there has been nothing done here to prove the poor tax payer that he does not pay head tax for nothing. [Pencilled-in comment by the DC: 'All the seven Gandah boys went to school however. This letter is one of the results.'] ... In view of this, we are not prepared to work jointly with the Lawra Na and hope to get our own division.[46]

As was to be expected, this petition found favour neither among the Lawra divisional chiefs nor with the district commissioner.[47] So, the Birifu Naa sent another petition, now to the Ministry for Local Government in Accra, which formulated the ethno-cultural conflicts with Lawra even more forcefully:

> Burifo is an entirely different tribe to that of Lawra and our customs are not the same and so since our amalgamation with the Lawra people there have been unceasing tribal feuds which often resulted in that the Burifoman was found guilty because he is inferior. ... Unlike the Lawra people, the culture of this state is entirely different. This difference resulting from our dialectal speech and tribal disconnection. We want our Local Council because we are prepared for it. We are sure the development in our area will be more advanced than it is now.[48]

This petition was not granted either because the new local council would have been too small and financially weak. Apart from that, the Lawra Naa pre-empted Birifu's moves towards independence by nominating the Birifu Naa to be the first chairman of the Lawra Confederacy District Council.

However, when K. Y. Baloro of Lambussie succeeded Gandah in this office, the latter started his next secession attempt, which failed this time due to opposition from influential chiefs in Jirapa Division. Now party lines also played a role, as the Birifu Naa ran for the CPP in 1954 and 1956, while his opponents in Lawra and Jirapa stood for the NPP.[49]

As the Birifu example demonstrates, the Lawra Confederacy and its four local councils were kept together by diplomacy and pressure, which succeeded as long as the majority of the divisional chiefs were interested in the continuity of the Confederacy. From the mid-1950s onwards, however, party fronts increasingly eroded the cohesion, eventually leading to the 1962 division into four separate districts. But the Lawra Confederacy's resurrection immediately after the fall of Nkrumah's government testifies to the endurance of administrative units once created by the British. Even during recent conflicts following President Rawlings' policy of decentralisation in the late 1980s, the four divisions comprising the former Lawra Confederacy constituted the framework within which districts and constituencies were defined.

Mass education and community development

Despite the continuity of chieftaincy structures, the role of the village as a unit of action was also strengthened, particularly in the context of community-development and mass-education programmes. To the colonial officials of the post-war period, education seemed the decisive lever of progress, not just for a chiefly elite but for the general population. Hence, new primary schools were opened by the first graduates of the Tamale Government Training College, and an extensive adult education programme – the mass-education campaign – was initiated. In many district towns and villages of the Northern Territories (as in the South), young teachers and school graduates gave evening instruction to interested illiterates in reading, writing and arithmetic. Following initial, rather spontaneous initiatives, in 1952 a mass-education officer was stationed in Lawra, where both teacher commitment and interest in learning seem to have been great.[50]

Mass education was to stimulate community development in 'an attack on ignorance, apathy and prejudice, on poverty, disease and isolation.'[51] In communal work campaigns led by mass-education officers, supported financially by the government, villagers were to build schools and water reservoirs, plant trees and fence in pastures to obtain fertiliser.[52] The 'self-help' discourse linked to these projects was not fundamentally different from the paternalist, populist development rhetoric of the inter-war years. What was new, however, was the campaign's extent and the degree of professionalisation and bureaucratisation as well as the emphasis on the village, which differed from the chief-centred approach characteristic of earlier campaigns.

Mass-education planners were convinced that the village, 'a genuine closely knit community' (Sautoy 1958: 13), not the clan, the tribe or the native state, was the traditional social unit of greatest significance, a conviction entailing institutional consequences. Under the aegis of the Department of Social Welfare and Community Development, structures parallel to the institutions of local government were created that reached down to the village level. Although supra-village development initiatives, such as those concerning infrastructure, were to continue being planned and implemented by the local and district councils, the budget for community development measures allocated directly by Accra often exceeded the money available to the local councils. Moreover, the CPP government exploited community development structures in order to bypass elected councillors and strengthen direct political control.[53] For the villagers, the parallel structure amounted to a system of double taxation; for in addition to the basic rate, they now had to contribute both more money and their labour to village communal projects. On the other hand, this personal commitment did visibly benefit their village, without the 'diversion' of tax payments to the local council, which seemed to offer little direct return.

The missionary work of the White Fathers also looked to the village as a unit of action. The catechists initiated the construction of village cemeteries and chapels, and from the 1950s the Catholic church undertook village development programmes. In 1956 the first credit union was founded in Jirapa, and beginning in 1962 a lay movement, Catholic Action, established itself in the North-West. In Nandom Parish especially Catholic Action groups sprang up in many villages, followed later by associations of Christian Mothers and Fathers, whose members strengthened friendly ties between the different village patriclan sections and initiated village projects. In brief, the Catholic church too privileged the village and created networks which cut across chiefdoms, providing an alternative structure to the chiefly hierarchy.[54] However, exactly how individual villages were to be circumscribed territorially and socially, as well as which sections belonged to which village, were highly controversial issues, even though the 'village' seemed to be an entirely self-evident unit.[55]

THE CONFLICT OVER HAMILE

The conflict over Hamile's political allegiance was fought out with particular bitterness because of its location on the international border. The prospect of higher tax and customs revenues whetted political appetites, while the multi-ethnic and multi-national character of the settlement challenged local conceptions of 'natives' and 'settlers'. In some phases of the conflict, Sisala landowners and chiefs insisted that Dagara farmers in Hamile were merely 'settlers' and so had limited political rights. However, in their desire to distinguish themselves from 'stranger traders', the Sisala regarded the same Dagara as autochthonous farmers, almost equal in rank to themselves. At other times, Dagara and Sisala farmers allied with Wala traders, namely as Ghanaians against non-Ghanaian immigrants. Common nationality was and is also sometimes evoked against the claims of the Sisala earth priests in Hamile who live in the former French colony of Upper Volta (Burkina Faso). The border situation therefore multiplied the potential identities, alliances and demarcations, making particularly clear the flexibility of the ethnic boundaries and categories, upon which actors drew.

The conflict over Hamile is the first local political dispute in Lawra District in which the African parties themselves produced ample documents – letters, petitions, polemics and position papers – thus enabling a detailed reconstruction of the arguments. At the same time, the course of the conflict makes clear what decolonisation meant on the ground, namely that African actors had become capable of acting in different political arenas, while the British were increasingly on the defensive. The conflict ended with the decision of the new CPP government to subordinate Hamile to the Lambussie Local Council, a move against which the colonial government had fought for seven years.

A market town on the border

Hamile was originally a small settlement founded by Sisala hunters and farmers, around the latter part of the nineteenth century. Hamile's first compounds were built north of a stream which later demarcated the international border, this forming the original nucleus of what Ghanaians today refer to as Hamile-French. Towards the end of the century the Sisala were joined by Muo, a Dagara farmer, warrior and blacksmith, who soon became the host of a Mossi family of farmers and weavers wishing to settle in the area.[56] For various reasons, Muo and his Mossi guests later asked their Sisala landlords if they could resettle further south, across the stream; and their new compounds and farms came to form the nucleus of Hamile-Ghana or Hamile-Zongo, as it is locally called.[57]

The two Hamiles, separated by the stream and a stretch of grassland, were divided between British and French territory along the 11th degree of latitude, as defined in the Anglo-French Convention of 1898.[58] Although colonial and post-colonial governments periodically attempted to tighten control of cross-border traffic, the border never severed the dense kinship and economic networks between the two settlements. Instead, the border has proven to be quite lucrative, thanks to the trading and smuggling across it. While land use and ritual ties that were connected with the earth shrine, which was located in the original settlement on French territory, ignored the border, colonial chiefdoms accepted the border as fact from the outset, and border communities soon used it as a shield against persecution, colonial taxes and forced-labour requirements.[59]

Perhaps even before, but certainly since the border demarcation in 1900, Mossi traders on their way to Kumasi with goats and cloth have been stopping over at Muo's compound and the resident Mossi family. Flourishing markets sprang up on both sides of the border.[60] With the completion of the road from Lawra to Hamile via Nandom and further to Bobo-Dioulasso and Ouagadougou, supra-regional trade and border traffic increased, especially after the French built a bridge over the Volta at Ouessa in the early 1930s. An increasing number of Mossi, Kantonsi, Wangara, Hausa and Wala settled in Hamile, on British territory, as farmers, weavers, tailors and merchants. Thus, in the late 1930s, the Lawra-Tumu District Commissioner reported that a 'large settlement has sprung up at Hamale, which is a cosmopolitan trading post used as a clearing house for goods imported from French country ... and the community is highly prosperous.'[61]

From the outset the British suspected this prosperity stemmed not only from legal trade, but also from smuggling. Furthermore, they feared the 'over-farming' of Hamile lands, since many traders also farmed.[62] They therefore decided Hamile's growth should cease, and that cross-border trade be controlled more strictly. Then, during the war, when the Governor of French West Africa sided with the Vichy regime, making Britain and France wartime enemies, border security became more important to the British than ever, and they insisted the responsible native authority do everything possible to defend British interests in Hamile.

Since its founding, Hamile-Zongo had been a part of Nandom Division, even though it continued to be controlled ritually by the Sisala earth priest in Hamile-French. The Kokoligu Naa, an important Nandom sub-divisional chief, had unquestioningly added Hamile to his own chiefly territory, probably because Muo belonged to the same patriclan of the Kusiele as himself. This arrangement was reinforced when, immediately after the First World War, in the interests of better border security, District Commissioner Duncan-Johnstone ordered the rest house in Kokoligu be rebuilt near Hamile. The Kokoligu Naa appointed Loni, one of Muo's sons (the old man having passed away), to supervise the construction and made him headman of Hamile. As was customary in many *zongo* settlements, Loni allowed the various groups of immigrant traders to name their own headmen, who were subject to Loni's authority.[63] Until the outbreak of the Second World War, the records mention no protest against this administrative hierarchy. However, this was to change dramatically with the new regulations governing border activity.

Increasing the native authority treasury's revenues by tightening control of the border also served the interests of Nandom Naa Imoru, who had been in office since 1940. He felt British (as well as his own) interests were not well served if Hamile residents continued to pay ritual allegiance to the village's Sisala earth priest, a French 'native', and therefore suggested this allegiance be transferred to a related earth-priest family in Happa, a neighbouring Sisala village on British territory.[64] In co-operation with District Commissioner Amherst and the Kokoligu Naa, Imoru also tried to encourage as many Hamile traders as possible to resettle in Nandom. Drastically higher leases and the threat of fines for those unwilling to move on the one hand, and low rents, cash gifts and a new market in Nandom on the other, were all measures designed to make this plan a reality.[65] Yet this stick-and-carrot policy did not encourage traders to resettle, but rather provoked demands that Hamile be separated administratively from Nandom and brought under the Lambussie Native Authority instead. Even the Hamile headman supported this demand, preferring to follow the Lambussie Kuoro, via the chief of Happa.

First petitions

Immediately after the war, the Hamile 'stranger headmen' petitioned the Lawra Confederacy Native Authority that the Nandom Naa now reduce the high rent and the other levies he imposed on them. The district commissioner urged the assembled chiefs to reject this petition, because the stream of traders coming to Hamile still needed to be kept in check.[66] A few months later, the Happa Kuoro demanded Hamile's political loyalty, arguing 'that he owns the land as Tengansob, and that rent is charged by the [Nandom] Native Authority to strangers, which is against his custom'.[67] For District Commissioner Charles, who later reconstructed the course of the Hamile dispute, it was clear that the traders had incited the Happa Kuoro to write this letter because they hoped that Happa and Lambussie would control them less strictly than the Nandom Naa.[68] In July 1946, the Happa Kuoro's demand was heard in the Nandom Naa's native court, because at that time Lambussie, and therefore also Happa, still belonged to Nandom Division:

> Happa Kuoro vs. Kokoligu People. The complainant states ... that the land Fetish [earth shrine] of Hamile is looked after by them, but that the people living there follow Kokoligu; which he dislikes. So he is claiming his land Hamile and the people living there, to follow Hapa [*sic*] instead of Kokoligu. Plea: – not liable. Judgement of Court: – Plaintiff should own his land fetish and should be responsible to claiming anything from the Defendant if the said Defts [Defendants] caused any damages against his land Fetish but the people staying on the land should still follow Kokoligu as was booked by the authority: Hamile people rejected to follow Happa.[69]

The Nandom Naa thus insisted that the rights arising from control of the earth shrine be separated from chieftaincy affairs, which would permit him to control Hamile politically, while earth-shrine affairs were dealt with by Happa. In response the Happa Kuoro countered that the legitimate right to the political allegiance of the area's inhabitants arose from control over the earth shrine and thus landownership.

The court's decision was only valid as long as Lambussie was subject to the Nandom Native Authority. Since the establishment of the Issala Tuntumer Native Authority in November 1947[70] Lambussie Kuoro Salifu attempted to bring Hamile under Lambussie's control, encouraging the Happa Kuoro to persevere with his demand. Wa District Commissioner Charles, for his part, was certain that Hamile should continue to be subject to Nandom, and he referred the matter to the Lawra Confederacy Native Authority, hoping they would side with him in their decision.[71] In fact, the 'advice' that Lawra Naa Karbo and his assessors drew up supported the Nandom court's opinion that earth-shrine and chiefly affairs be kept separate. Every concession to the Happa Kuoro, so the Lawra chiefs thought, would provoke endless disputes over political boundaries, an argument cited previously in the 1930s by District Commissioner Guinness in order to thwart Eyre-Smith's proposal to redraw the chieftaincies according to earth-shrine territories. In addition, the Lawra chiefs accused the Sisala of Lambussie of once, when the Lawra Confederacy was introduced, having opposed the all-Sisala state proposed by the British with the argument 'that they were Dagarti, and they would not mix with the Sisalas'.[72] Thus, they found it difficult to fathom why the Happa Kuoro should complain of Hamile's following a 'Dagarti' chief (namely the Kokoligu Naa).

In light of this argument, and the fact that the Lawra Naa had consulted only with Dagara chiefs, the Happa chief suspected a tribalist conspiracy to usurp historically certified Sisala land rights, which included not just Hamile, but all of Nandom Division. Why Hamile had for a time followed the Nandom Naa, was explained by the Happa Kuoro with reference to the political machinations of the 'Dagarti chiefs'. Now, however, the inhabitants of Hamile 'diametrically refuse to follow or go under the chief of Nandom until all of them will get finished on the earth and they are no more.'[73] In fact, Hamile Naa Perwere, the headmen of the Mossi and Wangara, and the Imam of Hamile had petitioned the Chief Commissioner to categorically declare their independence from Nandom, arguing the Happa Kuoro was the 'landowner' and that 'in any ... land dispute the Nandom Chief can never assist us'.[74] Furthermore, as Perwere's brother later added, the Hamile traders complained that the Nandom Naa demanded £3 in taxes per year, while traders in Nandom only paid ten shillings and that failure to pay led to the demolishment of one's compound. Taxes were actually collected 'for the improvement of the villages', but 'nothing practically has been done for we the people in Hamile', a complaint, as we have seen, the secessionists of Birifu also raised.[75]

The plebiscite

Wa District Commissioner Charles was taken aback that the 'Dagarti' of Hamile had decided to voluntarily follow a Sisala chief instead of their own tribesman in Nandom, and suggested to wait and see. Time would help overcome the 'dislike for Nandom, which may be purely a personal ill feeling for the Nandom Naa'.[76] However, the Chief Commissioner wanted a quick solution and ordered a plebiscite, so that the responsible native authority would learn 'to settle such a dispute themselves and by consent of the people concerned'.[77] The vote, held in September 1949, yielded no surprises: of 44 compound heads, only 3 wanted to remain with Nandom, the other 41 all voting for Happa. However, District Commissioner Charles refused to recognise the outcome because, as the Lawra Naa assured him, 'improper pressure had been brought to bear by the Happa Koro on the people of Hamile ... that if they did not vote for following him he, as their Tengansob (landowner), would put medicine on their land, and would take it away from them.'[78] Although Hamile Naa Perwere flatly denied such accusations,[79] his hopes that the British would ultimately implement the majority decision were to be dashed. The Chief Commissioner was persuaded by Charles' arguments and decided that Hamile would continue to be subject to the Nandom Native Authority.[80] Any resistance to Hamile's administration by Nandom was henceforth subject to legal prosecution.[81] Moreover, in order to quickly intervene in Hamile if required, a contingent of mounted police was stationed in Nandom.[82] When the Happa Kuoro announced, shortly afterwards, that he, and not the Nandom Naa, would collect taxes in Hamile, the district commissioner threatened to imprison him and to close down the market.[83]

However, the Happa Kuoro not only sought to use tax collection to effect a *fait accompli*, he also hired one of the Gold Coast's best known lawyers, Dr J. B. Danquah, co-founder of the UGCC. The middleman who arranged contact with Danquah must have been K. Y. Baloro, of the chiefly house of Lambussie, at that time representing the Lawra Confederacy in the NTC. Danquah's readiness to represent Happa was probably politically motivated: such an opportunity would enable him to build networks in this part of the Northern Territories, and in fact Lambussie Kuoro Salifu and K. Y. Baloro later did become strong supporters of the United Party, an outgrowth of the UGCC tradition.[84] In his first letter to the Chief Commissioner, Danquah asserted that decisions as to where a particular place belonged administratively in no way fell under the jurisdiction of the native courts, and that therefore the Nandom court decision concerning Hamile could at best be regarded the outcome of an 'administrative enquiry'.[85] Further, there was no reason why the referendum, which was also a form of 'enquiry', should not be given equal weight to the Nandom court's findings. In any event, a failure to implement the plebiscite's outcome would amount to a violation of 'natural justice, democracy and good conscience', and undermine the 'Issalla tribes" trust in the administration. In a petition to the Governor of the Gold Coast, Danquah summarised the Happa Kuoro's central argument as follows:

> that the principle of dual control over Hamile, one Chief exercising religious and property rights over the land and its inhabitants, with another Chief collecting the taxes and tributes and levies from the people living on the said land and deriving their wealth from it, be rejected as a sure means of creating a lasting cause of friction between the two adjacent Native Authorities;
>
> that the admission on all sides that the Hamile land belongs to the Happa-Koro, Petitioner herein, and, with him, the 'Land Fetish' of Happa, should be recognised as over-riding all other claims;
>
> that the immediate Chief over Hamile village must be the Happa-Koro, and through him to the Lambussie Subordinate Area Native Authority.[86]

Yet the tacit compromise that landownership and political authority need not be identical was a fundamental premise for the establishment of the Lawra Confederacy. The new Issalla Tuntumer Native Authority also defined its area of sovereignty as 'all lands subject to the Chiefs of Lambussie, Samoa, Billo, Happa and Bangwon',[87] an ambiguous definition, as the Chief Commissioner pointed out.[88] No one would dispute, the Chief Commissioner argued, that Hamile was situated on land 'owned by' Happa, but it had never been politically 'subject to' Happa. The two-thousand-year-old maxim, 'render unto Caesar the things that are Caesar's', therefore should also apply to Hamile. The Governor adopted this position, informing Danquah that he would not overturn the decision.[89]

The rejection of the Happa Kuoro's petition was to be announced at the next Lawra Confederacy Council meeting, and police contingents in Hamile were provided with reinforcements.[90] Nevertheless violence nearly did break out when the Nandom Naa and his entourage of sixty men, armed with bows and arrows, axes, machetes and rifles, arrived in Hamile to count the cattle. Only the confiscation of weapons and the arrest of six of the ringleaders prevented a bloodbath, according to the police officer in charge.[91] This incident encouraged the headmen of the Wala, Mossi and Wangara in Hamile to emphasise once again that 'we ... will not at any time go under any other chief besides the Happa-Koro.'[92] But District Commissioner Charles only commented that these 'strangers' were 'at perfect liberty to move into an area administered by the Lambussie Native Authority.' If, however, they wished to remain in Hamile, they would have to recognise the powers of the Nandom Native Authority.[93]

British and local attitudes towards the political rights of 'stranger traders' were ambivalent, as this comment shows. On the one hand, they empha-sised the political prerogative of the Dagara 'natives', excluding 'strangers' from decision-making. Yet on the other hand, they granted the right to vote in the plebiscite to anyone having lived in Hamile at least ten years, including 'strangers'. The British, for their part, had not yet begun to stress this distinction between 'national' and 'foreign' outsiders, but the ambi-valence that led them to grant the 'stranger traders' a say, only to withdraw it again, was itself enough to contribute to the conflict's escalation

Settlement history on trial

Although his petition to the Governor was rejected, the Happa Kuoro did not give up, but, again represented by Dr Danquah, submitted a complaint to the Lawra Confederacy Court against the Kokoligu Naa, asking that the court find

> the town and land of Hamile are the property of the ... plaintiffs and that the people of Hamile ... can only pay tribute and dues in respect of their living on the land of Hamile to the chief of Happa ... according to the laws and customs of the Issala tribes.[94]

The proceedings turned into a protracted debate over the history of Hamile, the chieftaincy, the earth shrine and land ownership.[95]

The chiefs of Kokoligu and Nandom insisted that the first chief of Kokoligu acquired his office not from Happa but from the British, as a 'government made chief', and as such controlled 'Hamile and all the people inhabiting thereon'.[96] In addition, the Kokoligu Naa referred to the work of his predecessors in building the Hamile rest house and the road from Hamile to Nandom – a modern argument holding that political loyalty be rendered in return for the ruler's provision of services and 'development'. Conversely, the Happa Kuoro insisted that chiefly authority was rooted in the office of the earth priest and stressed that the Kokoligu Naa's forefathers had only been able to settle with the permission of the Happa earth priests. Without the latter's backing they would not have become chiefs either and would not have come to rule Hamile. Endorsement, however, depended on their good behaviour, the Happa Kuoro therefore demanding this office be returned to its original rightful incumbent, because the Kokoligu Naa was being 'disobedient' and violating custom.

The Happa Kuoro's claim that land ownership implied political control bore ample material for conflict, because it presupposed clearly defined earth-shrine boundaries and hierarchies. However, in Hamile, as in many other settlements, this was and still is disputed, leading to fierce debates over whether, and where, Happa 'owned' the Hamile lands. The Happa Kuoro's first petition had contained the essence of his version of the settlement history, namely that all land in Kokoligu and Hamile once belonged to his forefathers. In Kokoligu they then transferred land to Dagara immigrants, though not in Hamile, over which Happa continued to have unrestricted ownership rights.[97] The Lawra Confederacy chiefs, for their part, did concede that the Happa Kuoro had been the earth priest responsible for Hamile at the time of the conflict, but otherwise sought to dodge the sensitive topic of land ownership. Only towards the end of the court proceedings did they raise the issue of Happa's and Hamile's settlement histories, to which the Happa Kuoro replied that his great-grandfather 'came to Happa where his uncles settled and [was] given part of the land to settle. So as they [the uncles] are not living again the land of Happa is ours.' The judges, knowing more about the settlement history than they admitted, posed follow-up by asking: 'So the land belonged to uncles from Gyawie and not your grandfather's, is that not so?' To this the Happa Kuoro replied: 'They [the uncles] gave us the land and so if you give something to your son you cannot take it away from him and so the land is mine.'[98]

I cannot analyse here the complicated settlement histories of Happa, Kokoligu and Hamile in detail.[99] In the present context most important is that Happa's earth priests made their ownership claims to Happa and Hamile land not *qua* first-comer status, but rather *qua* inheritance from their maternal uncles from 'Gyawie' (Jaffien in my interviews), who had no male heirs, and whose lineage had therefore 'died out'. The Sisala earth priests of Hamile, who for their part regarded the Happa earth priests as their maternal uncles, also originally settled on Jaffien land, in Kokoligu, until the expanding Dagara drove them out. Their uncles from Happa came to the rescue, offering them refuge on Hamile land. The Hamile earth priests thus were granted their village territory by Happa's earth priests, though they had their own earth shrine and were able to settle subsequent immigrants, such as Muo and his family, by their own authority. Muo and the first Mossi therefore presented their traditional post-harvest gifts, straying animals and other found objects to the 'French Hamile land gods.'[100]

Until well into the 1930s, the inhabitants of Hamile-Zongo continued to consult the Hamile Sisala earth priests on French territory in all earth shrine-related matters. It was only when, at the start of the Second World War, to quell cross-border traffic the British established a large new market in Hamile-Zongo, that the Sisala earth priests from Happa became involved. As Nandom District Commissioner Termaghre later explained, they set up the shrine for the new market, and 'arrangements were made with the Haute Volta land fetish priest so that his duties were delegated to the Sissalas in Happa for the question of land fetish customary performance'.[101] Newcomers to Hamile-Zongo were now to go to Happa's earth priest for all earth-shrine matters. Only Hamile's older inhabitants remained loyal to the earth-priestly family on the French side of the border, immediately after the war again bringing their gifts to them instead of to

Happa. This is what provoked the Happa Kuoro's complaint to the court, in which he invoked his historical position as the original 'landgiver', without of course mentioning that his rights to these gifts derived from the relative recent transfer made necessary by the war.

It is clear that relations between the earth shrines of Hamile and Happa changed over time, particularly as border policies changed. The Lawra Confederacy Court judges were probably aware of these shifts and the settlement history's complexity and therefore avoided clarifying precisely the Happa Kuoro's rights of 'ownership'. In any case, they did not issue his requested 'declaration of title' stipulating 'that the town and land of Hamile are the property of the first and second plaintiffs'. Instead, they maintained that Hamile belonged politically to Kokoligu and Nandom. Despite this, most of my Sisala informants remembered this judgement as a victory for Happa, maybe because a ministerial decision in their favour soon followed, but perhaps also because the negotiations at least recognised Happa as responsible for Hamile's earth-shrine affairs, a move which strengthened Happa's position in the dispute with the earth priests of Hamile-French.

The decision of the Minister of Local Government

When the Nandom Naa wanted to assert his rights in practice, he discovered that on the very day he set out to collect the poll tax in Hamile, the Hamile Naa and the 'stranger headmen' were already on their way to deliver the tax revenues directly to the Lawra Confederacy central treasury.[102] While the Happa Kuoro threatened that the only response was 'to meet face to face with bows and arrows',[103] the Hamile secessionists drafted a new petition, this time to the Minister of Local Government.[104] They hoped for support from the newly elected CPP government, not only against Kokoligu and Nandom, but also against the District and Chief Commissioners.

District Commissioner Charles responded to the petitioners by insisting that the boundaries of the new local councils must without exception follow those of the former native authorities, and that Nandom was simply, for geographical reasons, 'the natural place for Hamile to look to'. Moreover, the status quo entirely suited certain Dagara farmers in Hamile, who would not say so openly for fear of reprisals. Although outnumbered by the traders, 'they are the earliest settlers, and should have greater consideration than stranger settlers'. Thus, Charles ultimately deployed the same discourse as the Happa Kuoro – special political rights resulting from first-comer status – except that he considered the Dagara, not the Sisala, to be the first-comers to British Hamile, and therefore 'natives'.[105]

However, very much to the surprise of the British and the Nandom Naa, the Minister of Local Government decided in spring 1952 to subordinate Hamile to the Lambussie Local Council. Although his decision only directly applied to local council membership, it also affected the chiefly hierarchy, and both the Hamile Naa and the 'stranger headmen' were regarded henceforward as chiefs under the Happa Kuoro and Lambussie. The Nandom Naa protested vehemently: it was he and his forefathers who had made Hamile what it had become, and for this reason Hamile tax revenues should not go to Lambussie. Lawra Naa Karbo and Jirapa Naa Yelpoe drafted an ominous letter in the name of the Lawra Confederacy, supporting Nandom and threatening 'forewarned, forearmed'. The only reason for conflict, according to Karbo and Yelpoe, were the Wala traders, and if the government did not reconsider its decision regarding Hamile, they would have no choice but to expel all Wala from Lawra District.[106] Still, the minister's decision stood.

The Hamile conflict may have offered the new CPP government an opportunity to demonstrate its independence from the British; the minister may also have been persuaded by the petitioners' argument that their democratic decision had not been respected. Although there is no indication of political manipulation at the national level, some ten years later Nandom Naa Imoru's successor Polkuu was entirely convinced that Hamile had only been reassigned to the Lambussie Local Council because of the party-political machinations of the NPP opposition. According to Polkuu, 'at the time' Nandom Naa Imoru was 'the only CPP supporting chief' in the whole of Lawra District, and 'the Dombos, the Karbos and other United Party Chiefs' had conspired against him in order to prevent the possibility that 'the Nandom Naa would influence the minds of all the people he ruled on to the side of the Convention People's Party.'[107] In fact, the oppositional NPP, in which Dombo and Karbo were both active, was only founded in 1954, and in 1952 Karbo was still supporting Imoru's claims to Hamile. Yet Polkuu's projection of political power struggles onto past events indicates the depth of the schisms created by local and partisan struggles in Lawra District since the mid-1950s – an issue to which we shall turn in the following chapter.

8

'THE TIME WHEN POLITICS CAME': PARTY POLITICS AND LOCAL CONFLICT

In January 1955 Prime Minister Kwame Nkrumah visited Lawra District. The welcome organised by the British Government Agent was to be the last opportunity for many years to come that Confederacy chiefs would meet peacefully. A delegation of elders sent by the Lawra Naa whose son was serving the oppositional NPP in Parliament presented its concerns that Lawra District CPP activists could 'give the Prime Minister a vociferous welcome as Life Chairman of the Party'. Yet the CPP district executive kept its promise 'that they would do nothing to detract from the dignity of the Prime Minister's visit' so that the 'meeting between the Prime Minister and the Lawra-Na went off well.'[1]

Shortly after this visit, however, the already problematic relations between the Nandom Naa and the Lambussie Kuoro, as well as those between the Nandom Naa and the Lawra Naa, grew increasingly tense. Not only did old conflicts over territorial boundaries and the entitlement to tax revenues resurface, but an attempt was also made to oust the Nandom Naa – which in turn intensified Nandom's desire to secede from the Lawra Confederacy. The fronts between divisional chiefs hardened so that the Regional Secretary in Tamale advised his successor to get used to the idea of the dissolution of the Lawra Confederacy, which had from the outset been an 'artificial creation' anyway.[2] In fact, the Lawra Confederacy State Council was dissolved in 1960 and split into four independent local councils in 1962 – Lawra, Jirapa, Nandom and Lambussie. Lawra Naa J. A. Karbo could but respond with resignation: 'The Lawra Confederacy days are gone and gone forever'.[3]

This time of conflict during the 1950s and early 1960s is locally remembered as 'the time when politics came', 'politics' referring here to party politics. While the inhabitants of Lawra District did not view Ghana's independence to be a decisive historical break, 'the time when politics came' marked a profound shift, in which all the long-standing local political rifts discussed in previous chapters became charged with party politics. The instrumentalisation was mutual: parties – particularly the CPP – took advantage of local political tensions to gain a foothold, while local litigants looked to party friends in the regional and national arena for support in asserting their own interests. The involvement of supra-local power blocks imparted local conflicts with an unprecedented divisiveness.[4]

Against this background of hardening conflict, the expression 'the time when politics came' may be understood as an attempt to externalise the causes of unresolved local animosities. 'Politics' is thus construed as an external force, exerted by national power elites, broaching a 'harmonious' local community, guided by 'tradition'. This dichotomisation of 'tradition' and 'politics', which even today characterises local political discussions, applies mainly to the chieftaincy. It was the massive interference of the government in Accra and of ruling party cadres in chieftaincy succession conflicts that brought the victorious candidates to their posts – at least according to explanations proffered by the defeated candidates and their supporters who claim 'tradition' to be on their side. Similar arguments were advanced in debates regarding local council, district, and constituency boundaries. In short, whoever wishes to discredit his opponent accuses him of using 'politics' to further his interests, of disregarding local criteria of legitimacy by pursuing special-interest politics with the aid of allies at the regional and national level.

Ethnic fronts played less of a role in the partisan clashes between different factions of the educated elite, between the divisional chiefs and between earth priests and chiefs. On the whole, the lines along which local factions and partisan alliances formed crosscut those of ethnicity, even if ethnicity was on occasion instrumentalised for partisan aims, as we shall see. But, shared ethnicity could also temper conflict, a tendency that will be discussed in the next chapter.

THE BEGINNINGS OF PARTY POLITICS IN LAWRA DISTRICT

The British two-party system, established after the Second World War in what would become Ghana, made it easier to link national party politics with local conflicts. Political platforms were largely irrelevant to the initial decision of party membership. Ideologically, all the chiefly houses tended to the NPP, but local power struggles often resulted in one faction – initially usually the 'losing' one – joining the CPP. However, reconstructing the history of these alliances is difficult, not only because they are complex and contingent, but also because those involved harbour much resentment and their accounts of the events are often contradictory. Nevertheless, in this section I will attempt to trace the emergence of party factions that continue to shape the present-day local political landscape. First, however, I would like to outline the views and organisations of the young educated elite, from which the parties' primary political actors would be recruited.

Football and political education: the 'literates' of Lawra District
Up until the 1954 elections the young educated elite was less concerned
with factional politics than with defining its own identity and role in a
predominately patriarchal agricultural society. The number of 'literates', as
school-leavers like to call themselves, a term distinguishing them from the
'illiterates', was limited. In 1945 a mere 33 pupils from Lawra Confederacy
were, thanks to native authority scholarships, able to attend the senior
school or teacher training college in Tamale. Ultimately the Lawra
Confederacy's investment in education produced 5 teachers and 5
'Standard VII' boys who worked as native authority clerks.[5] In addition
there were also the graduates of the mission schools and the Catholic
teachers' seminar in Navrongo. Nandom, the division with the highest level
of education, boasted 49 young men and women who had reached Standard
III and 16 who had completed Standard VII or higher – less than 1 per cent
of the total population.[6]

However, after the war, educational opportunities expanded considerably with the establishment of five new public primary schools – in Birifu,
Eremon, Duori, Nandom and Lambussie. In 1952 a second Catholic
primary school for girls opened its doors, the existing girls' school – founded
in Jirapa in 1940 – being unable to accommodate the demand any longer.
With the opening of a Catholic middle school in Nandom (1950) and the
Lawra Confederacy Middle School (1952) the district finally had its own
institutions of post-primary education. In 1957 the establishment of a
second public middle school in Burutu near Nandom followed. The senior
school in Tamale was turned into the Northern Territories' first secondary
school in 1951, dubbed 'Tamasco' by its graduates. Two years later, the
Catholics followed suit in opening St Charles, also in Tamale. However, St
Charles only took pupils as far as the GCE (General Certificate of
Education) O-level, while at Tamasco students could study through the
GCE A-level and qualify to attend university. St Charles graduates, who
wished to study at university, thus usually transferred to Tamasco for their
final two years. In 1960, the first pupils from Lawra District passed their A-
levels and went on to study in Legon (Accra) or abroad.[7]

Almost all young teachers working in the Lawra District schools hailed
from Lawra Confederacy. Because they all came from the same area and
had passed through the same educational system, they knew each other
quite well. Even the relationship between the teachers at mission schools
and those at local council schools was quite warm, at least initially. 'They
wanted to identify themselves as a class': This is how one informant stated
the purpose of the first informal meetings between 'literates'. Teachers,
native authority clerks, as well as older middle and secondary school
students, who spent their holidays at home, wanted to set themselves apart
from the illiterate peasants. At the ever popular 'end-of-the-year parties' or

at the weddings of fellow literates, those in attendance ate rice instead of millet porridge, drank bottled beer instead of locally brewed sorghum beer and listened to 'modern' music. According to one informant, it was only later that these 'literates' associations' became concerned with the loftier mission of village development.[8]

Central to the sense of camaraderie among the local educated elite were football matches. For a long time this sport was pursued almost exclusively by the literates, encouraging friendly competition between pupils and teachers from different villages. The first matches between the Nandom Mission School and the Lawra Native Authority School were even promoted by District Commissioner Amherst, a football enthusiast, to create unity 'between the just and the unjust'.[9] Since then football matches have become regular events at the chiefs' conferences and at receptions in honour of the Chief Commissioner or other important visitors.[10]

Beyond football the young literates were also interested in political education. In 1943 both District Commissioner Amherst and Naa Imoru inaugurated V (Victory) Clubs in Lawra and Nandom respectively, which were charged with collecting donations for the British Army, but which also held monthly 'discussion circles'.[11] After the war, these activities continued under the Lawra Literary and Social Club, whose members even set up a club house. The club, reported District Commissioner Smeddle, had 'a good library, some indoor games, a tilly lamp, kerosene supply, a solvent cash account and enthusiasm.'[12] The topics of the various talks and discussions ranged from information regarding the British Labour Party to scientific matters.[13] A few years later, the Department of Extra-Mural Studies of the newly founded University College of the Gold Coast even sent to the Northern Territories a 'resident tutor', who in fourteen-day cycles drove through all the Northern district towns holding lectures on political history, constitutional law and the like. Between visits there were boxes of books that served to supplement the curriculum, which included, for example, the works of Rattray on the Asante, Sir Ivor Jennings' monograph on the British constitution and Erskine May's *Parliamentary Practice*. The three young tutors – William Tordoff (1951–2), Dennis Austin (1952–5) and Ivor Wilks (1955–8), who would later become well-known political scientists and historians – were politically inclined to the British Labour Party and saw it their mission to prepare the future political elite for independence.[14]

In the villages and towns the educated organised themselves in branches of the People's Education Association (PEA), which arranged the tutors' lecture series and the occasional weekend seminar with neighbouring branches.[15] Once a year PEA delegates from the Northern Territories, Ashanti and the Gold Coast Colony gathered at the annual summer school, which ran several days and whose daytime programme included a variety of courses and lectures held by politicians, judges and high-ranking civil servants, while evening highlights included such festive events as dances and plays.[16] The PEA branches were training grounds for future political activists. For example, S. W. D. K. Gandah, one of the Birifu Naa's sons, served as secretary of the PEA Tumu, and then, as personal secretary to S. D. Dombo, helped establish the NPP in Lawra and Tumu Districts.[17] In the Nandom branch of PEA both Polkuu – member of the Nandom chiefly family, headmaster of the Nandom Local Council School and CPP sympathiser – as well as Silvester Sanziri – teacher at the mission school and future member of the NPP – were active. Both ran in the 1954 elections against the NPP candidate Abayifaa Karbo, who at the time was serving as secretary of the Lawra branch of PEA. Due in part to the competition inherent in the electoral process, but mostly to their becoming embroiled in local political battles, the shared sense of being 'literates' was eventually superseded by party loyalties, and most of the PEA branches dissolved or transformed themselves into local branches of one of the two parties.

The candidates
Until the 1954 elections, the young teachers' and clerks' interest in political issues did not entail active involvement in party politics. S. D. Dombo, as discussed earlier, found himself quite accidentally in the role of the opposition. Some of my informants doubted that there was a single CPP member in the Lawra Confederacy before 1954. Severio Termaghre, who later became Lawra (and Nandom) District Commissioner, claims to have been one of the first CPP activists in the area. He was one of the first graduates from St Paul's Primary, and during his teacher training in Navrongo, 1947–9, came into contact with the UGCC and later the CPP. The latter's 'anti-imperialism' attracted him, he explained, because of the conflicts he had had with his white teachers and his subsequent superiors – Termaghre taught for some time in the Jirapa and Nandom mission schools. Despite his sympathies for the CPP, however, he decided to run for parliament in 1954 as an independent, 'in order to divide potential voters of Abayifaa Karbo'.[18]

The CPP candidate for the Lawra-Nandom constituency was the new Birifu Naa, Nonatuo Gandah. A news report accorded Birifu a local party branch with 300 to 400 members as early as 1952, a figure most likely stated to journalists by an optimistic CPP secretary at the Tamale headquarters.[19] Jack Goody, who conducted fieldwork in Birifu from August 1950 until the end of 1951 and who even became a CPP party member, reported that during his entire stay not a single party meeting took place.[20] Decisive for Nonatuo's CPP membership, at least according to his brother and NPP organiser S. W. D. K. Gandah, were monetary and power interests. When it became obvious that Abayifaa Karbo would run for the NPP, Nonatuo's aspirations could only be realised with the CPP's help.[21] Whatever the case might have been, the CPP demand for 'self-government now' must have been attractive for the Birifu educated elite who wanted to break away from Lawra and who hoped that a CPP government would grant them their own local council.

Which factions of the Nandom chiefly house were affiliated with which party, and since when, is controversial. Nandom Naa Charles Imoro, for instance, is certain that his father, Nandom Naa Imoru, had been a staunch CPP member from the very beginning.[22] Termaghre and others insisted, on the other hand, that Imoru moved closer to the CPP only after the 1956 elections in response to chieftaincy conflicts in which his internal opponents formed alliances with Lawra Naa J. A. Karbo and the NPP. However, all interviewees agreed that party preferences in the chiefly house of Nandom were closely linked to competition between Imoru and Karbo. When it became clear that Karbo's son Abayifaa would stand for the NPP, Imoru supported his cousin Polkuu's candidacy. Polkuu himself, according to one Nandom NPP supporter, 'wanted to go to parliament because why should Karbo go and he would not go, so he also stood – as an independent.'[23]

Abayifaa Karbo's reconstruction of the 1954 nomination of candidates emphasised that CPP party strategists plotted to break his father's pro-NPP influence. Nandom Naa Imoru had, like all the other chiefs, participated in the NPP inaugural congress in Tamale,[24] and found the CPP's plan to let his cousin Polkuu stand on the party ticket 'dangerous'. The CPP then hoped, Karbo explained, that the candidature of the Birifu Naa would split the Lawra vote, and Polkuu, 'coming from the chief's palace ... would collect the whole vote of Nandom. This was a CPP gamble, yes. And they lost!'[25]

Besides such party tactical considerations, hopes that the candidates would actually get into parliament must have also played a role. After all, all candidates in the Lawra-Nandom and Jirapa-Lambussie constituencies had been trained as teachers. Although one prerequisite for nomination was the resignation from state employment, teachers were often re-appointed after losing an election, meaning the risk was comparatively low and the potential gains rather lucrative – a parliamentarian's salary amounting to six times that of a teacher. Moreover, the older generation's success in politics encouraged their younger schoolmates to follow suit. Jirapa Naa Bapenyiri Yelpoe, for instance, standing as an independent candidate in Jirapa-Lambussie in 1954, recalled his determination to compete with the older and politically much more experienced S. D. Dombo: 'Because we were all schoolmates ... I felt I was capable of being a politician too.'[26]

With Silvester Sanziri, the fifth candidate in the Lawra-Nandom constituency, we see yet another motive: growing tensions between mission school graduates and chiefly sons coming out of native authority schools. Sanziri, like Termaghre, attended St Paul's Primary School, afterwards

Plate 5 Abayifaa Karbo, Member of Parliament, 1954 (with kind permission of Ghana Information Services, Accra)

continuing his education at the Navrongo Catholic Teacher Training College. From 1950 onwards, he taught in Nandom. When asked how he got started in politics, he recalled the influence of Peter Dery, later Archbishop of Tamale, who was entrusted with the supervision of the

B. YELPOE II JIRAPA - NA 1ˢᵗ Ju 1962

Plate 6 Jirapa Naa Bapenyiri Yelpoe, with the King George Medal for Chiefs (3")
and the King's Medal for African Chiefs for long and loyal service to Government,
1962 (with kind permission of Jirapa Naa B. Yelpoe)

Catholic schools in the North-West. Sanziri recalled that Dery admonished mission school teachers not to sit 'aloof ... and allow only ... the chiefs' sons to involve themselves in politics.' The White Fathers, as expatriates, had been careful to stay out of political matters and cautioned their students to do the same, but Dery 'believed that politics is ... for everybody, whether priest or civil servant or any other person'.[27] He did not endorse a particular political party, but sympathies among Catholic teachers clearly tended towards the NPP. However, since Karbo had already been nominated by NPP cadres, Sanziri had to stand as an independent. It was only in 1969 that Sanziri, now running directly for a party in the UP tradition, was elected to parliament as the first politician from Lawra District not affiliated with a chiefly house.

Election campaigns and results
Lawra Government Agent Wallace, acting as electoral officer, reported in May 1954 that the Jirapa Naa had complained of political party pressure – Wallace suspected the NPP, in the person of S. D. Dombo. Wallace recommended 'that he [Jirapa Naa] remain completely neutral and should not support any candidate or political party', or risk alienating those who did not share his political convictions.[28] Nothing could have been further removed from local political realities than this advice. Indeed, soon enough Wallace reported complaints from S. D. Dombo that the Jirapa Naa threatened to record the names of all those who would not vote for his son.[29] The Birifu Naa accused the Lawra Naa of similar tactics, although the latter naturally denied exerting any illegal influence upon voters.

But generally, voters were pressured by much subtler means: appeals to duty, loyalty and respect towards the chief partial to a certain candidate, towards the candidate as the 'son' of one's own patriclan, or towards the catechetists' or teachers' endorsement. Respect for the chief's opinion, however, was never absolute. Candidates Gandah and Dombo, for instance, were themselves influential sub-divisional chiefs able to mobilise their following against the party affiliations of their divisional chiefs. In Lambussie and Lawra, where divisional chiefs supported the NPP, their competitors who had been defeated in earlier succession conflicts, joined the CPP. Furthermore, some Lambussie sub-divisional chiefs, such as the Samoa Kuoro, backed the CPP out of protest against the Lambussie Kuoro's pretensions to authority. In Nandom, too, the divisional chief's wish was sometimes ignored, as Sanziri's comparatively strong electoral results testify. In many villages, families followed neither their headman's or divisional chief's dictum nor the catechetists' support for the NPP – some because they harboured a grudge against the chief, and others because, as former labour migrants in the South, they had become more familiar with the CPP.
'Voting ... was still mainly on the lines of family ties and traditional

loyalties', wrote the Lawra Government Agent after the 1956 elections, emphasising the low interest in party platforms.[30] However, voters had to decide between different 'traditional loyalties', and in some cases the question of party support even divided families, as the case of the Gandah brothers illustrates. Furthermore, even illiterates knew the party slogans and symbols – the cock for CPP and the fist for NPP. Although detailed party programmes may not have mattered, the local candidates' campaigns did impress the binary opposition between CPP and NPP upon many villagers. 'Food' was a metaphor often used in the electoral campaign. One informant recalled how Nandom Naa Imoru called on all to vote for Polkuu in the 1954 election, cautioning against the CPP with the argument 'that those who followed the party down South were boiling a cow's head in their soup [i.e. were rich] whereas we in the North had only got a goat's head [i.e. were left poor]'.[31] The North-South divide, to which Imoru referred, was the dominant theme in the NPP campaign. The campaign speakers knew that a majority of the men in each village once worked in the South and experienced discrimination against backward Northerners. Hence, NPP demands for a more gradual transition to independence and more development in the North were well received by illiterates. How much party propaganda influenced the final outcome of the election is a matter of debate; however, it is important to rectify the image of a pre-political peasantry, blindly following their chiefs, commonly held by district commissioners. 'Traditional loyalties' were important, but they cannot be regarded as the sole determinant, and they certainly did not prevent new forms of party discourse from taking root in the villages.

On 10 June 1954 the Northern Territories voted. In Lawra Confederacy over 90 per cent of registered voters went to the ballot, and in many places elections resembled 'a new festival', as one colonial officer described the mood at the time.[32] Ballot counts in Lawra-Nandom constituency registered 27.6 per cent (of 10,034 votes) for the NPP candidate Abayifaa Karbo; 24.2 per cent for the CPP candidate Nonatuo Gandah; 18.6 per cent for Sylvester Sanziri; 15.7 per cent for Konkuu Polkuu, and only 5 per cent for Severio Termaghre. S. D. Dombo won the Jirapa-Lambussie constituency for the NPP with 44.4 per cent of the vote (out of a total of 9,527 votes), defeating the independent candidate Bapenyiri Yelpoe.[33]

That Karbo won with a relatively small majority led the Birifu Naa Gandah to suspect that the Lawra Naa had manipulated the elections in his son's favour. The Lawra Government Agent pointed out that such an accusation required hard evidence and advised him to consult his party headquarters (which also felt that a formal complaint in court did not look promising). As a result, the Birifu Naa became even more determined to secede from Lawra.[34] Similarly embittered were the other defeated candidates and their supporters. Among the literates especially, friendships and common ties now fell to party politics. Relations between local council and mission schools in Nandom became increasingly tense. As Oscar Pagzu, a mission school pupil who later joined the CPP, related,

> it was a very bitter time. Members of the two parties could not sit down ... and be drinking beer together. ... Now I will not agree as an UP man to go and sit down and teach children from a CPP family. It started getting mad, particularly after 1956![35]

That party fronts hardened is also borne out by the fact that during the 1956 elections candidates no longer ran as independents. In Lawra-Nandom Constituency, Polkuu and Termaghre now openly supported the CPP candidate Gandah, while Silvester Sanziri mobilised his supporters for Abayifaa Karbo, who this time won 73.3 per cent of the votes.[36] Meanwhile, Jirapa Naa Yelpoe's son Bapenyiri, who had succeeded his father as chief in 1955, was not prepared to risk an electoral defeat, so R. G. Gariba, son of Sabuli Naa, the highest-ranking sub-divisional chief in Jirapa Division, stood for the CPP in Jirapa-Lambussie Constituency, but failed to win against Dombo.

Although the nomination process fed on old rivalries, it was the campaigns and the elections themselves that hardened the fronts between conflicting actors. Particularly after the 1956 elections, which even at the village level had been more polarised than those of 1954, the conflicts between divisional chiefs and within the divisions themselves intensified, a development foreshadowing the turmoil to befall party politics.

PARTY POLITICS, LAND DISPUTES AND SUCCESSSION CONFLICTS

Until 1958–9 the NPP/UP dominated Lawra District, while the CPP held an absolute majority everywhere else. In this political environment the formation of alliances and the consolidation of political fronts was exceedingly complex. In principle, whoever was defeated locally could try to take advantage of the opposing political majorities either in the district, the regional or the national arena. The following pages will illustrate how a whole array of prior conflicts – over land, administrative boundaries, taxation, the rights of earth priests and chiefs, as well as chiefly succession – fed into party politics and how in the process ethnic and traditional lines of argumentation mingled with newer political discourses on democracy and anti-imperialism.

The Dahile–Bapula conflict: a dispute over land use and taxes

Soon after the 1948 restoration of Nandom and Lambussie Divisions as separate administrative entities of equal status, disputes over administrative boundaries and the taxation of compounds along the border, which had already been a source of conflict in the 1930s, welled up once again.[37] Not all disputes were recorded, but the case of Dahile and Bapula – two Sisala villages along the Lambussie–Nandom border, in which numerous Dagara farmers had settled – were. Shortly before the 1955 agricultural season, Lambussie Kuoro Salifu told Nandom Naa Imoru that his subjects would no longer be allowed to farm Lambussie land. With this move Salifu hoped to force Dagara compounds in Dahile and Bapula to pay their taxes to the Lambussie Local Council instead of to Nandom. Moreover, he wanted to impress upon the territorially less well-endowed Nandom that in this respect it was at Lambussie's mercy. Every Nandome wishing to farm Sisala land, so Salifu claimed, 'should have his name registered there [in Lambussie] before farming to ensure paying his rates and liquor licences there'. When the conflict came before the Lawra Confederacy State Council, Salifu explained that he was left no choice in the matter, since he feared that 'one day Nandom people will claim the land to be theirs and may kill my children because of the farm.'[38] The basic pattern evident in this dispute would also characterise the disputes during the 1960s and 1980s: These were without fail provoked by the (re-)establishment of an administrative boundary between Nandom and Lambussie, with new factors exacerbating the conflict each time.

In 1955–6 one such factor was the emergence of party fronts. Salifu was counting on the support of the Lawra Naa – a friend, fellow NPP member and President of the Confederacy State Council – to assert his claims. Additionally, there were conflicts between the Nandom earth priests and the Nandom chiefly family, which were voiced in terms of party opposition and weakened the Nandom Naa's position in the land conflicts with Lambussie. Finally, the old Sisala chief of Dahile, on friendly terms with the Nandom chiefs and having once allowed Dagara compounds in his village to pay their taxes to Nandom, died in 1953,[39] and his successor supported Salifu's tougher course.

The Lawra Confederacy State Council established a commission of inquiry to investigate the root of the conflict. In one session Salifu testified that the Dahile earth priest had performed the groundbreaking rituals necessary to begin house construction for the thirteen Dagara compounds on which the dispute centred – six of these in Dahile and seven in neighbouring Bapula – meaning these compounds were politically a part of Dahile and therefore also Lambussie. Only because Lambussie Division was once subject to Nandom, did the compounds pay their taxes to Nandom, a situation to which it seems they had grown accustomed. But now, after regaining autonomy from Nandom, they had to pay allegiance to Lambussie. In response, Nandom Naa Imoru referred to an agreement between Lambussie Kuoro Yesibie and Nandom Naa Boro which allowed the Dahile Dagara peasants to 'be following and doing everything for the

Nandom Local Council'. The Dahile earth priest testified that his land extended 'as far as from here [Dahile] to the Volta'; yet he could not specify the border with Nandom, since 'the elderly people did not show us the boundary'. One of the heads of the compounds in question admitted that all Dagara in Dahile and Bapula respected the directives of the Dahile earth priest, but also declared that he was not prepared to 'follow' the Lambussie Local Council in political matters.[40]

The commission finally recommended the Nandom Naa recognise the Lambussie Kuoro's authority over the thirteen disputed compounds, but that peasants who merely farmed and did not reside on Lambussie land, should not be taxed.[41] The State Council adopted these recommendations, but Imoru protested vehemently, and the affected Dagara compounds refused to implement the decision.[42] Imoru's uncompromising stance was reinforced as the party fronts hardened. The commission's efforts were finally undone with the 1956 election campaign in which Imoru openly supported the CPP candidate. Whether Imoru requested the Government Agent's involvement or whether the latter did so of his own accord is uncertain, but the latter informed the State Council that it was not authorised to issue decisions regarding land conflicts.[43] With his position strengthened by this announcement Imoru wrote a forceful letter to the Lawra Naa re-stating his position and petitioned the Chief Regional Officer for the establishment of a Nandom State Council that would be autonomous from the Lawra Confederacy.[44] Lawra Naa Karbo felt the letter to be a personal insult and regarded the petition as a declaration of war.[45] He therefore made it his mission to ensure the Nandom Naa be destooled, counting on support from the Nandom earth priest, among others.

Nandom téŋgàndèm *versus Nandom Naa*
Tensions between earth priests and chiefs go back to when native authorities were first introduced, and when, as a result, earth priests were forced to share a portion of their income – such as that derived from market fees – with chiefs. Rent and building permit fees, which the native authorities collected from the growing number of Wala, Mossi, Wangara, Hausa and Yoruba traders who came to settle in Lawra District, became a lucrative source of income. Naturally, the earth priests wanted their share of this, and thus evoked their traditional rights vis-à-vis the construction of houses. Once the new local councils were introduced, the Nandom earth priests living in Nandomkpee demanded their village be awarded its own electoral ward, citing their status as 'original inhabitants and land owners of the whole area of Nandom'. They claimed to need their own representative in the Nandom Local Council, since up until then their right to have a say in matters regarding 'native customs concerning the land' had been denied.[46] Nandomkpee was eventually granted the right to present one of the two

councillors sitting on the ward of 'Nandom town'. However, the earth priests' views on the 'native customs' with respect to land provoked serious controversy. The building permit for the United African Company (UAC) became a particularly salient bone of contention between the earth-priestly and the chiefly family.

When the Lawra Government Agent submitted the UAC manager's building request to Nandom Naa Imoru, the latter responded that he and the *tèngánsòb* Soglikuu had approved it, but that Soglikuu wanted a yearly 'commission on the store'.[47] Shortly thereafter – in a move probably incited by the Nandom Naa – Dasoberi, the Government Agent's interpreter and member of the Nandom chiefly family, expounded the 'Native Custom of a Tingansob when building a new Compound', claiming that the earth priest was not actually entitled to any commissions beyond the customary sacrifices.[48] To 'receive any money for the use of the land', constituted a violation of 'Native Custom'. In a sharp response Soglikuu questioned Dasoberi's competence in matters regarding Nandom tradition, claiming that the rituals described by the latter were 'in the majority not the native customs of … this part of the district', and, moreover, the earth priest was indeed entitled to demand a commission on the tax that the Nandom Local Council collected from shopkeepers.[49]

The records provide no further information as to the subsequent course of events, but it is unlikely that Soglikuu asserted his standpoint in practice, and so he used the Dahile conflict a few years later to bolster his claims. In any event he complained to the commission of inquiry that he was never informed of the UAC's construction plans – just as he had not been informed earlier regarding those of the mission. When he protested against this state of affairs, Imoru demanded he submit the appropriate 'application',[50] which he did, but to which Imoru never responded. Finally, matters came to a head in a raucous confrontation, and Imoru 'told us that we could go on spoiling his work as a chief and he also in turn would go on spoiling our customary rights.'[51] Because of this past 'insult' Soglikuu now refused to support the Nandom Naa in the Dahile conflict. While the commission agreed with Imoru that Soglikuu should not be allowed to settle old scores, it warned Imoru that he 'should have little or nothing at all to do with building purposes', this being the concern of 'the Tengandem'.[52] Imoru must have regarded this admonition to be more than unacceptable meddling, as part of a political conspiracy against him – the majority of the State Council's commission of inquiry and the Nandom earth-priest family being NPP supporters. Then, just one year later the earth priests cited the conflict over the UAC store as one of the reasons why the Nandom Naa must be destooled.

Lawra Confederacy State Council versus Nandom Naa Imoru

Since Imoru announced his desire to secede, he and his supporters no longer participated in Confederacy State Council meetings and were thus not present when in February 1957 Lawra Naa Karbo had the case put on the agenda. A petition submitted by Nandomkpee Naa Kuuyele, a member of the Nandom earth-priest family, and signed by headmen and earth priests from fourteen villages in Nandom Division, demanded the Nandom Naa's destoolment.[53] Kuuyele and two petitioners, who accompanied him to Lawra, criticised first and foremost that the Nandom Naa had, without consulting the sub-divisional chiefs, decided that he wished to secede. In response the State Council suspended the Nandom Naa from office until his conflict with the sub-chiefs was resolved.[54]

The Nandom Naa's refusal to submit to this provisional removal from office became evident when he travelled to Accra for the independence day festivities, presenting himself as the Lawra Confederacy representative, in defiance of the State Council's decision that only the Lawra Naa should travel to Accra.[55] After Imoru's return from the capital, relations between the Lawra and Nandom chiefly families were so tense that minor provocation risked a violent response. Yet the refusal to show respect at a funeral, as Imoru interpreted the Lawra Naa's behaviour, was a serious one. During a funeral at the Nandom Naa's home the chiefs of Lawra and Jirapa, followed by a large entourage, travelled to a celebration in Ko, in Nandom Division, right past the site where the funeral was held. During the return to Lawra from Ko, some young men from the Nandom chiefly family attacked the Lawra Naa's dancers, apparently beating them mercilessly.[56]

At the next meeting of the Lawra Confederacy State Council in April 1957 all twenty signatories to the petition against Imoru were present. Of the Nandom State Council members only the Tuopari Naa showed up, thereby publicly demonstrating his desire to secede from Nandom Division. This time Kuuyule argued, referring to the attack on the Lawra Naa's dance troupe, that the strongest argument for the removal of Imoru was that '[t]here was blood shed which was against the Nandom Tengani'.[57] Petro from Dangko added that Imoru's actions were 'creating perpetual hatred for them all [the Nandom people]'. Kuuyele listed further complaints, which other petitioners repeated in various forms: the arbitrary secession from the Lawra Confederacy, the disregard of the earth priest in the matter of the UAC store, and finally Imoru's responsibility for Hamile's secession from Nandom Division. The State Council echoed these arguments and decided that

> in accordance with the customary law of our land and the rules of our chieftaincy, the turner of office of C. P. Imoru can no longer be trusted. ... only distoolment [*sic*] ... will bring about peace and order

in the affected division – Nandom. It was by the votes of we the chiefs of the Lawra Conf. District State Council and the majority of the people of Nandom Division that C. P. Imoru was installed chief. By our vote and the concencous [*sic*] of opinion of the Nandom people, we do hereby remove C. P. Imoru from his office as a chief.[58]

Interestingly, one of Kuuyule's complaints was not mentioned in the State Council's resolution, namely that regarding Imoru's attempts to induce all chiefs to vote for the CPP. Although the party political differences were one of the driving forces behind the attack on Imoru, they were officially not allowed to play a role in chieftaincy matters.

The question of what constituted and who had the power to define the 'rules of our chieftaincy' subsequently led to a vehement controversy between the British Government Agent and the Lawra Naa. While the State Council decided that the Gegenkpe Naa, as the oldest sub-divisional chief, would carry out the official duties of Nandom Division until a new divisional chief was instated,[59] the Government Agent countered 'that Government will continue to recognise the Nandom-Na as the properly appointed Head Chief of the Nandom Division'. The British administrator challenged the authority of the Confederacy State Council to remove a divisional chief from office, supporting his argument by quoting from the 'early history of the District as set out in the District Record Books'.[60] The Lawra Naa sharply reprimanded the Government Agent insisting that 'the law comes first before District Record Books' and that he should keep his 'personal opinions' to himself, since they only undermined the 'lawful authority of the Lawra Conf. State Council'. Moreover, these same District Record Books clearly showed that the late Jirapa Naa, the current Lambussie Kuoro and the now destooled Nandom Naa had all been instated following elections, in which all chiefs in the Confederacy had cast their votes.[61] What Lawra Naa Karbo did not mention was that the Confederacy State Council had since then done away with such 'balloting for chiefship'.[62] Besides, the divisional chiefs had never been able to agree upon the procedure to destool a chief.[63]

Imoru himself did not rely on 'customary law', but on the support of the newly elected CPP government. He appealed the Confederacy's decision to the Chief Regional Officer and certainly did not let the situation stop him from representing Nandom Division at the great durbar in Tamale that was to mark the end of the British treaties of protection with the Northern Territories.[64] For Imoru's opponents this simply constituted a further provocation. So, when the Chief Regional Officer finally visited Nandom, the petitioners awaited him. It is unclear whether Imoru really felt threatened or whether he just took advantage of the situation, nevertheless he managed to have the officer from Tamale arrest 'the troublemakers' for disturbing the peace. Reportedly a dozen men were arrested and fined ten pounds each; but the sentence was overturned in an appeal submitted with the help of lawyer and member of the opposition, Joe Appiah. On the very night the released men were to go to Lawra to be reimbursed the sum of the fine, a rumour spread like wildfire that the Nandom Naa was dead.[65]

While the above account may or may not be true, it is certain Nandom Naa C. P. Imoru died on Christmas Day in 1957 – 'after brief illness', according to a telegraph sent by the Government Agent to Tamale,[66] or, according to an official statement made six months later by his successor Polkuu, 'owing to internal troubles from malcontents of Nandom and external troubles from the other members of the Confederacy who resisted his ambition and determination to break away from the Confederacy'.[67] His son claimed that Imoru had been killed by 'African mechanics – poison and other things', 'because my father was the only CPP ... surrounded by UPs'.[68]

The conflict over succession to the Nandom chieftaincy[69]

Since the end of 1957 a Ghanaian Regional Commissioner appointed by the CPP government had replaced the British Chief Commissioner in Tamale. Abavana, the first appointee, was an old school friend of Severio Termaghre's, and he ensured that the controversy over Imoru's successor was brought before a government commission of inquiry – instead of the Lawra Confederacy State Council – which ultimately decided in favour of the pro-CPP candidate, Polkuu. Yuori ran against him, enjoying the support of the Nandom earth priests and all those pro-NPP headmen and chiefs who had petitioned against Imoru. While Yuori argued that the earth priests had chosen him to be the new chief – as tradition demanded – Polkuu insisted that Imoru had appointed him successor as he lay dying and had done so in the presence of his sub-divisional chiefs.[70]

Despite the Government Agent's reprimands, both candidates had themselves enstooled as chief of Nandom in March 1958 – Polkuu by his supporters among the 'royal family' and Yuori by the earth priest Soglikuu and the pro-NPP chiefs. What ensued was a drawn-out conflict over sinecures and the exercise of power.[71] Yuori complained that Polkuu was openly campaigning for a CPP candidate in the up-coming local elections 'exercising his powers as a Chief.'[72] Polkuu's supporters, however, insisted that the Regional Commissioner officially recognise their candidate immediately, arguing that Nandom was in need of a strong hand, particularly during elections.[73]

At the end of April S. D. Opoku-Afari, Appeal Commissioner of the Ministry of Local Government in charge, J. A. Z. Andan, a Dagomba chief, and Nana Kwadjo Ahinkora II, the Ohene of Asuboa in Ashanti Region, were called to serve on a commission that was 'to inquire into the correct method of selecting a Nandom-Na and to report whether Konkou Polkuu

Paul or Borrow Yuori is properly the occupant of the Nandom skin'.[74] The announcement alone was biased in two ways: first in deciding to keep the NPP-dominated Lawra Confederacy Council out of the matter, and second by interpreting the name K. P. Paul as Konkou Polkuu Paul. According to Yuori, the initials K. P. did not actually stand for Konkou Polkuu, but rather Kolor Polkuu; and since Kolor himself was no chief, his son Polkuu was not entitled to the office either.[75] But the commission ignored his objection, and beginning in late June – after the local government elections – it convened for ten sessions. Polkuu represented himself, while Yuori was counselled by Joe Reindorf, a pro-UP lawyer from the offices of Danquah and Owusu, a firm that had back in 1950 represented the Happa Kuoro in the Hamile conflict. Earth priest Soglikuu and members of the 'royal family' testified as witnesses.

Since according to official discourse politics was not to play a role in chieftaincy affairs, the commission debated the issue of chiefly succession only in terms of the proper definition of 'tradition'. The conflicting accounts of the Nandom chieftaincy's origin presented to the commission are very similar to those I heard some thirty years later[76] – they probably first came to a head in the conflict between Polkuu and Yuori. The controversy predictably centred on the Nandom earth priest's role in the enskinment of the Nandom Naa. Polkuu's case rested on arguing that the tèŋgánsòb exercised no influence on the choice and enskinment of the Nandom chief. He testified that the office of chief followed from the holding of other leadership positions, which had already in pre-colonial times been exercised by 'individuals who were rich, kind and obliging and commanded respect among the community', just as his great-grandfather Kyiir had done, who 'was virtually a chief of his people'.[77] Yuori countered that the 'people acknowledged the Tingansob as their Chief' and that it was 'the Tingansob who installed Chiir officially as the Nandom-Na.'[78] From this he concluded that traditionally 'the Tingansob selects a chief and presents him to the People'.[79] However, Yuori's further testimony by no means conclusively showed that this was indeed a valid tradition, as the commission emphasised, since, even according to Yuori, his father Boro had named his successor as he lay dying – a practice to which Polkuu had actually referred in making *his* case. The commission summarised '[t]he sum-total of the evidence' entirely in Polkuu's favour, stating, 'that the dying chief and the members of the Chief's family are responsible for the selection of a chief in Nandom'.[80] Polkuu had been made chief by means of *both* practices and was therefore to be judged 'properly the occupant of the Nandom Skin'.[81]

The commission's decision was upheld by the Governor and announced in the Ghanaian official gazette.[82] However, Yuori and his supporters appealed, no longer citing the earth priests' prerogative, but the idea that chiefs were elected to office. This notion, once introduced by the British, was now declared to be the 'customary way of election of a new Naa' in situations of 'rivalry about the chieftaincy' as well as an affirmation of the people's democratic rights. The chief, the petitioners insisted – alluding to popular CPP rhetoric – 'is not going to rule only the Royal Family but all the people and therefore we the masses are at liberty to give our wish which must be respected.'[83] The Regional Commissioner responded that the commission of inquiry's decisions were not subject to appeal;[84] and Yuori lacked allies in order to assert his views. Then, in the summer of 1959, the British Government Agent in Lawra was replaced by a CPP-appointed District Commissioner – Severio Termaghre, an unequivocal supporter of Polkuu's. As for Polkuu himself, he proceeded to destool Nandomkpee Naa Kuuyele, along with other chiefs who had supported Yuori. Their protests that the Nandom Naa had no right to destool them were ignored.[85]

As Yuori's supporters even today resentfully summarise the events: 'Polkuu was able to win through politics'. However, the latter soon endeavoured to make peace with his opponents, enabling him in time to consolidate his position to such an extent that he not only survived Kwame Nkrumah's overthrow unscathed, but was even called upon by the new government to serve on the constitutional committee. Polkuu was to remain in office longer than any of his predecessors, twenty-six years in total, and he held numerous public offices at both the local and national level. But maybe because he demonstrated that a chief could play such a prominent public role, the conflicts over his succession immediately resurfaced, and once again the defeated candidates accused Charles Imoro, whom the Rawlings government gazetted Nandom Naa, of having succeeded only because of clever political manoeuvring.[86]

TOWARDS CPP HEGEMONY: THE DISSOLUTION OF THE LAWRA CONFEDERACY

Lawra was the only district in the entire North, in which the UP still secured a majority in the 1958 local government elections; but the CPP was catching up.[87] The battle over political hegemony within the district became more bitter than ever. In order to undermine the political dominance of the Lawra Naa and the UP, CPP supporters endeavoured to effect the dissolution of the Lawra Confederacy State Council. But the local political 'underdogs' only profited briefly from their alliance with the CPP. As soon as the former NPP/UP activists joined the CPP, older hierarchies and power relations prevailed once again. This is quite evident in two conflicts: that over the establishment of a Nandom-Lambussie District and the renewal of the dispute over Hamile's administrative subordination. During these conflicts the parties not only argued along party lines, but also in terms of ethnic boundaries and the differing political rights of 'natives' and 'strangers'.

The demise of the Lawra Confederacy State Council
The April 1960 plebiscite that was to ratify the new Republican constitution
and elect a president was one of the last opportunities in which the
opposition could express itself publicly. In the North, an average of 85 per
cent voted for the new constitution and for Nkrumah as President,[88] but in
Lawra District this was only 65 per cent.[89] In Lawra Division the UP still
managed to secure just over half the votes. Support for Nkrumah came
primarily from Birifu, a staunch opponent to the Lawra Naa, and from
Konyukuo, an area populated by traders.[90] Even in Nandom Division the
UP managed to capture 38 per cent of the vote and secured a majority
primarily in Nandomkpee, Kogle, Ko and Gegenkpe. The CPP made the
greatest strides in Jirapa and Lambussie, where UP opposition shrank to a
quarter of the vote.

Now the Jirapa Naa, too, demanded the dissolution of the Lawra
Confederacy State Council – just as Nandom had done – arguing that the
Lawra Confederacy chiefs should not be represented in the newly
established Northern Regional House of Chiefs by a member of the
opposition like the Lawra Naa. Of course the Jirapa Naa was hoping that his
connections with the CPP would boost his position in the chiefly hierarchy
and ultimately land him a seat in the House of Chiefs.[91] But because party
differences still did not suffice to legitimate his being granted his own
paramountcy, he bolstered his demands with ethnic arguments, insisting
that Jirapa is a 'Dagarti Division', with 'customs and culture far different
from the Lobi' of Lawra; thus if Jirapa were to remain in the Lawra
Confederacy, 'our people will be doomed to follow different customs'.[92]
The village chiefs, too, masked their political aspirations in the garb of
culture and tribe, like some elders from the Lawra Division, who insisted
'that we are pure Dagarti', and complained 'that our continual relationship
with the Lawra Division who are Lobi will ever make us perpetual slaves
forever'.[93] These arguments, however, impressed neither the Lawra District
Commissioner nor the CPP executive who demanded that the Lawra
Confederacy State Council itself had to agree to the divisions' demands for
autonomy.[94]

Yet at the heart of these endeavours, so Polkuu argued diplomatically, lay
nothing more than Nandom's desire for 'more developments' and 'more
representation in the Northern House of Chiefs'. With the Jirapa Naa's
support , he finally secured the State Council's grudging approval to secede
from the Lawra Confederacy State Council pending government approval.[95]
The Lawra Naa could no longer forestall this development since his most
important ally, the Lambussie Kuoro, had come under strong pressure from
opponents within his own chiefdom. A number of rebellious sub-divisional
chiefs and members of the house of the late chief Bombieh, Salifu's pro-
Nandom predecessor, swiftly destooled Salifu for governing autocratically,

for removing headmen from office because of political differences and for misappropriating local council funds.[96] Lawra Naa Karbo attempted to stave off this political assault by objecting that the Confederacy State Council had not been properly informed, which prompted his opponents to follow the precedent set by the chiefs of Nandom and Jirapa and call for an end to the Lawra Confederacy State Council, using usual tribalistic language: 'We are of a different tribe and we shall therefore like to have a separate district by ourselves'.[97] Salifu protested vehemently,[98] but could no longer prevent the State Council's dissolution. In November 1960 the government in Accra overruled Lambussie's petition and sustained that Nandom-Lambussie and Jirapa were recognised as two autonomous State Councils.

Party politics and districts
The appointment of loyal party members as district commissioners provided the CPP government with the leverage it needed to expand political control throughout the country. Partly in order to intensify the CPP government's control and partly to accommodate local demands for separate administrative units, the number of district commissioners was increased. From mid-July 1959 until the end of 1962 the number of districts in the Northern and Upper Regions, into which the Northern Region had been divided in 1960, increased from twelve to forty-three. In Lawra District, too, a second commissioner was appointed in 1960 to serve Lawra-Jirapa, while Nandom-Lambussie continued to be under the jurisdiction of A. P. S. Termaghre.[99] The latter had pushed for this new arrangement, which cross-cut the constituencies of Lawra-Nandom and Jirapa-Lambussie, in order to undermine the influence of the two UP parliamentarians. In response, the Lambussie Kuoro tried to circumvent the administrative amalgamation with Nandom by arguing that merging with Tumu made more sense because of the greater ethnic affinities, an argument similar to that articulated by his predecessor Hilla in the 1930s.[100] Although Termaghre played the ethnic card whenever it served his own purposes best, he now took advantage of the Nkrumah regime's repugnance against tribalism in order to spoil the Lambussie Kuoro's plan: '[I]f Government would allow Districts or parts thereof to secede in order to join their tribes in other Districts then there would be no peace in the country and then tribalism would ruin administration'.[101] Certainly, just as Salifu had feared, Termaghre's efforts sought to secure Nandom's predominance in the new district – district headquarters were located in Nandom, and he treated the Lambussie Kuoro as if he were a divisional chief with the Nandom Naa his paramount.[102]

At first Lambussie Kuoro Salifu protested by boycotting the sessions of the newly established Nandom-Lambussie State Council.[103] However, in

the long term, he could only strengthen his political leverage by reconciliation with his rebellious sub-chiefs, and by securing allies from the upper
echelons of the ruling party. He thus applied for CPP membership.[104] Even
K. Y. Baloro, once Lambussie's leading UP politician, became a CPP
member and later even the Lambussie local party secretary.[105]

In the struggle against Nandom, the Lambussie Kuoro also resorted to
the well-tried tactic of refusing Dagara peasants permission to farm Sisala
land.[106] Reportedly, at his instigation, some Sisala earth priests even
hindered Dagara settlers from promptly burying their dead and cursed their
fields so that they could no longer be cultivated – actions which Termaghre
regarded to be 'tribalistic hatred actions' perpetrated by the Sisala against
Dagara farmers.[107] Tensions between Lambussie and Nandom increased
further, when Nkrumah announced near the end of 1961 that administrative districts were to be made to conform to voting constituencies.[108] Salifu's
opponents within Lambussie Division tried to hinder the establishment of a
new Jirapa-Lambussie District and petitioned the Regional Commissioner
that Lambussie remain part of Nandom, arguing that 'Nandom and
Lambussie are geographically fit to form one District, being only two miles
from each other', that 'we share the same social amenities, marketing for
example', and that 'Nandom and Lambussie have been bound together
traditionally for a very long time and still have love for these ties'.[109]
However, Salifu too petitioned the Regional Commissioner, complaining
that Termaghre was interfering in chieftaincy affairs[110] and that Lambussie
was being slighted when it came to development investments. In his view
Lambussie needed 'a District Commissioner who has a common understanding with my people to accelerate Government policy properly. Or we
go with any tribe beside Nandom'.[111]

The further course of events showed that Salifu's political machinations
would come to fruition. In 1962 Lambussie became an autonomous district,
and in 1963 the Lambussie Kuoro was officially recognised as paramount
chief.[112] Although Termaghre had warned that a small administrative entity
such as Lambussie was not financially viable and that its ethnic composition
– with a majority of Dagara peasants – did not favour a separation from
Nandom,[113] his influence with the Regional Commissioner did not suffice to
prevent the administrative separation of Nandom and Lambussie. Kweku
Mensah, a Dagaba from S. D. Dombo's home village Duori, was appointed
Lambussie District Commissioner, an appointment that raised fears among
Termaghre and other Nandome that the old UP alliance of Jirapa with
Lambussie would be resurrected. The power struggle now shifted to a bitter
face-off between Termaghre and Kweku Mensah, in which Mensah clearly
regarded himself the champion of Lambussie's interests, and it was largely
upon his doings that one year later Termaghre was transferred out of
Nandom.[114]

At the end of 1962 political fragmentation within the former Lawra District reached its climax: four autonomous administrative districts (Lawra, Jirapa, Nandom and Lambussie), four local councils,[115] four traditional councils and – as of 1965 – four constituencies. The Lawra District Commissioner lauded the CPP's ultimate victory over the opposition and the administration's responsiveness to the people's wishes – 'that the ordinary man in the street should be directly involved in the activities of the Council'.[116] In reality, however, the fragmentation served first and foremost to defuse local power struggles and the local elite's political ambitions – but only to a limited extent, since tax income was too low to even cover the salaries of local council employees, much less the financing of village development projects.

The Hamile conflict revisited

The conflict over Hamile's administrative jurisdiction re-ignited under the influence of party politics, provoked this time by fierce competition between Wala and Mossi traders over control of transportation, particularly the lorry stations. Lorry station operators collected fees from all lorries and buses that allowed passengers to get on or off or that loaded, unloaded or reloaded goods at the station. Often they even organised porters or accommodation for those passing through – all in all a very lucrative business. It is therefore hardly surprising that the operators of 'Station Number One', under the leadership of the Wala headman Zachary, would resort to any means to protect their monopoly, which was threatened when a Mossi businessman applied to the Lambussie Local Council for a permit to open 'Station Number Two'. While good relations with their hometown Wa, through which one had to pass when travelling south, were a definite advantage for the Wala, the Mossi tried to use their networks on French territory, particularly their connections to French customs, to their own advantage.[117] Furthermore, both sides secured local allies, which led to Hamile's split into two camps that became embroiled in a bitter conflict. The CPP camp was headed by the Mossi headman Sumaila, included most Mossi traders and recognised Peter Ziem to be the Hamile Naa. Moreover, this camp managed to win the support, at least for a time, of the Happa Kuoro, who wished to secede from the Lambussie Kuoro and return to CPP-dominated Nandom. The Mossi, Peter Ziem and the Happa Kuoro were supported in this endeavour by the Nandom Naa and District Commissioner Termaghre. The Wala traders, under Zachary's leadership, joined the NPP/UP and formed an alliance with Lambussie Kuoro Salifu against the Happa Kuoro, while in Hamile they supported Norbert Lalang as the new Hamile Naa, a man known for his loyalty to Lambussie. When the Lambussie Kuoro and the Wala UP activists left the NPP/UP to join the CPP late in 1959, the Happa Kuoro caved to their anti-Nandom, anti-Mossi and anti-

Dagara stance, and Hamile remained part of the Lambussie Local Council. In what follows I will examine the explosive combination of tribalistic, xenophobic, traditionalist and administrative arguments which were deployed in the course of the conflict.

The tensions between Happa Kuoro Huor and Lambussie Kuoro Salifu escalated into open conflict, when in 1957 Salifu destooled the Hamile chief Peter Ziem, bypassing the sub-divisional chief in charge, the Happa Kuoro. Huor saw the 'Walas who left their home town and came over here for trading' as 'the source of all these troubles'.[118] If the Lambussie Kuoro did not reinstate the Hamile Naa and if the majority of Hamile's inhabitants did not wish to return to Nandom, then Huor saw himself with no other option but also to secede from Lambussie.[119] Huor's bitterness grew, when his son Amissah, who ran for the CPP in the local council elections, lost to the Wala-backed UP candidate. Huor wrote to his fellow party member Termaghre, mobilising largely xenophobic sentiments against Zachary:

> Since he has only come into the town as a money finder, and has now put up many buildings in his own home town Wa, we have all come to a general feeling that his recent actions are only a means of putting the town in chaos, discord and confussion [sic]. Then, when his bad aims are achieved, he will quickly and safely run back to his home town Wa. ... We all as Ghanaians share a common interest as Ghanaians yet since this concerns only our town we do not on traditional lines share any common interest with him.[120]

What caused the Happa Kuoro a short time later to join Salifu's course and vehemently protest against the aspirations of Peter Ziem and the Mossi traders to secede is not clear. Perhaps the Lambussie Kuoro's threat to have him fined caused him to cave, or perhaps he was prepared to move towards reconciliation, since his son Amissah had been voted into the Lawra Confederacy Local Council after all and was even made its Vice-Chairman. In any event, he now ardently insisted that Hamile was a cosmopolitan settlement of strangers, not the product of a single ethnic 'tradition', nor was it a Dagara settlement, whose composition would favoured amalgamation with Nandom.[121]

The ethnic card – as well as partisan arguments – were now brought into play by Peter Ziem and the pro-CPP Dagara farmers in Hamile, as well as the Mossi and Yoruba traders, who also wanted a lorry station. Insisting that 'the factual inhabitants of Hamile are Dagare whereas the subjects of Lambussie are Sisaalas. Our customs do not agree', they felt Hamile should return to Nandom.[122] Hamile, so countered Zachary Wala and his supporters, was a Sisala settlement, in which the Dagara only constituted a minority. Peter Ziem and his supporters were not only inciting a border conflict between Lambussie and Nandom, but also resorting to 'tribalism'.[123]

Plate 7 K. Y. Baloro as teacher at the Lambussie Local Council primary school, 1950s (with kind permission of Lambussie Kuoro K. Y. Baloro)

Termaghre, prominent in the effort to win Hamile back for Nandom, contended that the traders had absolutely no say in Hamile's administrative and political affiliation. Before forwarding Zachary Wala's letter to the Regional Commissioner in Bolgatanga, he marked each of the signatories as either Wala or 'non-Ghanaian', i.e. Yoruba, Hausa or Mossi, requesting with respect to the latter to: 'Please inform those concerned in this petition to be much careful of how they have involve [sic] themselves to local politics and matters. ... They are non-Ghanaians'. He also felt the Wala should be warned 'to be careful because they are not entitled to any material rights in Hamile'.[124]

With the creation of Nandom-Lambussie District in late 1960, the situation in Hamile settled down, but just two years later, with the proposed redrawing of district boundaries, the conflict flared up anew. This time, Termaghre was even more aggressive in pitting 'Dagarti Native Settlers' against Sisala and 'Wala Mobile Traders', whom he blamed for Hamile's secession from Nandom.[125] The pro-Lambussie faction of Hamile traders and Norbert Lalang, the man they recognised as chief of Hamile, challenged Peter Ziem's right to act on behalf of Hamile's inhabitants: 'We are the rightful people to tell where we stand and not people like Peter Ziem, a self styled chief, who is only a tribal headman of the Dagarti in Hamile'.[126] The Lambussie Kuoro, for his part, accused Peter Ziem 'and his accomplice A. P. S. Termaghre' of propagating 'tribalistic ideas' and insisted that the Sisala did indeed have a right to Hamile: 'Hamile is for the Sissalis and not Lobi please'.[127]

The Lambussie Kuoro received backing from the new Lambussie District Commissioner Kweku Mensah, who made sure the pro-Nandom Mossi-dominated CPP executive was replaced by pro-Lambussie Wala traders. Mensah also convinced the Regional Commissioner to bar Termaghre from any further involvement in Hamile's affairs.[128] When Nandom Naa Polkuu tried to settle matters once and for all by announcing he would visit Hamile as part of his annual tax census, the Regional Commissioner, having been forewarned by Mensah, forbade him to set foot there.[129] He also sent two high-ranking police officers to Nandom and Hamile, to whom the Nandom Naa and Peter Ziem had to swear that for at least one year they would not say anything having remotely to do with Hamile.[130] The following day the new Local Council members were announced: Hamile was to remain part of Lambussie.[131]

Two years later, when the government decided to redraw constituency boundaries, Nandom Naa Polkuu started one last (unsuccessful) attempt to win back Hamile. According to the government, the constituencies needed to be adjusted to conform to new political realities as well as reflect population growth. Thus, the number of parliamentarians representing voters in Accra was to be increased from 104 to 198.[132] The issue of Hamile had already played an important role in 1953 during the initial drawing up of constituency boundaries by the Van Lare Commission. According to this commission's criteria, each constituency would be comprised of roughly the same number of inhabitants, but no single local council should be split between two constituencies, nor should local councils of different languages

Plate 8 Nandom Naa K. P. Polkuu, 1960s (with kind permission of Nandom Naa Dr Charles Imoro)

be amalgamated.[133] This meant that in Lawra Confederacy only Jirapa would have received its own constituency, the three other local councils being too small. To K. Y. Baloro, the Lawra Confederacy representative in the Northern Territories Council at this time, it was patently clear that in view of the intense conflicts over Hamile Lambussie could only join with Jirapa, and he set about using his influence to make this a reality.[134] That the Van Lare Commission finally adopted his arrangement with the Jirapa Naa was due in large part to the influence of one of its members, S. D. Dombo. It was in good part out of gratitude for Dombo's support that Baloro and Lambussie Kuoro Salifu became NPP supporters.

CPP supporters in Lawra Confederacy indeed regarded the first division of constituencies into Jirapa-Lambussie and Lawra-Nandom to have been a partisan manoeuvre in favour of the NPP, speculating that in a Nandom-Lambussie constituency a CPP candidate could have prevailed. Termaghre had thus in 1960 already suggested the constituencies be redrawn.[135] Moreover, a single Nandom-Lambussie constituency would be conducive to getting a Nandom representative to Accra while in a Lawra-Nandom constituency Nandom would have been short-changed. An initial proposal presented by the Ministry for Local Government actually suggested the creation of a single Nandom-Lambussie constituency, while Jirapa and Lawra were each to have their own.[136] The Lambussie Kuoro, however, convinced the new Commission that Lambussie should be amalgamated with Gwollo instead of Nandom, because 'the Lambussie people are Sissalas of the same ethnic group as the Tumus and the Gwollus while the Nandoms are Dagarti', judging the amalgamation of Lambussie and Nandom to be a colonial administrative error that 'caused endless friction between the two groups of people.'[137] But unfortunately the commission wanted to make Fielmuo, a settlement inhabited predominately by Dagara peasants, the constituency headquarters. In a final hearing, however, Salifu's son S. B. Dy-Yakah, who at this time was studying law at the University of Ghana and was representing Lambussie, managed to win a separate constituency for Lambussie that included Hamile.

Nandom Naa Polkuu's complaint that Hamile was 'a Dagarti village' and neither a part of Lambussie nor a part of the proposed Sisala constituency went unheeded.[138] According to him, Hamile was really called 'Muoteng', after the first Dagara settler, and belonged to Kokoligu. Only in retaliation against Imoru for his pro-CPP stance did UP politicians transfer Hamile to Lambussie in 1952. Polkuu therefore felt confident the 'battle' over Hamile would end in favour of Nandom, which had always been loyal to the CPP.[139] However, Polkuu lacked allies, and Hamile thus remained with Lambussie.[140] But at least Nandom, too, was awarded its own constituency – only without Hamile.

That the matter was not settled became evident following a rally, during which the newly elected Nandom Member of Parliament C. Y. Deri, a close relative of the Nandom Naa and the Regional Party Education Secretary, introduced himself to his constituency. CPP delegates from Hamile claimed Deri had stated that he would not rest until Hamile was once again under Nandom, and that the Regional Commissioner had already signalled his consent. 'We feel the statement was discriminatory and tribalistic', wrote Zachary Wala to the Regional Commissioner.[141] Amolubilla, the new Nandom District Commissioner, dismissed this as hysterical and unfounded.[142] Regional Commissioner Asumda, however, believed it prudent to reassure the Lambussie Kuoro that any statement on the Hamile issue supposedly made by Mr C. Y. Deri 'is his own opinion and is not subscribed to by either Government or my office'.[143]

Five months later the Nkrumah government was overthrown. Asumda and other political functionaries and parliamentarians – including Amolubilla, Termaghre and C. Y. Deri – were imprisoned for several months.[144] All district commissioners were removed from office and the number of districts reduced drastically. In doing so most district boundaries, including Lawra, reverted back to those of the colonial period. The four local councils of the Lawra Confederacy were replaced by two management committees, one for Lawra-Jirapa and one for Nandom-Lambussie, until a single Lawra District Council was finally re-established. The Lawra Confederacy State (now called Traditional) Council, too, was revived – unleashing the same internal competition that had plagued the Lawra Confederacy from the very beginning and that would effect its ultimate demise in the 1980s.

Although this return to larger administrative units dampened the potential for local political conflict, the rifts caused by partisanship cum local politics were too recent. Several 'losers' continued to harbour hopes of revenge for a long time to come. Nandom Naa Charles Imoro even believed this constituted an ontological constant in African politics: 'You see, we Africans don't forgive easily … When you belong to a different party then you consider the other person as an enemy till death'.[145] The younger generation of educated elites hoped such bitterness and life-long animosity merely represented the juvenile phase of party politics and that the political process could be 'civilised'.

In fact, the 1969 elections seem not to have split the constituencies in Lawra-Nandom and Jirapa-Lambussie as deeply as in the past. The winners were all older UP politicians, S. D. Dombo and Silvester Sanziri, both entering parliament backed by over 80 per cent of the vote.[146] Sanziri was also elected by many Nandome former CPP supporters, probably because they accorded greater importance to his Nandom origins than party affiliation. The 1969 campaign was more a face-off between generations than parties. Dombo's and Sanziri's opponents, S. B. Dy-Yakah from Lambussie and Anthony Bondong from Lawra, were young men who, during the time of the greatest local and party political conflict, were still students. Now they were looking to enter the political arena, which until then was dominated by the older generation. However, it would be another ten years, until the 1979 elections, before the younger generation occupied leadership positions and entered parliament in the two Lawra District constituencies. In the following chapter we will turn to this younger generation of educated elites and examine their ideals, organisations, and attempts to articulate a sense of ethnic community.

9

ETHNIC MOVEMENTS AND
SPECIAL-INTEREST POLITICS

In December 1979, more than 150 'sons and daughters of Nandom' working in Accra, Kumasi, Tamale, Bolgatanga and other Ghanaian cities travelled to their home town to join Dagara teachers, doctors and priests active in Nandom and neighbouring towns and villages in founding the Nandom Youth and Development Association (NYDA). Nandom Naa Polkuu urged those attending the inaugural assembly to abandon the 'armchair approach' and the 'path of individualism', which had hampered the 'total development of Nandom'. Jacob Yirerong, the chairman of the NYDA's Accra branch and the meeting's organiser, exhorted all to prove to hard-bitten sceptics that Nandome could join together. Dr Benedict Der, Professor of History at the University of Cape Coast – whose sweeping lecture explored everything from the historical origins of the 'Nandome Dagara', to the particularities of Dagara culture, to the youth associations – advised that Nandom should not stand back 'when other tribes in the North have Youth Associations'. These 'are not for dances' – a reference to the cultural activities of many migrant associations – 'but can be used as pressure groups'. Archbishop Peter Dery evoked the 'very high moral code' that characterised Dagara society even before its conversion to Christianity, warning further that parochialism and 'selfish criticism' would be 'inimical to unity and development'.[1]

However, as soon evident from the debates of the by-laws, defining 'Nandom' was a matter of heated discussion. Was this to be along political and territorial lines, corresponding to the chiefdom boundaries that dated back to the colonial era, or along ethnic lines so as to include Dagara farmers living in Lambussie? Moreover, that the first national executive was to be composed exclusively of NYDA activists in Accra was criticised by senior 'local literates', who preferred the executive have its seat in Nandom. Thus, the portents of conflict were already discernible on the political landscape. Nonetheless, hopes ran high 'that the birth of NYDA marks an important watershed in the history of this area'[2] and that, through the joint efforts of migrants and those who stayed behind, the association would be able to develop Nandom and obtain a 'bigger share of the national cake'. By the time the inaugural conference was to take place, the organisers, mostly young university-trained civil servants, priests, secondary school and university teachers, actually succeeded in including all important local political actors: the paramount chief, the earth-priest family, the Catholic Church and – in the person of Rear-Admiral Kevin Dzang, also from the chiefly family – a Nandome in the government. With the selection of Polkuu and W. K. Dibaar as chairmen of the meeting and the presence of many older local teachers, even former political opponents were brought to the table.

There was a great deal of optimism, particularly in the early years, and by the mid-1980s the NYDA had established nineteen branches across the country, with as many as 250 members travelling to Nandom each year for the annual conference. The NYDA-supported Rural Bank, which opened in Nandom in 1981, was regarded by association activists as a milestone on the path to development. Yet other ambitious projects would not be realised. And, as initial enthusiasm waned, moral appeals 'to accept the spirit of sacrifice and to eschew our petty differences that have tended to widen instead of bridge the gap of unity' became more frequent.[3] During the festivities to mark the association's ten-year anniversary, the NYDA chairman emphasised that ultimately it was not just about the creation of 'physical structures', but about education towards 'self-help projects'. His comment that 'the greatest achievement of the Association ... is that it is still in existence and goes marching on'[4] was in no way meant ironically. The NYDA indeed survived more than one test of strength. Today, some fifteen years later, most of the association's founding members agree that the NYDA, as an umbrella organisation, is either 'dead' or 'dormant'. Nevertheless, some local branches continue to meet, and members of a third generation of young, educated migrants, particularly those in the 'diaspora', have launched a new, more professional, but at the same time also more exclusive association, namely the FREED (Foundation for Rural Education, Empowerment and Development).[5]

Like the NYDA, other youth associations, founded in the 1970s and early 1980s in the Lawra Confederacy and elsewhere in the North-West, also suffered phases of crisis and inactivity.[6] To some degree difficulties stemmed from changes in the political climate: youth associations that were successful lobbyists during the Rawlings regime suddenly found it difficult to regain their footing under a government constituted by the NPP (New Patriotic Party), the former opposition. Yet of greater importance are the internal contradictions plaguing these youth associations.

The term 'youth', as has by now become apparent, is a socio-political category which situates the associations in the familiar Ghanaian framework circumscribed by 'chiefs', 'elders' and 'people'. 'Youth' refers to politically active commoners who consider themselves opinion leaders and are only in the widest sense also biologically 'young' men. (The ideology and chief activities of the associations are indeed in most cases focused on men, even though women may sometimes organise their own parallel meetings.) These youth associations pursue two objectives: to represent their community's interests to outsiders, and at the same time to define and internally flesh out this very community. This dual project exposes the structural contradictions of societies in the North-West encountered in earlier chapters – the complex intermingling of territoriality and ethnicity, of chiefdoms and segmentary organisation; the blurred boundaries between cultures and languages; the tensions between first-comers and late-comers, migrants and those who remain behind, the educated and the illiterate, Christians and 'traditionalists', the mission- and state-educated. Because these tensions potentially threaten the associations' very survival, the latter invest considerable energy in constructing a corporate identity to mitigate such pressures – hence the invocation of 'unity' and 'ethnic identity' in discourses, symbols and rituals. The cultural work of ethnicity that the associations and their members carry out – activities with lasting impact on how people in the region think about this concept – will be the focus of Chapter 10. This chapter explores the political debates on ethnicity, local citizenship and leadership which the youth associations provoked through their activities and ideas.

STUDENTS' UNIONS, MIGRANTS' ASSOCIATIONS AND PRESSURE GROUPS

The initiative to found youth associations generally came from the educated elite. In the process, previous types of organisation were re-defined, some of which now exist parallel to the new associations, overlapping in personnel, while others were replaced by them. Among the predecessors were the so-called literates' associations. While party fronts had prevented the first larger-scale clubs, founded by teachers and local council clerks after the Second World War, from consolidating, smaller village-based literates' associations created in the 1950s and early 1960s managed to survive and promoted mutual support and the development of their village. Yet the founders of subsequent youth associations garnered their organisationally most formative experiences not in these village associations, but in various school and student groups. The camaraderie among young, educated migrants that evolved out of a sense of shared roots and manifested itself in the founding of associations knew no party lines (at least not yet). Who associated with whom depended mainly on the number of pupils coming from the various regions. For example, at the Lawra Local Council Middle School, established in 1952, Dr Daniel Delle, one of the first pupils from Nandom, recalled: 'We met different people from different parts of the district who spoke different dialects. So we wanted to identify ourselves as Nandom people'.[7] At the Tamale Government Secondary School (TAMASCO), pupils from all over Lawra District joined together to organise transportation from and to home at the beginning and end of every term and also establish a fund to assist classmates with financial difficulties. A certain united front against pupils from other parts of the North – Lawra students constituted a disproportional number of school prefects, a fact that won them no sympathies – led the Lawra contingent to form a tight-knit group. In 1962 at the University of Ghana in Legon, on the other hand, students from all over the North founded the Northern Students Union, the small number of Northern students and the need to represent their interests vis-à-vis the scholarship secretariat being important factors in the group's formation. Interestingly, the Northern Students Union's first chairman was S. B. Dy-Yakah from the Lambussie Kuoro's house, who would later play a central role in the conflicts surrounding proposals to create a Nandom-Lambussie District.

As the number of students from particular parts of the North gradually increased, smaller-scale associations, such as the Nandom Students Union (NANSU), were founded and existed parallel to the Northern Students Union. This development first raised the issue of how precisely to define membership, a question later to plague youth associations. TAMASCO was dominated by pupils from chiefly families so that the associations and interactions of Nandom pupils tended follow the boundaries of the Nandom Traditional Area. However, Catholic school graduates also studied at the university. Their 'Nandom' was the old Nandom Parish that extended into the chiefdoms of Lambussie and Zini (under Tumu). NANSU ultimately adopted this wider definition of 'Nandom', a move due at least in part to two of its founders (and later co-founders of NYDA) being from families of Dagara settlers on Sisala land, who therefore had a vested interest in a geographically wide definition of NANSU membership. Even to the present day, NANSU's by-laws still extend membership to all ethnic groups, so that in principle it is possible for Sisala from Lambussie (the former Catholic parish of Nandom) to join.[8] However, fact is that Dagara students have predominated, in part because Dagara is the most commonly spoken language at association meetings, so that even those Sisala who understand Dagara have felt marginalised.[9] Sisala students from Lambussie founded their own association, the Issaw West Development Union (IWDU)[10] – a choice of name that links ethnicity and territory, since Issaw means Sisala – from which, however, Dagara students from Lambussie felt excluded.[11] Yet as long as student associations devoted themselves primarily to the well-being of their members at their place of study, conflicts over the definition of membership remained in check.

The fragmentation of the associations that resulted from an increase in the number of migrants from the same region of origin and/or ethnic group was a tendency also evident among the migrants' associations, as shown in Chapter 5. Before the youth associations were established, literates and illiterates were generally organised separately, the latter usually under a tribal head or along the lines of the patriclans, the former mostly in rather more formalised associations. However, one cannot draw too sharp a line between the two, since most migrants belonged and still belong to several associations. For example, a migrant from Kokoligu who works in Kumasi as a salaried administrative official may be a member of the Dagaba Catholic Union, which brings together Dagaba and Dagara from across the North-West; also be involved in the local NYDA association; third, cultivate close ties with the elders of his patriclan; fourth, support the Kokoligu Youth Association; and finally, make donations to the Dagara 'tribal head' in Kumasi. The local organisational landscape varies from place to place and depends both on the nature of the place of migration (large city, smaller administrative or mining centre, cocoa or yam cultivation area, etc.) and its political traditions (chieftaincy with a tradition of tribal heads for the 'strangers'; newer administrative centre without such institutions, etc.).

Finally, regionalist pressure groups constituted yet another predecessor to modern youth associations. In the late 1960s, after Nkrumah's overthrow, a number of lawyers, civil servants, businessmen and politicians founded the Northern Youth Association which sought to represent regional interests to the central government in Accra as well as to advise and influence future parliamentary representatives and members of government from the North. Following the removal of restrictions on political parties in 1969, the Northern Youth Association, plagued by political quarrels, disintegrated,[12] but was revived under the military regime of Acheampong (1972–8) as the Northern Study Group. However, when the Study Group's chairman, Dr Hilla Limann, was elected president of Ghana's Third Republic (1979–81), the group was eventually supplanted by more informal discussion circles among the Northern elite as well as by smaller-scale interest groups such as the ethnically defined youth associations of the Northern Region.[13] Nonetheless, the model of a supra-party lobby for regional interests in the central government, as pioneered by the Northern Youth Association, would inspire subsequent youth and development associations.

The nation-wide boom of the late 1960s (in the North, not until the 1970s) in the founding of youth associations was in no small measure due to the political context. Under Acheampong political parties were banned, as they had been under the National Liberation Council (1966–9). In view of the gaps and disruptions hampering the functioning of local government during the 1970s and 1980s, youth associations provided institutional continuity and an important forum that represented local interests to the government. Second, it was only towards the end of the 1960s, at least in the North, that the critical mass of secondary school and university graduates typically required to found smaller-scale youth associations was achieved.

In addition, although the Nkrumah government had generally been sympathetic towards Northern interests, by the late 1960s it became clear that the central government's support for development in the North was biased. When, for instance, the placement of the Upper Region's head-quarters at Bolgatanga channelled more resources towards the North-East than the North-West, many political activists from the latter began to feel that to offset such regional imbalances they should intensify local special-interest politics rather than rely solely on an 'all-Northern' representation of their interests. It is no coincidence, therefore, that North-Westerners were among the first in the North to found their own youth and development associations, such as the Upper West Youth Association in 1975, the Lawra Paramountcy Youth Association (LAPYA) and the Jirapa Youth and Development Association (JAYDA) in 1976, and the Nandom Youth and Development Association in 1978–9.

Unlike the preceding literates' associations, these youth associations strove to involve not only the educated, but also illiterate migrant workers and farmers in their work. The desire to provide an impetus towards development through the mobilisation of self-help projects distinguishes youth associations from pressure groups, which primarily rely on increasing the share of national resources allotted to their constituency, as well as from migrant associations, which focus on the well-being of members while they are away from home. Thus, to a certain extent, the new associations incorporate the characteristics of all previous organisational types; and it is precisely for this reason that internal tensions develop. At the same time, the longevity of these associations is due to the multiplicity of the tasks they fulfil. While these associations primarily strive to be ethnic movements that encourage self-help initiatives and work as pressure groups, in towns they also function as social, burial and savings clubs, and may moreover serve as job exchanges, *ersatz* families, discussion forums and starting points for political careers. Furthermore, in hardly any other organisations do urban elites reflect so assiduously on their rural origins or do elites and the grass roots together deliberate questions of reciprocity, redistribution and political morality. Thus, youth associations, resting on the idea of a shared ethnicity, are not only a potential resource for client networks and political mobilisa-tion, but also provide a basis for a moral community, or, to use Lonsdale's terms, they serve as institutions of both 'political tribalism' and 'moral ethnicity' (1996).

DEBATING ETHNICITY, LOCAL CITIZENSHIP AND LEADERSHIP

The North-West's incorporation into a larger political, economic and cultural context – initially the Northern Territories and the Gold Coast, later the Ghanaian state – did and still does influence local discourses and forms of organisation. Supra-local models of the 'native', the chiefdom and the 'tribe' became the framework in which local particularities could be expressed, especially vis-à-vis a non-local public. Migrant workers and the educated elite, who had the most intimate contact with the supra-local field, have been particularly active in the shaping of this new ethnic discourse. Away from home, they create relationships of solidarity which transcend clan and village, more so, at any rate, than local farmers. Also, they needed and still need ethnic groups in order to be able to identify themselves in relation to others. Back home, however, they become embroiled in local factionalism involving chiefly houses, earth priests and chiefs, natives and settlers who compete to control resources and for political influence. In what follows, I will look at three particular points of tension which have arisen from these conflicting loyalties and circumscribed youth association activities: conflicts in delimiting the communities which the associations seek to represent (territorial versus ethnic boundaries), tensions between the grass roots and the elite, and difficulties in translating so-called community interests into concrete projects in which the educated, migrant workers and farmers all genuinely share an interest.

Ethnic or territorial boundaries?

All youth associations in the North-West define their membership by birth, if not explicitly, then at least implicitly. The strength of the category 'indigenous', on which almost all youth associations fall back, lies in its ambiguity. As we shall see with the Dagara settlers in Lambussie, it can be interpreted more or less exclusively, while still ascribing to the association the quasi-automatic, 'natural' legitimacy which has been attached to the category 'indigenous' or 'native' since the colonial period. As the NYDA national executive put it, those who are indigenous to an area 'have a common basis' and 'a common heritage', 'think alike', 'share common interests' and therefore find it easier to associate. Besides, no 'indigenous ruler', the area chief, would without further ado permit anyone who is not indigenous to become involved in local development matters.[14] Youth associations, in aiming at development, therefore face the question of whether to admit 'settlers' or 'strangers' (including in-migrating wives) as members and, if so, under what conditions. Conversely, immigrants must decide whether to join an 'indigenous' youth association if they are invited to do so, or instead, join an organisation in their home community.

As already mentioned, at the NYDA's founding, there was lively controversy over whether only Dagara or all residents of Nandom should be admitted as members, and over how to define Nandom territorially: with reference to the Nandom Traditional Area or to the old Catholic parish that also included Lambussie and parts of Tumu. The wording finally adopted defined members as 'indigenous Dagara within ... the areas currently under the Nandom, Ko, Hamile and Fielmuo Roman Catholic Parishes' – that is, the former Nandom parish.[15] That some NYDA founders came from the Lambussie Traditional Area and would thus have been excluded from the Association by the adoption of a territorially narrowly defined membership criterion certainly played a role in this outcome. However, basic questions of ethnicity, political participation and local citizenship were also involved.

The criterion of Dagara ethnicity excluded from membership non-indigenous traders living in the Nandom and Hamile *zongos*. Even the revised by-laws of 1990, which accorded non-Dagara citizens at least honorary membership, denied them both active and passive voting rights as well as the right to 'represent NYDA ... in any capacity'. This ambivalence towards the '*zongo* community' for one had to do with the 1950s secession of Hamile traders, and for another stemmed from the general unease felt by rural, Christian Dagara towards urbanised, Muslim merchants. 'Traders have money', one of my informants told me, and it would therefore be 'suicidal' not to demand they make a contribution to local development; however, 'with money you will want power ... and we don't want that tomorrow people who are not indigenous will begin to create problems for us'.[16]

Yet in contrast, the parish criterion opened NYDA membership to Dagara who had been living for some decades on Sisala land in the neighbouring Lambussie Traditional Area and in the chiefdom of Zini (under Tumu). Here, where the Sisala regard Dagara farmers as 'settlers', excluding them from allodial land rights and full political participation, the NYDA questioned the legitimacy of differentiating between autochthones and 'strangers'. 'Nobody has created the ground', insisted the NYDA executive in a conversation with me.

> The Sisala also came from somewhere and settled. ... So you [the Sisala] are also a settler just like me. ... After I have lived with you for over a hundred years, you turn around and tell me I am a settler and you own the place – that's what I am not going to accept. And that is what you can see between the Arabs and the Israelites.[17]

Although NYDA activists assured everybody that integrating the Dagara living on Sisala land into their association in no way implied territorial claims, the Sisala political elite nonetheless perceived this inclusive definition of NYDA membership as inimical to their interests. Yet which association should Dagara settlers join? The by-laws of the reactivated IWDU stipulated that members not be allowed to belong to any 'second youth association which is totally outside this area'. As a result, the Dagara in Lambussie were effectively excluded, at least those who felt loyal towards Nandom and the NYDA. However, one IWDU committee member insisted that this constituted self-exclusion and that his association was in principle 'open to any person within or from Issaw West' (i.e. Lambussie), not only the Sisala. As it was, he argued, a quarter of the inhabitants of Lambussie (and according to NYDA data, more than half) were Dagara, and the Sisala could not, and did not want to, exclude them from joint efforts to develop the area. Nonetheless, the Dagara 'don't become members of the IWDU because they ... wouldn't like to be so closely associated with the Sisala, but prefer to be in close association with their kinsmen in the Nandom area.'[18] At any rate, whether all this amounted to exclusion by the Sisala or self-exclusion by the Dagara, in the mid-1980s Archbishop Peter Dery and opinion-leaders from the Lambussie area attempted to found a purely territorial, not ethnic, association with equal rights for both Dagara and Sisala. However, after a burst of initial enthusiasm, this endeavour failed because of intensifying conflicts over the new districts, and the *status quo ante* of uneasy co-existence between the NYDA and the IWDU prevailed.[19] The revised NYDA by-laws amended the controversial parish clause, re-defining members as 'Nandome resident in and outside Nandom' and equating the Dagara in Lambussie with migrants in other parts of the country. Yet not even this could resolve the tensions between ethnic and territorial definitions of the community whose interests the NYDA claimed to represent.

In ethnically more homogeneous traditional areas like Lawra and Jirapa, youth associations tend to have shunned explicitly ethnic definitions of membership. Yet even here a shift in the political environment can lead to changes in definition that certainly make membership more inclusive with respect to social class, but also render it more exclusive with the introduc-tion of indigenousness as a criterion. The old Jirapa Literates' Association, for example, initially concentrated on ensuring the well-being of local teachers, clerks and hospital employees, some of whom were actually from Jirapa, while others were from neighbouring chiefdoms. In time, however, association activists began to regard the restriction to 'literates' as unten-able, particularly in view of efforts to effect the establishment of a Jirapa district. These activists sought to integrate in their endeavour chiefs, influential opinion-leaders and financially powerful traders, which a literacy requirement would have excluded. Additionally, in the course of re-launching the JAYDA as a youth association, its territorial basis was also re-defined. The previous Literates Association, which had been greatly influenced by educated Catholics, was modelled on the Catholic parishes, whose boundaries cross-cut chiefdoms and districts. The Youth Association, by contrast, now organised itself along the boundaries of the Jirapa Traditional Area, which were to serve as the basis of a new district, while at the same time introducing 'indigenousness' as a membership criterion. More recently, the by-laws were revised so as also to allow long-term, non-indigenous residents of Jirapa to become members. *De facto*, however, they were still excluded from leadership positions.

These cases show that the ethnic and territorial definitions of community upon which youth associations are based may harbour considerable potential for conflict. In the migration context, from which most associations originated, such potentially conflicting definitions of membership were not important. Whether the shared identity coincides in both territory and ethno-linguistic make-up is largely irrelevant to solidarity and sociability when away from home. However, this question becomes decisive as soon as youth associations direct their activities to their regions of origin.

'Mass movement' or 'elitist club'?

Youth associations regard 'self-help' as central to 'development' and therefore seek to mobilise the grass roots, since, as a mineworker in Obuasi aptly put it, 'the literates alone cannot develop the place for the illiterates to come and stay in, so we all have to come together'.[20] Yet, despite the open invitation for 'illiterates' to participate in association activities, in practice it is the educated elite that decides organisational policy, a state of affairs that fits well with their view of themselves as 'leaders'. Youth association activists, by virtue of their education and knowledge of the modern world, feel a natural calling to become 'leaders'. Moreover, they sense a moral obligation to repay the community for the privileged status they have achieved through education, something most could not have accomplished without help from their extended families back home.[21] Such support of the home region consists not only in exerting political pressure 'so that we will also get our proper share of the national cake',[22] but also in 'educating' the grass roots to help themselves by changing their 'attitudes' and 'mentality'. In this sense, the NYDA executive commented, the youth associations must gradually develop into a 'mass movement' under the guidance of the educated elite:

> We would want to be a mass movement. We would want to be a grass-roots organisation. But ... it has to be started from ... those of us who are privileged, privileged in the sense that we are more informed about issues than the grass roots. We want to share this information with the grass roots and pull them along, with the times. ... From the onset, it can never be a grass-roots organisation. It is a pressure group ... the mouthpiece of the grass roots.[23]

However, who exactly may be counted amongst those called upon as 'leaders' is controversial and feeds into conflicts between various factions of the educated elite. Often, an older generation of teachers and white-collar workers employed in the home region compete with a younger, university-educated, urban-based elite over the right to represent the grass roots and the home region. For example, 'local literates', as younger NYDA activists have complained, are accustomed and therefore insufficiently responsive to the precarious conditions in their home region and are inadequately informed about national politics; it is merely out of their 'petty jealousies' that they dispute the right to represent Nandom with more educated migrants. Those thus criticised, on the other hand, grumble about the arrogance of the 'Accra boys' in general and the national executive in particular, 'who want to lord it over us'. They are reproached for having lost contact with local realities, only coming once a year for the general meeting and expecting 'to be treated like invited guests'.[24]

There have also been conflicts over claims to leadership between association activists and chiefs, whose co-operation is vital to the successful functioning of any association. For example, members of the JAYDA executive reported the initial difficulties in integrating the chiefs into the new youth association's activities:

> [The chiefs] were thinking on local grounds. We were thinking differently, we who are educated, we have a better way of thinking than they. But they felt we were too high for them and that we were trying to live like Europeans ... the chiefs felt that we didn't respect them enough.[25]

At the heart of this dispute between youth association activists and chiefs was therefore the very basis of authority: 'modern', European knowledge versus seniority and familiarity with local traditions. In light of this criticism, the JAYDA strove to ensure that greater attention was accorded the views of the chiefs and village population by establishing an advisory board to the national executive, which was to consist of delegates representing all divisions in the Jirapa Traditional Area. The NYDA, too, wanted to work with the chiefs, though conflicts over Nandom Naa Polkuu's successor impeded their efforts. The NYDA executive's attempts to reconcile competing factions of the chiefly house proved unsuccessful, and the association had to invest all its energies to avoid splitting over this issue as well. Rear-Admiral Dzang and other members of the Nandom chiefly family withdrew entirely from NYDA activities, because, according to some critical commoners, their leadership claims had been frustrated. They countered that, although members of the chief's house had initially promoted the founding of the NYDA, they were then organisationally sidelined by a few individuals 'who just wanted to promote themselves as the leaders'. Here old rivalries between the educated Catholic elite and those graduates of state-run schools linked with the chiefly house stirred once again, though also at stake was the relationship between chiefs and other institutions in the modern Ghanaian state. As the current Nandom Naa put it: 'What does the chief want? Development! So they [the youth associations] are branches ... of the chief. And in fact, whoever is Nandom Naa, he is patron of NYDA.'[26] Yet NYDA activists insisted that they are not simply 'the Nandom Naa's executors', but operate at the same level in co-operation with him.

Basically, the oft-cited 'grass roots' seem quite ready to recognise their educated relatives' greater expertise and claims to authority, at least in certain 'modern' fields of action. 'They sent you to school and they believe that you know better and that whatever you come to say, they should listen to you.'[27] Only in financial matters, as my informants readily admitted, do three decades of problematic experiences with embezzling village development committees and tax-collectors dampen grass-roots support. Yet the tensions between educated youth association activists and the grass roots do not stem solely from financial problems. Urban branches in particular, which mobilise many migrant workers, have become a forum to dispute the proper relationship between the elite and the 'less privileged' in terms of the legitimacy of disparate life-styles and social comportment, the obligation of mutual respect and appropriate forms of solidarity. An example from the NYDA's history will clarify the issues at stake.

When the brother of a NYDA activist working in Cape Coast died in Accra, one of the NYDA founding fathers, from the same patriclan, who also lived in Accra, provided him with a proper funeral, even before the deceased's brother arrived from Cape Coast. Later he discussed the matter with other educated Nandome in Accra: 'When we, the supposed big men, are in trouble, we can't go back to Nima', where most Northern labour migrants in Accra live, 'because they cannot help us – funerals are very expensive'. So he proposed forming a 'little club', whose members would provide mutual financial support in just such cases and which would also 'serve as a think tank for NYDA'.[28] In the early 1990s, the Accra Nandome Social Club (ANSOC), the product of this initiative, had twenty members, all university graduates in higher occupational positions who could no longer draw on grass-roots material solidarity, but who received requests from poorer clan and village comrades for financial and moral support. In addition to the mutual aid provided to members, a fund was established to support needy students. ANSOC was also active in its self-proclaimed role as a NYDA 'think tank' or 'kitchen cabinet', as some members call it. Yet as an ANSOC member admitted self-critically, 'the whole concept of a club of status-bearing members of NYDA that more or less meets in the comfortable sitting room of one of the members with their wives serving refreshments ... is looked upon with ... a great deal of acrimony or condemnation from the majority of ordinary NYDA members.'[29] In Wa, Bolgatanga and Tamale too, the university-trained elite from Nandom formed their own clubs, usually called 'inner groups', to advise the NYDA executive. In a meeting of the NYDA executive with 'opinion leaders' in Nandom, the establishment of these clubs was criticised: It appears, 'that one has to belong to a certain "high" class before you qualify to contest for positions on the national executive'. Such 'think tanks' are thus viewed as problematic, since they imply 'that some people are not capable of thinking and those who can think should go ahead and think for everybody'.[30]

ANSOC's strategies 'to bridge this gap' involved the admission of the NYDA Accra branch executive into the club as well as efforts to play a regular part in general branch meetings and to make larger financial contributions to the association account. Yet, as one sceptic explained, ANSOC continues to be perceived as an elitist club:

> We are caught in this contradiction. We are supposed to be promoting the empowerment of the poor, defenceless rural people, yet we are perceived by the same people as bigwigs around Accra who meet and have a good time. ... That is our major failure and it limits our political clout and reduces us to just another club of petty bourgeois, lonely isolated people in the jungle of Accra city. At best we can only serve as a kind of pressure group lobbying in the corridors of power here and there – which is not our ambition. ... The ambition would be really to integrate our work with the mass of NYDA and to be seen not as some remote elitist club, but to be seen – I don't want to say 'mouthpiece', but identical in interests and aspirations. But so far we have not achieved this ideal.[31]

Now fifteen years later, the dilemma evident in this comment has yet to be resolved. While ANSOC is still alive and well, the NYDA is defunct, many critics blaming its downfall precisely on the continued existence of such 'inner groups'. This dilemma, however, is not unique to youth associations but confronts all organisations that aim at broad participation while striving to act as an effective special-interest group. Reconciling internal democracy, which must accommodate dissent and ambivalence, with effectiveness in negotiations with the outside world, which requires unity and quick decision-making, is all the more difficult in heterogeneous organisations such as the youth associations.

Organising common interests
'To promote the social, economic, educational and cultural development in Nandom' and 'to protect the rights and interests of the people in the area': Such were the chief aims articulated not just in the NYDA by-laws, but also in those of other youth associations. Yet what precisely were these 'common interests'? Defining specific projects that were both deemed feasible by a majority of members and could at the same time mobilise the grass roots was made difficult, not only by the processes of social differentiation already discussed, but also by differences between the interests of migrants, and those of the population back home.

Not only have most youth associations been founded outside the home region, following in the footsteps of preceding migrant associations, it is also there that they generally had and continue to have the greatest appeal. Beyond their role as providers of assistance in times of personal crisis, the urban branches of youth association also serve as places for social and cultural activities. Thus, youth associations were (and still are) often extremely popular among migrants for reasons that initially had little to do with 'development', although members did make occasional donations to support specific projects at home. To non-migrants such mutual support is generally found within kinship networks and a whole series of village and multi-village associations, such as the Christian Mothers, Catholic Action and prayer groups, all of which are concerned with the personal welfare of their members. Here, in the home region, youth associations are attractive primarily for their development goals and are thus confronted with a complex of potentially conflicting loyalties which usually play a less prominent role away from home.

In any case, none of the youth associations in the North-West have succeeded so far in creating a truly active grass-roots home branch. Because most associations lack large-scale financial support, they must mobilise the local population for 'self-help'. To achieve this the NYDA, as part of its annual convention, used to organise exemplary work actions, at which, for instance, in Nandom clay bricks were made for a post office, while in some nearby villages trenches were dug for latrines. However, when NYDA activists returned South most projects were left unfinished, and after a number of years such actions were no longer initiated. Later, there were avid discussions as to whether the possible educational benefits warranted a revival of such work actions, or whether such tactics were silly and, even more importantly, whether they encouraged a 'spoon-feeding' mentality. It was finally decided that the NYDA should refrain from carrying out projects itself, and instead encourage and co-ordinate village initiatives, as well as establish contacts with government and international development agencies; though not much has yet been done in this respect. Larger projects, which require outside support, provoke controversy regarding their location, as do projects for which local funds need to be mobilised. A retired mine worker, who was chairman of the NYDA branch in Tarkwa before he returned to his home village, stated the problem rather directly:

> I don't think I will have any interest in the NYDA again because in my village, if we need a latrine and we contribute, we can get it. And if I send my money to Nandom, you know, I don't go to Nandom and shit.[32]

Such conflicts over project location and the lack of interest at the grass-roots level reflect the fact that in most areas of the North-West the supra-clan and supra-village commitment which the youth associations aim to develop, be this ethnically or territorially based, has no pre-colonial roots.

Here, unlike in chiefdoms with a long historical tradition, the supra-village 'local patriotism' felt vis-à-vis the traditional areas, whose gradual emergence was sketched out in previous chapters, is essentially restricted to paramount chiefs and the educated elite. Moreover, the feeling is repeatedly undercut by conflicting loyalties that focus to varying degrees either on smaller domains (villages) or on other networks (patriclans).

DECENTRALISATION: THE RESURGENCE OF CONFLICTS BETWEEN NANDOM AND LAMBUSSIE

With the slogan 'bring the government to the people', the Rawlings government announced in the late 1980s the creation of new districts. This sparked vigorous lobbying and political mobilisation at the local level. In view of the difficulties in translating 'common interests' into concrete development plans, the youth associations happened on a project with the potential to counteract the centripetal forces threatening to paralyse their organisations, namely the struggle to obtain a district of their own. Actually, the JAYDA's efforts did succeed in making Jirapa the administrative centre of a new district. A similar high-profile success story would also have helped the NYDA gain legitimacy, but none was to present itself. Instead, the district question provoked a bitter dispute, pitting the association against the Nandom Naa, many local literates, Archbishop Peter Dery, the neighbours in Lambussie and the administration. It was to be a battle of interests whose wounds would not heal quickly.

In what follows I shall first relate the events, so that we may subsequently look more closely at two particularly controversial issues: the territorial delimitation of administrative units and the social delimitation of local political communities. Should the traditional ritual prerogatives and property rights of 'first-comers' translate into privileges regarding modern political decision-making? Or, should immigrants, particularly if they constitute a sizeable majority, have equal political rights to these 'first-comers', since all are citizens of the same nation-state? These are some of the difficult questions raised by the recent decentralisation project which have yet to be solved. These questions are also at least partly responsible for the crises that have plagued the youth associations. Moreover, the same issues that shaped the debates over the definition of youth association membership also appeared under a slightly different guise in district conflicts, where they became important to debates over the relevance of ethnic versus territorial criteria that constitute local citizenship.

A chronology of events

Three criteria guided the demarcation of the new districts: population, economic viability and existing infrastructure. The 1984 population census recorded 67,721 inhabitants in Nandom-Lambussie Local Council and

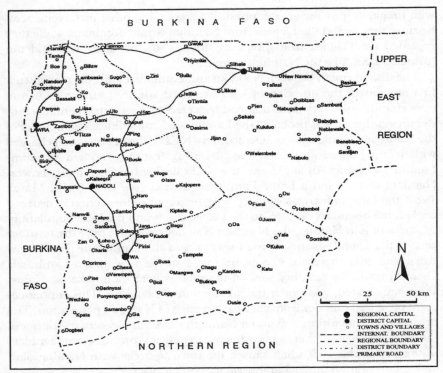

Map 9 The new districts of the Upper West Region, 1989
Source: Town and Country Planning Department, Wa

88,453 in Lawra-Jirapa Local Council (the old census units from the early 1960s were retained). Clearly, the population of Lawra District was sufficient to create two or even three new districts. However, neither Nandom nor Lambussie alone had the required 50,000 inhabitants and therefore needed a partner if they were to break away from Lawra. The NYDA presented a petition to create a Nandom or, 'if the need arises', a joint Nandom-Lambussie District.[33] However, given the bitter disputes between Nandom and Lambussie in the 1950s and 1960s, it is not surprising that this petition aggravated old grievances.

Although the petition mentioned a combined Nandom-Lambussie district only as one of two possible options, this was the one actually favoured by NYDA activists. Such a joint district had advantages in terms of infrastructure and proximity, but the NYDA also supported it, because it would encompass in one politico-administrative unit the numerous Dagara from Nandom living on Sisala land in Lambussie villages. Sisala politicians in Lambussie, on the other hand, preferred the creation of a joint district with Jirapa, despite the greater physical distance and other inconveniences, because they feared the Dagara from Nandom would dominate, while they regarded the Dagaba from Jirapa as 'friends' or 'brothers' who did not 'disturb' them 'like the Nandom people do'.[34]

The disagreement between Nandom and Lambussie over the new district first arose over the question of who exercised administrative jurisdiction over Hamile – the very issue that had triggered off protracted conflicts four decades earlier. It was probably the Lambussie Kuoro himself, a member of the National Commission on Democracy (NCD), the organisation charged with defining the new districts, who advised against the proposed Nandom-Lambussie district. In any event, the NCD decided in favour of a Lawra-Nandom district and a Jirapa-Lambussie district (see Map 9). In March 1987, the Lawra District Secretary went on a tour of inspection in order to explain the boundary changes to the village chiefs and the local population. At a meeting in Hamile, the Nandom Naa declared that only the territory east of the Hamile-Nandom road was part of the Lambussie Traditional Area, and that therefore it now belonged to the new Jirapa-Lambussie District, while the territory west of the road, where the market and most shops are located, was under the jurisdiction of Nandom. This announcement provoked outcries from various segments of Hamile's population. The prospect of re-incorporation under Nandom stirred unpleasant memories of the Nandom Naa's father, whose draconian policies towards Hamile traders in the 1940s and 1950s had caused the town to break with Nandom and seek incorporation under Lambussie in the first place.

The Nandom Naa's claim to Hamile was almost immediately followed by the mass seizure of farms from Dagara cultivating Sisala land, just as the new agricultural season had started. The matter was brought to the Lawra District Secretary, who confirmed that, according to a 1951 'High Court' decision, Hamile belonged to the Lambussie Traditional Area,[35] and exhorted the Nandom Naa and his chiefs to comply with the ruling that 'all of the Hamile township and its environs not ... be divided in any way between Lambussie and Nandom'. The Lambussie Kuoro, for his part, should allow Dagara farmers to continue farming Sisala land.[36] After further 'peace talks' between Sisala chiefs and landowners and Dagara farmers, the administrators felt that the matter had been solved.[37]

However, such optimism proved premature. Tensions were fuelled anew by further petitions and counter-petitions, drafted by the NYDA and the Sisala-dominated IWDU, and by 'confidential' meetings of association activists with the Regional Secretary in Wa who refused to rescind the original decision with regard to the district. And although the dispute was officially settled, the land conflicts continued. Again at the start of the following agricultural season in 1988, a sizeable number of Dagara farmers cultivating Sisala land was not allowed to work their fields. One conflict, in

Taalipuo, a village on the border between the Nandom and Lambussie chiefdoms, was particularly salient. Here, the disagreement centred on the administrative ties of several Dagara compounds, much as it had during the conflicts of the 1950s. Did these houses belong to Lambussie via Nabaala, the Sisala village that claimed to have granted the Dagara farmers permission to settle there originally? Or, did they belong to Nandom via the Nandom earth priest, who likewise claimed to have established the compounds in question? The Sisala felt the compounds should pay their taxes to the new Jirapa-Lambussie District and coerced Dagara farmers to comply by denying them permission to farm bush fields further inside Sisala territory.[38]

The District Security Committee, alerted by the youth associations and the paramount chiefs, organised a series of meetings with the aggrieved Dagara farmers and the Sisala landowners, as well as the earth priests from Nandom, Nabaala and Lambussie. However, the resulting agreements were never implemented since rival local dignitaries disputed the authority of those at the meeting. As the earth priests, who are traditionally responsible for the settlement of land disputes, could not resolve the matter either, other institutions were brought into play: the paramount chiefs, the political authorities at the district, regional and even the national levels, and the youth associations, which stood as the legitimate spokesmen of the aggrieved farmers. However, none of these could resolve the conflict: During the 1989 agricultural season, the Taalipuo and other Dagara farmers cultivating Sisala land were yet again barred from the fields.

The Gordian knot was finally cut by Archbishop Peter Dery, a man of mixed Dagara and Sisala ancestry who commands much respect throughout the region. After preliminary talks with both sides, he managed to summon the Nandom and Lambussie paramount chiefs to a meeting on 'neutral grounds' – the Catholic mission – though this was located in Hamile, precisely the town where the dispute over district boundaries had begun. Dery greatly simplified matters by concentrating on the Taalipuo issue. He treated the district matter as closed and avoided the complexities of settlement history and ethnic relations, reminding the chiefs and others present that 'land is the creation of God for the use of human beings'. Eventually, the chiefs agreed that three of the disputed Taalipuo compounds should be placed under the jurisdiction of Lambussie District and that in return 'the Lambussie Traditional Area will revoke all existing seizures of farm lands of immigrant and settler farmers'.[39] The agreement was implemented, and since then no overt conflicts have erupted in the disputed area. However, the property rights of first-comers and the socio-political status of long-term 'settlers', particularly immigrants' children and grandchildren, continue to be a source of tensions and have sparked innumerable squabbles.

Contested boundaries

One of the issues at stake in the Taalipuo conflict, and in the controversies over the new districts generally, was their precise territorial delimitation. Which of the existing boundaries should become the basis for defining the new districts territorially – the pre-colonial earth-shrine territories being important to the establishment of property rights to land, or the chiefdoms introduced in the colonial period, or the post-colonial electoral constituencies? As explained in earlier chapters, these boundaries are not coincident but cross-cut each other.

During the first decades of the colonial regime, chiefly rule was personal rather than territorial, and chiefdoms were defined by lists of sub-chiefs and villages subordinate to them. This practice continued into the 1950s, when local and district councils were defined on the basis of the existing chiefdoms. The exact course of these boundaries had never actually been physically demarcated, and any such exercise was bound to cause never-ending disputes, as the frequent conflicts over the placing of road signs bearing village or district names indicate. In colonial times, chiefdom and district boundaries were defined pragmatically. When it came to maintenance work, for instance, neighbouring villages were made to agree on a specific spot on the road, easily recognisable by some landmark such as a stream or a big tree, up to which each side would be responsible. Such places came to be regarded as indicators of the relevant boundaries.

In the Taalipuo conflict, the Dagara indeed referred to such a spot on the road between Taalipuo and Nabaala as proof that their forefathers actually owned the disputed land and that the village belonged to Nandom. However, the Sisala rejected this claim, insisting on their first-comer status. They reminded the Dagara that it was the Lambussie earth priests who had once given Nandom its earth shrine, implying that no real boundary separated these two areas. Consequently, there was nothing separating Taalipuo and Nabaala. Decisive in their eyes was that the Sisala from Nabaala and Billaw had given the Dagara permission to settle in Taalipuo.[40]

This argument exemplifies an alternative approach to demarcating administrative units, one not based on chiefdoms, but on allodial land ownership. Yet even these boundaries are neither straightforward nor uncontested. For one, there may be debate over claims of first-comer status and the legitimacy of subsequent property transfers. If, for example, the Sisala claim the land up to the Black Volta as theirs, then this is because they insist that although their ancestors transferred an earth shrine to the Dagara, the shrine-giver's community retains certain rights over the territory. Moreover, they not only accuse the Dagara of disregarding these rights, but also of having appropriated further land without the authorisation of the original Sisala landowners – accusations which the Dagara vehemently reject. While disagreement between Sisala and Dagara regarding these claims and accusations and the history of land ownership more generally had little effect on everyday access to farmland, when it came to redrawing district boundaries, this became a controversial issue.

Furthermore, as the Taalipuo conflict showed, the exact course of village and earth-shrine boundaries, which the Sisala insisted district boundaries should follow, is often contested. These boundaries were traditionally imagined not as linear, but rather as a series of 'meeting points' in the bush. Village affiliation of houses and fields along these relatively open borders usually depended on which earth priest had originally granted permission to cultivate or build. Thus, the social networks arising from these spiritual services can and do create rights and obligations between the service provider and the service beneficiary, which in turn can translate into territorial ties. In the Taalipuo conflict, this is what set off such intense debate over which earth priest – the one from Nabaala or the one from Nandomkpee – had given the compounds in question the right to settle. Such service relationships generate the authority to impart numerous rights (including the right to build houses, to farm and to bury the dead). Yet neither are these relationships unambiguous or unalterable, nor is their translation into territorial affiliation straightforward, so that a compound's territorial affiliation, for example, is not always clear. Inhabitants can, depending on the context and interests involved, refer to different services as evidence to bolster competing claims to property rights.

In the conflicts between Nandom and Lambussie, each of the interested parties tried to present the criteria for delineating the district boundaries as 'natural', as ensuing automatically from legitimately attained property rights or colonially established political hierarchies. However, all criteria are contestable and subject to negotiation and the manner in which any one of these will subsequently be effectively translated into territorial ties highly uncertain. As such the final outcome of such conflicts as the ones between Nandom and Lambussie depend on local power relationships as well as the mobilisation of regional and national political contacts.

Autochthony and citizenship

Any decision on the territorial delimitation of new administrative units entails important consequences for their social and ethnic composition, raising delicate questions as to the political rights of land-owning 'natives' versus immigrant farmers. This was the second issue at stake in the conflicts over new districts. In the district assemblies as proposed by the NCD, the inhabitants of a district, being citizens of Ghana, all have the same fundamental rights and duties. Differences in ethnic identity and questions of autochthony are regarded to be irrelevant. It is exactly this model of political participation by citizens with equal rights to which the NYDA and the Dagara generally referred. Sisala politicians, on the other hand, emphasised specific rights ensuing from their status as property owners and first-comers to the region. Even today, the most these politicians concede to the Dagara in the Lambussie Traditional Area are positions as headmen, and not as 'full-fledged' chiefs, even in villages with a sizeable Dagara majority. As far as modern administration is concerned, the Sisala fear that should Dagara and Sisala participate equally in a single common district, it would further bolster Nandom's dominance, because the Dagara living in the Lambussie Traditional Area could join with their 'brothers', the Dagara of Nandom, to gang up against the Sisala.

At the heart of these powerful sentiments are tensions arising from the unequal development of Nandom and Lambussie. Due to extensive conversion to Catholicism, the Dagara of Nandom enjoyed earlier and more widespread access to education than the Sisala. They have therefore had access to a greater variety of employment opportunities, and have secured more infrastructure for their villages and Nandom. Sisala politicians also viewed the Dagara as being more skilful lobbyists and as using this to 'take land away' from the Sisala. This is why they wished to block the establishment of a common district at all costs.[41] Yet when it came to the Dagaba of Jirapa they harboured no such fears; though a good ten years after the introduction of the new districts, they did begin complaining of a certain marginalisation in securing government positions and the development of infrastructure.

NYDA activists saw the emphasis on ethnic difference as a political strategy initiated by a small Sisala elite: '[T]he vast majority of ordinary people are quite capable of making up their minds without resorting to ethnic identities'. Most importantly, they insisted that after more than sixty years of settlement it was simply unjust to continue to classify people as 'settlers', effectively excluding them from full political participation. Furthermore, they claimed that ownership rights, and therefore rights of political participation, were linked to the active cultivation of the land, not first-comer status as such:

> Most of the Dagaaba[42] in the Nandom-Lambussie area have made the place their home since the early part of the 19th century. The Sissala [sic] ... themselves ... migrated into the area from somewhere else. ... The fact that they arrived before us and established a few communities in the wild bush that the area at that time was, does not justify the landowner-tenant relations that some would like to see existing between the two areas. In fact, the pioneer Sissala settlers could not have tamed and put under cultivation the wild bush that the area was without the Dagaabas. Descendants of these intrepid conquerors of the land cannot now be dismissed, generations later as mere settlers, as is now currently happening in Taalipuo.[43]

Although NYDA leaders accused the Sisala of using land for political leverage, the Lambussie Kuoro insisted that Sisala landowners' concerns regarding land access were justified, because 'the land is becoming short ... so if you give up all your land and it is exhausted, you yourself will have nowhere to go.'[44] Archbishop Peter Dery argued similarly, but also agreed with the NYDA that political relations as well as ethnicity were also important concerns. He saw the 'root of the problem' in the 'discriminatory attitude of the Dagara towards the Sisala' and in the 'second thoughts' of the 'NYDA young men', who 'planned to pull Lambussie under Nandom'.[45]

The central point at issue in all these discussions is: How is the community that exercises effective political control in a given district to define itself? Does it do so in terms of autochthony and ethnicity, or in terms of basic equality and a shared vision of the future, leaving aside the historical intricacies of ownership rights to the land? The growing popularity of primordialist discourses of autochthony, which was evident in the conflicts surrounding the creation of new districts in the North-West, has been observed in many other parts of Africa, too. Various authors have proposed that the preoccupation with local rootedness intensifies with the need for reassurance and identity under the pressures of globalisation (Geschiere and Gugler 1998; Geschiere and Nyamnjoh 2000). In North-West Ghana, however, globalisation plays only an indirect role in the alternating cycles of increasing exclusivity or inclusiveness evident in local political debates. Rather, the configuration of first-comers versus late-comers we see negotiated in the authochthony discourses is a phenomenon with pre-colonial roots that became politically re-signified during the colonial period.

As we have seen in earlier chapters, even in the pre-colonial period first-comer status was important for land ownership and ritual control. Nevertheless, the in-migrating Dagara did become allodial landowners by various means: by ethnic assimilation (thus becoming members of the first-comer community), the purchase of land and earth shrines from the Sisala, or the forceful expulsion of the latter. Colonial pacification put a halt to this process of autochthonisation. The colonial category 'native' drastically simplified the complex pre-colonial strategies of social belonging, and, even more importantly, politicised the rights arising from settlement history. In the context of the native-state model, it is only the natives, as first-comers and land owners, who rightfully enjoy full citizenship and political participation in a chiefdom. Since the British model did not foresee multiple group memberships and mobility, even living in a chiefdom for several generations did not suffice to achieve native status. Some primordial, genealogical link to the purported first-comers was necessary. Conversely, groups living elsewhere for an extended period still counted as natives in their old homes. The more difficult it was for one to become a native elsewhere, the stronger the inclination to retain one's status as a native in one's community of origin, and the more the category's significance shifted from a territorial to a descent-based community. As a result, the Sisala claimed to be the only natives of Lambussie, insisting that the in-migrating Dagara from Nandom, regardless of the duration of their stay, were 'settlers' who, although they owed allegiance to the Lambussie Kuoro, should not enjoy the same rights to participate in local affairs as the Sisala natives. Furthermore, they felt that such a prerogative should not be limited to chieftaincy matters, but also encompass modern political institutions. At the district level, this means that while the Dagara may be represented by their own assembly – men and women – they should not be allowed to furnish, for example, the District Chief Executive; at the national level, many Sisala insist that a Dagara should not represent their constituency in Parliament.

In the conflicts over local councils and district boundaries in the 1950s and 1960s as well as in the recent land conflicts, it is this ideological model to which local political actors continued to appeal. It remained an argumentative resource for those it privileged politically, while those it potentially excluded – immigrants and strangers – tended to deploy civic and democratic discourses, both during the conflicts of the decolonisation period as well as, and ever more forcefully, in recent decades. Mahmood Mamdani (1996) regarded the difference between 'citizen' and 'subject' (the primordially-ethnically defined 'native' in a chiefdom) as the most important legacy of the colonial 'bifurcated state' and the decentralised despotism of the 'native authorities', and he associated this binary opposition with the rural–urban dichotomy. While urban elites propagated democratic discourses of civic equality, rural areas continued to be dominated by chiefs that constituted their authority through primordial, traditionalist discourses. But as seen in the case presented here, the lines of conflict actually cross-cut such dichotomies. Youth association activists and regional politicians, chiefs and commoners, rural inhabitants and urbanites, farmers and the educated elite alike deploy both traditionalist and democratic discourses, depending on the context and interests at stake.

For the NYDA, these conflicts over territorial and social boundaries, districts and land constituted a test of strength whose debilitating consequences have yet to be overcome. For better or worse, the division of districts had to be accepted, and many even blamed the NYDA that Nandom was not given its own. The next defeat soon followed: When electoral constituencies were redrawn, Lambussie and Jirapa were each given their own, but not Nandom, despite a NYDA petition. NYDA activists complained about the 'monstrous instincts of our neighbours', the 'internal detractors' and the 'Judases' who were aiming to sell out the NYDA,[46] and they insisted that 'our only salvation now lies in our galvanising a united front upon which greater laurels can be achieved'.[47] However, these problems confronting the NYDA and other youth associations stem not from a lack of personal engagement on the part of association members, nor do they have much to do with particular failings in their internal organisation. Rather, these difficulties are the offshoots of the legacy left by the colonial native-state model, a legacy having produced a discourse of autochthony and 'local patriotism' that up until the present day competes with discourses propounding the equality of citizens in modern nation-states.

10

THE CULTURAL WORK
OF ETHNICITY

In the summer of 1989 Dr Gbellu, a doctor from Nandom living in
Germany invited Dagara friends and family as well as their German wives
and children and even Dagara migrants from other parts of Europe to come
together at his home for a 'Dagara family meeting'. For two days more than
twenty adults gathered, as they had done in previous years, in order to
celebrate and to reflect on Dagara culture and history. During the 1989
meeting, to which I had been invited, a number of those attending held
avidly discussed lectures on topics such as traditional religion, initiation
rituals, patri- and matriclans and Dagara historical origins. Here too the
relationship between territoriality, political organisation and ethnicity, the
very issues analysed in previous chapters of the present work, was, as the
following excerpt from the meeting shows, a controversial matter and part
of an ongoing process of negotiating their self-understanding and historico-
cultural heritage:

> P.S.: What I would like to know from you is where ... the Dagara stay,
> where do you find the Dagara? ... Suppose I do not know who the
> Dagara are, then you could tell me: it is in this area that the Dagaras
> live?
> S.B.: ... it's a very wide thing, but obviously we shouldn't exaggerate.
> We just want to stress that we live in three countries, Ghana,
> Burkina Faso and Ivory Coast. ...
> D.D.: If you start from Hamile and you go all the way down to Bole
> and still beyond Bole, all to the West, there you find Dagara ...
> S.B.: His problem is that there are also other people there. Where is
> the border? [much stirring and lively discussion]
> D.D.: ... Naturally you don't find a people in the world today which is
> 'pure' ... Even in Nandom itself ... you find Ewes there, you find
> Yorubas there, but because they are in the minority, they are not
> taken as important, they are living in Dagaraland.
> P.S.: What I am after: certainly there are so many Dagara here [in
> Gammelshausen, Germany], but we will not say that this place is
> Dagara. ... Where are the borders between the Dagara people and
> other tribes ... ?

J.G.: It is difficult. Even the kingdoms, the Mossi kingdoms and the rest, you will never find that the border ends here sharply. It doesn't exist in nature like that. .... There is always a transit area [lively discussion] ...

D.D.: ... You see, if the Dagara had a kingdom and had laid-down boundaries, then we could say this is Dagaraland. But within a particular area, Dagara are living there, and we for convenience's sake call it Dagaraland. It mustn't be Dagaraland, in the sense that the land is our property. No. It could be that Dagara are found there, but it is not Dagaraland, because we haven't formed any empire. ... Historians and anthropologists have always been to the mind that we are acephalous. ... Perhaps the Dagara had an empire, but we haven't been able to establish that.[1]

Dr Delle's proposal to thus use the term 'Dagaraland' in a limited sense only, or not at all, met with objections. Others suggested that language be the deciding criterion, the idea being that Dagaraland encompasses all villages, the majority of whose inhabitants are native speakers of Dagara, whatever the dialect. But even this idea did not go unchallenged. Such lively debate had previously also arisen regarding the proper name for the Dagara and their origins. Time and again the discussions returned to the question of ethnic boundaries, social location and belonging: Who are the Dagara? Where do they come from? Who may be considered a member of the Dagara community? Why do they speak different dialects? Which cultural traditions distinguish them from their neighbours, and which customs are to be preserved?

The cultural work of ethnicity, which provided the impetus for the 'Dagara family meeting', is also the focal point of cultural festivals, which have developed since the 1970s in North-Western Ghana. They have become an arena where ethnic identities are articulated within a framework negotiated by the state and the media. At the same time, this public form of self-representation propels internal processes of defining and integrating the various ethnic communities. Hence, the aims of the Kakube Festival, as explained by the event's initiator, the Nandom Naa, in his opening remarks: 'To reconsider traditional culture' and 'to foster unity between our people and our neighbours'. The festival was inspired by the traditional thanksgiving sacrifice in honour of family ancestors, but the highlight of the festivities was – much like in the older Kobine Festival in Lawra – a large, public dance competition, in which dozens of groups from the Nandom Traditional Area, neighbouring chiefdoms and even Dagara villages in Burkina Faso participated (Lentz 2001b). Over the years the festival has become an important site of cultural self-affirmation, a celebration of the Dagara community's vitality (many migrants return to Nandom for the event) and a demonstration of pride in being 'we Nandome'. This became particularly clear in the NYDA chairman's address during the great durbar that opened the festival in 1991, at which – as is customary for such events – representatives of the district administration and the regional government and officials from Accra were among the guests:

> The first basic step in a bid to achieve development in a community is the sense of oneness and coming together, the consciousness of a common cultural identity. ... It is in line with this that NYDA is fully behind the chiefs in the revival and celebration of our age-old Kakube Festival. ... We shall do everything possible to develop the celebration of the Kakube Festival to appreciable standards to attain national and international recognition. ... This occasion gives the youth of the Traditional Area an opportunity to partake and learn more about our cultural heritage and we are happy and proud to have all these invited guests in our midst to witness the rich culture of the Nandome. This occasion has given us a sense of belongness [sic] and identity. It is a reminder to all sons and daughters, all Nandome, of our cultural origin and our commitment to the development of Nandom.[2]

Discussions like those at the 'Dagara family meeting' in Germany or the NYDA chairman's call to raise the festival 'to appreciable standards' show that local cultural heritage is not taken for granted; it is negotiated, via a process that includes innovation and the redefinition of traditions. This holds true not just for the dances performed at the above-mentioned festivals, but also for questions regarding the historic migrations of the groups living in the North-West or their pre-colonial political traditions. That local intellectuals reflect on these issues with self-confidence, and occasionally with self-criticism, is a relatively recent development. In contrast, the kind of political instrumentalisation of ethnicity examined in previous chapters was marked by chiefs and local politicians referring back rather uncritically to colonial ethnic categories. However, since the 1970s members of the regional educated elites have explicitly subjected the ethnic constructs produced by outsiders to re-evaluation. Dagara and Dagaba intellectuals in particular have been quite diligent in this matter, producing numerous ethnographic, historiographic and ethno-theological studies. The Sisala and Wala – probably because there are far fewer Western-trained academics among them – have not been quite so prolific, or at least have not recorded their activities in writing to the same extent. For this reason the present chapter focuses primarily on the cultural work undertaken by Dagara and Dagaba intellectuals.[3]

Their activities have not brought forth a monolithic account of the origins and culture of the Dagara/Dagaba. Specific local perspectives have given rise to different versions of history, while cultural and historical arguments have also served as an idiom to express diverging political

Plate 9 Chiefs during the Kakube Festival, Nandom, 1994
From the left (sitting): Jirapa Naa B. Yelpoe, Nandom Naa Dr Imoro, Lambussie
Kuoro K. Y. Baloro, Nadawli Naa, Kokoligu Naa, Billaw Kuoro (Photo: Carola
Lentz)

interests. There is, as we shall see, considerable debate on names, origins,
pre-colonial social organisation, and so forth. Their 'primordialisation',
then, does not preclude that ethnic categories and boundaries continue to
be contested. Moreover, the educated elite can not enlist wider constituencies in their ethnic projects by simple imposition. Ethnic idioms of social
belonging must convince, emotionally and intellectually, by their plausibility
and their link with the realm of ordinary experience. Thus, on the one hand,
they have to somehow accommodate and incorporate older social networks
(such as the patriclan), village oral history(ies) and popular concepts of
'tribal customs'. Yet on the other hand, in order to make a Dagara identity
nationally or even internationally communicable, ethnic difference must be
constructed within generally accepted models of 'Ghanaian cultures'. The
cultural construction of ethnicity, then, is a multi-faceted, contested
process.

THE POST-WAR CULTURAL AND LINGUISTIC TURN
The larger context in which this local cultural work of ethnicity takes place
is marked by new discourses regarding ethnicity that unfolded in Ghana,
and in West Africa generally, during the post-war period of local government reforms – discourses which effected the depoliticisation of 'tribes' as a

concept while at the same time refining ethnic categorisations. 'Tribes' now became 'ethnic groups' or 'cultures', at least in official discourse. Although 'tribes' certainly lived on in popular discussions and in local political strategies, officially they were no longer regarded to be the natural founda-tion of political community (except when referring to the past). Instead, they came to be viewed as groups distinguishable by linguistic characteristics and cultural traditions, which need to be taken into account, but also partly 'modernised' in the interests of long-term economic development and the cultivation of a national cultural heritage. The counterpart that was now politically relevant to the nation-state was not the 'native' or the 'tribesman', but rather the 'citizen' – whether a city-dweller or a farmer – and, if reference was made to the 'natural' community as the cornerstone of development, then this was not the tribe, but rather the village.

This trend is evident in the 1960 population census – the last to ask about ethnic identification. While until then 'tribes' had been an established census category, now its use was explicitly defended. The figures on 'tribes in Ghana' were to serve academic purposes only, namely, 'to give the research worker in the social sciences ... a few basic data on population groups which are ... generally referred to as tribes or tribal groupings'.[4] This cautious wording must on the one hand be understood in the context of the Nkrumah regime, which through the 1957 Avoidance of Discrimination Act devised an effective means to check political opposition by banning religious, regionalist and ethnic parties. On the other hand, Nkrumah's dictum that 'tribes, like nationalities may always remain in a country, but it is tribalism – tribal politics – that should be fought and destroyed' (1970: 59–60) reflects a view on which there is broad consensus and which continues to guide Ghanaian politics today.

The shift in official discourse reflected, to a certain degree, increasing doubts in anthropology about the analytical usefulness of the term 'tribe'. However, tribes were still retained as units of research, as the 'X' for whom ethnographic descriptions should be valid. This paradox of deconstructing while maintaining the concept of tribe (or ethnic group) is particularly evident in Meyer Fortes' and E. E. Evans-Pritchard's *African Political Systems* (1940). The introduction criticised the assumption of clear-cut territorial-political cum cultural boundaries, which the then current notion of the tribe implied. Yet at the same time, the individual contributions to the volume continued to use colonial tribal names, census data and maps to define their units of research. This approach also shaped the International African Institute's Ethnographic Survey of Africa series which was to provide an overview of the knowledge available about the 'tribal societies of Africa'. Contributions to the Survey implicitly reified tribes, despite the authors' introductory criticism of this terminology. 'Tribes tended to emerge inside the green covers', writes Elizabeth Tonkin, 'through the standard constitutive categories of kinship, political structure, traditions of origin and the like which imply and get their meaning from the assumption that there are bounded social units' (1990: 141–2). Tonkin blames this reification above all on the desire for a complete description of the African world and the functionalist paradigm that sought to be holistic in its analysis of social systems.

The Survey's study of the Gold Coast's Northern Territories written by Manoukian (1951) adopted colonial ethnic categories more or less uncritically. Manoukian's defence that her classification into tribes followed linguistic criteria remained, at least as far as defining the Wala, Birifor and Dagaba was concerned, a mere assertion. It did not fundamentally challenge the ethnic categories used by the first colonial officers. Even Jack Goody, who carried out field research in the North-West in the early 1950s, grappled with the paradox of deconstructing these categories while still retaining them. He convincingly established that it was not tribes *per se*, but a flexible, situation-specific and context-dependent system of group formation with variable, directional actors' and observers' names that shaped and still shapes local societies. Conventional ethnic names such as Lobi and Dagarti could only be understood properly if one regarded them as concepts with which local actors designated their neighbours in particular situations with regard to specific cultural practices (1956: 16–26). But, says Goody further, this situational labelling does not give rise to a clear, permanent, ethnic nomenclature. A person can thus be described in one context as Dagarti and in another as Lobi. For purposes of anthropological comparison, however, Goody felt it necessary to devise his own nomenclature. With his distinction between the LoDagaa (further sub-divided into the LoDagaba and LoWiili) with dual descent and the patrilineal Dagaba, he returned finally to the old colonial distinction between Lobi and Dagarti. And while Goody initially emphasised that this was a classification imposed by the observer, he later seemed to be convinced that the actors consistently defined themselves in the same manner. The anthropological question regarding the dividing lines between various 'culture areas' was relatively unproblematic as far as the LoDagaa were concerned, at least according to Goody, since it was 'answered by the people themselves' (1962: 4), with reference to differences in rules of descent.[5]

Compared to the colonial classification the only thing new here is the culturalist justification which is presented with the authority of ethno-graphic expertise. However, one should not overestimate the impact of these early professional attempts to classify the North-West ethnologically. Goody's nomenclature only really gained acceptance in British ethnographic literature, while Francophone authors largely ignored it and the Ghanaian census of 1960 only adopted it partially.[6] Today, as we shall see, these categories are relevant only insofar as Dagara intellectuals cite them as a

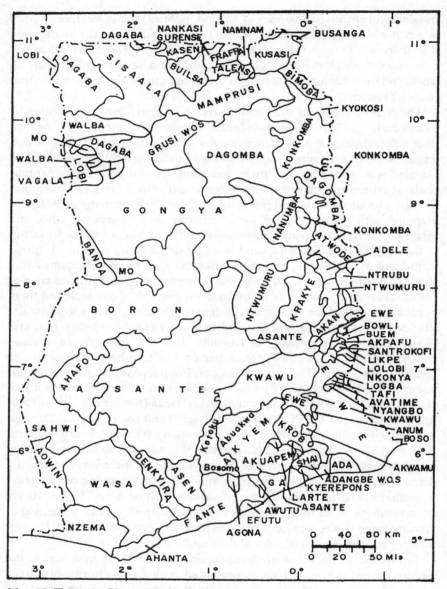

Map 10 Tribes in Ghana, 1960
Source: 1960 Population Census of Ghana, Special Report E

prime example for the arbitrariness of Western ethnographies, which serves as a counterpoint to their own terminology.

The population census of 1960 also shows how persistent colonial ethnic categories really were, and in fact still are. Although the census promised a 'multicriteria classification', according to 'language, traditional or historical classification and geographic affinity or origin', in fact, the classifications that had up until then been prevalent were adopted so that the census distinguished between 'Dagaba', 'Walba' (Wala) and 'Lobi'.[7] Under the category Lobi we find placed 'several ethnic groups', namely Birifor, Yangala, Miwo, Lowili and Lo Dagaba, whereby – as had been the case in the early colonial systems of classification – Lobi-speakers (Miwo) and Dagara-speakers comprised a single category that was regarded as distinct from the Dagaba, who also happened to speak Dagara.[8] A look at the census map (Map 10) also shows that under the category 'Lobi' were subsumed not only 'real' Lobi immigrants from Upper Volta, which had settled in the area south of Wa back in the 1920s, but also the remnants of the British 'Lobi' and 'Lobi-Dagarti' in Lawra District. That the latter now only comprised a mere 4.8 per cent of Lawra's population, while 81.4 per cent were classified as 'Dagaba' indicates that the popular trend towards 'Dagabafication', which Duncan-Johnstone observed back in the 1920s, had continued.[9] The extirpation of all vestiges of a matrilinear, and therefore presumably 'primitive', Lobi heritage from the cultural self-definition of the Dagara will be the focus of the following pages.

Census and census map also show that the basic idea of a mosaic of clearly delineated ethnic groups continued to dominate. On the 1960 census map we find no indications of fluid ethnic boundaries, inter-ethnic marriages or multi-ethnic settlements, on the contrary: with its clear dividing lines it reified the ethnic landscape to a greater extent than did the earlier British maps, which indicated ethnic names, but did not sketch linear boundaries. Even today this map, reproduced in dozens of handbook articles and monographs, continues to shape popular notions regarding ethnicity in Ghana.

DAGABA OR DAGARA? STRUGGLING FOR A NAME

Time and again Dagara and Dagaba intellectuals complain that the Asante and other groups from the South 'have certain pejorative terms for us, they call us *ntafo* or *pepeni* ... Dagarti or even Dangati, and they write these things'.[10] These intellectuals feel the need to counter the popular view expressed by these derogatory labels that the Dagara / Dagaba are primitive and backward. Moreover they regard consensus among themselves about the proper group name and group boundaries as a prerequisite to gaining a respectable place among the Ghanaian 'tribes'. As the discussants during the 'Dagara family meeting' in Germany expressed it:

The problem may be within [us] because we have not been able to identify ourselves and tell them what to say. ... So anybody calls us by any name, some of them pejorative, some not, but we accept them. So the problem is to define who we are.

Names are vital to the definition of 'who we are' and to the creation of ethnic communities. Naming (and mapping) collectives was integral to the (re-)configuration of the political landscape, as we have seen in earlier chapters of this book. However, the question as to which term should be adopted as the proper ethnic name – Dagara, Dagaba or some other label – is controversial, particularly among the educated elite. The controversy is about group boundaries and the degree of exclusivity (should the 'Lobr' speakers from the Nandom and Lawra traditional areas be included in the Dagaba community or do they form a separate group?) as well as about dominance within the group (which section's name should be made the name for the whole group?).

There is consensus that colonial tribal categories and anthropological classifications have been rather divisive and that external observers generally had a 'lopsided interest in the dissimilarities' of different sub-groups (Kuukure 1985: 26). '[C]ustomary and dialect variations', insists Paul Bekye, have been 'mistaken by the European colonial administrators and ethnologists for different ethnic groups', but the 'Dagaaba' themselves have always known 'that they are one people even if they exhibit customary and dialect variations' (1991: 95–6). Many intellectuals have looked to language as a unifying element. They agree that Lobi, spoken in areas west of the Black Volta, and Dagara (or Dagaare) are two different languages, and that the latter breaks down into a variety of mutually intelligible dialects. But there is debate whether this language should be called Dagara or Dagaare. Moreover, there are different classifications of the dialects, and there is disagreement whether Wale and Birifor are dialects of Dagara (Dagaare) or languages in their own right (Bemile 2000). Yet even if these questions could be answered unequivocally, language is as ambiguous a marker for group boundaries as culture or descent. It is quite common for people to speak several dialects and languages; mobility has militated against a neat correspondence between language and territory; and patriclan networks extend across all dialects. It is impossible, therefore, to define ethnic boundaries 'objectively', for instance in accordance with linguistic and cultural affinities, and all proposals to adopt a common ethnic name are implicitly political, even if the arguments appear cultural.

Goody's complicated and contrived nomenclature offers many discussants a welcome point of departure, in order to present their own proposals as a return to the 'simple facts'. The only indigenous name Goody retained was 'Dagaba', because it was 'in fact the name by which these people refer to themselves', as he conceded, and because he had not yet carried out a sufficiently 'detailed investigation' to attempt any further 'sub-division' (1956: 26). With respect to the name 'Dagara', on the other hand, Goody wrote that the term was sometimes used 'by the LoDagaba for internal reference', but insisted that it was a recently adopted name, 'by which they were known to a neighbouring people' and that its usage was 'far from frequent' (ibid.: 25). Not surprisingly, this dismissal has been particularly criticised by intellectuals from among Goody's LoDagaba, of the Nandom area, who want to dissociate themselves from the stigma of primitivism surrounding all things 'Lo' or 'Lobi' (Hawkins 2002: 95–102). They assert that Dagara has in fact since time immemorial been the accepted self-designation (and the name of their language), popular in the villages of the North-Western corner of the Upper West region and in South-Western Burkina Faso, but also suitable as a unitary ethnic name for a wider community, including the Dagaba (Der 1989, Somda 1989). However, Dagaba intellectuals from the Jirapa and Kaleo areas have proposed their own ethnonym as unitary ethnic designation. And, in fact, thanks to the Catholic mission starting its activities in Jirapa, Dagaba (also spelled 'Dagaaba') has enjoyed more currency so far, at least within Ghana, particularly in English-language public discourse, because the missionaries were the first to put the language – more precisely, the Jirapa dialect – into writing, and in consequence adopted Dagaba as the most inclusive ethnic name. That the Dagara and Dagaba intellectuals' debate over ethnic boundaries and names is a struggle over cultural self-assertion and political ties becomes particularly clear in a locally published pamphlet written by the late Gabriel Tuurey, a teacher from Kaleo.

In his *Introduction to the Mole-speaking Community* (1982),[11] Tuurey called upon his local readers to overcome differences of dialect and descent in order to unite in the struggle for a separate Upper West Region. Searching for the most inclusive name for his constituency, Tuurey used the term Dagaba only occasionally and preferred to speak of the 'Mole-speaking community', because he wanted to include the politically powerful Wala who would not want to identify with the designation 'Dagaba'. While Dagara intellectuals from Nandom largely ignored the Wala in the construction of their ethnic community, Tuurey's emphasis on the blood relationship and linguistic ties shared by all 'Mole-Dagomba peoples' was primarily directed against the distinction between Wala and Dagaba. But Tuurey hesitated to include the people from the Nandom and Lawra areas, whom he called Lor-Dagaba, borrowing from Goody's nomenclature. The Lor-Dagaba, Tuurey claimed, emerged from marriages between the indigenous Lobi and 'Mole-speaking elements' that had immigrated from the Dagomba area. Echoing colonial stereotypes of the Lobi as the most primitive of all tribes, Tuurey wrote that the Lobi were matrilineal, knew no 'governmental organization' and were therefore 'a wily treacherous people capable of waylaying anybody to settle a personal or imaginary score' (1982: 22). Furthermore, Tuurey emphasised, these traits did not disappear when the Lobi intermarried with the 'Mole speaking elements': the Lor-Dagaba 'drew from both Lobi and Mole cultures', speak a 'hybrid of Mole and Lobi', and 'freely refer to themselves either as Dagara or Lobi' (ibid.: 33). This indicated that they were not only less civilised than the rest of the 'Mole speaking community' but also unreliable allies. Tuurey thus attempted to rid the 'Mole speaking community' of all 'Lobi elements', even if this conflicted with his original intention to promote the most inclusive sense of ethnic unity possible.

As one of the primary differences between the Lobi and the Dagaba Tuurey cited the matrilinearity of the former (and the patrilinearity of the latter), whereby for him – in classic evolutionist fashion – matrilinearity represented a lower level of development. In light of such value judgements it is not surprising that the issue of matrilinearity provoked a great deal of interest and was discussed in a series of articles on 'Dagaaba identity' in a journal published by the Wa Diocese.[12] Gaspard Dery (1987), a geography teacher at Nandom Secondary School, also ruminated over the issue. His primary concern was to prove that all 'Dagaba tribes' were in fact patrilinear, including the 'Lobi', 'Lobr' and 'Lobi-Dagarti': in all, patriclans were exceedingly important, residence was virilocal and the inheritance of land and compounds patrilineal. Only moveable wealth was inherited through the matriline in some groups, and then only if there were no full brothers. Dery thus did not criticise the stigmatisation of 'Lobi cultural traits', but rather contended that those to whom Tuurey and others had ascribed this cultural heritage were in reality organised patrilineally.

Benedict Der, coming from a village near Nandom, also basically agreed with the criticism of the term Lobi, but took Tuurey to task for echoing the colonial view that the people of Nandom and Lawra were originally 'Lobi' and for excluding them 'from those he thought were or are the real Mole-Dagbane speakers' (1989: 7). According to him, Tuurey was misled by the differences in dialect and failed to see that the Dagaba patriclans of Kaleo, Nadawli and Jirapa were the same as those of the Dagara from Nandom and Lawra (ibid.: 14–15). Der for his part insisted that those whom Tuurey pejoratively called Lor-Dagaba were in actual fact pure Dagara who had immigrated from the Dagomba area and never intermarried with Lobi autochthones. He claimed that they had indeed immigrated earlier than Tuurey's southern Dagaba and that the latter in reality descended from the original Dagara and later immigrant groups. Therefore,

> if a common ethnological term has to be found to describe them as a people, one would suggest Dagara ... Failing that, the compound name Dagara-Dagaba can be used. The early Dagaba were, in effect, the grandchildren, the nephews, nieces and cousins of the Dagara. (ibid.: 21)

Der presented these arguments to Dagara and Dagaba intellectuals from both Ghana and Burkina Faso at a 1988 conference in Wa, which was to serve as a cornerstone for ethnic unification and the cross-border exchange of ideas.[13] But the agreement reached by participants to adopt 'Dagara' as unitary ethnic name petered out in practice, at least as far as English-language public discourse is concerned. Even Dagara intellectuals some-times still use Dagaba as a collective term, when they wish to mobilise the widest possible ethnic front for their political cause. In other contexts, however, they insist that Dagara is the only correct term for the entire ethnic group. The educated elite from the area around Jirapa, Nadawli and Kaleo, on the other hand, interpret Der's thesis as amounting to an unacceptable pretension to hegemony. Pressure for the creation of new districts and constituencies, the struggle for influence within existing ones, as well as conflicts about which dialect to privilege in church, adult education or language courses at university, keep the debate regarding names and ethnic boundaries alive.

This debate is not only of interest to intellectuals and politicians. Many labour migrants to the gold mines, for instance, have insisted that Dagara and Dagaba (or 'Lobi' and 'Dagarti', when they speak in English) constitute two distinct, albeit similar tribes. Each group tends to have its own chief and voluntary associations. In this and similar contexts, Dagaba migrants continue to call Dagara from Nandom and Lawra *lobr* (Lobi), a term as pejorative today as when the British introduced it. In turn, the latter retort by calling the Dagaba *mwelere*, literally: 'hitting with an axe', a name that refers to someone who is slow or who takes advantage of others. While Dagaba and Dagara are the indigenous ethnonyms which the local people themselves generally use when speaking in their own language, the colonial term 'Dagarti', ironically, appears to be the most neutral and inclusive ethnic name in English-language conversations.

ORIGINS: CONTESTED ACCOUNTS

Defining 'who we are' involves knowing 'where we come from' and much of the controversy over ethnic identities is cast in terms of a debate on history. Here again, the intellectuals' struggle to find a convincing account of the origins of the Dagara/Dagaba arises partly from the absence of political centralisation and a single, official account of the past, and partly from the current jockeying between various local factions for dominance. Among Dagara villagers, as we have seen, 'history' exists in the form of many migration narratives told by different patriclan segments, which portray the piecemeal agricultural migration of small kin groups. Reference to a previous home may serve as the basis for extra-village networks, but on the whole the accounts are much less concerned with origins *per se* than with rights in the here and now. However, colonial historiography found its inspiration in the origin myths of centralised polities rather than the local patriclan migration narratives and was shaped by European images of *Völkerwanderung* – a history ultimately driven by the expansion of more highly developed states, while stateless tribes such as the Lobi or Dagarti were consigned to the role of victims. Colonial officials therefore found it difficult to explain the puzzling ethnographic make-up of the North-West without recourse to a history consisting of large-scale collective migration, conquest and intermarriage. Until very recently, West African university and secondary school history textbooks continued to focus on the development of states, whereas stateless groups appear as a general mass of 'people without history'. It is against both backgrounds, village oral traditions and colonial historiographies, that the efforts of Dagara and Dagaba intellectuals to rewrite history must be understood.

While some of these new historiographies perpetuate evolutionist or cultural-diffusionist models of 'tribal' migration (Tuurey 1982, Naameh 1986, Der 1989), others dismiss colonial (and European anthropologists') conjectures on the grounds of 'what the Dagara themselves say about their origins' (Somda 1989: 6; Hébert 1976). All attempt to restore historical agency to the Dagara and other local groups and present their historiographies as authentic articulations of their respective communities. Yet at the same time such endeavours to write a tribal history and integrate this into a master narrative of 'the History of West Africa' are problematic for oral traditions, which have never known absolute chronologies and which are primarily concerned with local boundaries and hierarchies. How this problem is confronted varies from author to author: some stick closely to lineage narratives, others combine village legend with elements taken from colonial historiography, while yet others make only cursory reference to oral traditions and develop their own view of tribal history (Lentz 1994a).

One of the first concerted history projects took shape in the mid-1960s, when two young Dagara priests from Upper Volta, under the guidance of the French White Father Jean Hébert, collected patriclan migration accounts in about fifty Dagara villages on both sides of the Ghanaian-Upper Volta border. The resulting document aimed to 'help the Dagara country to know its past a little better, serve as a basis for a broader knowledge of the Dagara, and contribute to the development of an authentic Dagara future' (Hébert 1976: 2). After an introductory outline, in the 'ethnographic present', of Dagara social and political institutions which was designed to refute stereotypes of their anarchy and primitiveness, the main text documented in detail migration data, genealogies and praise songs down to the village and patriclan level. Asserting that Dagara actually means *da-gaara*, a man in revolt (ibid.: 30), Hébert believes that the Dagara once seceded from the Dagomba kingdom, but he also quotes oral evidence that at least some of the Dagara clans originally came from Accra (ibid.: 33–40).

However, most subsequent Ghanaian authors have adopted the Dagomba rather than the Accra thesis. Tuurey, for instance, vividly narrates how towards the end of the fifteenth century the new ruler over the Dagomba, Na Nyagse, 'brutally put down' an indigenous rebellion against his assertion of power. The Dagaba-to-be followed their 'natural desire for political freedom and free enterprise ... and much like the Beni-Israel without a Moses went westwards', to settle in their present abode in the North-West (1982: 30–1). Der (1989), however, asserts that it was not the Dagaba now living in Nadawli, Kaleo and Jirapa, but the Dagara from the Lawra and Nandom areas who originally migrated from the Dagomba kingdom.

Yet not all Dagara intellectuals find the exodus thesis all that convincing. Naameh, for example, does not believe that the Dagara or Dagaba once migrated en masse to settle on uninhabited or abandoned land. Instead, he maintains that the Dagara are of mixed origins, descended from the region's indigenous peoples – according to Naameh the Gurunsi, Bobo and Lobi – as well as Dagomba, Mande and Mossi immigrants (1986: 136). Because present-day Dagara society embodies all these influences of 'Paleo-Sudanese' and 'Neo-Sudanese' cultures, no segment could claim 'to be more Dagara than other groups' (ibid.: 104).

Despite such disagreement quite a number of Ghanaian Dagara intellectuals espouse the Dagomba rebellion thesis. What makes it attractive? First, the exodus as one tribe upholds the unity of the ethnic community: linguistic and cultural differences are explained by later contact with subsequent immigrants in the new environment.[14] Second, the image of 'rebellion' casts the statelessness of North-Western peoples in a new light: it is no longer an indication of a low level of political evolution, but bears witness to an immanent democratic predisposition. Third, the Dagomba origin thesis is quite compatible with the north-western direction reported by many patriclan migration narratives. In addition, a Dagomba origin has the advantage of lying within present-day Ghanaian territory. And finally, it fits well with the school and university textbook versions of West African history. Hence, it manages to present the past of a stateless people within a framework dominated by the historiography of states without betraying this acephalous past or indigenous accounts of migration.

Exactly how the wider local public of Dagara farmers and labour migrants viewed these new tribal histories put forth by intellectuals is difficult to assess. Some of my village informants claimed to have never heard of the Dagomba rebellion thesis, while others insisted on distinguishing between migration narratives as handed down by their forefathers and the Dagomba story usually heard from educated Dagara. In any case, the various accounts of origins – indigenous and intellectual, clan and collective – co-exist as two different registers of historical narrative, and a single individual can and will invoke different registers in different contexts.

While lineage narratives buttress the assertion of local boundaries and land rights, 'tribal' histories present the Dagara as a political community within a modern state. During the Taalipuo conflict, for example, farmers, earth priests and local chiefs invoked the settlement histories of individual families in order to bolster their respective claims. However, in the petitions circulating at the regional and national level, the Sisala argued from the perspective of 'tribal history', in order to establish their status as 'autochthones' and substantiate their criticism of the Dagara as recent 'Lobi' immigrants from Burkina Faso, while the Dagara counter-petitions asserted the Dagomba origins of their ethnic community.

CONFRONTING STEREOTYPES, REFORMING 'DAGARA CUSTOMS'

While the articulation of a tribal history is still largely the affair of intellectuals, virtually everybody indulges in discussions of ethnic stereotypes and characteristic 'customs' – that is, in defining the 'contents' of ethnic identity. Many sorghum beer bar chats or daily conversations express and debate a whole set of emotional, intellectual and behavioural characteristics that are allegedly typical of the Dagara (or Wala, Sisala, Ashanti ...) personality and social relations. Such characteristics usually crystallise out of comparisons with 'peculiarities' of other ethnic groups, thus creating a relational system of ethnic differences and psychologies.

One of the notions most frequently expounded by Dagara peasants, labour migrants and intellectuals, men and women alike is that they are an extremely hard-working people, while most Southerners, in general, use their well-developed intelligence only for finding a way to live off other people's work. Dagara labour migrants are the nation's 'hewers of wood and carriers of water', as the intellectuals have it. They usually regard the Wala as traders and money-lenders, interested in profit-making, and ready to exploit honest labour. By contrast, Dagara themselves claim not to know how to borrow money, much less how to trade or lend money at interest. Despite owning vast stretches of land and having produced a growing number of commercial farmers, the typical Sisala is – in the eyes of many ordinary Dagara – not a peasant, but someone who only burns charcoal, produces soap, and plants some yams here and there. Insulting proverbs and stories, quite popular among Dagara villagers, have it that the Sisala are a cowardly people whom the Dagara would have chased much further east if the British hadn't stopped them. Conversely, Dagara male elders pride themselves on being hard-working farmers and, at least in the past, formidable warriors. Women are proud to conform to the *pogminga* ideal, which embodies notions regarding the ideal behaviour of the Dagara woman: tireless hard work in the household for husband and family, hospitality, modesty, friendliness, respect towards elders, and humility regarding the assertive presentation of her own successes (Behrends 2002a). In any case, Dagara men and women believe that the ability to endure hardship learnt from farming in a harsh climate enables them to become good mine workers or urban sorghum beer brewers as well as successful students and civil servants. Moreover, Dagara assert that their success is attained through personal effort, never through protection or favouritism.

Socially and politically, most Dagara consider themselves to be individualists, to the degree that agreement on communal projects is difficult to achieve and the advancement of the group as a whole suffers. Dagara regard themselves as open-minded and eager to adopt new techniques or forms of organisation. But once difficulties crop up, innovations are quickly abandoned, so that many developmental or other associations are short-lived. Educated and well-to-do Dagara complain about the 'PhD-syndrome', the 'pull-him-down' tactics employed by their fellow tribesmen who allegedly criticise anyone who excels economically or otherwise. Individual progress, so the argument runs, is thus hampered, and leaders are always regarded with distrust. Because they value honesty and straightforwardness so highly, Dagara are not well-suited to become effective politicians (who need to lie). In short, the very ethic of hard work and honesty, as well as an innately democratic spirit, which nearly all Dagara – literates and illiterates, men and women, villagers and urbanites – hold to be the very essence of Dagaraness, are at the same time regarded as the reason for the group's subordinate position in the national arena, because they obstruct the willingness to resort to favouritism deemed necessary to advance the cause of one's own people.

Many of these attributes are sufficiently malleable to suit different contexts and argumentative strategies, and there is a good deal of debate and disagreement on the Dagara psychological make-up. Written accounts of Dagara characteristics produced by intellectuals are, of course, more sophisticated; but even these are essentially based on the above-mentioned attributes.[15] Hard work, honesty, individualism, and courage stand out as fairly incontrovertible core elements, and apparently have done so for quite some time. In part these arose from everyday experience and basic cultural patterns – the history of expansive land appropriation, the labour-intensive cultivation of dense virgin bushland, the high regard for economic and political autonomy of household heads (*yirdem*), the close co-operation between patriclans, but also, if necessary, the violent self-defence against neighbouring kin. In part, they invert negative or appropriate positive hetero-stereotypes, and, not surprisingly, some of their embryonic forms can be traced to early colonial discourse on the 'Lobi' and 'Dagarti'. Many Dagara intellectuals (and in their own way, labour migrants and villagers too) are at pains to cultivate acceptable and revise problematic attributes that are deemed unbecoming of a civilised, well-educated Christian community. Somda, for instance, interprets the alleged readiness to resort to bow and arrow as arising from a pronounced sense of honour. That which neighbouring centralised polities and colonial officials stigmatised as intolerance of authority and incidence of 'primitivism', is re-interpreted as morally well-founded egalitarianism and commendable individualism that does not preclude solidarity (1975: 17–33). Such revisions of colonial stereotypes, however, have sometimes even gone as far as to deny a past that also encompasses feuds and violence. In his preface to Tuurey's account of Dagaba origins, Bishop Kpiebaya, for instance, emphasises 'the peace loving character of the people of the Upper-West' and even asserts that 'the different clans who settled in the area did not fight among themselves except in self defence against greedy marauders', i.e. slave raiders (in Tuurey 1982: 7). Yet few if any older villagers would ascribe to this 'victims'' perspective; they in contrast are quite proud of their ancestors' wartime prowess.

The decision which attributes to embrace and which to revise, and in which situation to foreground these characteristics, correlates closely with current strategies of survival and advancement. Many Dagara pin their hopes on education and on advancement by participation in rather than by withdrawal from the 'system' (the church, the administration, the schools, etc.). Obviously, a public image of belligerence or primitivism would be counter-productive, even though Dagara villagers and youth association activists do sometimes semi-publicly make recourse to memories of pre-colonial violent encroachment on Sisala land. Similarly, the 'hard-work' motif was originally closely connected with the pre-colonial history of agricultural expansionism and frontier spirit of the Dagara and Dagaba, but later instrumentalised by the colonial state, in the development of the North-West into a labour reservoir and the disciplining of the colonial subject. Subsequently, the Dagara re-interpreted it as a source of pride, even using it as an argument in the struggle to overcome their dependency: the 'hard workers' present themselves as morally superior to those who profit off their labour's fruits, thereby justifying claims to a fair share.

Ethnic stereotypes and characterisations, however, are not only an important means of defining the group's position in the wider regional and national arena, but are also a way of coping with increasing internal heterogeneity. Such characterisations bridge the widening gap between the educated elite, the labour migrants and the illiterate peasants by asserting that all share the same basic character traits. The NYDA, for example, evoked the 'hard work' motif by creating a logo that consisted of a hoe crossed with a cutlass, set in front of an unfurled banner carrying the slogan 'in unity and hard work we grow', and framed by the association's acronym together with the motto 'unity for development'. T-shirts carrying this logo on the front proved to be a really big seller among members. Such a 'common heritage' is believed to transcend differences in economic standing, life-style and personal philosophy, which actually distinguish the well-to-do urban-based educated Dagara from their illiterate, poorer rural kin. Such is obviously a normative rather than descriptive understanding of ethnicity, which can also be invoked by the 'grass roots' to serve interests of their own.

Defining 'who we are', however, requires more than just broadly affirming a 'common heritage' and a specific ethnic character. Particular cultural institutions need to be pinpointed as uniquely Dagara or Dagaba. Again, this is not an easy task: A 'Dagara culture' cannot be neatly distinguished from other 'cultures', because, for one, neighbouring groups share similar norms and practices, and for another, within the Dagara/ Dagaba community-to-be many customs differ from village to village or even patriclan to patriclan. Forging a self-conscious ethnic community that is proud of its 'unique values and customs which can contribute to others', as Archbishop Dery put it, implies a certain standardisation of these very cultural norms and practices.[16]

A first attempt at standardisation was the colonial codification of 'native laws and customs' discussed in Chapter 4. The definition of 'native custom' was to guide the chiefly courts, with quite immediate consequences for the reconfiguration of authority and the control of local resources. This aimed not only at preservation and standardisation, but also at reform, namely transforming or abolishing practices that were considered unhygienic, unhealthy or otherwise uncivilised. The colonial codification of customary law took place in the midst of heated debate between colonial officers and chiefs, on the one hand, and the White Fathers and their converts, on the other – a state of affairs, which provoked detailed explication of Catholic versus 'native' practice.

The recent normative descriptions of 'traditional culture' by Dagara intellectuals are no longer intended to serve as guidelines for behaviour in the present, but as substantiations of the past. As Bravman's study of similar processes in Kenya put it, 'custom' is being transformed 'from an active body of norms, outlooks and sanctions into a common cultural heritage' (1998: 251). These new conceptions of Dagara culture[17] are shaped in part by the repercussions of the colonial codification of 'custom' as well as by Catholic values, but are also formulated out of critiques of colonial stereotypes and of Jack Goody's authoritative monographs published in the 1950s and 1960s. They aim at projecting a new public image of who the Dagara are, and often justify future (political) projects by rooting them in 'tradition'. Therefore, notions regarding the tribal past are highly contested, particularly with respect to the representation of the pre-colonial political order (for instance, the question whether chiefs existed, or not) (Lentz 2003a), but also with respect to issues such as marriage and divorce, gender relations, funerals and inheritance. Furthermore, it is difficult not to notice that reformulations of Dagara 'traditions' are tacitly Catholic: It is remarkable that many contemporary ethnographic texts downplay, for instance, polygamy. Similarly, descriptions of 'traditional' Dagara domestic life rarely mention slaves and pawns, despite their historical importance, at least in the nineteenth century, and their prominent role in current genealogical disputes. Some practices such as clitoridectomy, which still occur, are ignored by almost all ethnographies, whether colonial or Catholic, European or indigenous.[18] Not surprisingly, Dagara 'traditional religion' is a particularly prominent site where Christian values are projected onto the pre-Christian past.[19]

Contemporary ethnographies by local scholars, much as those written previously by European anthropologists, tend to present a rather homogeneous, static and harmonious portrait of authentic 'Dagara customs'. Yet this does not preclude the same authors and the general public from engaging in vigorous debates about the necessity of reforming some of these 'traditions', such as the length of funerals and the cost of the brideprice (Hawkins 2002: 279–80, 287–8). A reformist attitude also dominates the cultural policies of the youth associations. The NYDA, for instance, sought 'to encourage the propagation and progressive development of the traditions of the Dagara in the area', and the JAYDA quite explicitly cited as one of its missions 'to preserve as far as possible the traditions and culture of the people of this area, but to change those aspects of our traditions and culture that impede the progress and modernization of the area'.[20]

Yet youth association activists are well aware that reforms and, eventually, a self-conscious 'common cultural identity' only develop if there is communication between villagers, the educated elite and migrant workers. As a NYDA member in Obuasi insisted, younger migrants born in the South must first be properly culturally socialised through the youth associations:

> at our meetings we talk to them that it is our responsibility to learn our culture. And these funerals, the local dancing and other things, it's part of our culture. So we don't have to sit on our oars and say that it's for those who have been born back up North. They have to be doing it. … Being born down here doesn't mean you are not a Dagaare or anything of that sort. You must learn your culture![21]

Even the educated, explained a former NYDA chairman, must first learn to hold their 'own culture' in high esteem. Their interest could then have a beneficial effect on the self-awareness of villagers:

> Once we are educated and mix with other people, we seem to be forgetting about our identity, our culture. The people at home are shocked with your interest in what they thought is an ordinary life, and you are out of it. Once you are educated, you are out of it. So when you

show interest ... when they see: 'Oh, this man, we thought he is educated and he will never like it' ... Then they begin to appreciate what they have had.[22]

This new-found appreciation for Dagara culture, the deepening of home-ties and the creation of a new cultural awareness, are successes which many Dagara intellectuals regard as the most important outcomes of the work done by youth associations.

It is, however, no coincidence that my Dagara interlocutors, when citing examples of the kind of 'common heritage' to be learned, only refer to appropriate rules of behaviour at funerals, dances and the like. In matters of daily life, the life-styles of the educated elite, migrants and farmers back home differ to such an extent that one can hardly speak of a shared culture at all. For instance, while Dagara professionals tend to insist on the necessity of radical reforms along the lines of the nuclear family, their less well-to-do relations attempt to use the Dagara extended kinship 'system' in order to claim support from their better-off kin (Lentz 1994b, Behrends 2002b). Such overt debate and tacit struggle over the current meaning and the practical implications of cultural norms co-exist with the general conviction that the Dagara/Dagaba have 'a unique culture' which needs to be 'preserved', as Archbishop Dery has said. What the intellectuals and the youth associations want to 'preserve' and refine as cultural traditions are language, local dances, songs, proverbs, stories, clothing, craft products, in short, and above all, a kind of local 'folklore'. The framework in which this 'cultural identity' is defined, the means by which differences from other localities and ethnic groups are expressed, always have national and also international dimensions, even when the 'material' is of local origin.

THE MULTIPLE MEANINGS OF ETHNICITY

What, then, does ethnicity mean in North-Western Ghana today? Despite their rigid façade, ethnic identities have been, and still are, varied, polysemic and subject to modification. Ethnic discourses generally argue in an essentialist manner and purport the non-negotiability of identities defined by right of birth. Yet, despite the ubiquity of this discourse, the communities thus created are not necessarily constructed along the same principles and actually vary in their inclusiveness. The interweaving of pre-colonial and colonial models of belonging – ranging from clans and clan alliances, first-comer/late-comer relations and territorial proximity as defined by earth-shrine parishes, chiefdoms, districts, and Catholic congregrations – has created a complex system of available identifications that local actors mobilise in defining group membership and justifying collective action.

On the face of it, the question of which 'ethnic' identity will be invoked seems to obey the often cited principle of 'nested identities': the closer to one's original home, the more narrowly the boundaries will be drawn. A member of the Kusiele patriclan from the village of Kokoligu, for instance, would identify himself in Europe as an African or Ghanaian, in Accra as a Northerner, in Tamale as an Upper Westerner, in Wa as a Dagaba/Dagara or a Nandome, in Nandom as a Kusiele or Kokoligule, and in Kokoligu as someone from the Zogpiele section and the house of Kuunyaa. However, this example also shows that these presumably layered identities actually stress very different boundary-constituting criteria – sometimes kinship or territory, at other times linguistic and cultural characteristics. Moreover, each of these identifications are polysemic, a characteristic that makes ethnicity such a strategically effective idiom in building communities.

Thus, claiming to be a Nandome can, for example, refer to membership in a group of patriclans which have marked out a collective route of migration and, after many decades of intermarriage and co-residence, share close social and ritual ties. This group of Nandome may exclude late-comers and villages located at the periphery of the Nandom chiefdom. Alternatively, Nandom can be understood linguistically and culturally, as the community of those who speak the 'Nandom' dialect, attach importance to matriclans and play a particular kind of xylophone – a definition of 'Nandome' which would include many more houses and villages than the first one. Third, Nandom may refer to the old Nandom parish, and thus include Dagara villages once served by the missionaries stationed in Nandom who do not speak the 'Nandom' dialect or even Sisala and may not share any of the just mentioned cultural traits. Finally, Nandom could also be understood politically with reference to the Nandom Traditional Area. If one were to think of the first three possible interpretations in territorial terms, the communities thus defined would extend far beyond the border of the Nandom Traditional Area. Conversely, not everyone residing in the Nandom Traditional Area necessarily identifies him- or herself as a Nandome, or at least not in every context. Non-indigenous traders and civil servants, for instance, may feel themselves excluded from 'Nandom affairs' discussed by the 'natives'. Villages on the periphery, even though they may have kinship ties with families residing in Nandom 'town', may still prefer to characterise themselves more generally as Dagara and criticise the Nandom-centredness of the political elite.

Similar idiomatic versatility is evident with respect to 'Dagara' and other ethnic categories. Which interpretation of ethnicity resonates in any specific situation is a factor of the given context as well as the position of the speaker or actor. Thus, for migrants, regardless of their level of education, ethnicity is primarily an idiom associated with home ties and cultural roots, which is ultimately to find its ritual attestation in a dignified burial in their village of origin. Labour migrants often translate 'home' into Dagara as *sããkum-yir*, 'the house of the grandfathers', ethnicity thus being understood as an extension of kinship. However, other migrants organise themselves not according to patriclans or kinship groups, but to common, often loosely defined, territorial origins even though these may cross-cut politico-administrative boundaries.

Second, ethnicity serves as an idiom of moral community that aims at bridging the growing social inequality between the educated elite and their poorer rural kin. Even sceptical local intellectuals, who with some self-irony regard themselves as 'detribalised', admit that ethnic discourses are emotionally effective and prevent the creation of classes. In this way, not only do poor migrants and farmers deploy the ethnic idiom to demand protection and the redistribution of resources, the educated too invoke it to assert their right to educate and represent 'less fortunate' tribesmen and tribeswomen. But here again, there are numerous possibilities for drawing the boundaries that define such community. The well-to-do may prefer a wider definition of Dagara, because the ensuing obligation of redistribution then becomes rather diffuse, while poorer farmers will tend to assert a more narrow definition in terms of membership shared by the patriclan or village in order to emphasise their entitlement to assistance.

Finally, ethnicity may be deployed as an idiom of political mobilisation and making demands on the state. In this context, territorial interpretations of ethnic communities predominate, but cultural-linguistic definitions can become arguments in calls for the rearrangement of political boundaries or the definition of political participation, as we have seen in the conflicts over the creation of new districts.

None of these aspects of ethnicity can be entirely effective without the others. An ethnicity that is politically operative requires the cultural construction of community and must connect with discourses of personal identity and solidarity. These different fields – personal belonging, moral community and political interest groups – must be linked by attaching the emotionally laden concept of 'home' to an administrative territory (such as a traditional area) and to political demands. By virtue of their education and knowledge of the modern world, the educated elite is often in a better position than other actors to define ethnic identifications through boundaries, names, histories or a canon of cultural practices. However, their influence as ethnic entrepreneurs and their leeway in manipulating cultural categories and forms of self-understanding are restricted by the necessity to anchor symbols, historical narratives and rituals in the experiential world of all those at whom the discourse is directed.

In this world of experience, ethnicity is by no means the only idiom in which belonging is expressed, as I have shown throughout this book. The older elements of social belonging like the patriclan and earth-shrine area are still significant, and not always deployed in the ethnic sense. Moreover, people also belong to groups, networks and organisations explicitly not defined in ethnic terms, such as the Catholic Church, the freemasons and other lodges, alumni associations of particular secondary schools, political parties, occupational associations and unions. For most people such groups are just as important in managing their daily lives as their identities as Northerners or Upper Westerners, Dagara, Dagaba or Sisala, Nandome, Lambussiele, Jirbaale or Losaale. Precisely because ethnic categories do not dominate daily life entirely and, even more importantly, because of the comparatively low degree of ethnic violence have these categories in North-Western Ghana been so flexible and variable up to now. While during the violent ethnic conflicts of the 1980s and 1990s in the Northern Region and during the on-going civil war in the neighbouring Ivory Coast, fixed ethnic ascriptions became matters of life and death, the North-West has so far been spared this fate. Knowledge of these tragedies taking place so very near by has caused anxiety and affected discourses concerning ethnic belonging and interests. This has intensified the search for peaceful solutions and moved leading political actors to avoid polarising discourses and divisive actions.

EPILOGUE

During my last visit to Ghana, I found all my friends and acquaintances avidly discussing the results of the December 2004 presidential and parliamentary elections and the appointments of ministers, ambassadors and district chief executives that would follow. Why had the candidates of the NDC (National Democratic Congress), the once ruling, but now oppositional party won such a clear majority in the North, specifically in the Upper West Region? How had the three serving NDC parliamentarians from the former Lawra District managed to get re-elected, even though, as some of my interlocutors believed, the governing NPP (New Patriotic Party) was in a much better position to promote the interests of their constituencies? What role did money, the NDC party apparatus and the voluntary associations established by the Rawlings government play in all this? Did the NDC still profit from policies introduced by Rawlings that established the Upper West Region and brought electricity and roads to the area? Was the NPP still disadvantaged by its image as an 'Ashanti' party, a fact that would hurt its appeal among Northern migrants in the South, subject as they were to discrimination at the hands of just this group? The educated elite, too, according to some of my friends, bore a grudge against the NPP, because President Kufuor had complained about a supposed lack of qualified politicians from the Upper West and had only co-opted into his government representatives from this area rather late. Now the question remained whether Kufuor would punish the region for its 'loyalty' to the NDC, or whether representatives nevertheless would be included in his new administration. The elections, then, raised many questions and sparked moral narratives regarding political representation, participation and the just distribution of national resources. The issues debated included the position of Northerners and Upper Westerners in the national arena; the degree to which the various Upper Western districts and ethnic groups were represented in the regional government (was this appropriate, or were they perhaps over-represented?); and discussions as to whether local parliamentary candidates were competent and whether they were the legitimate representatives of their constituencies in the national parliament.

In these discussions and in the political jockeying over government positions, the old generation of politicians – the chiefs, chiefs' sons and members of chiefly families, who had dominated politics in the North-West from decolonisation until the 1990s – no longer played a significant role. Lawra Naa Abayifaa Karbo, who in the 1950s had so valiantly stood for the NPP and then the UP against the Nkrumah supporters, lived to witness Kufuor's victory in 2000 and was rewarded for his unwavering political commitment with a position in the Council of State. However, his influence had waned, and he was unable to secure an electoral victory for the local NPP candidate. In December 2004, the aged leader passed away, like most once so influential politicians in the district – Lambussie Kuoro Baloro, lawyer Salifu Bawa Dy-Yakah, Duori Naa S. D. Dombo, Jirapa Naa Bapenyiri Yelpoe, among others. Many younger civil servants, lawyers and other professionals, who now compete for positions and run things in the region, are not bound to chiefly houses. In all three constituencies comprising what was once Lawra District the NDC candidates won, despite the more or less explicit NPP endorsement of the paramount and many divisional chiefs. Under the Rawlings government the system of local and regional administration expanded considerably, creating opportunities for broader segments of the population – including members of families quite distant from the chiefs – to embark on a political career. As the number of local notables and Upper Westerners engaged in the civil service as well as in the professions in the South has increased, the number of potential patrons able to encourage villagers and labour migrants to support a specific party has done so as well. This makes it even more difficult to predict popular political leanings than in the past.

As the ranks of the educated elite have grown, so too has competition for political influence. A potential candidate's party affiliation is now influenced not only by his family's political tradition or other social loyalties, but also follows from very practical considerations such as maximising one's chance of nomination – or so critics say. Similarly, parties do not necessarily select their candidates on the basis of long-standing loyalty, but rather choose promising local opinion leaders or highly educated professionals, who, although not previously involved in party activity, are considered to be the most viable in the national arena. The fault lines once dividing members of chiefly houses and 'commoners', as well as graduates of state and mission schools, seem to have become irrelevant, given the increased variety of educational opportunities and concomitant academic vitae. Instead, it seems that conflicts over the legitimacy of claims to leadership status between, on the one hand, civil servants and teachers who live and work in the region and, on the other hand, those university graduates occupying better-paid posts in Accra, Kumasi and other major cities, are increasing. Certain locally anchored candidates have supposedly tried to score points by accusing their opponents of being elitist, out of touch with local realities and of denying parliamentarians who happen not to hold PhDs, the ability to successfully represent their home constituency in the national arena. In addition to such tensions between 'local literates' and 'Accra boys', which were so significant in the youth associations of the 1970s and 1980s, a further political rift has developed, at least among the Dagara and Dagaba, namely that between the educated elite residing in Ghana and migrants living in Europe or the US, who refer to themselves as the diaspora. The latter, for example, established the Foundation for Rural Education, Empowerment and Democracy (FREED), which recently began financing two public libraries as well as a radio station serving Nandom and its environs. Their plan to establish a 'think tank' dedicated to dealing with issues affecting Nandom and the Upper West Region has provoked heated debates among the Dagara in Ghana. The controversy centres on democracy and professionalism within the organisation, accountability and who is to have a say in local politics, as well as the issue of whether the organisation is sufficiently in touch with local village, or at least Ghanaian reality. Moreover, the issue has been raised whether the increasing involvement of educated Dagara and Dagaba in party politics – particularly their involvement in competing parties – is inimical to ethnic unity and the attainment of political influence, or whether such a development is integral to a modern democracy and an unavoidable part of the battle over regional interests.

In this context the debates over the territorial-administrative versus the ethnic basis of development and political representation that took place in the 1970s and 1980s have continued. FREED activists, for example, would like to expand their development activities beyond the Nandom paramountcy into 'Greater Nandom Area', as they call the former Nandom Catholic parish that includes Lambussie and part of Tumu – a term implying a certain agenda that has stirred some unease among the Sisala elite and those Dagara with no particular ties to Nandom. Fears of Nandom dominance thus still abound, which it seems served the Lambussie NDC candidate – a Dagaba teacher married to a Sisala lawyer and former district secretary – quite well, as she has cultivated a campaign image of being a champion of Sisala interests. She has apparently also tried to win over Dagara farmers by suggesting that a victory for the NPP candidate – a Dagara from Hamile – would provoke reprisals from Sisala landowners, who would, as in the 1980s, deny Dagara farmers access to their fields. The NPP candidate, for his part, had to exert enormous effort to undo the damage done by the rumour that he would use his victory to consolidate Dagara dominance by establishing a Nandom-Lambussie district and 'taking away' Sisala land. The complexity of the local political landscape becomes clear when one considers that it was in fact the Sisala, and the new Lambussie Kuoro in particular, who in spite of such ominous hearsay supported him rather than the NDC candidate. The latter, however, secured the majority vote among those Dagara farmers, and among Dagara women in particular, whom election analysts expected to support their 'brother' from Hamile.

Speculations regarding why the 'ethnic card' failed to trump in this and other constituencies led to discussions regarding the role ethnicity plays and should play in the North-West, and in Ghana more generally. With some degree of simplification, the stances on this issue roughly follow one of two positions, a more 'inclusive' culturalistic one and a more 'exclusive' political one. The inclusivist stance emphasises what is common to Dagara and Dagaba, Sisala and Wala. Its adherents point to the strong ties created by marriage and friendship that bridge the boundaries of dialect and ethnic identity, and they evoke a past shaped by common origins, a shared history of mobility and successful adaptation to a difficult natural environment. Evoking the 'melting pot' metaphor, they positively value, not ethnic purity, but the incorporation of strangers, cultural assimilation and ethnic permeability and emphasise the overarching similarities in norms, values and historical experiences of all ethnic groups in the North-West, at both the local and regional levels. Ethnic differences, according to this view, should not be allowed to polarise people, but should be tolerated, and such cultural diversity treasured. With their slogan 'unity in diversity', 'inclusivists' propagate what Richard Werbner has recently termed 'moral interethnicity' (2004: 69). They aim to strengthen local and regional patriotism, across ethnic boundaries, and thus advance the collective struggle for the recognition of all Upper Westerners in the national arena. Although this support for minority rights does not imply an anti-Southern stance, it does demand ethnic tolerance and equal opportunity for Northerners in a state that is dominated by Southerners.

Although promoting regional unity and combating tribal favouritism and discrimination are projects that 'exclusivists' would also support, they tend to place more emphasis on the political implications of ethnic differences, particularly at the sub-regional level. Furthermore, they foreground differences in historical trajectories, attaching more importance to when the various groups established themselves in the region. In their view first-comership constitutes the most important criterion for full land ownership. Influenced by the colonial native-state model, they tend to conflate ethnic identity and 'autochthony', considering this the basis on which full political rights should be accorded. In short: at the local level, exclusivists tend to distinguish between 'first-class' and 'second-class' citizens, but they also draw this distinction with respect to who should be accorded the right to represent the local community in the larger political arena.

'Exclusivist' notions of ethnicity tend to be more prominent among regional 'minority' groups such as the Sisala and Wala, but they are also held by the Dagara/Dagaba, depending on the context of the debate as well as the specific interests at stake. So, when it comes to positioning the Upper West as a region within the Ghanaian nation-state, 'inclusivism' is the more effective strategy as it can mobilise a larger constituency, while 'exclusivist' discourses may be more suitable when it comes to securing a share of the spoils at the regional or local level. However, such contextual considerations aside, the stances of Upper Westerners regarding the nature of citizenship or minority group rights differ. There is heated debate as to whether 'autochthony' and ethnic belonging should play any role at all in determining rights to political participation and access to resources, or whether ethnicity should be bracketed out of the political process altogether so that civic rights are defined solely on the basis of shared citizenship in a modern nation-state, with certain allowances for displays of cultural identity and linguistic difference being acceptable. It is interesting to note, however, that whether ascribing to more culturalist or more political notions of ethnicity, neither the Dagara nor the Sisala, who both straddle the international border, have ever initiated attempts at cross-border ethnic unification. Although some Sisala politicians have tried to discredit the Dagara for their allegedly 'non-Ghanaian' origins, and the latter have sometimes expressed pride that their culture is both a regional and international phenomenon, secessionism has never been an option. For both Dagara and Sisala, their national loyalties are self-evident and non-negotiable, and they are proud to be Ghanaians. Even if they disagree over the role to be accorded to regions and cultural difference in Ghanaian democracy, they agree with their compatriots that these differences must be settled peacefully and that neither ethnic nor other communal ties can justify violence – a commitment that has strengthened as the spectre of civil war looms from across the border in the Ivory Coast, Togo and other West African countries.

NOTES

INTRODUCTION

1. DC Lawra-Tumu to DC Wa, 1 Oct. 1947, Northern Regional Archives, Tamale (RAT), NRG 8/2/101: 3.
2. Interview of 17 Nov. 1990, Tamale. For details on the 'Dagomba origin' hypothesis, see Ch. 10 of this volume.
3. For overviews of research on ethnicity in Africa, see Young 1986, Lentz 1995a, Berman 1998 and Spear 2003; on ethnicity in Ghana, Greene 1996, and Lentz and Nugent 2000.
4. See Comaroff 1992: 49-67 and Berman 1998 for a similar resumé.
5. For a more extensive discussion of Hawkins' perspective and treatment of sources, see my review (Lentz 2004).
6. The *longue durée* of African power politics has mostly been examined using the examples of centralised societies, and it is the work of historians on African kingdoms – such as Peel's seminal study of the Ijesha-Yoruba (1983), Staniland (1975) on Dagbon, and Wilks (1989) on Wa – which have shaped my perspective.
7. On the recent discussions of historical 'truth', the imperatives of historical narratives and the limits of imagination see, for instance, White 1987; with reference to African history, Vansina 1985, Cohen 1991, Jewsiewicki and Mudimbe 1993, and Hamilton 1998.
8. Earlier travel reports by Europeans (e.g. Binger 1892) or African traders (in Wilks 1967) at best only marginally touch on present-day North-Western Ghana. Most Hausa manuscripts, with the aid of which Holden (1965), Wilks (1989) and Pilaszewicz (1992) have reconstructed the history of the city-state of Wa and the incursions of Babatu and Samori, were only composed after the turn of the century, under the encouragement of British colonial officials.
9. Monson's (2000) study of the historicity of memory in Southern Tanzania is a good example of the strength of such an analytical approach. See also my own work (Lentz 2000a, 2001a) on the oral traditions concerning the founding of Nandom and Ouessa.
10. On this point, see also Goody 1987 and Harneit-Sievers 2002.

CHAPTER 1

1. Goody recently criticised 'the "if-the-Government-Agents-hadn't-been-there" approach to the present', practised by himself and other anthropologists of his time, as ahistorical (1990: 1–2). However, this has not stopped either himself or his students from holding on to a rather idealised view of the segmentary Dagara.
2. See, for example, Somda 1975, Dabire 1983, Kuukure 1985, Ansotinge 1986, Mukassa 1987 and Kpiebaya 1991.

3. See Goody 1956, 1962; A. Tengan 2000.

4. On this, see Lentz 1999.

5. Thus, for example, the earth priest of Lambussie traces the origins of his forefathers back to Sankana, a Dagaba village north of Wa (interview with Nansie Issifu Tomo, 29 Nov. 1994). The family of the Billaw Kuoro, a Sisala chief, is closely related to the family of the Nandom Naa (interview with Manoh Forkoh and Kager Banuosin, 3 Dec. 1994).

6. On this, see also the discussion of the corresponding Sisala terms and cosmology in E. Tengan 1990, 1991.

7. Here I am following Goody's translation (1957 etc.) of *tèŋgánsòb* as 'custodian of the earth shrine' or 'earth priest', though this terminology neglects the political dimensions of the office.

8. Kuba and Lentz (2002) provide an overview of the settlement history of the region and the relations between Dagara pioneers and older settlers. On the controversial settlement history of Nandom, see Lentz 2000a; on Ouessa (Burkina Faso), see Lentz 2001a. For examples of negotiations over relations between first-comers and late-comers, see also Goody 1957, Hébert 1976; E. Tengan 1991: 81–4; Kuba, Lentz and Werthmann 2001.

9. See Ch. 3 of this volume and Lentz 1999: 158–64.

10. See Bening 1973; E. Tengan 1991: 57–61, 197–8; Hien 1996: 49–65, for opposing views with respect to traditional boundaries in the Black Volta region.

11. Letters dated 30 Oct. 1929 and 29 Dec. 1929, RAT, NRG 8/2/27.

12. On this, see also Dabire 1983: 155–6, 183–94, and Rohden 1992.

13. On this, see also Goody and Goody 1996.

14. Public Record Office, London (PRO), CO 96/493, enclosure 3 in Gold Coast no. 41 of 19 Jan. 1910.

15. Rhodes House Library (RHL), MSS Afr. P. 626, Papers of Harold Blair, a twenty-two-page manuscript on the Northern Territories, without title or date.

16. See also Holden 1965: 64–5; Seavoy 1982: 20–1.

17. Ruelle had already criticised the fact that such names, given by outsiders, were often 'imaginary' and the categorisations arbitrary (1904: 668).

18. On this, see Wilks 1989: 16–17, 51–2; Fikry 1969: 223, 238, 270–3.

19. There are hardly any sources on the effects of these raids in the North-West in the seventeenth and eighteenth centuries (Der 1998); only developments in the second half of the nineteenth century can be reconstructed to some extent from Islamic manuscripts and oral traditions.

20. On the controversies concerning the causes and starting point(s) of Dagara migrations, see Lentz 1994a.

21. On this, see Tamakloe 1931: 45–55; Holden 1965; Wilks 1989: 91–115; Rouch 1990; and Pilaszewicz 1992.

22. Wilks dates the destruction of Wa to 1887 (1989: 106–8, 116); see also Pilaszewicz 1992: 72–80.

23. See Wilks 1989: 125. Although none of my informants in Lambussie and Jirapa was able to confirm the existence of such garrisons, local warriors may well have joined the Sofa troops.

24. On political developments west of the Volta and in the 'Grunshi country' later colonised by the French, see Duperray 1984: 48–100; Kambou-Ferrand 1993a, especially pp. 187–256; Saul and Royer 2001: 51–73.

25. St John Eyre-Smith, Comments on the Interim Report on the Peoples of the Nandom and Lambussie Divisions of the Lawra District, 1933, National Archives of Ghana, Accra (NAG), ADM 11/1/824, § 8–9.

26. The name *yeri* is probably derived from a Mande word literally meaning

'scattered, dispersed'. In the North-West, *yera* (singular) is usually associated with merchants and/or Muslims. On Mande immigration to Jirapa and Wa, see the Wala traditions mentioned by Wilks (1989: 35–6, 57–9); also Abobo 1994. On Dagara-Yeri in Burkina Faso, see Hébert 1976: 150–61, Knösel 2001.

27. Interview with Bapenyiri Yelpoe II, 19 Dec. 1994, Jirapa.

28. See Wilks 1989: 112–15, 145–8 (especially note 23). Binger mentions a trade route from Kong to Bobo-Dioulasso and one from Wa to Walembele, Sati and Ouagadougou (1892, I: 372). Neither affected either Lawra or Nandom.

29. On this, see Goody 1972: 75–6.

30. McCall (1981: 370–3) is not able to verify his claim that Lawra was part of the Wala state in the pre-colonial period. Even the British doubted similar claims by the Wala, and all attempts to make the Wa Na the paramount chief of the North-West failed because of bitter resistance on the part of the chiefs of Lawra District (see Chs 2 and 7 of this volume).

31. See also Lentz 1993: 190–5; Goody 1956: 113. On 'strongmen' among the Tallensi, see Hart 1978: 191, 198–9. Sahlins' ideal type of the Melanesian 'big man' (1963) seems entirely applicable here.

32. See, for example, Lovejoy's definition (1983: 1–14) of slavery, as well as the instructive study by Bonnafé (1993) on slavery among the Lobi. On the recent discussion of slavery among Dagara intellectuals, see Der 1998, Somda 2000 and V. Somé 2001, which, however, stress the Dagara's role as victims, not perpetrators.

33. Interview with Tuopari Naa Dery, 25 Dec. 1996.

34. Interviews with Nestor Kuunyaa, 29 Dec. 1994, Kokoligu-Zogpiele; Siengang Naaisine and Aasogr Nibaalieru, 18 Dec. 1994, Tantuo; Darte Bason Boyuo, 2 Dec. 1994, Lambussie; Nansie Issifu Tomo, 29 Nov. 1994, Lambussie; Dennis Tiewiir and Dora Doglier, 9 Dec. 1992, Burutu-Danyegang; Lawra Naa Abayifaa Karbo, 23 Dec. 1994 (in English); Nabaala Kuoro Banii Kambang, 4 Dec. 1994; Baba Lere and Naab Omne, 24 Dec. 1994, Dikpe; and Yobo Kiebang, 24 Dec. 1994, Yirkpee.

35. Interviews with Lawra Naa Abayifaa Karbo, 23 Dec. 1994 and 4 Jan. 1998; with Kokoligu Naa Michael Zuwera, 24 Dec. 1996; with Hamile Naa Yuozeg John (and son Pascal), 26 Dec. 1994; and with Somé Nifaakang, Ouessa, 21 Nov. 1997.

36. See Mallam Abu, in Pilaszewicz 1992: 61, 104–5; Holden 1965: 66–71.

37. See Holden 1965: 77.

38. See Eyre-Smith, Comments, §§ 25, 26 (NAG, ADM 11/1/824), where the annual tribute of Lambussie to Babatu is given as 300 slaves, numerous cattle and a large sum of cowries. See also Holden 1965: 79–80; Tamakloe 1931: 54.

39. See Wilks 1989: 121–2, 125.

40. I was not offered any etymological explanation for this name. My Sisala informants in Lambussie and Billaw spoke of *zabaka* and also used this name generally for Gonja.

41. As, for example, in Dikpe (interview with Baba Lere and Naab Omne, 24 Dec. 1994) and Duori (interview with Duori Naa S. D. Dombo, 26 Feb. 1994, London, in English).

42. Interview with Gabriel Tangsege and James Bayuo, 18 Dec. 1994. The name 'cutter of necks' was usually explained with reference to the particular cruelty of the Sofa. However, Lawra Naa Abayifaa Karbo explained it with reference to the fact that, while Babatu usually attacked Lawra from the east, the Sofa arrived unexpectedly from the south and therefore from behind, from the neck (interview, 23 Dec. 1994).

43. Interview, 29 Nov. 1994. Patrick Viiru from Nandom insisted that some people

from Lambussie had joined Samori's troops and then 'run over' to the British (interview, 10 Dec. 1992).

44. Interviews with Nabaala Kuoro Banii Kambang, 4 Dec. 1994; and with Billaw Kuoro Forkoh Manoh, 3 Dec. 1994. Mwinpuo Le-ib of Nandomkpee reported that a brother of Gaamuo, from the family of the Nandom earth priests, joined the Zaberma (interview, 11 Dec. 1989).

45. On local marauders in general, see also Watherston 1907–8: 352–3. On Boyon of Ulu, see also Dasah 1974, though he does not recognise Boyon's services as a mercenary for Babatu and sees Boyon as the ruler of a 'kingdom' stretching as far as Nandom. A very different picture emerges from the report of a British punitive expedition to Ulu of June 1899. PRO, CO 879/58, no. 585 African (West), no. 141, enclosure 1: 246–8. On Sougoulé of Samoa, see 'Correspondence concerning Samor', Apr.–Jul. 1898, PRO, CO 879/54, African (West), no. 564 (no. 5, 11, 30, 76), as well as interview with Samoa Kuoro Saku Tigwii and elders, 28 Nov. 2001.

46. Interview with Abayifaa Karbo, 23 Dec. 1994 (in English). Such horses' tails are still waved by chiefs and dancers on ceremonial occasions.

47. Interviews with Kporkpar Tang, Dome Tang and others, 22 Dec. 1994, Eremon; with Baba Lere and Naab Omne, 24 Dec. 1994, Dikpe; with Soyeru Buolu and Tantuoyir, 27 Dec. 1989, Tantuo; with Dennis Tiewiir and Doria Doglier, 9 Dec. 1992, Burutu-Danyegang; and with Gabriele Tangsenge and James Bayuo, 18 Dec. 1994, Ko.

48. Interview with Yobo Kiebang, Lawra-Yirkpee, 24 Dec. 1994.

49. On the dynamics of slave raids and the slave trade in non-centralised societies in West Africa, see also Hubbell 2001; Klein 2001.

CHAPTER 2

1. Northcott to Colonial Secretary, 31 Jul. 1898, PRO, CO 879/54, no. 564 African (West), no. 143, enclosure 1: 252–3; see also Watherston 1907–8.

2. Draft Northern Territories Proclamation, PRO, CO 879/67, no. 649 African (West): 40.

3. Black Volta District, Monthly Reports, March 1902 (NAG, ADM 56/1/460) and March 1903 (NAG, ADM 56/1/451).

4. On these treaties, see Major Jenkinson to Colonial Secretary, 2 Dec. 1897, no. 101, enclosure; Commissioner Northcott to Colonial Secretary, 16 Jan. 1898, no. 248 and enclosures; Governor Hodgson to Colonial Secretary, 7 Feb. 1898, no. 171 and enclosures; all in PRO, CO 879/52, no. 549 African (West).

5. Northcott to Colonial Secretary, 4 Mar. 1899, PRO, CO 879/58, no. 585 African (West), enclosure in no. 79: 141.

6. Northcott to Colonial Secretary, 9 Jul. 1899, PRO, CO 879/58, no. 585 African (West), no. 96: 183.

7. Governor Hodgson to Colonial Secretary, 14 Jul. 1900, PRO, CO 879/64, no. 633 African (West), no. 39: 51. See also Morris to Governor, 12 Jul. 1901, PRO, CO/879/67, no. 649 African (West), enclosure 2 in no. 81; Governor to Morris, 19 Aug. 1901, ibid., enclosure 3; Morris to Governor, 30 Sep. 1901, ibid., enclosure 1 in no. 97; and Governor to Morris, 8 Nov. 1901, ibid., enclosure 2.

8. Irvine to Colonial Secretary, 4 Mar. 1905, PRO, CO 96/428, Gold Coast Confidential of 12 Apr. 1905, enclosure 3.

9. Northern Territories, Annual Report 1901, PRO, CO 98/10: 11.

10. Black Volta District, Monthly Report, Mar. 1901, NAG, ADM 56/1/416.

11. On this, see also Wilks 1989: 142, 148–9.

12. Because of the inconsistent spelling of place names, many of the settlements

listed in the monthly reports are not easy to identify.

13. See Black Volta District, Monthly Reports, Jan. to Sep. 1901, NAG, ADM 56/ 1/416.

14. Ibid., May 1901.

15. Morris to Governor, 16 Apr. 1904, NAG, ADM 56/1/2: 130.

16. DC Lawra, Duncan-Johnstone, Intelligence Report, Jun. 1921, Lawra District Record Book, NAG, ADM 61/5/11: 286.

17. Morris to Governor, 16 Apr. 1904, NAG, ADM 56/1/2: 130.

18. Black Volta District, Monthly Report, Jun. 1902, NAG, ADM 56/1/460.

19. On this, see the punitive expedition to Ulu of May 1899 PRO, CO 879/58, no. 585 African (West), enclosure 1 in no. 141: 246-8.

20. Black Volta District, Monthly Report, Apr. 1903, NAG, ADM 56/1/451.

21. Morris to Berthon, 27 Oct. 1903, PRO, CO 96/417, enclosure 2 in Gold Coast Confidential of 11 Mar. 1904.

22. Berthon to Chief Commissioner Northern Territories (CCNT), 29 Dec. 1903, PRO, CO 96/417, enclosure 1 in Gold Coast Confidential of 11 Mar. 1904. Nandom appears for the first time on the 1905 map of the Northern Territories, though different names were still being used up to about 1910.

23. According to some informants, 'Chilla' was actually a nickname for a shrewd, subversive individual who knew how to circumvent regulations to his own advantage. Apparently Kyiir (in colonial documents 'Cheriri' or 'Cheiriri'), a local 'strongman' and later the first chief of Nandom, as well as his settlement were given this name – an early reference to the source of Kyiir's power.

24. Governor Rodger to Morris, 11 Mar. 1904, enclosure 3, PRO, CO 96/417. The tour of inspection was accorded the greatest attention in colonial circles from Accra to London, because of an incident on the Anglo-French border on the Black Volta.

25. Berthon to CCNT, 29 Dec. 1903, ibid., enclosure 1. Berthon's 'Grunshi' are identical with the 'Sissalla' or 'Issalla' of later documents.

26. Morris to Governor, 16 Apr. 1904, NAG, ADM 56/1/2: 130.

27. Black Volta District, Annual Report 1904, NAG, ADM 56/1/410.

28. Black Volta District, Monthly Report, Feb. 1905, NAG, ADM 56/1/412.

29. Report on Lobi Mission, Mar. 1905, NAG, ADM 56/1/50. For a discussion of Read's ethnography, see Ch. 3 of this volume.

30. See Ch. 3 of this volume.

31. Report on Lobi Mission, Mar. 1905, NAG, ADM 56/1/50.

32. Ibid. Into the 1920s, Lawra usually appeared as 'Lorha'; unless quoting directly, I shall use the current spelling.

33. Report on Tour of Inspection, Feb. to May 1906, NAG, ADM 56/1/43: 15–16.

34. Northern Territories, Annual Report 1906, PRO, CO 98/16: 5.

35. Black Volta District, Annual Report 1906, NAG, ADM 56/1/422: 2.

36. Jackson to Read, Report of Tour of Inspection, 11 Jun. 1907, NAG, ADM 56/1/ 451.

37. Report on Tour of Inspection, Feb. to May 1906, NAG, ADM 56/1/43: 13.

38. Report on Tour of Inspection, 11. Oct. to 6 Nov. 1906, NAG, ADM 56/1/50. For the local view of this meeting, see pp. 49–50.

39. Ibid.

40. Northern Territories, Annual Report 1907, PRO, CO 98/16.

41. Ibid. Less than ten years had passed since Babatu's attacks, and the British campaign to recruit mine workers caused anxiety in many places that slaves were being taken again. Similarly, men were only prepared to serve as porters if the British engaged them for a short period and sent them, along with their pay, back

to their home village immediately their contract was completed. On this, see Black Volta District, Annual Report 1904, NAG, ADM 56/1/410.

42. Northern Territories, Annual Report 1906, PRO, CO 98/16: 3.

43. Northern Territories, Annual Report 1907, PRO, CO 98/16.

44. Report on Lobi Mission, Mar. 1905, NG, ADM 56/1/50.

45. See Lentz 1993 for an extensive analysis of the oral traditions of the Nandom chieftaincy.

46. Interview, 27 Nov. 1989, Nandom-Pataal.

47. Interview with Severio Termaghre, 12 Dec. 1989, Nandom (in English).

48. This, at any rate, is what Kyiir himself claimed when Read interviewed him in Wa in Dec. 1905 (see NAG, ADM 61/5/2: 250).

49. Interview with Soglikuu Saakum and Kuur Der, 17 Dec. 1994, Bilegang.

50. Interview with Gaamuo Kog and Gaamuo Der Tubor, 28 Nov. 1989, Nandomkpee.

51. Interview with Mwinpuo Le-ib, 11 Dec. 1989, Nandomkpee.

52. Interview with Soglikuu Saakum and Kuur Der, 17 Dec. 1994, Bilegang.

53. On this, see Correspondence Relating to the Delimitation of Boundaries under the Anglo-French Convention of 14 June 1898, Mar. 1899–Dec. 1900, PRO, CO 879/65, African (West) no. 642; Black Volta District, Monthly Report, Sep. 1902, NAG, ADM 56/1/460, and Archives du Centre National de la Recherche Scientifique et Technologique (CNRST), Ouagadougou, Délimitation des Frontières, Série B, III/1, *Historique (1890–1904) de la délimitation de la frontière Soudan-Gold Coast (1924)*.

54. In Lawra matters are admittedly more complicated, because, although the office of chief is inherited patrilineally, that of earth priest must be transferred within the Hien matriclan, to which the first settlers in Lawra belonged.

55. Interviews with Lawra Naa Abayifaa Karbo, 23 Dec. 1994; Yobo Kiebang, 24 Dec. 1994, Yirkpee; Lambussie Kuoro K. Y. Baloro, 28 Nov. 1989 and 2 Dec. 1994; Lambussie *totina* Nansie Issifu Tomo, 29 Nov. 1994; Jirapa Naa Bapenyiri Yelpoe II, 19 Dec. 1994; Jirapa *tendana* Pordor Mwinyele, 21 Dec. 1994, Tampui.

56. Interview with Dennis Tiewiir, 9 Dec. 1992, Burutu-Danyegang. An informant from the house of the earth priest also reported that the British had given Daga salt (interview with Dibaar, 29 Nov. 1994, Nandomkpee). On the role of presents of sugar and salt in pacifying Dagaba settlements to the south, see also Wilks 1989: 142–3.

57. Interview with Patrick Viiru, 10 Dec. 1992, Nandom.

58. Interview, 27 Nov. 1989, Nandom-Pataal.

59. The 'Nandom Local Government Chain of Command' laid down in 1918 by District Commissioner Duncan-Johnstone still listed the chief of Tom – later demoted – as 'head chief' under Nandom; see Lawra District Record Book, NAG, ADM 61/5/11: 40. See also DC Lawra to CCNT, 1 Jul. 1938, RAT, NRG 8/2/58; Lawra Confederacy State Council, Membership Apr. 1952, RAT, NRG 7/10/1; Nandom State Council, 29 Nov. 1960, RAT, NRG 7/2/6; Declaration of Customary Law of the Nandom Traditional Council, 2 Aug. 1963, RAT, NRG 7/2/7.

60. Interview with Panyaan Naa Edward Dery Yirbekya and others, 23 Dec. 1996.

61. Interviews with Gegenkpe Naa Yabepone Babai Tuolong III and others, 26 Dec. 1996; Tantuo Naa Tampula Nituorna Benee III and others, 27 Dec. 1996; Tantuo *tèŋgánsòb* Siengang Naaisien, 18 Dec. 1994; Kokoligu *tèŋgánsòb* Nestor Kuunyaa, 29 Dec. 1994; Kokoligu Naa Michael Zuwera, 24 Dec. 1996; Augustin and Stanislas Debzie, Kokoligu, 13 Jan. 1998.

62. Interviews with Guo Naa Sugem Gyiele III, 24 Dec. 1996, and Tuopari Naa Naabone Dery and others, 25 Dec. 1996.
63. Report on Tour of Inspection, 11. Oct. to 6 Nov. 1906, NAG, ADM 56/1/50.
64. NAG, ADM 61/5/8, Lawra District Diary, 10 Dec. 1917.
65. Interview with Gabriel Tangsege and others, 18 Dec. 1994.
66. Interview with Baba Lere, George Kuudaar and others, 24 Dec. 1994, Dikpe.
67. Interview with Lawra Naa Abyaifaa Karbo, 23 Dec. 1994. The topic of the opposition of the earth shrine, peacefully established by the first-comers, to horses embodying the violence and imperial power of 'foreign' invaders is part of mythology and ritual throughout the West African savanna region.
68. Interview with Nabaala Kuoro Kanii Kambang and others, 4 Dec. 1994.
69. Interview with Happa Kuoro Hilleh Babrimatoh, 30 Nov. 1994.
70. Interview, 3 Dec. 1994.
71. Interview, 2 Dec. 1994.
72. Black Volta District, Annual Report 1906, NAG, ADM 56/1/422.
73. On this in general, see also Kuklick 1991: 16–20, 242–78; Kuper 1988.
74. CCNT to Governor, 3 Aug. 1914, enclosure 3 in PRO, CO 96/548, no. 42088: 17–20.
75. Northcott thus adopted the claims to sovereignty that the Mamprussi ruler had himself formulated; see Northcott to Colonial Secretary, 20 May 1898, CO 879/ 54, no. 564 Africa (West): 98.
76. Commissioner Northern Province (CNP) to CCNT, 7 Nov. 1928, RAT, NRG 8/2/20.
77. Northcott to Colonial Secretary, 31 July 1899, PRO, CO 879/54, no. 564 African (West): 254.
78. For example, this argument was used to remove the 'Lobi' settlement of Tangisa from the realm of the 'Dagarti King' of Nadawli (Black Volta DC Taylor, Report on Tour of Inspection, Apr.–May 1906, NAG, ADM 56/1/43: 17–18.
79. As, for example, in all Gold Coast Civil Service Lists and Chiefs' Lists from 1906 to the end of the 1920s.
80. On this, see Watherston to Governor, 7 Mar. 1905, PRO, CO 96/428, enclosure 4 in Gold Coast Confidential of 12 Apr. 1905; Watherston 1907–8: 353–5; Bening 1977.
81. On this, see Bening 1975a, 1983.
82. Watherston, Report on Tour of Inspection, Mar.–Apr. 1906, NAG, ADM 56/1/ 43: 13–14.
83. Read, Report on site for station at Lorha and tour Jan. 1907, NAG, ADM 56/1/163.
84. Ibid.
85. Progress Report on the Northern Territories, Apr. 1907, NAG, ADM 56/1/515.
86. On the events in Bongo in the North-East, see Northern Territories, Annual Report 1916 (Colonial Reports); R. Thomas 1983. On the 'Bole revolt' of 1917, in which resistance to the conscription of soldiers was coupled with conflicts between the chiefs, see R. Thomas 1975a: 72–5; Iliasu 1975.
87. Lawra District, Quarterly Report, 30 Jun. 1919, NAG, ADM 56/1/452; also Lawra District, Informal Diary, 8, 9 and 18 Aug., 14 Sep. 1920, RAT, NRG 8/ 4/15. On the military maneouvres in Upper Volta, see also Kambou-Ferrand 1993b; on the Volta-Bani 'anticolonial war' (1915–17), see Saul and Royer 2001.
88. Lawra District, Informal Diary, 9 Aug. 1920, RAT, NRG 8/4/15; also Quarterly Report, 31 Mar. 1921 (NAG, ADM 56/1/452).
89. See Lawra District, Informal Diary, 14 Sep. 1920, RAT, NRG 8/4/15; also Northern Territories, Annual Report 1920: 16 (Colonial Reports).

90. Lawra District, Informal Diary, 14 Sep. 1920, RAT, NRG 8/4/15.
91. Northern Territories, Annual Report 1913: 22 (Colonial Reports).
92. Lawra District, Annual Report 1918, NAG, ADM 56/1/453.
93. See Northern Territories, Annual Reports 1925–6, 1927–8, PRO, CO 98/50. Part of the increase in road length between 1918 and 1926 is explained by the merging of Lawra and Tumu Districts in 1921.
94. See Lawra District, Annual Report 1918, NAG, ADM 56/1/453; Watherston 1907–8: 367.
95. Read to CCNT, 13 Jul. 1907, NAG, ADM 56/1/451.
96. Lawra District, Quarterly Report, 31 Mar. 1919, NAG, ADM 56/1/452.
97. Northern Province, Quarterly Report, 30 Jun. 1921, NAG, ADM 56/1/425. However, population figures must be treated with caution because many chiefs apparently either exaggerated them to stress their own importance or kept them low for of fear of a poll tax.
98. Lawra District Record Book, NAG, ADM 61/5/11: 40, 254.
99. Read to CCNT, 5 May 1914, NAG, ADM 56/1/477.
100. In Lawra District, the title 'divisional chief' for the highest rank was only finally introduced in 1934, when it systematically replaced the titles of 'head chief' and 'paramount chief'. Previously it had only been used occasionally, although the DC Lawra had suggested it back in 1922; see DC Lawra-Tumu to CNP, 26 Aug. 1922, and the latter's reply of 6 Sep. 1922, NAG, ADM 56/1/452.
101. Quarterly Report, 30 Sep. 1917, NAG, ADM 56/1/452.
102. Report on Tour of Inspection, 11 Jun. 1907, NAG, ADM 56/1/451; see also Ch. 3 of this volume.
103. On Lambussie, see entries from 1916 to 1937 in the Lawra District Record Book, NAG, ADM 61/5/11: 82–4, 92; Lawra-Tumu District, Quarterly Reports, 30 Jun. and 30 Sep. 1921, ADM 56/1/425; DC Lawra to Commissioner Northern Province (CNP), 2 Jan. 1922, with enclosures, ADM 56/1/307. For other examples of resistance, see Lawra District, Annual Report 1918, NAG, ADM 56/1/453.
104. Lawra District, Quarterly Report, 30 Jun. 1917, NAG, ADM 56/1/452; Lawra District, Informal Diary, 12 Dec. 1917, ibid.
105. Eyre-Smith to CNP, 15 Nov. 1927, RAT, NRG 8/2/18.
106. See, for example, the case of Kokoligu, where the son of a chief who had been removed was opposing the new office-holder; DC Lawra to Commissioner North-Western Province (CNWP), 13 Dec. 1917 NAG, ADM 56/1/163; Lawra District, Quarterly Reports, 30 Jun. and 30 Sep. 1918, ADM 56/1/452, and interview with the Nestor Kuunyaa, 29 Dec. 1994, Kokoligu. On the bitter power struggle between Tizza and Jirapa, see CNP to CCNT, 1 Feb. 1927, NAG, ADM 56/1/301; Eyre-Smith to CNP, 31 Dec. 1926, ibid.
107. Duncan-Johnstone to CNWP, 6 Aug. 1918, NAG, ADM 56/1/425.
108. Ibid.
109. Duncan-Johnstone to CNWP, 28 Feb. 1919, ibid. In 1960, one faction of the inhabitants of Lissa expressed the desire to be made subject to Nandom instead of Lawra, though this never came to pass. See Yob Babana and others to Minister of Local Government, 1960, RAT, NRG 7/2/6.
110. Lawra District Record Book, Jun. 1921, NAG, ADM 61/5/11: 254.
111. In 1929, following prolonged conflicts with Ulu, Karni became an independent division, though only for a few years, being placed under Jirapa in 1934. See Lawra-Tumu District, Annual Report 1929–30, RAT, NRG 8/3/25.
112. North-Western Province, Annual Report 1908, NAG, ADM 56/1/434.
113. However, even as late as 1912, the inhabitants of Sabuli beat up a constable

who was trying to recruit porters; the district commissioner returned to Sabuli a few days later with five constables and arrested eleven men, who subsequently received prison sentences between one and six months. See Lawra District, Quarterly Report, 31 Mar. 1912, NAG, ADM 56/1/452.

114. This was especially the case in settlements on the border with Wa District, where far less road work was demanded than in Lawra (Lawra District, Informal Diary, 2 Jul. 1920, RAT, NRG 8/4/15).

115. See, for example, Lawra District, Annual Report 1914, NAG, ADM 56/1/453: 6.

116. See, for example, Lawra District, Quarterly Report, 31 Mar. 1918, NAG, ADM 56/1/452.

117. NAG, ADM 61/5/11: 360.

118. Lawra District, Quarterly Report, 31 Dec. 1917, NAG, ADM 56/1/452.

119. See, for example, Lawra District, Quarterly Report, 30 Sep. 1916, NAG, ADM 56/1/452; exchange of letters concerning chiefs, Lawra-Tumu District, 1927–31, NAG, ADM 56/1/290; Lawra District Complaints Book, 1931–6, NAG, ADM 61/5/15: 66–76.

120. Eyre-Smith to CNP, 21 Mar. 1927, NAG, ADM 56/1/290.

121. Lawra District Record Book, 16 Mar. 1931, NAG, ADM 61/5/11: 373

122. On this, see also Ch. 4 of this volume.

123. Lawra District Record Book, NAG, ADM 61/5/11: 83–4.

124. Lawra District Informal Diary, 8 Mar. 1921, NAG, ADM 56/1/425.

125. Lawra-Tumu District, Quarterly Report, 30 Sep. 1921, NAG, ADM 56/1/ 425.

126. DC Lawra-Tumu to CNP, 2 Jan. 1922, with enclosures, NAG, ADM 56/1/ 307.

127. Lawra District Record Book, NAG, ADM 61/5/11: 84.

128. Eyre-Smith to CNP, 23 Apr. 1927, NAG, ADM 56/1/290.

129. Eyre-Smith to CNP, 18 Jul. 1927, ibid.

130. For the Birifu Naa's medicine shrine, see Gandah 1967/1993: 24–6, 51–2, 70– 4; CCNT to Secretary of Native Affairs, 9 May 1941, RAT, NRG 8/19/11. On the magic ascribed to Tumu Kuoro, see Grindal 1972: 62 ff., and, more generally, the examples in Hawkins 2002: 170–80. Nandom Naa Imoru, in office from 1940 to 1957, acquired his protective medicine from a Muslim whom his colleague and clan brother Denyuu had settled in the neighbouring canton of Niégo in the French colony (interview with Somé Adama and others, Dabileteng, 19 Feb. 1999).

131. See DC Lawra-Tumu to CNP, 26 Nov. 1928, RAT, NRG 8/2/27. Such penalties were particularly at issue in the conflict between Tizza and Jirapa (CNP to CCNT, 1 Feb. 1927, with enclosures, NAG, ADM 56/1/301).

132. CCNT to CNP, 5 Nov. 1927, RAT, NRG 8/2/18.

133. Lawra District, Quarterly Report, 30 Sep. 1916, NAG, ADM 56/1/452; see also Lawra District Complaints Book, 1931–6, NAG, ADM 61/5/15: 66–76; on this, see also Gandah 1967/1993: 43–6.

134. Lawra-Tumu District, Informal Diary, 15 Nov. 1925, NAG, ADM 56/1/467 (quoted after R. Thomas 1973: 95).

135. Interviews with Nandom Naa Dr Imoro, 4 Dec. 1989; and with Dennis Tiewiir, 9 Dec. 1992, Burutu.

136. DC Lawra-Tumu Eyre-Smith to CCNT, 25 Aug. 1927, RAT, NRG 8/2/14 (Tugu Affairs). Eyre-Smith estimated the farms of the Lawra Naa at about 325 acres, those of the Tugu Naa at as much as 640 acres. Boro's successor Konkuu is said to have had a farm of 200 acres in Varpuo alone (Lawra-Tumu

District, Informal Diary, 7 Oct. 1933, RAT, NRG 8/4/62). However, chiefs acquired access to land not only through their office, but also through kin ties.

137. Interview with Gbeckature Boro, 7 Dec. 1992 (in English).

138. Lawra District, Informal Diary, 3 Jan. 1921, NAG, ADM 56/1/8.

139. See Gandah 1967/1993: 47–8, 104, and personal communication; also Goody 1975: 98.

140. Eyre-Smith to CNP, 15 Oct. 1927, RAT, NRG 8/2/18; see also 'Tugu Affairs', RAT, NRG 8/2/14.

141. Eyre-Smith to CCNT, 3 Sep. 1927, RAT, NRG 8/2/14. On the role of the village elders, see Eyre-Smith to CNP, 26 Nov. 1928, RAT, NRG 8/2/27; on the earth priests, see Eyre-Smith 1933.

142. CNP to CCNT, 16 Sep. 1927, RAT, NRG 8/2/14.

143. Eyre-Smith demanded fixed salaries for chiefs and the replacement of road work with a monetary tax; see his communication to the CNP, 17 Nov. 1927, RAT, NRG 8/2/18; also Eyre-Smith 1933: 41–5.

144. CCNT to CNP, 24 Sep. 1927, ibid.

145. On the district commissioners, see Fortes 1936: 27–8; Kuklick 1979: 3–11, 68–84.

146. On Duncan-Johnstone, see Staniland 1975: 83–4; Tashijan 1998.

147. On this, see Ranger 1983, especially pp. 229–46; on the Indian durbar, see Cohn 1983.

148. Lawra District, Annual Report 1918, NAG, ADM 56/1/453: 26, 31.

149. Lawra District Record Book, NAG, ADM 61/5/11: 236, 210.

150. Lawra District, Annual Report 1918, NAG, ADM 56/1/453: 26. Courts were built in the villages of the head chiefs of Jirapa, Nandom, Lawra, Lambussie and Tugu, as well as in Gegenkpe, Kokoligu, Tantuo, Birifu, Duori and Tizza, apparently because their chiefs wanted to further their ambitions to acquire a higher rank.

151. Ibid.

152. Ibid.: 27–8. See also Hawkins 2002: 242–3 on the new native courts.

153. Ibid.: 28–31; Lawra District, Informal Diary, 21 Nov. 1919, NAG, ADM 61/5/8; Lawra District, Quarterly Report, 30 Jun. 1918, NAG, ADM 56/1/452; Lawra District Record Book, NAG, ADM 61/5/11: 230–7. Other chiefs who were not head chiefs also stationed messengers in Lawra, namely Kokoligu, Tizza and Gegenkpe.

154. CCNT to Colonial Secretary, 3 May 1933, RAT, NRG 8/2/58.

155. When the chiefs of Tizza and Ulu died in 1920, their medallions went to the chiefs of Birifu and Nandom (Danye had to return his when he resigned). In 1921 Birifu's and Tugu's two-inch medallions were replaced with three-inch ones, and the chief of Duori received a new two-inch one. On these developments and the practices associated with the award of medallions, see Lawra District, Informal Diary, 12 Jul. and 4 Aug. 1920, RAT, NRG 8/4/15; Lawra District, Quarterly Report, 30 Jun. 1921, NAG, ADM 56/1/425; DC Lawra-Tumu to CCNT, 17 Nov. 1927, RAT, NRG 8/2/18; Diary CNP, 18 Apr. 1928, RAT, NRG 8/4/22.

156. Report on Political Conference in Navrongo, 23 and 24 Dec. 1929, enclosure H in CNP to CCNT, 14 May 1931, RAT, NRG 8/2/32; CNP to DCs, 27 Apr. 1931, RAT, NRG 8/2/58.

157. DC Lawra-Tumu to CCNT, 3 Jun. 1938, RAT, NRG 8/2/58. See also Ch. 7 of this volume.

158. On this, see Northern Territories, Annual Report 1926–7: 12 (Colonial Reports). Instead of taking the subordinate chiefs' three-inch medallions away

from them, which might have provoked discontent, the DC was to ceremonially hand over the certificate of appointment signed by the Chief Commissioner to the Lawra Naa and Nandom Naa, and publicly read it out (CCNT to DC Lawra-Tumu, 17 Jun. 1938, RAT, NRG 8/2/58).

159. The smock (Dagara: *dàga-kpàrv*) is a man's shirt made of cotton strips, the back and chest usually being decorated with abstract motifs. It is widespread today in Northern Ghana, Burkina Faso and Northern Nigeria. The name was no doubt adopted because this West African garment closely resembles the English smock, a farmer's overall decorated with bunched material, over-sown pleats and embroidery.

160. DC Lawra-Tumu to CCNT, 13 Apr. 1933, RAT, NRG 8/2/58.

161. See Lawra-Tumu District, Informal Diary, 24 May 1943, 1944, RAT, NRG 8/4/100; on Empire Day in Tamale, see Gandah 1992: 179–83. Unfortunately, Goody's published edition of Gandah's autobiography (Gandah 2004) skips those eight chapters of the original manuscript which deal with the years 1940–7, and with life in the Tamale senior boys' boarding school. With respect to these chapters, therefore, I have quoted the manuscript; in all other cases the published version.

162. Northern Territories, Annual Report 1925–6: 15–16. See also *Visit of His Royal Highness the Prince of Wales to the Gold Coast, 1925*, Accra: Government Printer 1925.

163. See Gandah 1967/1993: 68–70.

164. Annual Report 1937–8: 13–14 (PRO, CO 98/72), and on Lawra in particular, Gandah 2004: 49–51; on the royalist 'invention of tradition' in Great Britain itself, see Cannadine 1983, especially pp. 139–55.

165. North-Western Province, Annual Report 1915, NAG, ADM 56/1/424; Lawra District, Annual Report 1918, NAG, ADM 56/1/453: 18–19; also R. Thomas 1975a. On irregularities in chiefs collecting the 'donations', see DC Lawra-Tumu to CNP, 12 Aug. 1927, enclosure of 20 May 1927, NAG, ADM 56/1/307.

166. DC Wa to CCNT, 12 Sep. 1947, RAT, NRG 8/2/96.

167. Lawra-Tumu District, Informal Diary, Apr.–Aug. 1939, NAG, ADM 61/5/16.

168. Lawra-Tumu District, Informal Diary, Aug.–Sep. 1942, RAT, NRG 8/4/100.

169. DC Wa to CCNT, 12 Sep. 1947, RAT, NRG 8/2/96.

170. Lawra-Tumu District, Informal Diary, 5 Aug. 1942, RAT, NRG 8/4/100.

171. Lawra-Tumu District, Informal Diary, 4 Jun. 1942, 7 Nov. 1943, 24 May 1944, 9 May 1945. RAT, NRG 8/4/100.

172. See Gandah 2004: 97–8.

173. Lawra-Tumu District, Informal Diary, 26 Aug. and 31 Oct. 1943, 9 May 1945, RAT, NRG 8/4/100.

174. See Lawra District, Quarterly Report, 31 Mar. 1919, NAG, ADM 56/1/452; Gandah 1967/1993: 46–7.

175. Lawra District, Informal Diary, 12 Jun. 1920, RAT, NRG 8/4/15.

176. Lawra-Tumu District, Annual Report 1920, NAG, ADM 56/1/453: 8–9.

177. Northern Territories, Annual Report 1908, PRO, CO 98/17; see also North-Western Province, Annual Report 1908, ADM 56/1/434.

178. Northern Territories, Annual Report 1938–39, PRO, CO 96/758, no. 31196: 5–6.

179. Ibid.

180. Interview with S.W.D.K. Gandah, 26 Feb. 1994, London; see also Gandah 1992: 179–83.

181. A colonial officer who was just passing through reported that at a festival in

Lawra during Ramadan in 1918 not 5 per cent of the Lobi taking part in the archery event could hit the target: 'they were said to be out of practise owing to recent absorption in farming' (PRO, CO 96/600, no. 34483: 46).

182. Lawra District, Informal Diary, 11 Jul. 1920, RAT, NRG 8/4/15.

183. Lawra District, Informal Diary, 22 Jul. 1920, RAT, NRG 8/4/15.

184. CCNT Walker Leigh claimed that these receptions were Duncan-Johnstone's invention (CCNT to CNP, 5 Nov. 1927, RAT, NRG 8/2/18), but S. W. D. K. Gandah, the son of the Birifu Naa, attributed them to his father (Gandah 1967/ 1993: 57–60).

185. Diary of the CCNT, 28 Sep. 1932, Duncan-Johnstone Papers, Rhodes House Library, Oxford, MSS. Afr. S. 593.

CHAPTER 3

1. Lawra District Record Book, NAG, ADM 61/5/11: 251; on Issa, see Watherston's report of April 1907, NAG, ADM 56/1/43: 13.

2. Birifu Naa N. Gandah and thirteen headmen to Commission of Enquiry on Local Government, 4 Nov. 1951; RAT, NRG 8/2/101.

3. An extensive version of some parts of this chapter has already been published in Lentz 1999.

4. Most studies of West African colonial ethnography focus on the anthropological theories that structured the authors' perceptions of reality; see, for instance, van Hoven (1990) on the works of Delafosse, Monteil and Labouret; and Kuklick (1991: 182–278) on the usefulness of a unique mixture of evolutionary and diffusionist theories for the legitimation of colonial policies. More generally on anthropology and British colonialism, see, for instance, Kuper 1983: 99–120; Goody 1995. Alexandre (1970) and Osborn (2003) discuss the role of African interpreters and other employees in the creation of colonial knowledge.

5. See Staniland 1975: 48–51; also Kuklick 1979, Chs 1, 3, 5. On the preparatory courses, see also the reports on his experience of S. A. Fox, RHL, MSS Afr. S. 2084: 1–2) and C. G. R. Amory, PRO, CO 96/738, no. 31196: Appendix A, Northern Territories, Annual Report 1936–7, enclosure in Gold Coast no. 545 of 1 Sep. 1937).

6. Colonial Reports, Annual, No. 1194, Northern Territories of the Gold Coast, Report for 1922–3, London: His Majesty's Stationary Office 1924: 26.

7. See PRO, CO 96/655, no. 32612. The examinations also covered 'native customs'; see the Informal Diary of the Commissioner of the Southern Province, 11 and 28 Jan. 1928, Duncan-Johnstone Papers, RHL, MSS Afr. S. 592.

8. Duncan-Johnstone, Eyre-Smith and Armstrong spoke Hausa, while Amherst spoke Dagbani (information from S. D. W. K. Gandah, 26 Feb. 1994, London). H. A. Blair, who had a fair knowledge of Dagbani and was stationed for a year in Lawra, could communicate without an interpreter (see NAG, ADM 61/5/16: Lawra-Tumu District Informal Diary, 16 Sep. 1938).

9. In this respect, my own findings clearly diverge from the thesis that posits the 'ignorance' of the colonial bureaucracy. See, for instance, Spittler 1981: 89–119 on the French colonial bureaucracy; in a similar vein, Hawkins (1996) brings Rattray's supposed ethnographic expertise into play against the supposedly erratic and superficial knowledge of the district commissioners. More generally on administrative ethnography, see Pels 1996.

10. Binger 1892, II: 36. Whether the 'Lama' were identical with the Sisala, whom Dagara-speakers often called 'Langme', must remain speculation. Only Ferguson quotes Binger's 'Lama'; thereafter this name disappears from the maps.

11. Her Majesty's Secretary of State for the Colonies to the Governor of the Gold

Coast, 5 Apr. 1892, cited in Arhin 1974: 66. On Ferguson's origins, education and activities, see also R. Thomas 1972.

12. Quoted in Wilks 1989: 7. See also Ch. 1 of this volume, and Ferguson's report, cited in Arhin 1974: 137–8.

13. Report on a Lobi mission, Apr. 1905, NAG, ADM 56/1/50.

14. Read to CCNT, 22 Nov. 1908; enclosure 3 in Gold Coast no. 41 of 19 Jan. 1910, PRO, CO 96/493, part 1 A.

15. Report on districts travelled through during March and May 1905, NAG, ADM 56/1/50.

16. Read to CCNT, 22 Nov. 1908; enclosure 3 in Gold Coast no. 41 of 19 Jan. 1910, PRO, CO 96/493, part 1 B.

17. On this, see Ruelle 1904: 657–69; Labouret 1931: 15–43; Fiéloux 1980: 18–37; Kambou-Ferrand 1993b, 1993c.

18. This may have been based on 'Lobr', the term for the northern Dagara dialect today and possibly at the time as well; on this, see S. Bemile 2000.

19. PRO, CO 96/417, enclosure 1 in Gold Coast Confidential of 11 Mar. 1904.

20. Ibid.

21. On this, see also Kuklick 1991: Chs 3, 5.

22. Read to CCNT, 22 Nov. 1908, enclosure 3 in Gold Coast no. 41 of 19 Jan. 1910, PRO, CO 96/493, part I B.

23. Ibid., enclosure 7 (contained in the Lawra District Record Book, NAG, ADM 61/5/11: 296). The first station book of the new Lawra District dedicates twenty-one pages to the question of tribal marks, containing sketches of faces and bodies – for example, a drawing with the caption 'Nandom man' – and attempts to correlate different styles of ornaments with ethnic groups and areas, however without success (NAG, ADM 61/5/1: 8–29). On this, see also the plates in Hawkins 2002: 73–83.

24. Northern Territories, Annual Report 1905: 8.

25. Report on districts travelled through on tours of inspection during March and May 1905, NAG, ADM 56/1/50.

26. See the Gold Coast Civil Service List of 1910–11, Accra (Government Press) 1910: 353.

27. NAG, ADM 56/1/453: 18, 26.

28. In the Lawra Native Authority School, opened in 1935, pupils from Nandom were classified as Lobi-Dagarti, those from Lawra as Lobi, and those from Jirapa as Dagarti (interview with S. W. D. K. Gandah, 26 Feb. 1994, London).

29. Report on districts travelled through on tours of inspection during March and May 1905, NAG, ADM 56/1/50; Taylor to CCNT, tour of inspection, 29 Apr. to 14 May 1906, NAG, ADM 56/1/43: 8.

30. NAG, ADM 56/1/91, Laws and Customs, Northern Territories, 1908.

31. On this, see also generally Appadurai 1996: Ch. 6.

32. On the methods used in conducting the early censuses, see Government of the Gold Coast, *The Gold Coast: Census of Population 1948, Report and Tables*, Accra: Government Printer 1950: 7; generally on the problems of Gold Coast censuses before 1960, see Engman 1986: 37–47, 59, 76–9, 94. Although the census should have been taken in April 1921, Duncan-Johnstone apparently already began having counts made in August 1920. Presumably a further count was taken in 1921, which would explain the differences between Duncan-Johnstone's figures and the published results.

33. Duncan-Johnstone and other district commissioners would alternately spell ethnic composites, such as Lobi-Dagarti, with or without hyphen. My own spelling follows the orthography of the specific document quoted.

34. Gold Coast Census 1921, Reports and Returns, Accra: Government Press 1923: 132.
35. Lawra District Record Book, NAG, ADM 61/5/11: 253. The absolute figures varied depending on the source. In the official census report the number of Lobi totalled 32,140 (Gold Coast Census 1921, Reports and Returns, Accra, Government Press 1923: 129–33); in the retrospective look back at 1921 that was published in the 1931 census this figure is given as 39,952; similarly on the basis of the 1921 census, District Commissioner Dasent assumed a total of 38,823 Lobi (26,154 Lobi and 12,669 Lobi-Dagarti; DC Lawra-Tumu to CNP, 24 Jun. 1924, RAT, NRG 8/2/32).
36. Dasent to CNP, 24 Jun. 1924, RAT, NRG 8/2/32.
37. Lawra District Diary, 20 Dec. 1918, NAG, ADM 61/5/8. See also Cardinall 1920: viii–ix, who traced the popularity of tribal names like Fra-Fra, Grunshi and Kanjaga as family names back to the fact that recruits were using them as a means of protecting themselves from witchcraft.
38. Lawra District Diary, 8 Jan. 1935, NAG, ADM 61/5/12.
39. See, for example, Appendix C, Lawra Native Authority Estimates, Northern Territories, Annual Report 1936–7, PRO, CO 96/738, no. 31196.
40. CNP to DCs, 12 Jun. 1931, RAT, NRG 8/2/27.
41. Lawra-Tumu District, Annual Report 1938–9, RAT, NRG 8/3/78: 1–2.
42. Northern Territories, Annual Report 1935–6, RAT, NRG 8/3/53: 89. On the immigration, see Colonial Secretary to CCNT, 14 Nov. 1929; CCNT to CNP, 22 Nov. 1929, RAT, NRG 8/2/20. See also Evans 1983.
43. 1960 Population Census of Ghana, Special Report E, Accra: Census Office 1964: D 9–10.
44. PRO, CO 96/493, Gold Coast no. 41, Governor Robertson to the Colonial Office, 19 Jan. 1910, enclosures 3, 7. On this questionnaire, see also Kuklick 1991: 199–200.
45. Read to CCNT, 5 Dec. 1914, NAG, ADM 56/1/105. On this, see also Wilks 1989: 142–3, 148–9.
46. PRO, CO 96/493, Gold Coast No. 41, Governor Robertson to Colonial Office, 19 Jan. 1910, enclosure 7, remarks on the answers to part II, 3 and 4.
47. Supplement to above questionnaire, in NAG, ADM 56/1/91.
48. Ibid.
49. Ibid., enclosure 7.
50. Ibid., part II, section 7. Incidentally, Read was the first author to mention the distinction between the matrilineal inheritance of moveable property among the Lobi and the generally patrilineal inheritance among the Dagarti, which, for Jack Goody, would later become the most important criterion for the distinction between the 'LoDagaba' and 'LoWiili'.
51. Ibid.
52. CO 96/493, Gold Coast no. 41 of 19 Jan. 1910, enclosure 3, part II, section 3.
53. Ibid., 'Remarks on the answers to part 2, 3 and 4 that are common to the Pagan Dagarti, Lobi, in some cases Walas who have not come under the influence of Mahommedanism'.
54. In a second copy of the same typed manuscript (enclosure 7, in Gold Coast No. 41 of 19 Jan. 1910, PRO, CO 96/493), the hunter is called 'Kontol', which is also what my informants called him.
55. Presumably Batié, a place west of the Black Volta.
56. In the second copy (PRO, CO 96/493), 'Tindana' ('earth priest') is mentioned instead of 'Ulliamae'.
57. Lawra District Record Book, NAG, ADM 61/5/11: 251.

58. Jack Goody and S. W. D. K. Gandah (2002: 337–80) recorded a *bàgr* recitation in Lawra which contained a long narrative about the 'coming of the Kusiele'. More generally on the *bàgr*, see Goody 1972; Goody and Gandah 1980.

59. Interview, 24 Dec. 1994.

60. Such legends were also created in many other new chieftaincies: see Rattray 1932: 468–81 for examples of Sisala legends; Schott 1977: 154–7 and 1993 on the Builsa.

61. St. John-Parsons 1958: 46–8.

62. Intelligence Report of Jun. 1921, Lawra District Record Book, 256, NAG, ADM 61/5/11.

63. See Tauxier 1912: 360–1; Delafosse 1912: 141–2.

64. Lawra District Record Book, 11 Oct. 1913, NAG, ADM 61/5/1.

65. CCNT to Governor, 3 Aug. 1914; PRO, CO 96/548, no. 42088, enclosure 1: 15.

66. Cf. also Ruelle 1904; Tauxier 1912.

67. Delafosse's short text on migration movements contains many inconsistencies; see also Labouret's criticism (1931: 15–17) of Delafosse.

68. Lawra District Record Book, NAG, ADM 61/5/11: 285.

69. Ibid.: 256–8.

70. Lawra District, Informal Diary, 9 Aug. 1920, RAT, NRG 8/4/15.

71. See ibid., entries for Aug. and Sep. 1920.

72. Lawra District Record Book; NAG, ADM 61/5/11: 286–7.

73. Ibid.: 254–6.

74. Government of the Gold Coast, Report for the Northern Territories for the Period Apr. 1928 to Mar. 1929, Accra: Government Printer 1929: 11. Rattray died in a gliding accident in 1938.

75. NAG, ADM 56/1/179: Report by the Special Commissioner for Anthropology for the year 1929–30 (cited hereafter as 'Report'; printed version in PRO, CO 98/50): 20, 2. This text was adapted for the introduction to *The Tribes of the Ashanti Hinterland* (1932) with little alteration. Here I am citing the Report, since it refers more explicitly to the political context than the book.

76. Ibid.: 2.

77. Diary of the Acting CCNT, 1 Oct. 1932, Duncan-Johnstone Papers, RHL, MSS Afr. S. 593. In fact, Rattray refused to acknowledge not only ethnographic notes to be found the district station books, but also Cardinall's *The Natives of the Northern Territories of the Gold Coast* (1920), which had contained many of the 'discoveries' later claimed by Rattray.

78. Report: 7–9.

79. Ibid.: 19, 21.

80. Ibid.: 6, 12.

81. Ibid.: 13.

82. Ibid.: 18. Cf. the CCNT's marginal note: 'probably rubbish' (ibid.: 19). In the book version, Rattray (1932: xx) even claimed that the same 'stranger-invaders' who set up the Dagomba and Mamprussi states had also founded the Akan kingdoms. For a critique of Rattray's romanticising views on the Asante kingdom, see McCaskie 1983.

83. Report: 14.

84. Ibid.: 15–16.

85. NAG, ADM 61/5/12, Lawra District Diary, 27 Oct., 6 and 18 Nov. 1929; and R. S. Rattray, Manuscripts, Royal Anthropological Institute (London), MS 109/18, notebook 24: 1774, and MS 109/2, notebook 8: 122–48, on work in Tiole (spelt 'Tuole' in the notebook); MS 109/18, notebook 24: 1714–16, 1746, on work in Han.

86. NAG, ADM 61/5/12, Lawra District Diary, 6 Nov. 1929.
87. For example, Rattray noticed that a whole clan does not necessarily share the same 'taboo' (1932: 405), that 'Lober' clans have no totems, just common names (ibid.: 426), and that the taboos change when clans split, so that common origins cannot be concluded from the present-day taboos.
88. 'Interim Report on the Peoples of Nandom and Lambussie', § 1; NAG, ADM 11/1/824, cited hereafter as Guinness 1932. On the origins of the report, see Lawra-Tumu District, Informal Diary, 11–17 Oct. 1932, RAT, NRG 8/4/62.
89. Guinness 1932: § 11.
90. Ibid.: § 9.
91. See Ch. 4 of this volume.
92. Ibid.: §§ 22–37.
93. Eyre-Smith to the Secretary for Native Affairs, 2 Mar. 1933, § 23; NAG, ADM 11/1/824, cited hereafter as Eyre-Smith, Comments. On the polemical critique of Eyre-Smith, see also the exchange of letters between the CCNT and the Secretary for Native Affairs, as well as H. A. Blair's commentary in NAG, ADM 11/1/824.
94. Eyre-Smith, Comments: §§ 2, 5, 17, 24.
95. Guinness 1932: § 10.
96. Guinness 1932: § 41.
97. The historical sketch can be found in Eyre-Smith to CNP, 22 Sep. 1927, NAG, ADM 56/1/307 (cited hereafter as Eyre-Smith 1927); the memorandum was published in revised form as Eyre-Smith 1933.
98. Guinness 1932: Apology.
99. Eyre-Smith, Comments: § 8, 24.
100. Lawra-Tumu Informal Diary, 14 and 20 July 1927, RAT, NRG 8/4/28; see also Eyre-Smith, Comments: § 11 and Eyre-Smith 1927: 2.
101. See Eyre-Smith, Comments: §§ 12, 13.
102. Eyre-Smith, Comments: § 24.
103. Eyre-Smith, Comments: §§ 8–10.
104. H. A. Blair, in a manuscript on the Northern Territories, no place, no date, RHL, MSS. Afr. S. 626.
105. Many colonial historiographies indeed end with the colonial takeover of power, which put an end to warfare and the pursuit of slaves. See, for example, Delafosse 1912, Cardinall 1931, Ward 1949.
106. Guinness 1932: § 41.
107. RAT, NRG 8/2/14, Tugu Affairs; see also Hawkins 1996: 205–7.
108. Eyre-Smith to NCP, 15 Oct. 1927, RAT, NRG 8/2/18; Eyre-Smith to CNP, 26 Nov. 1928, RAT, NRG 8/2/27.
109. Eyre-Smith, Comments: § 32.
110. Eyre-Smith, Comments: § 29.
111. Eyre-Smith, Comments: § 36.
112. Eyre-Smith, Comments: §§ 17–18, 20, 35; Guinness 1932: §§ 225, 40. See also Lentz 2000a and Ch. 4 of this volume.
113. Guinness 1932: § 4.
114. Ibid.: § 6.
115. Eyre-Smith, Comments: § 4.
116. Guinness 1932: § 43. The fact that the 'Tindana map' indicating the exact boundaries of earth-shrine parishes, which had already been ordered by Provincial Commissioner Whittall in 1928, was never drawn up indicates that these boundaries were not as clearly defined as Eyre-Smith's model suggested; see CNP to DCs, 29 Dec. 1928, 30 Oct. 1929, RAT, NRG, 8/2/27.

117. Guinness 1932: § 39.
118. Eyre-Smith, Comments: § 39.
119. Ibid.: §§ 40–3. See also Ch. 6 of this volume.
120. See, for instance, Der 1977, 2001.

CHAPTER 4

1. Minutes of a Conference at Tamale, 11 Mar. 1921; NAG, ADM 56/1/258.
2. On this, see Staniland 1975: Ch. 5; Ladouceur 1979: 52–61.
3. On Cameron, see Iliffe 1979: 318–41; Pels 1996.
4. Duncan-Johnstone, Memorandum on the introduction into and the development of native administration in the Southern Province, 14 Apr. 1930, RHL, MSS Afr. S. 593.
5. CSP Informal Diary, 9 and 21 Jan. 1930, RHL, MSS Afr. S. 593.
6. Slater to Colonial Office, 15 Feb. 1932, PRO, CO 96/702/7215.
7. DC Lawra-Tumu to DC Wa, 1 Oct. 1947, RAT, NRG 8/2/101: 3.
8. DC Lawra-Tumu to CNP, 24 Jun. and 6 Aug. 1924, enclosure in CNP to CCNT, 14 May 1931, RAT, NRG, 8/2/32.
9. DC Lawra-Tumu to CNP, 16 Oct. 1927, RAT, NRG 8/2/18.
10. CNP to CCNT, 7 Nov. 1928, RAT, NRG 8/2/20.
11. Report of Northern Province conference of 23 and 24 Dec. 1929, cited in CNP to CCNT, 14 May 1931, RAT, NRG 8/2/38.
12. Ibid.
13. DC Lawra-Tumu to CNP, 3 Jul. 1931, RAT, NRG, 8/2/27.
14. DC Lawra-Tumu to CNP, 17 Aug. 1931, RAT, NRG, 8/2/27.
15. CSP, Informal Diary, 21 Nov. 1931, RHL, MSS Afr. S. 593.
16. CCNT to CNP, 11 Feb. 1932, RAT, NRG 8/2/52.
17. DC Lawra-Tumu to CNP, 22 Mar. 1932, ibid.
18. Northern Territories, Annual Report 1933–4, PRO, CO 96/719, no. 21791: 29; see also CCNT Order No. 4 of 31 Jan. 1934 (Lawra Confederacy Native Authority) and CCNT Order No. 16 of 20 Jul. 1934, decreeing the four Subordinate Native Authorities as of 1 Sep. 1934.
19. On the structure of the native authorities in general, see Jones 1938, Packham 1950, Staniland 1975: 86–102, on the Lawra Confederacy Lawra-Tumu District, Annual Report 1938–9, RAT, NRG 8/3/78; on the native courts in Lawra, Hawkins 2002: 178–9, 242–3, 265–6.
20. A divisional chief in Lawra District received £3 a month, three times as much as a sub-divisional chief, as well as a bonus for performing 'special duties' such as treasurer or supervising a native authority experimental farm. Unpaid work for chiefs was now limited to five days a year, and the DCs no longer assisted chiefs in gaining compliance to demands; see Northern Territories, Annual Report 1936–7, CO 96/738, No. 31196: 71, as well as Lawra Confederacy, Complaints Book, 1931–6, NAG, ADM 61/5/15: especially 66–76.
21. Lawra-Tumu District, Informal Diary, 23 Mar. 1938, NAG, ADM 61/5/16.
22. CSP, Informal Diary, 20 Aug. 1932, RHL, MSS Afr. S. 593, Duncan-Johnstone Paper; see also Direct Taxation Propaganda Notes, c. 1932, RAT, NRG 8/2/38.
23. In the Lawra Confederacy, the divisional chiefs had already brought in £1,013 within seven weeks after the introduction of the tax in 1936, a good 20 per cent more than originally estimated; see Northern Territories, Annual Report 1936–7, PRO, CO 96/738, No. 31196: 46–7. Many of the coins used in payment dated from 1920, presumably the savings of returned soldiers. Such money, as well as the wages earned by labour migrants, were often hoarded, because the currency

relevant to the local economy continued to be cowries; Lawra-Tumu District, Informal Diary, Apr. 1937, RAT, NRG 8/4/76.

24. See, for example, the amounts in Lawra-Tumu District, Annual Report 1938–9, RAT, NRG 8/3/78, and generally 'Northern Territories Native Treasuries', *West Africa*, 22 Jan. 1938: 44.

25. Lawra-Tumu District, Annual Report 1938–9, RAT, NRG 8/3/78: 9.

26. The headmen received a 5 per cent commission to ensure a vested personal interest that tax lists were complete and payment punctual. On the technical details of tax collection, see Lawra-Tumu District, Annual Report 1938–9, RAT, NRG 8/3/78: 7–9, and Informal Diary for Sep. and Oct. 1937, 1938 and 1939, NAG, ADM 61/5/16.

27. Lawra-Tumu District, Annual Report 1938–9, RAT, NRG 8/3/78: 31–2.

28. DC Lawra-Tumu to CCNT, 7 Jun. 1933, RAT, NRG 8/2/52.

29. CCNT Order No. 16 of 1934.

30. Lawra-Tumu District, Informal Diary, 20 Nov. 1937, NAG, ADM 61/5/16; see also Informal Diary, 11 Feb. 1938, RAT, NRG 8/4/83.

31. Handing-over Report, DC Lawra-Tumu, 7 Nov. 1938: 19, RHL, MSS Afr. S. 626, papers of H. A. Blair.

32. Lawra-Tumu District, Informal Diary, 22 and 24 Jun. 1939, RAT, NRG 8/4/83.

33. Guinness 1932: § 25. For more details on Guinness's investigations, see Ch. 3 of this volume.

34. Ibid.: § 22–5. The full verbatim version of this story, as well as a detailed discussion of present-day versions of the settlement history of Nandom that I recorded among various Sisala and Dagara families, can be found in Lentz 2000a.

35. Interview, 28 Nov. 1989, with Lambussie Kuoro K. Y. Baloro in Lambussie; interview, 29 Nov. 1989, with Nansie Issifu Tomo and his elders in Lambussie; interview, 2 Dec. 1994, with Darte Bason Boyuo, Ali Tumarah, Edmund Ebito and others in Lambussie; also Bening 1976: 18.

36. Eyre-Smith, Comments: § 17.

37. Guinness 1932: § 33, 39. The acquisition of an earth shrine in exchange for substantial payments in cowries or a wife of the earth-shrine recipient was very much a theme in the interviews I have conducted on settlement histories in numerous Dagara and Sisala settlements in Ghana and Burkina Faso since 1997; on these, see Kuba and Lentz 2002; also the case study of Ouessa in Lentz 2001a.

38. Guinness 1932: § 40.

39. Eyre-Smith, Comments: § 17–18.

40. Ibid.: § 20.

41. Ibid.: § 35.

42. Interview with Lambussie Kuoro K. Y. Baloro, 24 Nov. 1994; on this, see E. Tengan 1991: 92–105.

43. The earth priest of Lambussie whom I interviewed, Issifu Nansie Tomo, mentioned a longer interregnum period before the term of office of his father, Nansie; interview, 29 Nov. 1994.

44. Interviews with Darte Bason Boyon, 2 Dec. 1994, and Nansie Issifu Tomo, 29 Nov. 1994. See also Lawra District Commissioner Armstrong's *Report on the Peoples of the Lambussie and Nandom Divisions in the Lawra-Tumu District*, 1934, NAG, ADM 11/1/824: 3.

45. See Ch. 2 of this volume.

46. DC Lawra-Tumu to CNP, 21 Apr. 1931, NAG, ADM 56/1/309.

47. Interview with Lambussie K. Y. Baloro, 28 Nov. 1989.

298 NOTES TO PAGES 116-23

48. See, for example, Lawra District, Informal Diary, 17 Jan. and 5 Feb. 1930, NAG, ADM 61/5/12, as well as my interviews in Taalipuo (David Nowe, Benjamin Kpiimogle *et al.*, 17 Dec. 1994), Kyetuu-Kuuziegang (Gyile Bagna, Kosi Debmole *et al.*, 25 Feb. 1999), Kyetuu-Tuolegang (Maasaagyir Depula *et al.*, 14 Jan. 1998), Fielmuo (Aansokang Dagnikuu, Faata Biku *et al.*, 14 Jan. 1998) and Piina (Ignacius Zaabaar, 15 Jan. 1998; Constancio Debuo *et al.*, 15 Jan. 1998).
49. On this, see also Bening 1976: 19; E. Tengan 1991: 119-23; A. Tengan 2000: 261-94.
50. The terms 'allodial title' or 'allodial ownership' are common Ghanaian legal parlance and refer to land titles beyond which there is no superior interest. According to most customary land tenure systems, allodial title is vested in communities, represented by chiefs or earth priests, according to the regionally different political traditions. For an overview of Sisala-Dagara relations with respect to settlement history, land tenure and earth shrines, see Kuba and Lentz 2002.
51. Native Land Tenure, NAG, ADM 56/1/375: 12. On this, see also the definition of 'native' in the Northern Territories Land and Native Rights Ordinance of 1931, PRO, CO 96/702/7187.
52. On this, see also E. Tengan 1991: 122, 130-4.
53. Interview with Michael Naateryel, 24 Nov. 1989, Kulkya.
54. Lawra-Tumu District, Informal Diary, RAT, NRG 8/4/76.
55. Lawra District Record Book, 20 Oct. 1935, NAG, ADM 61/5/11: 92.
56. Lawra District Record Book, 28 May 1930 and 7 Oct. 1934, ibid.: 84, 92.
57. Lawra-Tumu District, Informal Diary, 10 Mar. 1936, RAT, NRG 8/4/76; see also Lawra District Record Book, 10 Mar. 1936, NAG, ADM 61/5/11: 92.
58. See Armstrong, *Report on the Peoples of the Lambussie and Nandom Divisions in the Lawra-Tumu District*, 1934, NAG, ADM 11/1/824.
59. On Dasoberi, see Lawra-Tumu District, Informal Diary, 14 Jan. 1935, RAT, NRG 8/4/76; on Konkuu, see Lawra-Tumu District, Annual Report 1930-1 and 1931-2, RAT, NRG 8/3/27; Northern Territories, Annual Report 1935-6, RAT, NRG 8/3/53: 49; Northern Territories, Annual Report, 1936-7, PRO, CO 96/738 No. 31196; and Lawra-Tumu District Annual Report 1938-9, RAT, NRG 8/3/78: 6.
60. Lawra District Record Book, 30 Jun. 1936, NAG, ADM 61/5/11: 92. The Informal Diary criticises Hilla's 'slackness'; 30 Jun. 1936, RAT, NRG 8/4/76.
61. Lawra District Record Book, 30 Jun. 1936, NAG, ADM 61/5/11: 92.
62. 12 Jan. 1937, ibid.
63. On the legal situation, see DC Lawra-Tumu to DC Wa, 1 Oct. 1947, RAT, NRG 8/2/101: 1-2.
64. Ibid.: 2.
65. Tekowah Grunshie to CCNT, 31 Jan. 1938, NAG, ADM 56/1/301.
66. Tekowah Grunshie to CCNT, 15 Feb. 1938, ibid.
67. CCNT to Tekowah Grunshie, 9 March 1938, ibid.
68. Interview, 30 Nov. 1994.
69. Interview, 28 Nov. 1989.
70. Interview with Darte Bason Boyuo and Ali Tumarah, Lambussie, 2 Dec. 1994.
71. Lawra-Tumu District, Informal Diary, 13 May 1943; NAG, ADM 61/5/16; see also ibid., 3 May 1943.
72. Interview, 31 Aug. 1993.
73. Interview, 2 Dec. 1994.
74. Interview, 22 Dec. 1989.

75. DC Lawra-Tumu to DC Wa, 1 Oct. 1947, RAT, NRG 8/2/101: 2–3.

76. Ibid.: 3.

77. Zubeviel to Lambussie State Council, 6 Sep. 1961, RAT, NRG 7/3/3.

78. Salifu Botsea to Regional Commissioner Upper Region, 14 Nov. 1961, RAT, NRG 7/2/6.

79. DC Lawra-Tumu to DC Wa, 1 Oct. 1947, RAT, NRG 8/2/101: 3.

80. RAT, NRG 8/2/101; see also Supplement of the Gold Coast Gazette no. 91 of 29 Nov. 1947: 1082–3.

81. Interview with Darte Bason Boyuo and others, 2 Dec. 1994.

82. Ibid., and interview with Bawa S. Dy-Yakah, 31 Aug. 1993; no written documents concerning this election remain in the archives.

83. Northern Territories, Annual Report 1929–30, PRO, CO 98/55: 9.

84. See Handing-over Report, Lawra-Tumu District, 7 Nov. 1938, RHL, MSS Afr. S. 626; Northern Territories, Annual Report 1937–8, PRO, CO 98/72: 33–4.

85. DC Lawra-Tumu to CCNT, 30 Aug. 1938, RAT, NRG 8/2/73.

86. Lawra-Tumu District, Informal Diary, 16 Sep. 1938, NAG, ADM 61/5/16.

87. 30 Aug. 1938, ibid.

88. 14 Aug. 1938, ibid.

89. 11 Jan. 1939, ibid.

90. On this, see Lawra-Tumu District, Informal Diary, 14 Jan. 1935 and 10 Mar. 1936, RAT, NRG 8/4/76.

91. DC Lawra-Tumu to CCNT, 14 Jan. 1939, RAT, NRG 8/2/73. Even the compound owners of the entire division participated in the election to the Nandom Naa; DC Lawra-Tumu to CCNT, 23 Dec. 1940, ibid.

92. DC Lawra-Tumu to CCNT, 30 Aug. 1938, RAT, NRG 8/2/73.

93. Lawra-Tumu District, Informal Diary, 3 Jun. 1940, NAG, ADM 61/5/16.

94. Lawra-Tumu District, Annual Report 1938–9, RAT, NRG 8/3/78: 6–7.

95. See Lawra-Tumu District, Informal Diary, 1937–44, NAG, ADM 61/5/16; 1940–7, RAT, NRG 8/4/100.

96. Governor to Colonial Office, 2 May 1939, PRO, CO 96/755/31096/3. On the colonial development policy in the Northern Territories in general, see Bening 1975b, Der 1987, Sutton 1989.

97. Northern Territories, Annual Report 1936–7, CO 96/738, no. 31196: 112.

98. Northern Territories, Annual Report 1936–7, PRO, CO 96/738, no. 31196: 17: 68.

99. DC Dagomba to CCNT, 22 Oct. 1936, cited in Staniland 1975: 92.

100. Lawra-Tumu District, Informal Diary, 12 Sep. 1942, NAG, ADM 61/5/16.

101. Lawra-Tumu District, Annual Report 1938–9, RAT, NRG 8/3/78: 8–9.

102. See, for example, Lawra-Tumu District, Informal Diary, 3 Dec. 1937, RAT, NRG 8/4/76.

103. Lawra-Tumu District, Informal Diary, 6 Aug. 1942, NAG, ADM 61/5/16.

104. Ibid., 13 Apr. 1943.

105. On the colonial 'invention' of customary law, see Roberts and Mann 1991: 19–23, also Moore 1986: especially pp. 38–42, 317–19. On Lawra District, see Hawkins 2002: 118, 120–1, 281–3.

106. See Duncan-Johnstone's description of the 'bari fetish' (bàgr) among the Lobi (1918) (Lawra District Record Book, NAG, ADM 61/5/11: 220–2) and Corson's discussion of the 'burial customs' of the Lobi, Dagarti and Issala, with additions by Duncan-Johnstone (1915–18) (ibid.: 291–4).

107. Of the 36 native authority rules decreed between 1935 and 1951, 10 concerned caravanserais, lorry stops and ferries, 7 'village sanitation' and the protection of

trees, woodlands and soil, 6 the income from markets and abattoirs, 5 the issuing of fishing and hunting licences, 5 the manufacture and sale of 'native intoxicating liquor', and 3 other matters; RAT, NRG 8/2/48.

108. Handing-over Report, Lawra-Tumu District, 7 Nov. 1938, RHL, MSS Afr. S. 626: 4–5.

109. Lawra-Tumu District, Annual Report 1941–2, RAT, NRG 8/3/108.

110. Lawra-Tumu District, Informal Diary, 23 Jul. 1944, NAG, ADM 61/5/16.

111. On the colonial codification of marriage and divorce in Lawra District, see Hawkins 2002: 254–8.

112. Lawra-Tumu District, Annual Report 1938–9, RAT, NRG 8/3/78: 31.

113. DC Lawra-Tumu to CCNT, 17 Apr. 1935, RAT, NRG 8/2/52.

114. Ibid.

115. Lawra Confederacy Native Administration, Minutes of Conference 10–12 Sep. 1940, RAT, NRG 8/5/17.

116. Lawra Confederacy State Council, 25 Jun. 1954, RAT, NRG 7/10/1.

117. GA Lawra to Chief Regional Officer, 5 Jun. 1955, RAT, NRG 7/2/1.

118. On this, see also Pels 1996, who convincingly criticises Ranger's thesis (1983) of the reification of 'invented traditions'.

119. The comprehensive recording of 'traditional rules' in writing has only been achieved since the 1950s, since the courts were required to elucidate the bases of their decisions; on this, see Hawkins 2002: Chs 7, 8.

120. Marriage laws of the Lobi and Dagarti tribes resident in the Lawra Federation Native Authority Area, Lawra District Record Book, NAG, ADM 61/5/11: 388–94.

121. In Nandom Division, Tuopari and Zimuopere; in Lawra Division, Eremon, Donweni, Lissa, Bazim, Tampia and Nanyari.

122. Jackson mentioned, for example, that among the Lobi there was no obligation for the groom to work in his father-in-law's fields and listed an initial bridewealth of 3 chickens and 7 shillings (about 7,000 cowries), as well as 3 cows following the birth of the first child (Lawra District Record Book, NAG, ADM 61/5/11: 296).

123. Lawra-Tumu District, Informal Diary, 18 May 1944, NAG, ADM 61/5/16. On marriage, see also Hawkins 2002: Ch. 7.

124. Ibid.: 13 and 14 Jul. 1944.

125. Lawra District Record Book, NAG, ADM 61/5/11: 394.

126. On the contradiction between the written documentation of the law and the oral arbitration of conflicts, see Goody 1969. District Commissioner Amherst's complaint against the overturning of a native court ruling following a strike by lightning, which was interpreted as punishment for an incorrect court ruling, is evidence for the fact that decisions of the native courts could not, for example, be enforced against the advice of diviners; Lawra-Tumu District, Informal Diary, 15 Jul. 1942, NAG, ADM 61/5/16.

127. See, for instance, Dery 1987; Kpiebaya 1991.

128. See Bening 1990: 10–11; R. Thomas 1975b: 431; Gandah 1967/1993: 85–7.

129. See Lawra-Tumu District, Informal Diary, 26 Nov. 1938, RAT, NRG 8/4/83. On the history of the education system in the Northern Territories see Northern Territories Annual Report 1937–38, PRO, CO 98/72: 51–8; also R. Thomas 1975b, Bening 1990.

130. On this, see Lawra-Tumu District, Informal Diary, 22 Mar. and 20 Apr. 1943, NAG, ADM 61/5/16; also Gandah 1967/1993: 93–4.

131. Lawra-Tumu District, Annual Report 1938–9, Appendix C, RAT, NRG 8/3/78. Even when District Commissioner Amherst insisted that more girls be

enrolled in school, it was primarily the daughters and nieces of chiefs that profited from this; see Lawra-Tumu District, Annual Report 1942–3, RAT, NRG 8/3/122.

132. Minutes of the Lawra Native Authority estimates conference, 18–21 Mar. 1939; RAT, NRG 8/3/78. An extreme example is Birifu Naa Gandah: of the eight sons that he was allowed to send to school, two received scholarships for being 'heirs' and one for his performance. Lawra Naa Karbo and Nandom Naa Konkuu each also had three sons in school, all on scholarships.

133. The Lawra Confederacy spent over half the grant-in-aid allocated for the 1947–8 fiscal year on school education, in particular for scholarships for the continuing school in Tamale; in Tumu, on the other hand, only one quarter of the budget was set aside for education; see Northern Territories Territorial Council, minutes of meeting 1946, CO 96/808, 31608.

134. Lawra District, Informal Diary, 23 Jun 1920, RAT, NRG 8/4/15.

135. RAT, NRG 8/3/78.

136. Although in the late 1930s the Lawra school employed a Sisala teacher from Tumu, the Sisala pupils were not brought together in a class of their own, but continued to form a minority with respect to the Dagara speakers. Only in 1946 was Tumu granted its own boarding school.

137. See Gandah 2004: 36–56.

138. Lawra-Tumu District, Annual Report 1938–9, RAT, NRG 8/3/78: 16.

139. Lawra-Tumu District, Informal Diary, 12 May and 5 Jun. 1944, NAG, ADM 61/5/16.

140. On this, see Ladouceur 1979: 59; Bening 1990: 61–2; Gandah 1992: 260–1; also my interview with a strike-leader from that time, namely Lawra Naa Abeyifaa Karbo, 22 Dec. 1989.

141. Lawra-Tumu District, Informal Diary, 4 Dec. 1942, NAG, ADM 61/5/16. The only state-run teacher training college in the Gold Coast was located in Achimota; a corresponding institution was only set up for Tamale in 1942. On the British phobia for Achimota, see also R. Thomas 1975b: 464–7; Bening 1990: 118–27.

142. Lawra-Tumu District, Annual Report 1937–8, quoted in R. Thomas 1975a: 459 fn. 144.

143. Memorandum on the introduction into and the development of native administration, 14 Apr. 1930, RHL, MSS Afr. S. 593, Duncan-Johnstone Papers; on this, see also Staniland 1975: 98–101.

144. See Lawra-Tumu District, Annual Report 1939–40, RAT, NRG 8/3/100: 15–16, 20.

CHAPTER 5

1. Northern Territories, Annual Report 1923–4: 21 (Colonial Reports).

2. Ibid.

3. Northern Territories, Annual Report 1905, PRO, CO 98/14: 9.

4. On the history of the Ghanaian mines, see Crisp 1984; Dumett 1998. On mine workers from the North, see Robotham 1989; Lentz and Erlmann 1989.

5. CCNT to Secretary of Mines, 8 Nov. 1905, NAG, ADM 56/1/3; on this, see also R. Thomas 1973.

6. Speech of CCNT of 12 Apr. 1906, enclosure in Circular Memo to DCs of 13 Jun. 1906, NAG, ADM 56/1/4 (cited in R. Thomas 1973: 81). See also CCNT report on tour of inspection, detail of tour in Mar. and Apr. 1906, NAG, ADM 56/1/43.

7. Report on tour of inspection, Mar.–Apr. 1906, NAG, ADM 56/1/43: 14.

8. Northern Territories, Annual Report 1906, PRO, CO 98/16: 9.
9. Report on tour of inspection, Nov. 1906; NAG, ADM 56/1/50.
10. Tour of inspection, 26 Feb. 1907, NAG, ADM 56/1/50.
11. Table of Secretary of Mines, enclosure 7, in Gold Coast Confidential of 3 Feb. 1910, PRO, CO 96/493.
12. The CCNT wrote of as many as 10,000 victims, with 'whole families dying in a single day'; Northern Territories, Annual Report 1907, PRO, CO 98/16; see also DC Lawra, Report on tour 5–9 April 1907, NAG, ADM 56/1/50.
13. CCNT to Colonial Secretary, 2 Dec. 1909, enclosure 3, in Gold Coast No. 11 of 5 Jan. 1910. Later the subsidy was graded by the duration of migrants' work in the mines, in order to reduce the rate of 'desertions'.
14. On this, see also R. Thomas 1973: 81–2.
15. Enclosure 7 in Gold Coast Confidential of 3 Feb. 1910, PRO, CO 96/493; Watherston, Report on Northern Territories Labourers, enclosure 2 in Gold Coast No. 11 of 5 Jan. 1910, ibid.
16. North-Western Province, Annual Report 1908, NAG, ADM 56/1/434; Watherston to Colonial Secretary, 2 Dec. 1909, enclosure 3 in Gold Coast 11 of 5 Jan. 1910, PRO, CO 96/493.
17. CNWP to CCNT, 1 April 1910, NAG, ADM 56/1/84.
18. Joint Report of Acting CCNT, Secretary for Mines and Transport Officer, 17 Jan. 1910, PRO, CO 493 (cited in R. Thomas 1973: 87).
19. Regulations and instructions as to the supply of labourers from the Northern Territories of the Gold Coast to the Mines, enclosure 4 in Gold Coast Confidential of 3 Feb. 1910, PRO, CO 96/493; see also the exchange of letters of 1916–19 between CCNT and the mine managers in NAG, ADM 56/1/84; on this, see R. Thomas 1973: 84–9.
20. In Lawra District, for which the Census of 1921 listed a population of 57,708, at least 7 per cent of the population died of influenza; Lawra District, Annual Report 1918, NAG, ADM 65/1/453; see also Northern Territories, Annual Report 1918 (Colonial Reports); Patterson 1983.
21. Guggisberg to Colonial Office, 21 May 1920, PRO, CO 96/612, No. 29844: 7–9.
22. Lawra District, Informal Diary, 26 Jun. 1920; see also 22 May, 24 and 25 Jun., and 1 Jul. 1920; RAT, NRG 8/4/15.
23. Lawra District, Annual Report 1920, NAG, ADM 56/1/453; Northern Territories, Annual Report 1920.
24. Lawra-Tumu District, Quarterly Reports, 31 Mar. and 30 Jun. 1921, NAG, ADM 56/1/452 and 425; see also Lawra-Tumu District, Informal Diary, 20 Apr. 1921, NAG, ADM 56/1/271.
25. Ibid., 24 and 26 Nov. 1921. On the working conditions in the mines, see also Crisp 1984: 21–32, 35–51.
26. Enclosure 1 in Gold Coast No. 453 of 29 Jun. 1925, PRO, CO 96/655, No. 32860.
27. On this, see also R. Thomas 1973: 100–2.
28. Report on Northern Territories recruited labour for the mines, 31 Dec. 1925, NAG, ADM 56/1/383.
29. CCNT to Colonial Secretary, 3 Oct. 1927, ibid.
30. CCNT to CNWP, 9 Nov. 1915, NAG, ADM 56/1/84.
31. Lawra-Tumu District, Informal Diary, 18 Nov. 1929, NAG, ADM 61/5/12.
32. Figures taken from R. Thomas 1973: 80, 89.
33. See Robotham 1989: 42. Altogether, the number of mine workers reached its height with practically 40,000 at the end of the 1930s, before levelling off to around 20,000 in the 1950s; see Crisp 1984: 57, 77, 127.

34. However, there are no reliable figures on this migration. For estimates, see below; generally on the demand for labour from commercial cultivation in Southern Ghana, see Sutton 1983.
35. North-Western Province, Annual Report 1908, NAG, DM 56/1/434; North-Western Province, Annual Report 1911, NAG, ADM 56/1/449; Lawra District, Quarterly Report, 31 Dec. 1913, NAG, ADM 56/1/452.
36. See Northern Territories, Annual Report 1914: 28 (Colonial Reports).
37. North-Western Province, Annual Report 1915, NAG, ADM 56/1/424.
38. See, for example, Northern Territories, Annual Report 1925–6 (Colonial Reports); Northern Territories, Annual Report 1929–30, PRO, CO 98/55. Statistics were kept in the 1920s because the ferries were one of the most important sources of income for the Northern Territories.
39. On this see Hilton 1966: 44.
40. Lawra-Tumu District, Informal Diary, 10 Aug. 1943, NAG, ADM 61/5/16; Report on Census of Population, Gold Coast 1948, Report and Tables, Accra: Government Printer 1950: 75.
41. Figures taken from Hilton 1966: 45. An economic survey for 1948 lists 11 per cent Dagarti and 7 per cent Lobi migrants, the highest rates of migration for the Northern Territories as a whole; Report on a Preliminary Economic Survey of the Northern Territories of the Gold Coast, 1950, PRO, CO 96/817, No. 31196/4.
42. On the quality of the census data, see Engman 1986: 106–16; on more recent data on migration for the North-West, see Songsore 1983; Kasanga and Avis 1988.
43. On this, see Lentz and Erlmann 1989.
44. The proportions in Nandom and Lawra probably corresponded to those in the North-East of the Northern Territories, where Meyer Fortes determined in a micro-census for Tongo in 1935 that 15 per cent of adult men were working outside their home regions, and that of the men remaining in Tongo, 34 per cent had previously migrated for a shorter or longer period of time (1936: 39–40).
45. See, for example, Lawra-Tumu District, Quarterly Report, 31 Mar. 1921, NAG, ADM 56/1/452.
46. Northern Territories, Annual Report 1913: 9; see also Lawra District, Annual Report 1914, NAG, ADM 56/1/453.
47. DC Lawra to CNWP, 26 Oct. 1915, NAG, ADM 56/1/163.
48. Ibid.
49. Ibid.
50. CNWP to CCNT, 2 Nov. 1915, ibid.
51. CCNT to CNWP, 9 Nov. 1915, ibid.
52. See CCNT to Colonial Secretary, 2 Dec. 1909, enclosure 3 in Gold Coast No. 11 of 5 Jan. 1910, and enclosure 4 in Gold Coast Confidential of 3 Feb. 1910, PRO, CO 96/493.
53. CCNT to S. H. Ford, 4 Jan. 1917, NAG, ADM 56/1/84.
54. Northern Territories, Annual Report 1918 (Colonial Reports).
55. Northern Territories, Annual Report 1919: 5 (Colonial Reports).
56. Northern Territories, Annual Report 1937–8, PRO, CO 98/72: 3.
57. See Bening 1975b, Plange 1984, Konings 1986, Sutton 1989 and Saaka 2001 for different positions in more recent debates.
58. Northern Territories, Annual Report 1929–30, CO 98/55: 20.
59. Northern Territories, Annual Report 1925–6: 18 (Colonial Reports).
60. Lawra-Tumu District, Informal Diary, 6 Mar. 1942, NAG, ADM 61/6/16.
61. Ibid., 9 Sep. 1943. Conversely, G. N. Burden, Chief Regional Officer of the

Northern Territories from 1950 to 1953, stated: 'Huts falling down, fields left uncultivated, all the signs of absentee menfolk. I never came across this in the Northern Territories' (from an interview dated Aug. 1971, RHL, MSS Afr. 1435).

62. Northern Territories, Annual Report 1918: 19. For examples from Tizza, see Enclosure C in CNP to CCNT, 1 Feb. 1927, NAG, ADM 56/1/301; on Lambussie, see Lawra-Tumu District, Informal Diary, 3, 13 May 1943, NAG, ADM 61/6/16.

63. On the role of clothing, see also Goody and Goody 1996.

64. North-Western Province, Annual Report 1914, NAG, ADM 56/1/480: 3–4.

65. Lawra-Tumu District, Annual Report 1938–9, RAT, NRG 8/3/78: 32.

66. I have not been able to determine the origin of this word, which is neither Dagara nor Hausa nor Twi. Several of my interview partners used *girmati*, with its connotation of 'forced labour', to describe the recruitment for work in the mines or in railway construction carried out by the village chiefs, this being different from independent migrant labour.

67. Interview with Tantuoyir, Soyeru Buolu and others, Tantuo, 27 Nov. 1989.

68. Interview with Samuel Dagarti, Tarkwa, 15 Aug. 1988. 'Looking nice' refers not only to clothes, but also to the skin, which became discernibly sleeker after a long stay in the damp South.

69. Interview, Obuasi, 14 Sep. 1988.

70. One of over twenty songs on themes of migration that I recorded in Oct. 1989 with Maria Emilia Nifaasie, Lydia and Scholastica Yob in Hamile; *gubogubo* is an onomatopoeic word, which here is mocking clothes that are always the same.

71. On Tarkwa, see enclosure 3 in Gold Coast No. 11 of 5 Jan. 1910, PRO, CO 96/493; also Lentz and Erlmann 1989: 99–100; more generally, also Crisp 1984: 71–5.

72. On the associations, see also Ch. 9 of this volume.

73. For more detail, see see Lentz and Erlmann 1989: 90–102. Especially in the mines, the tribal heads could earn wealth of their own by imposing a more or less compulsory 'tax' on the wages and other payments made to the migrants.

74. Kofi Dagarti was also a prosperous man and seems to have run a small transport business as early as 1929; see Lawra-Tumu District, Annual Report 1929–30, RAT, NRG 8/3/25; see also Schildkrout 1978: 198–220.

75. On similar processes among the Frafra, a collective term for Tallensi and neighbouring Nabdam, Gurensi and Nankanni, see Hart (1971).

CHAPTER 6

1. Some parts of this chapter have been published as 'Christianity, colonial rule and ethnicity: the mission of the White Fathers among the Dagara (Ghana/Burkina Faso)', in Toyin Falola (ed.), *Christianity and Social Change in Africa: Essays in Honor of J. D. Y. Peel*. Durham: Carolina Academic Press, 2005, pp. 441–69.

2. Detail of tour of inspection in Mar. and Apr. 1906, NAG, ADM 56/1/43: 9; letter of Oscar Morin to Mgr Bazin, Navrongo, 4 Jun. 1906, Vicariat apostolique du Soudan Français, Chronique trimestrielle 1904–09, Archives Générales des Missionaires d'Afrique, Rom (A.G.M. Afr.), AO2: 226. See also Der 1983: 94–5; on the (pre-)history of the White Fathers in the neighbouring French colony, see M. Somé 1996.

3. After fifteen years of proselytising, the White Fathers only counted 422 baptised individuals and about 500 catechists; see Northern Territories, Annual Report 1922–3 (Colonial Reports).

4. On this, see R. Thomas 1975b: 432–6; Der 1983: 40–7; Naameh 1986: 166–8.

5. On this, see History of Navrongo etc., A.G.M. Afr., Dos. 291/6; John McNulty, *The fiftieth anniversary of the evangelization of North-West Ghana*, Jirapa 1979, A.G.M. Afr., N 189/3; also Lesourd 1938; Paternot 1949: 27–8; Der 1974; McCoy 1988: 33–4; Naameh 1986: 169; Der 1983: 118–24.

6. Préfecture Apostolique de Navrongo, Rapport Annuel, A.G.M. Afr., AO 15. For Sean Hawkins (1997; 2002: Ch. 6), the successful provision of medical care is the first and foremost reason for the success of the White Fathers' mission. He sees the second reason in the population's dissatisfaction with the colonial political system, especially the chiefs (see also pp. 156–60).

7. See Der 1983: 56–7; McCoy 1988: 50–1.

8. See Préfecture Apostolique de Navrongo, Rapport Annuel, A.G.M. Afr., AO 15; Der 1983: 48. The DC estimated the number of catechumens at 12,000 to 13,000; Lawra-Tumu District, Annual Report 1931–2, RAT, NRG 8/3/27. The catechumenate consisted of three stages and took four years altogether. After participating for three to six months in the Sunday instruction for the catechism and undertaking two days work for the mission, the converts received a medal with a picture of the Virgin Mary. After a total of two years' instruction and passing an examination they received a rosary, and finally, after a further two years' instruction and change to a Christian way of life, they were baptised. On this, see Rapport du sup. Rég. P. Blin, Nov. 1933–Jan. 1934, A.G.M. Afr. Dos. 198/7; McCoy 1988: 315; Lesourd 1938; Paternot 1949: 136–9.

9. Here I draw on material collected in biographical interviews with early converts, who were all labour migrants before becoming Christians. However, obviously not all labour migrants converted. A systematic study of the relationship between Christianisation and labour migration in the North-West has yet to be undertaken. For the relationship between the mission and individualisation, see also Meyer's study (1999) on the Protestant mission among the Peki-Ewe.

10. DC Lawra-Tumu to CCNT, 8 Sep. 1932, NAG, ADM 56/1/301.

11. It is also striking that the converts only destroyed the ancestral shrines in their homes after acquiring their medals. Naameh (1986: 196–7, 204–5) therefore assumes that the Christian medals were seen as powerful 'fetishes'.

12. Interview, Tamale, 7 Jan. 1995.

13. CCNT, Diary, 25.7 and 4 Aug. 1932, RHL, MSS Afr. S. 593.

14. Lawra-Tumu District, Informal Diary, 16 and 21 Jul. 1932, RAT, NRG 8/4/62.

15. There are different versions of the exact timing and the identity of the affected village (or villages): McCoy's recollections (1988: 109–24, 247–9, 285–6) mention Daffiama and then numerous other villages; Paternot (1949: 123–31), Der (1983: 49–50) and Naameh (1986: 179–84) write about Jirapa itself.

16. DC Lawra-Tumu to CCNT, 8 Sep. 1932, NAG, ADM 56/1/301. See also Duncan-Johnstone, Diary, 10 Aug. and 14, 15 and 19 Sep. 1932, RHL, MSS Afr. S. 593.

17. Interview, Tamale 7 Jan. 1995. On Porekuu, see also McCoy 1988: 75–83.

18. Lawra-Tumu District, Informal Diary, 26 and 30 Jul. 1932, RAT, NRG 8/4/62.

19. See, for example, Der 1983: 48–57; Naameh 1986: 206–24; Bekye 1991: 269–309.

20. Eyre-Smith to Secretary for Native Affairs, 2 Mar. 1933, NAG, ADM 11/1/824, § 40–3. This interpretation is shared by Hawkins (1997: 55–65).

21. CCNT to Secretary for Native Affairs, 1 Apr. 1933, NAG, ADM 11/1/824.

22. CCNT, Diary, 30 Sep. 1932, NAG, ADM 56/1/301; see also CCNT to Colonial Secretary, Gold Coast Confidential, 14 Dec. 1934, enclosures 1 and 3, PRO, CO 96/720/31002. On the perspective of the missionaries, see McCoy 1988: 133–8.

23. Guinness to CCNT, 8 Sep. 1932, NAG, ADM 56/1/301.
24. On this, see McCoy 1988: 99–102.
25. Lawra-Tumu District, Informal Diary, 6 May 1935, RAT, NRG 8/4/76. On this, see also Der 1983: 135–8.
26. Lawra-Tumu District, Annual Report 1938–9, RAT, NRG 8/3/78: 34.
27. Barsalou to CCNT, 4 Sep. 1934, enclosure 6 in Gold Coast Confidential of 14 Dec. 1934, PRO, CO 96/720/31002.
28. See Préfecture Apostolique de Navrongo, Rapport Annuel, 1932–3, A.G.M. Afr., AO 15; also Northern Territories, Annual Report, 1932–3, RAT, NRG 8/3/46. However, following his visit to the new mission stations, the Regional Superior of Navrongo, P. Blin, warned against exaggerating the figures; Rapport sur la Préfecture de Navrongo, November 1933–January 1934, A.G.M. Afr. Dos. 198/7.
29. On the training of the catechists, see McCoy 1988: 94–103; Naameh 1986: 257–61.
30. See Préfecture Apostolique de Navrongo, Rapport Annuel, 1932–3, A.G.M. Afr., AO 15; also Der 1983: 62–4.
31. Lawra-Tumu District, Annual Report 1938–9, RAT, NRG 8/3/78: 34–7.
32. Préfecture Apostolique de Navrongo, Rapport Annuel, 1950–1, A.G.M. Afr., AO 15. This figure obviously includes the children of the first converts.
33. 1949: 23–4, 149–50. Paternot's listing of the 'main characteristics of our Dagari' (1949: 33) did not differ from colonial ethnographies (see Tauxier 1912, Delafosse 1912, Labouret 1931).
34. McCoy 1988: 230, 311 fn 2 to Ch. 2.
35. On this, see Naameh 1986: 198–224; Mukassa 1987: 124–38; Der 1983: 53–8; Dabire 1983: 226–55; Bekye 1991: 274–309. On the construction of a uniform 'traditional religion' by Dagara priests, see Goody 1975, R. Somé 1991, and Hawkins 1996, 1998.
36. Strong criticism of this distinction and of McCoy's comments on Birifu can be found in Gandah (1967/1993: 64–8). Gandah, himself a son of the Birifu Naa, whom McCoy accused of religious intolerance, joined the Ahmadiyya movement in 1941 while a schoolboy in Tamale, this although many of his brothers are Catholics.
37. DC Wa to CCNT, 5 Feb. 1937, RAT, NRG 8/19/7. See also McCoy 1988: 136–8, on the quarrel with DC Ardron.
38. See Wilks 1989, Chs 5, 6 and 7; also Ch.1 of the present volume. In addition, when the mission station opened in Kaleo, Wa was preoccupied with internal conflicts. The success of the Ahmadiyya mission among one of the competing Wala factions exacerbated the local power struggle.
39. Interview, Tamale, 7 Jan. 1995. On this, see also E. Tengan 1991: 25–30, 208–15.
40. See Lesourd 1938; Paternot 1949: 23–33; McCoy 1988: 35–8.
41. On this, see Lesourd 1938; Paternot 1949: 141–53.
42. On the so-called 'Ouessa conference', see Diaire de Ouagadougou, 17 and 14 Jan. 1933, A.G.M. Afr.; Lesourd 1938; McCoy 1988: 125–8; Naameh 1986: 185–7; M. Somé 1993: 104–12. On the further development of the mission stations at Dissin and Dano, see M. Somé 1993: 307–17.
43. On this, see Der 1983: 52, 61. Lawra only became a parish of its own in 1966.
44. Interview with Archbishop Peter Dery, Tamale, 7 Jan. 1995. On Jirapa, see McCoy 1988: 48–9.
45. Lawra-Tumu District, Annual Report 1938–9, RAT, NRG 8/3/78: 6. See also Northern Territories, Annual Report 1936–7, PRO, CO 96/738, No. 31196: 73.

46. Lawra-Tumu District, Informal Diary, 28 Mar. 1935, RAT, NRG 8/4/76; see also 20, 26 Mar. 1935, ibid.
47. Lawra-Tumu District, Annual Report 1938-9, RAT, NRG 8/3/78: 37.
48. On this, see Ch. 9 of this volume.
49. See Lentz 1995a: 211-12.
50. The Nandom Naa complained that the Sunday market was not paying market fees to the native authority and was competing with the six-day market; see Lawra-Tumu District, Informal Diary, 12 and 17 Sep. 1934, RAT, NRG 8/4/62. For the later accommodation, see Informal Diary, 19 and 21 Jan.1940, also 2 Apr. 1942, NAG, ADM 61/5/16.
51. On this, see also the report of a service held in Nandom by DC Amory, Northern Territories, Annual Report 1936-7, Appendix A: 13, PRO, CO 96/738 No. 31196; see also the photographs of masses held in Dissin and Dano in Lesourd 1938.
52. On this, see McCoy 1988: 98-9; Der 1983: 272-3, 294-8.
53. On this, see Lawra-Tumu District, Annual Report 1941-2, RAT, NRG 8/3/108: 5; Informal Diary, 25 Jan. 1944, NAG, ADM 61/5/16.
54. On this, see S. Bemile 2000: 211-22.
55. CCNT to Colonial Secretary, 9 Mar. 1937, RAT, NRG 8/19/7; see also Gold Coast Confidential, 14 Dec. 1934, with enclosures, PRO, CO 96/720/31002.
56. Lawra-Tumu District, Informal Diary, 28 Dec. 1934, RAT, NRG 8/4/62; see also 13 Dec. 1934, ibid.; 6 Jan. 1935, RAT, NRG 8/4/76.
57. Lawra-Tumu District Informal Diary, 13 Dec. 1934, RAT, NRG 8/4/62; see also Informal Diary, 6 Jan. 1935, RAT, NRG 8/4/76. For the Christian view of 'pagan' funerals, see Lesourd 1938, Appendix.
58. See, for example, Lawra-Tumu District Informal Diary, 20 and 28 Mar. 1935 (at Lissa), RAT, NRG 8/4/76; DC Lawra-Tumu to CCNT, 18 Apr. 1935, NAG, ADM 56/1/301 (at Karni).
59. Lawra-Tumu District, Informal Diary, 12 Jun. 1935, RAT, NRG 8/4/76.
60. Bishop Morin, Memorandum, 14 Dec. 1936, RAT, NRG 8/19/7. Six of the ten conflicts listed by Morin concerned questions of marriage and divorce, which had not yet been brought up at all in the local negotiations.
61. DC Wa to CCNT, 5 Feb. 1937, RAT, NRG 8/19/7.
62. DC Lawra-Tumu to CCNT, 6 Feb. 1937, ibid.
63. Colonial Secretary to Bishop Porter, Cape Coast, 25 Oct. 1937, ibid.
64. See Annual Report Northern Territories 1937-8, PRO, CO 98/72: 34, 88-90.
65. See Lawra-Tumu District, Annual Report 1938-9, RAT, NRG 8/3/78: 34-6; Informal Diary, 13 and 17 Jan. 1940, 1 and 2 Feb. 1940, 23 Apr., 4 Nov. and 29 Dec. 1942, and 16 and 18 May 1944, NAG, ADM 61/5/16.
66. Morin Memorandum, 14 Dec. 1936, RAT, NRG 8/19/7.
67. CCNT to Colonial Secretary, 9 Mar. 1937, RAT, NRG 8/19/7: 1, 4.
68. DC Wa to CCNT, 5 Feb. 1937, RAT, NRG 8/19/7.
69. CCNT to Colonial Secretary, 9 Mar. 1937, RAT, NRG 8/19/7: 11; see also DC Lawra-Tumu to CCNT, 18 Apr. 1935, NAG, ADM 56/1/301.
70. DC Lawra-Tumu to CCNT, 6 Feb. 1937, RAT, NRG 8/19/7.
71. On this, see also Comaroff and Comaroff 1992: 265-95.
72. On this, see Berman 1992.
73. See Lesourd 1938; Paternot 1949: 67-75; McCoy 1988: 64-9. However, DC Eyre-Smith is known to have severely punished witch hunts; see Lawra-Tumu District, Informal Diary, 20 Jul. 1932, RAT, NRG 8/4/62.
74. On this, see the examples in McCoy 1988: 149-65.
75. Lawra-Tumu District, Annual Report 1938-9, RAT, NRG 8/3/78.

76. DC Lawra-Tumu to CCNT, 6 Feb. 1937, RAT, NRG 8/19/7.
77. For Fortes's text and the extensive comments of various district commissioners, see RAT, NRG 8/2/81.
78. See McCoy 1988: 149–53, 161. On the ambivalent significance of the mission for the status of Dagara women and the development of Christian education for girls in Lawra District, see Behrends 2002a.
79. On this, see Lesourd 1938; Paternot 1949: 225–6; Girault 1959; Naameh 1986: 117–224.
80. See McCoy 1988: 123; Der 1983: 61–2.
81. See Barsalou to CCNT, 4 Sep. 1934, enclosure 6 in Gold Coast Confidential, 14 Dec. 1934, PRO, CO 96/720/31002; see also Lesourd 1938; Naameh 1986: 240–2; also Goody 1975 on the initial role of Christianity as simply an additional cult, not a wholly new one.
82. The missionaries explained very precisely to converts the restrictions on the rights of the chiefs and unofficially backed them up before the native courts too. See, for example, Northern Territories, Annual Report 1935–6, RAT, NRG 8/3/53: 49.
83. Lawra-Tumu District, Informal Diary, 4 Nov. 1942, NAG, ADM 61/5/16.
84. After the late 1950s, and especially in the wake of the Second Vatican Council, the local clergy explicitly discussed a re-evaluation of local cultural practices that the White Fathers had forbidden as 'heathen'; see Naameh 1986, Chs 7, 8; P. Bemile 1987, Mukassa 1987, Bekye 1991, Kpiebaya 1991.
85. CCNT to Colonial Secretary, 18 Oct. 1934, enclosure 3, in Gold Coast Confidential, 14 Dec. 1934, PRO, CO 96/720/31002.
86. CCNT to Revd Father Barsalou, 13 Aug. 1934, enclosure 5, ibid.
87. Power to Colonial Secretary, 18 Sep. 1934, enclosure 2, ibid. On the conflicts over the school in Nandom, see also R. Thomas 1975b: 640–4; Der 1983: 181–90; McCoy 1988: 145–7.
88. Father Irenaeus Songliedong, in McCoy 1988: 290.
89. Interview with Father Gervase Sentuu, Hamile, 24 Dec. 1993. As in the native authority schools, the boarding regime followed the model of the English boarding school, but it did not borrow from the chieftaincy.
90. On this, see Der 1983: 205.
91. Literacy was taught in Dagara, however. According to McCoy (1988: 145), this was due above all to the restrictions imposed by the colonial government. Some of my own informants saw in this an attempt by the White Fathers to prevent their graduates from working as government employees (which nonetheless happened) rather than as catechists.
92. See McCoy 1988: 287.
93. In 1942–4, because of a shortage of teachers in Nandom due to the war, only five new pupils per parish were accepted. After 1944 the number was increased, though for a long time the demand for education exceeded the supply. Exceptions to the rule that only one child per family could attend school were only made for catechists. Interviews with Jacob Yirerong, Accra, 7 Feb. 1990; Anselmy Bemile, Hamile, 12 Oct. and 6 Dec. 1989; Alexis Nakaar, Bonn, 2 Aug. 1989; and John Sotenga, Wa, 4 Jan. 1990.
94. On this, see McCoy 1988: 145–6, 282–3, 288.
95. On the priests' seminary, see McCoy 1988: 14–15, 200–1; Der 1983: 412–28; on teacher-training, see Bening 1990: 111–18.
96. On this, see Bening 1990: 112–13; also my interview with Severio Termaghre, Nandom, 12 Dec. 1989.

CHAPTER 7

1. Quoted in Ladouceur 1979: 79.
2. Parts of these chapters have been published in Lentz 2002.
3. Address of the CCNT at the first NTC sitting, 16 Dec. 1946, PRO, CO 96, 808/ 31608. For the history of the NTC see Northern Territories, Annual Report 1955, RAT, NRG 8/3/222, and Ladouceur 1979: 72–5.
4. On the Coussey Committee, see Apter 1972: 170–7; Ladouceur 1979: 74–5.
5. J. A. Braimah in a NTC meeting, 4–6 Jan. 1950, quoted in Ladouceur 1979: 94.
6. Report of a Committee of the NTC appointed to make recommendations concerning Local Government in the Northern Territories, Accra 1951, NAG, ADM 5/3/124: 1–2.
7. By the mid-1950s, only five or six Northerners had attended secondary school. About 200 teachers had a B-Certificate (two years teacher training college after completion of Standard VII) but only 20 had the A Certificate, which required one additional year of studies. A single Northerner was enrolled in a university; see Ladouceur 1979: 87–8; R. Thomas 1975b; Bening 1990.
8. On the beginnings of CPP in the North, see *West Africa*, 26 Jan. and 2 Feb. 1952; Ladouceur 1979: 80–3, 88–9. On CPP in Lawra District see Ch. 8 of this volume.
9. Interview with S. D. Dombo, 26 Feb. 1994, London. For more detail, see North-West District Annual Report 1950–1, RAT, NRG 8/3/178; on the 1951 elections in general see Apter 1972: 179–85, 199–202, 222–8.
10. Quoted in Ladouceur 1979: 115; interview with S. D. Dombo, London, 26. Feb. 1994.
11. See Ladouceur 1979: 112–21, 129–36.
12. See Austin 1961 and 1976: 140–50; Ladouceur 1979: 143–5, with respect to the Lawra Confederacy see Ch. 8 of this volume.
13. On the opposition parties, see also Rathbone 2000: 65–7 and, from the perspective of the Asante-based National Liberation Movement, Allman 1993: 111–14, 186.
14. On chieftaincy policies generally during the Nkrumah regime, see Rathbone 2000.
15. See Ch. 8 of this volume and Lentz 2000b on the 1958 Nandom chieftaincy succession dispute.
16. See Clerk of Lawra Confederacy Local Council to Nandom Naa, 2 Jun. 1961, RAT, NRG 7/2/7. Unlike the president, the district council chairman was elected, but here again chiefs and their sons dominated the scene: in 1952–3 Birifu Naa was chairman, in 1953–8 K. Y. Baloro from the Lambussie Kuoro's family, and in 1958–61 the Birifu Naa again.
17. Of the 12 representatives elected to the Lawra Confederacy District Council in 1952–57, 2 were chiefs and at least 5 the sons or close relatives of chiefs; it is possible that other relatives of chiefs were among the 5 other elected councillors; see RAT, NRG 7/10/2. In the Interim Lawra Confederacy Council, elected in 1957, among the 12 representatives were 7 chiefs and one chief's son; see Report on Local Government Elections, 18 Dec. 1957, RAT, NRG 8/3/302.
18. Local Authority Year Book 1960–1, Lawra Confederacy Local Council, RAT, NRG 7/3/4.
19. See Lawra District, Annual Reports 1953–4 und 1956–7, RAT, NRG 8/3/199, 215.
20. Lawra Confederacy State Council, 26 Jun. 1952, RAT, NRG 7/10/1; Lawra District, Annual Report 1953–4, RAT, NRG 8/3/199. In 1960, the Lawra

Confederacy Local Council decided to pay village chiefs only in shares of tax income (6d. in the £); see Lawra Confederacy Local Council to Divisional Chiefs *et al.*, 30 Aug. 1960, RAT, NRG 7/2/1.

21. Lawra District, Informal Diary, 6 Oct. 1954 as well as 23 Jul. 1954 and 19 Aug. 1955; RAT, NRG 8/4/113.

22. A. P. S. Termaghre to Comrade K. Amolubila, Guiding Notes: the Hand-Over of Nandom Administrative District, 26 Mar. 1964, RAT, NRG 7/3/5: 3.

23. J. A. Karbo, Representations to the Commission of Enquiry on Local Government [n.d., probably 1951], RAT, NAG 8/2/101: 1.

24. North-West District, Annual Report 1950–1, RAT, NRG 8/3/178: 1.

25. Quoted in North-West District, Annual Report 1950–1, RAT, NRG 8/3/178: 1.

26. North-Western District Council, 17 Jun. 1950, RAT, NRG 8/5/32: 2. The Coussey Committee proposed 'Class A Authorities' (district councils) for areas with 100,000 to 200,000 inhabitants each. Lawra Native Authority had 89,187 inhabitants, Tumu 30,341, and Wa 85,479, according to the 1948 census (Gold Coast 1948, *Report and Tables*, Accra: Government Printer 1950: 75).

27. RAT, NRG 8/5/32: 4–5.

28. Ibid.: 3.

29. Ibid.: 4.

30. Karbo was referring to the Hamile conflict; see pp. 188–98.

31. RAT, NRG 8/5/32: 2– 3.

32. Ibid.

33. Ibid.: 6–7.

34. Ibid.: 9.

35. Ibid.

36. Ibid.: 7–8.

37. Ibid.

38. Ibid.: 12. More than thirty years later, a similar discussion was to take place in preparing the establishment of the Upper West Region. Again it dwelt on the fear that if the administrative headquarters were to be located in Wa, Wala hegemony might be cemented. And again in the end Wa remained the headquarters, mainly because of the existing infrastructure.

39. Report of a Committee of the NTC appointed to make recommendations concerning Local Government in the Northern Territories, 1951, NAG, ADM 5/3/124: 2.

40. *Gold Coast Gazette* No. 29 of 18 Mar. 1952, Gazette Notice No. 627.

41. Report of the Commission of Enquiry into Representational and Electoral Reform [Van Lare Commission], Accra: Government Printing Department 1953: 17. Only the local council electoral wards were not always congruent with the sub-divisions of the chiefdoms, because the first were based on population, the second on historical alliances and the power politics of the paramount chief. These differing bases provided leeway for political manoeuvring: for example, when villages demanded a better position in the chieftaincy hierarchy by invoking their status as electoral wards or, on the other hand, a sub-division demanded a councillor of its own despite its low population.

42. On Samoa see Chief of Samoa to DC Lawra, 14 Nov. 1951, RAT, NAG 8/2/101.

43. For a similar mix of discourses, see the examples from Togoland and the Volta region in Nugent 2002: 141–5.

44. North-West District, Annual Report 1950–1, RAT, NRG 8/3/178: 6–7.

45. See DC Lawra an CCNT, 24 Sep. 1949, RAT, NRG 8/2/58. See Ch. 2 of this volume for the politics connected with chiefly medals.

46. Birifu Naa N. Gandah and eleven headmen and tendanas to CCNT, 9 Jul. 1951, RAT, NRG 8/2/101.
47. DC Lawra and DC Wa, 3 Aug. 1951, ibid.
48. Birifu Naa N. Gandah and thirteen headmen to Commission of Enquiry on Local Government, 4 Nov. 1951, ibid. Nonatuo Gandah's culturalist discourse may have been influenced by Jack Goody, who spent most of his field trip to the North-West, from Aug. 1950 to Sep. 1951, in Birifu.
49. See Lawra District, Informal Diary, 23, 27 and 31 Jul. as well as 5 Oct. 1954, RAT, NRG 8/4/113. On a third unsuccessful petition by the Birifu Naa, see Lawra District, Annual Report 1955–6, RAT, NRG 8/3/216.
50. On mass education in general, see Sautoy 1958: 83–105; on the activities in Lawra District, see Lawra District, Informal Diary, 22 Mar. 1954, RAT, NRG 8/4/113; Gandah 2004: 119–20, 191–3.
51. Kojo Botsio, Minster of Education and Social Welfare, before the Legislative Assembly in 1951, cited in Sautoy 1958: 3.
52. See Sautoy 1958: 117–22, 136–56, for typical village projects and campaigns; see also Lawra District, Informal Diary, 12 and 13 Feb. 1954, RAT, NRG 8/4/113, on the 'dam fever'.
53. On the institutional structure, see Sautoy 1958: 62–82.
54. On Catholic Action, see Bekye 1987: 17–24, 48–55; also Der 1983: 326–9, 353–8.
55. For an overview of the debates about, and political creation of, the African 'village', see Oppen 1996.
56. Interviews in Hamile-Ghana with Anselmy Bemile, 12 Oct. and 5 Dec. 1989; Hamile Naa John Victor Yuozeg, 26 Dec. 1994; Alhaji Dramani Abudulai, 28 Dec. 1996; interviews in Hamile-Burkina with Hamile Kuoro Puli Nagie and *totina* Bawaar Bei, 29 Dec. 1996; Salifu Ouedraogo, Kadre Ouedraogo and Adama Ganeme, 24 Jan. 1998. For the settlement history, see also Lobnibe 1994: 5–16, 29–32.
57. The Hausa word *zongo*, meaning a settlement of Muslim migrants 'from the north', was already used by the British to refer to Hamile.
58. For the history of the border and the demarcation, see 'Historique de la délimitation Soudan-Gold Coast', Léo 1924, CNRST, Ouagadougou, Délimitation des Frontières de Haute-Volta, Série B III/1; also Governor, Gold Coast, to Chamberlain, 28 Jan. 1901, with enclosures, PRO, CO 879/65, No. 13.
59. For a fuller history of the border and of recent cross-border land conflicts, see Lentz 2003b.
60. See Lawra District Record Book, NAG, ADM 61/5/11: 41, 44; also Lawra District, Informal Diary, 4 Jun. 1921, NAG, ADM 56/1/271.
61. Lawra-Tumu District, Annual Report 1938–9, RAT, NRG 8/3/78: 23. In 1931, 13 Dagara, 5 Mossi and 3 Hausa compounds were counted; in 1948 there were only one Sisala and 17 Dagara compounds, compared with 41 houses belonging to 'foreigners', that is, Mossi, Wala, Hausa and others; see Lawra District Record Book, NAG, ADM 61/5/11: 44; also DC Wa to CCNT, 12 May 1949, RAT, NRG 8/3/128.
62. Lawra-Tumu District, Annual Report 1944–5, RAT, NRG 8/3/128.
63. Interviews with Anselmy Bemile, 8 Dec. 1992, and Hamile Naa John Victor Yuozeg, 26 Dec. 1994.
64. The history of this transfer is traced in a letter of Nandom Naa Imoru to the Minister of Local Government, 26 Mar. 1952, RAT, NRG 8/2/73, and in the Intelligence Reports, Jul.–Aug. 1962, RAT, NRG 7/3/5.
65. See Lawra-Tumu District, Informal Diary, 16 May 1941; 17 and 20 Mar., 2

Apr., 10 and 11 Jun. 1942; 4 Jan. 1943; NAG, ADM 61/5/16; also Lawra-Tumu District, Informal Diary, 9 Aug. 1945, RAT, NRG 8/4/100.

66. Lawra-Tumu District, Informal Diary, 9 Aug. 1945, RAT, NRG 8/4/100.
67. Quoted in DC Wa to CCNT, 28 Oct. 1949, RAT, NRG 8/2/100.
68. DC Wa to CCNT, 28 Oct. 1949, ibid.
69. Nandom Native Authority Court, 26 Jul. 1946; Appendix in DC Wa to CCNT, 28 Oct. 1949, RAT, NRG 8/2/101.
70. On this, see Ch. 4 of this volume.
71. DC Wa to CCNT, 28 Oct. 1949, RAT, NRG 8/2/101: 2.
72. Lawra Confederacy Native Authority, Written Advice – Hamile Dispute, 24 Mar. 1949, ibid.
73. Happa Kuoro to CCNT, 25 Mar. 1949, ibid.
74. Hamile Naa and others to CCNT, 25 Mar. 1949, ibid.
75. Naalang Dagarti to DC Lawra, 27 Nov. 1950, ibid.
76. DC Wa to CCNT, 9 May 1949, RAT, NRG 8/2/101.
77. CCNT to DC Wa, 20 May 1949, ibid.
78. DC Wa to CCNT, 28 Oct. 1949: 1–2, ibid.
79. Hamile Naa Perwere to CCNT, 27 Sep. and 25 Oct. 1949, ibid.
80. CCNT to DC Wa, with copy to Happa Kuoro, 22 Nov. 1949, ibid.
81. DC Lawra to DC Wa, 30 Nov. 1949, ibid.
82. North-West District, Annual Report 1950–1, RAT, NRG 8/3/178: 6.
83. Lawra Newsletter, Mar. 1950, ibid.
84. See Ch. 8 of this volume. For Danquah's similar legal and political activities in the Volta region and in Togoland, see Nugent 2002: 136–7.
85. CCNT to Dr Danquah, 14 Jan. 1950; Dr Danquah to CCNT, 25 Jan. 1950; RAT, NRG 8/2/101.
86. Chief of Happa to Governor of the Gold Coast, Mar. 1950: 10–11, ibid.
87. CCNT, Order No. 14 of 1947, RAT, NRG 8/2/73.
88. CCNT to Colonial Secretary, 22 Apr. 1950, RAT, NRG 8/2/101.
89. CCNT to Dr Danquah, 21 Jun. 1950, RAT, NRG 8/2/101.
90. DC Wa to DC Lawra, 3 Jul. 1950, ibid.
91. Station Officer Lawra to Superintendent, Gold Coast Police, 3 Sep. 1950; Superintendent to CCNT, 20 Sep. 1950, ibid. The DC Wa disputed the accuracy of the police report in a letter to the CCNT dated 19 Sep. 1950.
92. Sakare Wala, Lanla Dagarti, Osumani Moshie and Tara Wangara to CCNT, 20 Sep. 1950, ibid.
93. DC Wa to CCNT, 20 Oct. 1950, ibid. See also CCNT to Sakare Wala et al., 30 Oct. 1950, ibid.
94. Dr Danquah to Registrar, Lawra Confederacy Court, Nov. 1950, RAT, NRG 7/2/5.
95. Verbatim Extracts of Proceedings on Hamile Affairs, Lawra Confederacy Court Book, 15 Dec. 1950, ibid.: 4. The district commissioner later declared the judgement null and void, because the court had not been composed according to the regulations. In July 1951 there was a second hearing, but the decision was upheld 'Hamile should follow Nandom'; Lawra Confederacy Court A, 2nd Proceedings, 2 Jul. 1951, ibid. On the Happa Kuoro, see DC Lawra to DC Wa, 3 Aug. 1951; DC Wa to CCNT, 17 Aug. 1951, RAT, NRG 8/2/73.
96. Verbatim Extracts of Proceedings on Hamile Affairs, Lawra Confederacy Court Book, 14–15 Dec. 1950: 1, RAT, NRG 7/2/5.
97. Happa Kuoro to DC Wa, 2 Dec. 1949, RAT, NRG 8/2/101.
98. Verbatim Extracts of Proceedings on Hamile Affairs, Lawra Confederacy Court Book, 14–15 Dec. 1950: 3, RAT, NRG 7/2/5.

99. On this point, I have conducted numerous interviews in Hamile and the neighbouring Sisala and Dagara settlements in Ghana and Burkina Faso, in the context of my more recent research into settlement history and land rights.
100. Verbatim Extracts of Proceedings on Hamile Affairs, Lawra Confederacy Court Book, 14–15 Dec. 1950: 2, RAT, NRG 7/2/5.
101. Short History of Muayiri (Hamile), Appendix in Nandom District, Intelligence Reports, Jul.–Aug. 1962, RAT, NRG 7/3/5. See also Nandom Naa Imoru to Minister of Local Government, 26 Mar. 1952, RAT, NRG 8/2/73.
102. DC Lawra to DC Wa, 22 Jan. 1951, ibid; see also North-West District, Annual Report 1950–1, RAT, NRG 8/3/178: 6.
103. Happa Kuoro to DC Lawra and DC Wa, 27 Nov. 1951, RAT, NRG 8/2/101.
104. Lanlan Dagarti, Taara Wangara, Osumani Moshi and Mogtari Waka to the Minister of Local Government, 6 Jun. 1951, RAT, NRG 8/2/73; see also Naalan Dagarti and others to Local Government Committee, 5 Nov. 1951, ibid. Although the brother of the late Hamile Naa Perwere, who led the secessionists, is listed in the letterhead sometimes under Lanlan and sometimes under Naalang Dagarti, these are all actually the same person.
105. DC Wa, Confidential Minute on Local Government, 28 Nov. 1951, ibid.
106. Letter dated 2 Apr. 1952 (presumably to CCNT and Minister of Local Government), RAT, NRG 8/2/73.
107. Nandom Naa to Secretary of Delimitation Commission, Ministry of Justice, 8 Dec. 1964, RAT, NRG 7/2/5.

CHAPTER 8

1. Lawra District, Informal Diary, 28 and 29 Jan. 1955, RAT, NRG 8/4/113.
2. Regional Office, W. Peters, Handing-over Notes, 14 Mar. 1959, RAT, NRG 7/2/1.
3. Lawra Local Council, 17 Jan. 1962, RAT, NRG 7/4/7.
4. Generally on the links between party politics and local conflicts in the North, see Ladouceur 1979, Chs 6 and 7; in the North-East, Austin 1961 and 1976: 140–50; in Wa, Wilks 1989: 185–95; in Dagbon, Staniland 1975: 133–68; and on similar developments in Southern Ghana, Dunn and Robertson 1973 as well as Rathbone 2000: esp. 32–43, 59–88.
5. Lawra-Tumu District, Quarterly Reports, Oct.–Dec. 1945, RAT, NRG 8/3/148.
6. Gold Coast 1948, *Report and Tables*, Accra: Government Printer 1950. Even in 1960 only 1,348 men and 560 women in Lawra Confederacy over the age of 15 – 3.2 per cent of that particular age group – had attended or were still attending school (*Population Census of Ghana 1960*, Accra: Government Printer 1964).
7. On this generally see Bening 1990, Chs 7–11.
8. Interview with John Bosco Baanuo, 14 Dec. 1992, Accra.
9. Lawra-Tumu District, Informal Diary, 8 Sep. 1943, NAG, ADM 61/5/16.
10. See ibid., 7 Oct. , 7 Nov. and 8 Nov. 1943 as well as 27 May 1944.
11. Lawra-Tumu District, Informal Diary, 26 Aug. 1943 and 31 Oct. 1943, NAG, ADM 61/5/16.
12. Lawra District, Quarterly Reports, Oct.–Dec. 1945 and Apr.–Jun. 1946, RAT, NRG 8/3/148.
13. Lawra District, Informal Diary, 13 Oct. 1946, RAT, NRG 8/4/100; see also 23 Sep. 1945.

14. Personal communication, Ivor Wilks, Mar. 1991 and May 1993, Evanston, USA.
15. On this see Gandah 2004: 186–7 as well as Lawra District, Informal Diary, 6 Jun. 1954, RAT, NRG 8/4/113.
16. See Gandah 2004: 206–11.
17. Ibid.: 186, 227–8.
18. Interview on 12 Dec. 1989, Nandom.
19. *West Africa*, 2 Feb. 1952: 85.
20. See Goody 1982: 17–18.
21. Interview with S. W. D. K. Gandah, 4 Oct. 1995, London.
22. Interview on 22 Dec. 1993.
23. Interview with W. K. Dibaar, 29 Nov. 1994, Nandomkpee.
24. According to a report in *West Africa* (15 May 1954: 444), Imoru even made a public address on behalf of the North-West.
25. Interview on 22 Dec. 1989, Lawra.
26. Interview on 19 Dec. 1994, Jirapa.
27. Interview on 10 Dec. 1994, Tamale.
28. Lawra District, Informal Diary, 5 May 1954, RAT, NRG 8/4/113.
29. Ibid., 2 and 4 Jun. 1954.
30. Government Agent Lawra to Chief Regional Officer, Tamale, 30 Jul. 1956, RAT, NRG 8/22/58.
31. Interview conducted by Barbara Habig with the earth priest of Varpuo, 3 Nov. 1989.
32. Peters, Report on Elections 1956, RHL, MSS Afr. S.1126.
33. RAT, NRG 8/22/34; see also Peters, Report on Elections 1956.
34. Lawra District, Informal Diary, 18 Jun. as well as 1, 13, 23, 27, and 31 Jul. 1954, RAT, NRG 8/4/113.
35. Interview on 13 Dec. 1989, Segru.
36. *Daily Graphic*, 19 July 1956.
37. See Ch. 4 of this volume.
38. Lawra Conf. State Council, 4 May 1956, RAT, NRG 7/4/5.
39. Deaths and Appointments of Chiefs Lawra District, RAT, NRG 7/2/1.
40. 'Report of the Committee of Enquiry of the Lawra Conf. State Council appointed to examine the land dispute between the Nandom-Na and the Lambussie Koro', May 1956, RAT, NRG 7/4/5.
41. Ibid.
42. Lawra Conf. State Council, 3 Sep. 1956, ibid.; see also Lawra Naa to Lambussie State Council among others, 1. Oct. 1956, ibid.
43. GA Lawra to President Lawra Conf. State Council, 28.Oct.1956, ibid.
44. Unfortunately there were no copies of either of these letters on file, but the contents were deducible from the replies.
45. Lawra Conf. State Council, 9 Jan. 1957, ibid.
46. Kuuyele to GA Lawra, 25 Sep. 1951, RAT, NRG 8/2/101.
47. Nandom Naa to GA Lawra, 10 Jun. 1952, and Soliku Dagarti, Tingansob, to U.A.C. Manager, 10 June 1952, RAT, NRG 7/1/2.
48. B. Dasoberi to GA Lawra, 18 June 1952, ibid.
49. Soliku, Tingansob Nandom, to Clerk of GA Lawra, via Nandom Naa, 22 July 1952, ibid.
50. He was probably referring to a response to the application for a 'certificate of occupancy', which the Occupation of Land and Native Rights Ordinance required prior to commencement of construction in urban areas; on this see the corrsponding memorandum by the CRO Tamale, 15 Aug. 1957, RAT, NRG 7/1/3.

51. 'Report of the Committee of Enquiry of the Lawra Conf. State Council appointed to examine the land dispute between the Nandom-Na and the Lambussie Koro', May 1956, RAT, NRG 7/4/5.
52. Ibid.
53. The signatories came from Nandomkpee, Dangko, Goziir, Tantuo, Ketuo, Kogle, Monyupelle, Tom, Ko, Varpuo, Kusele, Betaglu, Bo and Kokoligu. Although there were no copies of the petition in the archives, the contents and the signatories were summarised in the minutes of the Lawra Conf. State Council meeting, 3 Apr.1957, ibid.
54. Lawra Conf. State Council, 21 Feb. 1957, ibid.
55. Lawra Conf. State Council, 3 Apr. 1957, ibid.
56. Interviews with Nandom Naa Dr Charles Imoro, 22 Dec. 1993, and Gbeckature. Boro, 7 Nov. 1992, Nandom.
57. Lawra Conf. State Council, 3 Apr. 1957, RAT, NRG 7/4/5.
58. Ibid.
59. President Lawra Conf. State Council to Nandom State councillors, 5 Apr. 1957, RAT, NRG 7/4/5.
60. GA to President Lawra Conf. State Council, 6 Apr. 1957, ibid.
61. President Lawra Conf. State Council to GA, 6 Apr. 1957, ibid. On this see also Ch. 4 of this volume. In fact, Imoru, who in 1940 competed with late Nandom Naa Boro's son Yuori, did come to power in a truly competitive election in which all Nandom Division compounds, the Nandom headmen, sub-divisional chiefs and neighbouring divisional chiefs were eligible to vote, and which Imoru had won with 627 to 402 votes in his favour. See DC Lawra-Tumu to CCNT, 23 Dec. 1940, RAT, NRG 8/2/73.
62. Lawra Conf. State Council, 25 Jun. 1954, RAT, NRG 7/10/1.
63. Finally in 1940 a minimal consensus was reached that a chief's 'criminal conviction' should be sufficient grounds for his removal from office, but that generally destoolment charges required a hearing during a 'public meeting' and the 'approval of the Central Government'; Lawra Conf. Native Administration, 10–12 Sept. 1940, RAT, NRG 8/5/17. This procedure had, however, never been applied.
64. See Ladouceur 1979: 140–1.
65. Interview with W. K. Dibaar, 29 Nov. 1994, Nandomkpee.
66. GA to CRO, 27 Dec. 1957, RAT, NRG 7/2/1.
67. 'Report of the Committee appointed to enquire into the Nandom Skin dispute, Lawra Conf.', 1958: 4–5 (in the following cited as Report 1958).
68. Interview with Nandom Naa Dr Charles Imoro, 4 Dec. 1989, Nandom.
69. For details on this and other conflicts over Nandom chiefly succession see Lentz 2000b.
70. Report 1958: 5. Of Nandom's eight sub-divisional chiefs (since 1960: divisional chiefs) only Tuopari did not support Polkuu and was thus demoted from a division to a sub-division; Puffien, on the other hand, was rewarded for its support of Polkuu and made a division.
71. State Council of Chiefs Nandom to GA Lawra, 20 Mar. 1958; GA Lawra to RC Tamale, 22 Apr. 1958, RAT, NRG 7/2/2.
72. Boror Yuori to GA Lawra, 28 May 1958, ibid.
73. Nandom State Council (Chiefs of Gegenkpe, Guo, Kokoligu, Panyati, Tantuo, Puffien, Zimuopari, Varpuo) to RC Tamale, 22 Apr. 1958, ibid.
74. Notice No. 866 in *Ghana Gazette* No. 37, 28 Apr. 1958; quoted in telegram RC Tamale to GA Lawra, 5 May 1958, ibid.
75. Boror Yuori to GA Lawra, 3 Jun. 1958, ibid.

76. See Ch. 2 of this volume.
77. Report 1958: 2–3.
78. Report 1958: 6.
79. Report 1958: 9.
80. Ibid.
81. Ibid.: 11–12.
82. *Ghana Gazette* No. 76, 30 Aug. 1958.
83. Kuuyele *et al.* to GA Lawra, 25 Oct. 1958, RAT, NRG 7/2/2.
84. RC Tamale to GA Lawra, 21 Nov. 1958, ibid.
85. Nandomkpee People to GA Lawra, 15 May 1959, RAT, NRG 7/3/1.
86. For specifics see Lentz 1993: 177–9, 208–11.
87. On this see Ladouceur 1979: 169–71.
88. See Ladouceur 1979: 205–6.
89. Plebiscite and presidential election, 19 and 27 Apr. 1960; RAT, NRG 7/5/4; see also DC Lawra to RC Tamale, 30 Apr. 1960, ibid.
90. Ibid.
91. Jirapa State Council, 10 Nov. 1958, RAT, NRG 7/10/3.
92. Jirapa Naa and Chiefs of Sabuli, Han, Ulo, Karni, Tizza, Tugu and Gbari to RC Tamale, 10 Nov. 1958, ibid.
93. Elders of Ko to DC Lawra, 13 Oct. 1959, RAT, NRG 7/2/1; see also the petition submitted by Lissa, which preferred to follow Nandom over Lawra, Yob Babana *et al.* to Minister of Local Government, n.d., RAT, NRG 7/2/6, as well as Nandom District Intelligence Reports, Aug. and Sept. 1961, RAT, NRG 7/3/5.
94. DC Lawra to Jirapa Naa, 30 Mar.1960, RAT, NRG 7/10/3.
95. Lawra Conf. State Council, 5 Nov. 1959, RAT, NRG 7/4/5.
96. Lambussie Electorate to DC Lawra and RC Tamale, 3 Oct. 1959, RAT, NRG 7/2/1.
97. Chiefs of Samoa, Bangwon, Billaw, Koro, Konguol, Suggo, Dahile and Happa to Minister of Local Government, Accra, 30 May 1960, RAT, NRG 7/4/5.
98. Lambussie Kuoro to President Lawra Conf. State Council, 1 Jun. 1960, ibid.
99. In order to increase administrative efficiency the Greenwood Report (1957) recommended reducing the number of local councils. As a result the four local councils of Lawra District were amalgamated into the Lawra Confederacy Local Council in 1958; a division back into smaller local councils only occurred in 1962.
100. See Ch. 4 of this volume.
101. Nandom District, Intelligence Reports, Dec. 1960 and Jan. 1961, RAT, NRG 7/3/5: 1.
102. Letter dated 30 Jan. 1961, RAT, NRG 7/2/6; see also DC Nandom to RC Upper Region, Intelligence Reports, Apr., May and Jun. 1961, RAT, NRG 7/3/5; DC Nandom, 3 Jul. 1961, Short Guiding Handover Notes, ibid.
103. Nandom State Council, 29 Nov. 1960, RAT, NRG 7/2/6; see also Nandom District, Intelligence Reports, Dec. 1960–Jan. 1961, RAT, NRG 7/3/5.
104. Lambussie Kuoro to RC Upper Region, 4 May 1961, RAT, NRG 7/5/6. See also Lambussie Kuoro to DC Nandom, RC Upper Region, Duori Naa *et al.*, 5 Apr. 1961, RAT, NRG 7/5/6.
105. CPP District and Branch Party Executives, 1964–5, RAT, NRG 7/5/8.
106. Nandom District, Intelligence Reports, Feb. and Mar. 1961, RAT, NRG 7/3/5; see also Marcel Debaru *et al.*, Cheboggo, to DC Nandom, 12 May 1961, RAT, NRG 7/3/3.
107. Nandom District, Intelligence Reports, Apr. and May 1961, draft, RAT, NRG

7/3/5 as well as a letter to the Nandom Naa and the Lambussie Kuoro dated 28 Apr. 1961, RAT, NRG 7/2/2.

108. Nandom District, Intelligence Reports, Nov. and Dec. 1961, RAT, NRG 7/3/ 5. On administrative reforms in general see also Ladouceur 1979: 199–200.

109. Billaw Kuoro, Samoa Kuoro, Konguol Kuoro, Piina Naa *et al.* to RC Upper Region, 29 Dec. 1961, Nandom District, Intelligence Reports, Nov. and Dec. 1961, Appendix, RAT, NRG 7/3/5.

110. In Piina, a village inhabited largely by Dagara, Termaghre had tried to replace the Sisala chief, appointed by the Koro Kuoro and Lambussie Kuoro, with a Dagara chief; on this see Zubeviel to Lambussie State Council, 6 Sep. 1961, ibid. and the Koro Kuoro's statement dated 14 Nov. 1961, RAT, NRG 7/2/6.

111. Lambussie Kuoro to RC Upper Region, 25 Jan. 1962, RAT, NRG 7/3/3.

112. Secretary to RC Upper Region to DC Lambussie, 27 Nov. 1963, RAT, NRG 7/2/8.

113. Nandom District, Intelligence Report, Jun. 1962, RAT, NRG 7/5/6.

114. Nandom District, Intelligence Reports, Jul. and Aug. 1962, RAT, NRG 7/3/5; see also Termaghre to Amolubila, 26 Mar. 1964, ibid.

115. Executive Instruments Nos 309, 311, 313 and 325 dated 11 Oct. 1962, NAG, ADM 4/1/605.

116. Lawra Local Council, 17 Dec. 1962, RAT, NRG 7/4/7.

117. On this see the accusations of Zachary Wala, Liman Wangara *et al.* to GA Lawra, 24 Jan. 1957, RAT, NRG 7/3/1 as well Happa Kuoro to GA Lawra, 1 Jun. 1957, ibid.

118. Happa Kuoro Huor to GA Lawra, 11 Sep. 1957, RAT, NRG 7/3/1; see also Huor to the GA Lawra, 20 Jun. 1957, ibid., and Peter Dagarti, Sumaila Moshi *et al.* to GA Lawra, 4 Jul. 1957, ibid.

119. Happa Kuoro Huor to GA Lawra, 8 Aug. 1957, ibid. See also the responses by Lanlang Dagarti, Amadu Wangara Naa *et al.* to GA Lawra, 29 Jul. 1957, ibid; and by the Lambussie Kuoro to GA Lawra, 4 Jan. 1958, ibid. Huor countered by accusing the Wala headman Zachary and the Lambussie Kuoro of mobilising their subjects against the CPP in the run-up to the local council elections; Happa Kuoro to Lambussie Kuoro, 7 Apr. 1958, ibid; Happa Kuoro and Totina Naweleh to Kwame Nkrumah, with a copy addressed to Imoru Egala (M. P. Tumu), 21 Apr. 1958, RAT, NRG 8/2/110.

120. Happa Kuoro to DC Lawra, 14 Sep. 1959, RAT, NRG 7/3/1.

121. Happa Kuoro to RC Upper Region, 6 Jul. 1960, RAT, NRG 7/2/5.

122. Hamile Na Peter Ziem, Moshie Na Sumailla, Lagos Na Issifu, elders Naatone, Yirkuu, Jonas Ninfaasie and CPP members to RC Tamale, 4 Jan. 1959, RAT, NRG 7/2/1.

123. Alhaji Zakaria Wala *et al.* to RC Upper Region, 20 Jul. 1960, ibid.

124. Ibid.; see also DC Lawra to RC Upper Region, 20 Sep. 1960, ibid.

125. Short History of Muayiri (Hamile), Appendix to Nandom District, Intelligence Reports, Jul.–Aug. 1962, RAT, NRG 7/3/5.

126. Alhaji Motali *et al.* to RC Upper Region, 8 Oct. 1962, RAT, NRG 7/2/5; Naalang [Lanlang] Dagarti to RC Upper Region, 8 Oct. 1962, ibid.

127. Lambussie Traditional Council to RC Upper Region, 8 Oct. 1962, ibid.

128. RC Upper Region to DC Nandom, 29 Sep. 1962, and DC Lambussie to RC Upper Region, 2 Oct. 1962, ibid.

129. See written communications dated 5, 12, 13 and 16 Oct. 1962, ibid.

130. Secretary to RC Upper Region an DC Nandom, 10 Oct. 1962; DC Nandom to RC Upper Region, 11 Oct. 1962, RAT, NRG 7/3/5.

131. Executive Instrument No. 311, 11 Oct. 1962, NAG, ADM 4/1/605.

132. On this see Ladouceur 1979: 200, 207.
133. Commission of Enquiry into Representational and Electoral Reform (Van Lare Commission), Report, Accra: Government Printing Department 1953: 17; on the North-West see ibid., Appendix F.
134. Interview dated 2 Dec. 1994 as well as interview with Jirapa Naa Bapenyiri Yelpoe on 19 Dec. 1994.
135. Nandom-Lambussie District, Intelligence Reports, Dec. 1960–Jan. 1961, RAT, NRG 7/3/5.
136. A.F. Greenwood, Proposals for the Delimitation of Parliamentary Constituencies, 16 Jul. 1963, RAT, NRG 8/22/43.
137. Report of Delimitation Commission 1964, NAG, ADM 5/3/113: 15.
138. Nandom Naa to RC Upper Region, 31 Aug. 1964, RAT, NRG 7/2/5.
139. Nandom Naa to Delimitation Commission, Accra, 8 Dec. 1964, ibid.
140. DC Lambussie to RC Upper Region, 16 Jul. 1965, ibid., as well as letters dated 6 Dec. 1965 and 18 Feb. 1966, RAT, NRG 7/2/5.
141. Zachary Wala to RC Upper Region, 17 Sep. 1965, ibid.; see also an almost identical communiqué written by the Tribal Heads, Hamile Zongo, 18 Aug. 1965, and one by the Lambussie Kuoro, 24 Aug. 1965, ibid.
142. DC Nandom to RC Upper Region, Aug. 1965, ibid.
143. RC Upper Region to Lambussie Kuoro, 29 Sep. 1965, ibid.
144. See Ladouceur 1979: 212–14. Asumda even remained imprisoned until 1968.
145. Interview on 4 Dec. 1989.
146. *Ghana Gazette*, 19 Sep. 1969.

CHAPTER 9

1. First Annual General Meeting of NYDA, 27–30 Dec. 1979, Minutes: 1–5.
2. NYDA National Executive, Annual Report 1981: 10.
3. NYDA National Executive, Annual Report 1980: 7.
4. Address by the National Executive of the NYDA to a durbar of chiefs and young people from the Nandom Traditional Area, 30 Dec. 1988: 1.
5. On FREED, whose geographically widely dispersed activists communicate mainly via the internet, see www.gnafreed.org.
6. For further details regarding the history of youth associations in Lawra District, see Lentz 1995b; on the political context of youth associations in Northern Ghana in general, see Lentz 2000c.
7. Interview, 30 Jul. 1989, Trier.
8. Nandom Students Union, new by-laws, passed on 28 Dec. 1988.
9. Interview with Jacob Yirerong, 7 Feb. 1990, Accra.
10. My informants could not agree on whether the Association was called the Sisala Youth Association from the outset or had initially been called the Lambussie Students Union; interviews with S. B. Dy-Yakah (2 Dec. 1992), Jacob Boon (23 Nov. 1989) and Vito Banu (30 Jan. 1990).
11. Peter Der in a group discussion with the NYDA executive, 15 Nov. 1989, Wa.
12. See Austin 1976; Ladouceur 1979: 113, 218–33.
13. Interviews with Lawra Naa Abayifaa Karbo, 22 Dec. 1989; S. B. Dy-Yakah, 2 Dec. 1992, Tamale, and 31 Aug. 1993, Berlin; and Rear-Admiral Rtd, Kevin Dzang, 15 Dec. 1992, Accra.
14. Discussion with the NYDA National Executive, 15 Nov. 1989, Wa.
15. Constitution of the NYDA, ratified 28 Dec. 1979, Articles 1, 2.
16. Interview with Joe Zagbuor, 22 Dec. 1989, Lawra.
17. Discussion, 15 Nov. 1989, Wa.
18. Interview with Vito Banu, 30 Jan. 1990, Accra.

19. Interviews with Prof. Benedict Der, 17 Jan. 1990, Cape Coast, and Luke Kor, 21 Dec. 1994, Piina, on the Bussie Traditional Area Development Association (BUTADA).
20. Interview with Leo Abeikpeng, 14 Sep. 1988, Obuasi.
21. On how the educated elite views itself, see also Lentz 1994b; on educated Dagara women and their organisations, Behrends 2002b.
22. Group discussion, 15 Nov. 1989, Wa.
23. Ibid.
24. Interviews with Dr E. N. Gyader, 13 Nov. 1989, Wa; Jacob Yirerong, 7 Feb. 1990, Accra; Oscar Pagzu, 13 Dec. 1989, Segru; Felix Nifaakang, 18 Dec. 1989, Burutu.
25. Discussion with Bruno Ninnang and others, 11 Nov. 1989, Wa.
26. Interview with Nandom Naa Dr Charles Imoro, 4 Dec. 1989.
27. Interview with John Sotenga, 1 Dec. 1992, Tamale.
28. Interview with Alexis Nakaar, 24 Nov. 1992, Accra.
29. Interview with Aloysius Denkabe, 21 Jan. 1990, Accra.
30. Minutes of a meeting of opinion leaders in Nandom and NYDA National Executives, 25 Aug. 1991.
31. Interview with Aloysius Denkabe, 21 Jan. 1990.
32. Interview with G. B. Kwao, 20 Nov. 1989, Guo.
33. NYDA, Petition for the Creation of a District for the Nandom Traditional Area, presented during the NYDA national delegates' conference, Dec. 1986: 6.
34. Interview with Jacob Boon, DC Jirapa-Lambussie, 23 Nov. 1989.
35. In fact, the case was never brought before the High Court, but decided by the Lawra Confederacy Court A; for more details, see Ch. 7 of this volume.
36. Lawra District Secretary to Lambussie Kuoro, Nandom Naa and others, 5 May 1987.
37. *People's Daily Graphic*, 11 Jul. 1987.
38. On the Nabaala-Taalipuo conflict, see also Kunbuor 2003: 120–5.
39. Summary of decisions taken at a meeting of Lambussie Kuoro, Nandom Naa and their respective Tindanas with His Grace Archbishop P. P. Dery, Hamile, 23 Jan. 1990.
40. See the minutes of the District Security Committee visit to Taalipuo, 5 May 1988.
41. These arguments are summarised in a letter by the Upper West Regional Secretary to Ag. Director, Castle Information Bureau, Accra, 10 May 1989.
42. In this letter the use of the term 'Dagaaba' – instead of Dagara – indulges the ethnic terminology dominant in the public sphere and reflects NYDA's desire to mobilise the widest possible ethnic front for their political cause. In other contexts NYDA activists insisted that Dagara is the only correct term for the entire ethnic group, including the Dagaba of Jirapa. For more details on this, see Ch. 10 of this volume.
43. NYDA National Chairman to Ag. Director, Castle Information Bureau, Accra, 26 May 1989.
44. Interview, 28 Nov. 1989, Lambussie.
45. Interview, 17 Nov. 1990, Tamale.
46. NYDA Delegate's Conference, 29 Dec. 1990, Minutes: 2, 6.
47. Meeting of Nandom opinion leaders and NYDA national executives, 25 Aug. 1991: 1.

CHAPTER 10

1. Discussion during the 'Dagara family meeting', 1 Jul. 1989, Gammelshausen.
2. From a copy of the speech kindly provided by John Sotenga, the former NYDA chairman.
3. Parts of this chapter have been previously published in Lentz 1997.
4. 1960 Population Census of Ghana, Special Report 'E', *Tribes in Ghana*, Accra: Census Office 1964: ix (in the following cited as Special Report 1960).
5. For more details on Goody's ethnic nomenclature, see Lentz 1998: 377–85 and Hawkins 2002: 42–4, 92–5.
6. On British authors see for example Hagaman 1977, Evans 1983 and Hawkins 2002. Despite the vehement criticism on the part of Dagara intellectuals regarding Goody's nomenclature, Hawkins continues to use it to this day, insisting that it best reflects the fluid cultural boundaries and the fact that the Dagara have still yet to come to a consensus regarding their ethnic name. Differing from Goody, however, Hawkins also counts the patrilineal Dagaba among the LoDagaa (2002: 3–6; 1996: 233 fn. 3). On French authors see for example Labouret 1958: 32–4 and Sabelli 1986.
7. Special Report 1960: xi–xii. On more recent works regarding the dialect and geography of Dagara, Lobiri and similar languages see the overview provided in Lentz 1998: 389–93.
8. Ibid.: xxvii–xxix. According to Goody (1954: 5) the Gonja referred to Birifor and Lobi immigrants from Upper Volta who recently migrated to the area south of Wa as 'Miiwoo', while Yangaala or Nyangaala was a Gonja nickname for Dagara speakers (Special Report 1960, A 2).
9. Special Report 1960: D 9–10. See also Ch. 3 of the present work.
10. Quoted from a discussion during the 'Dagara family meeting', Gammelshausen, 30 Jun. 1989. Many Dagara think that *ntafo* (Twi) means twins and refers to the Northerners undertaking labour migration only in pairs or groups; they translate *pepeni* as 'only a visitor'. When cross-checking this with Twi-speakers, different explanations emerged: one informant claimed that *ntaafo* referred only to the Gonja, as a people living between two rivers (*ntaa* = two), that *ntafo* could be a corruption of *NTifo*, 'people from the Northern Territories (NTs)', and that *pepeni* could actually mean *potoni*, 'barbarian'. Owusu 1970: 101, 150–1 describes *pepefo* as a derogatory name for 'Northerners' in general and for the Hausa in particular.
11. 'Mole' is synonymous with Mooré, the language spoken by the Mossi which is closely related to Dagara/Dagaare.
12. See the 1983–5 issues of the journal *The Diocese* (Wa).
13. A number of the papers presented at this conference – including Benedict Der's theories – were published in a new journal edited by Dr Sebastian Bemile, *Papers in Dagara Studies*.
14. There are obvious parallels with the cultural production of ethnic histories in other African societies; for a Ghanaian example see Sandra Greene on the role of the Notsie origin myth among the Ewe (1996: 65–8, 137–8, 148–52).
15. See, for instance, Ansotinge 1986, Somda 1975: 13–37, and, on the basis of the interpretation of proverbs and folk tales, Dabire 1983: 61–111.
16. Interview on 17 Nov. 1990, Tamale.
17. See, for instance, the accounts of B. Somé 1969, Dabire 1983, Dery 1987, Bekye 1991: 109–130, and Kpiebaya 1991.
18. An exception is Labouret 1931: 307–9 whose gruesome description is virtually never referred to by subsequent authors. See also Hawkins 2002: 249–51.

19. See, for instance, Naameh 1986, Dabire 1983, Bekye 1991, to name just a few of the numerous dissertations written by Catholic priests on Dagara religion; see Goody 1975, R. Somé 1991 and Hawkins 1998 for a critical view.
20. Quoted from the constitutions of the NYDA and JAYDA, respectively.
21. Interview with Leopold Abeikpeng, 14 Sep. 1988, Obuasi.
22. Interview with John Sotenga, 1 Dec.1992, Tamale.

ABBREVIATIONS

ANSOC	Accra Nandome Social Club
CCNT	Chief Commissioner Northern Territories
CNP	Commissioner Northern Province
CNWP	Commissioner North-Western Province
CPP	Convention People's Party
CSP	Commissioner Southern Province
DC	District Commissioner
GA	Government Agent
IWDU	Issah West Development Union
JAYDA	Jirapa Youth and Development Association
NANSU	Nandom Students' Union
NCD	National Commission on Democracy
NDC	National Democratic Congress
NPP	Northern People's Party (1954–7; since 1992: New Patriotic Party)
NTC	Northern Territories Council
NYDA	Nandom Youth and Development Association
PEA	People's Educational Association
RC	Regional Commissioner
UAC	United African Company
UGCC	United Gold Coast Convention
UP	United Party

GLOSSARY

Please note that words used only once are explained in the text and do not appear in the Glossary.

no comment:	the Dagara dialect most commonly used in Nandom
J.:	the Dagara dialect most commonly used in Jirapa
S.:	Sisala (the dialect commonly used in Lambussie)

bàgr	initiation society
fàŋ	power, strength
kpɛ̃ɛ́	big, great
kuoro (S.)	rich man, chief
kyielo (S.)	lit.: hawk; pejorative term referring to the Dagara
laŋ (*laŋme*)	lit.: to sit or stick together; pejorative term for the Sisala
mʋɔpʋɔ nıbɛ	lit.: bush-men; migrants, strangers
naa (*naminɛ*), *na* (J.)	rich man, chief (pl.)
saan (*saamɛ*)	stranger (pl.)
-sòb (*-dèm*)	owner, proprietor, custodian (pl.)
tendana (J.)	earth priest
tèŋ	earth, land, soil
tèŋgán (*tèŋgáme*) (pl.)	lit.: skin of the earth; earth deity, earth-shrine area
tèŋgánsòb (*tèŋgándèm*)	earth priest (pl.)
tèŋgán yele	matters of the earth priest, matters of the earth shrine
totina (S.)	earth priest
yele	affair, speech
yi-kpɛ̃ɛ́	great house, original house
yir (*yiiri*) (pl.)	house, patrilineage
yirsòb	head of a house
yirdèm	residents of a house
zongo	lit. (Hausa): caravanserai; a settlement of Muslim traders

DIVISIONAL (PARAMOUNT) CHIEFS
OF LAWRA DISTRICT

Nandom
Kyiir [Chiir, Chiri, Cheriri] (1903/1905–8)[1]
Danye [Danniseh, Dannieh, Denye] (1908–18)
Boro [Boroh, Borrow, Bawra] (1918–30)
Konkuu [Kongkung] (1931–40)
Puobe Imoru [Imoro, Moro, Moru] (1940–57)
Polkuu Konkuu Paul (1958–84)
Dr Charles Puoure Imoro (1985–)

Lambussie
Gbeliñu [Balinu, Galinnu, Galina] (1903/1905–15)
Kantonbie [Kantombieh] (1915–27)
Yesibie [Ysibie] (1927–35)
Hille [Hilleh, Hilla] (1936–7)
Bombieh [Bombae] (1937–48)
Salifu (1948–68)
K. Y. Baloro [Baleero] (1969–2000)

Lawra
Daka [= Nale?] (1903/1905–c.1907]
Gari [Garri, Gare] (c.1907–18)
Naamwine [Nanweni] (1918–27)
Binni [Binney, Lobibinni] (1927–34)
J. A. Karbo (1935–67)
Zame Karbo, as 'regent' (1968–77)
Abyaifaa Karbo (1977–2004)

Jirapa
Ganaa [Gana] (1907–38)
Yelpoe [Yelpwe, Ayelpwe] (1938–55)
Yelpoe Bapenyiri (1955–99)

---

1 In brackets: a given name's most prevalent orthography, as found in various written documents; in parentheses: the terms of office, as could be deduced from the colonial records and interviews.

REFERENCES

Abobo, Salvius Anthony Claret. 1994. 'A history of the Jirapa Traditional Area from the early settlement to 1980'. BA dissertation, University of Cape Coast, Department of History.

Alexandre, Pierre. 1970. 'Chiefs, commandants and clerks: their relationship from conquest to decolonisation in French West Africa', in Michael Crowder and Obaro Ikime (eds), *West African Chiefs: Their Changing Status under Colonial Rule and Independence*, pp. 2–13. New York: Africana Publishing Corp.

Allman, Jean. 1993. *The Quills of the Porcupine: Asante Nationalism in an Emergent Ghana*. Madison: University of Wisconsin Press.

Anderson, Benedict. 1983. *Imagined Communities: Reflections on the Origin and Spread of Nationalism*. London: Verso Editions.

Ansotinge, Gervase T. 1986. 'Wisdom of the ancestors: an analysis of the oral narratives of the Dagaaba of Northern Ghana'. PhD thesis, University of California, Berkeley.

Appadurai, Arjun. 1981. 'The past as a scarce resource', *Man* 16, 201–19.

—. 1996. *Modernity at Large: Cultural Dimensions of Globalization*. Minneapolis: University of Minneapolis Press.

Apter, David E. 1972. *Ghana in Transition*, 2nd rev. edn. Princeton: Princeton University Press.

Arhin, Kwame (ed.). 1974. *The Papers of George Ekem Ferguson, a Fanti Official of the Government of the Gold Coast, 1890–1897*. Leiden: African Studies Centre.

Asiwaju, A. I. 1983. 'The concept of frontier in the setting of states in pre-colonial Africa', *Présence Africaine* 127–8, 43–9.

Austin, Dennis. 1961. 'Elections in an African rural area', *Africa* 29, 1–18.

—. 1976. *Ghana Observed: Essays on the Politics of a West African Republic*. Manchester: Manchester University Press.

Bayart, Jean-François. 1993. *The State in Africa: The Politics of the Belly*. London: Longman.

Behrends, Andrea. 2002a. 'Pogminga: the "proper Dagara woman": an encounter between Christian thought and Dagara concepts', *Journal of Religion in Africa* 32, 231–53.

—. 2000b. *Drahtseilakte. Frauen aus Nordghana zwischen Bildung, Beruf und gesellschaftlichen Konventionen*. Frankfurt am Main: Brandes & Apsel.

Bekye, Paul K. 1987. *Catholic Action: An African Experiment in the Lay Apostolate*. Rome: Leberit Press.

—. 1991. *Divine Revelation and Traditional Religions with Particular Reference to the Dagaaba of West Africa*. Rome: Leberit Press.

Bemile, Paul (ed.). 1987. *From Assistant Fetish Priest to Archbishop: Studies in Honour of Archbishop Dery*. New York: Vantage Press.

Bemile, Sebastian. 1990. 'Dagara orthography', *Papers in Dagara Studies* I (2), 1–31.

—. 2000. 'Promotion of Ghanaian languages and its impact on national unity: the Dagara language case', in Carola Lentz and Paul Nugent (eds), *Ethnicity in Ghana: The Limits of Invention*, pp. 204–25. London: Macmillan.

Bening, Raymond B. 1973. 'Indigenous concepts of boundaries and significance of administrative stations and boundaries in Northern Ghana', *Bulletin of the Ghana Geographical Association* 15, 7–20.

—. 1975a. 'Location of district administrative capitals in the Northern Territories of the Gold Coast (1897–1951)', *Bulletin de l'IFAN* 37, série B (3), 646–66.

—. 1975b. 'Colonial development policy in Northern Ghana, 1898–1950', *Bulletin of the Ghana Geographical Association* 17, 65–79.

—. 1976. 'Land tenure system and traditional agriculture of the Sissala', *Bulletin of the Ghana Geographical Association* 18, 15–34.

—. 1977. 'Administration and development in Northern Ghana, 1898–1931', *Ghana Social Science Journal* 4, 58–76.

—. 1983. 'The administrative areas of Northern Ghana, 1898–1951', *Bulletin de l'IFAN* 45, séries B (3–4), 325–56.

—. 1990. *A History of Education in Northern Ghana, 1907–1976*. Accra: Ghana University Press.

Berman, Bruce. 1992. 'Structure and process in the bureaucratic states of colonial Africa', in Bruce Berman and John Lonsdale, *Unhappy Valley: Conflict in Kenya and Africa*, pp. 140–76. London: James Currey.

—. 1998. 'Ethnicity, patronage and the African state: the politics of uncivil nationalism', *African Affairs* 97, 305–41.

Berry, Sara S. 2001. *Chiefs Know Their Boundaries: Essays on Property, Power and the Past in Asante, 1896–1996*. Oxford: James Currey.

Binger, Le Capitaine. 1892. *Du Niger au Golfe de Guinée*, 2 vols. Paris: Librairie Hachette.

Bonnafé, Pierre. 1993. 'Une société hétérogène. La division Woò-Deè chez les Lobi', in Michèle Fiéloux *et al.* (eds), *Images d'Afrique et sciences sociales. Les pays lobi, birifor et dagara*, pp. 123–38. Paris: Karthala.

Bravman, Bill. 1998. *Making Ethnic Ways: Communities and Their Transformations in Taita, Kenya, 1800–1950*. Oxford: James Currey.

Brubaker, Rogers and Frederick Cooper. 2000. 'Beyond "identity"', *Theory and Society* 29, 1–47.

Cannadine, David. 1983. 'The context, performance and meaning of ritual: the British monarchy and the "invention of tradition", c. 1820–1977', in Eric Hobsbawm and Terence Ranger (eds), *The Invention of Tradition*, pp. 101–64. Cambridge: Cambridge University Press.

Cardinall, A. W. 1920. *The Natives of the Northern Territories of the Gold Coast*. London: Routledge.

—. 1931. *The Gold Coast, 1931*. Accra: Government Printer.

Cohen, David William. 1989. 'The undefining of oral tradition', *Ethnohistory* 36, 9–17.

—. 1991. 'La Fontaine and Wamimbi: the anthropology of "time-present" as the substructure of historical oration', in John Bender and David E. Wellbery (eds), *Chronotypes: The Construction of Time*, pp. 205–25. Stanford: Stanford University Press.

— and E. S. Atieno Odhiambo. 1989. *Siaya: The Historical Anthropology of an African Landscape*. London: James Currey.

Cohn, Bernard S. 1983. 'Representing authority in Victorian India', in Eric Hobsbawm and Terence Ranger (eds), *The Invention of Tradition*, pp. 165–209. Cambridge: Cambridge University Press.

Comaroff, John and Jean Comaroff. 1992. *Ethnography and the Historical Imagination*, Boulder: Westview Press.

Cooper, Frederick. 1994. 'Conflict and connection: rethinking colonial African history', *American Historical Review* 99, 1516–45.

Crisp, Jeff. 1984. *The Story of an African Working Class: Ghanaian Miners' Struggles 1870–1980*. London: Zed Press.

Dabire, Constantin Gbaane. 1983. 'Nisaal – L'homme comme relation'. PhD Thesis, Université Laval.

Dasah, James. 1974. 'Ulo: the history of a Dagaba kingdom'. BA dissertation, University of Ghana, Department of History.

Delafosse, Maurice. 1912. *Haut-Sénégal-Niger*, vol. 1. Paris: Emil Larose.

Der, Benedict. 1974. 'Church–state relations in Northern Ghana 1906–1940', *Transactions of the Historical Society of Ghana* 15, 41–61.

—. 1977. 'The "stateless peoples" of North-West Ghana: a reappraisal of the case of the Dagara of Nandom'. Unpub. manuscript, University of Cape Coast, Department of History.

—. 1983. 'Missionary enterprise in Northern Ghana, 1906–1975: a study in impact'. PhD thesis, University of Ghana.

—. 1987. 'Agricultural policy in Northern Ghana during the colonial era', *Universitas* 8, 3–18.

—. 1989. 'The origins of the Dagara – Dagaba', *Papers in Dagara Studies* I (1).

—. 1998. *The Slave Trade in Northern Ghana*. Accra: Woeli Publishing Services.

—. 2001. 'The traditional political systems of northern Ghana reconsidered', in Yakubu Saaka (ed.), *Regionalism and Public Policy in Northern Ghana*, pp. 35–65. Frankfurt am Main: Peter Lang.

Dery, Gaspard. 1987. *Inheritance and Marriage among the Dagaaba of Northern Ghana: Second Opinions to Existing Theories*. Accra: Ghana Publishing Corporation.

Dorward, D. C. 1974. 'Ethnography and administration: a study of Anglo-Tiv "working misunderstanding"', *Journal of African History* 15, 457–77.

Dumett, Raymond E. 1998. *El Dorado in West Africa: The Gold-Mining Frontier, African Labor and Colonial Capitalism in the Gold Coast, 1875–1900*. Oxford: James Currey.

Dunn, John and A. F. Robertson. 1973. *Dependence and Opportunity: Political Change in Ahafo*. Cambridge: Cambridge University Press.

Duperray, Anne-Marie. 1984. *Les Gourounsi de Haute-Volta*. Wiesbaden: Franz Steiner.

Engman, E. V. T. 1986. *Population of Ghana, 1850–1960*. Accra: Ghana Universities Press.

Evans, Philip. 1983. 'The LoBirifor/Gonja dispute in Northern Ghana: a study of inter-ethnic political conflict in a post-colonial state'. PhD thesis, University of Cambridge.

Eyre-Smith, R. St John. 1933. *A Brief Review of the History and Social Organisation of the Peoples of the Northern Territories of the Gold Coast.* Accra: Government Printer.

Fardon, Richard. 1996. '"Crossed destinies": the enlarged history of West African ethnic and national identities', in Louise de la Gorgondière et al. (eds), *Ethnicity in Africa: Roots, Meanings and Implications*, pp. 117–46. Edinburgh: Centre of African Studies.

Fortes, Meyer. 1936. 'Culture contact as a dynamic process', *Africa* 9, 24–55.

— and E. E. Evans-Pritchard (eds). 1940. *African Political Systems.* London: KPI.

Gandah, S. W. D. K. 1967/1993. 'Gandah yir: the house of the brave'. Unpub. manuscript.

—. 1992. 'The silent rebel'. Unpub. manuscript.

—. 2004. *The Silent Rebel.* Accra: Subsaharan Publishers.

Geschiere, Peter and Joseph Gugler (eds). 1998. 'The politics of primary patriotism', *Africa* 68, special issue, 309–19.

Geschiere, Peter and Francis Nyamnjoh. 2000. 'Capitalism and autochthony: the seesaw of mobility and belonging', *Public Culture* 12, 423–52.

Girault, Louis. 1959. 'Essai sur la religion des Dagara', *Bulletin de l'IFAN* 21, série B (3–4), 329–56.

Goody, Jack. 1954. *The Ethnography of the Northern Territories of the Gold Coast, West of the White Volta.* London: Colonial Office.

—. 1956. *The Social Organisation of the LoWiili.* London: H.M. Stationery Office.

—. 1957. 'Fields of social control among the LoDagaba', *Journal of the Royal Anthropological Institute of Great Britain and Ireland* 87, 75–104.

—. 1962. *Death, Property and the Ancestors: A Study of the Mortuary Customs of the LoDagaa of West Africa.* Stanford: Stanford University Press.

—. 1969. '"Normative", "recollected" and "actual" marriage payments among the LoWiili of Northern Ghana, 1951–1966', *Africa* 39, 54–60.

—. 1972. *The Myth of the Bagre.* Oxford: Clarendon Press.

—. 1975. 'Religion, social change and the sociology of conversion', in Jack Goody (ed.), *Changing Social Structure in Ghana*, pp. 91–106. London: International African Institute.

—. 1982. 'Decolonization in Africa: national politics and village politics', *Cambridge Anthropology* 7, 2–23.

—. 1987. *The Interface between the Written and the Oral.* Cambridge: Cambridge University Press.

—.1990. 'The political systems of the Tallensi and their neighbours 1888–1915', *Cambridge Anthropology* 14, 1–25.

— 1995. *The Expansive Moment: Anthropology in Britain and Africa 1918–1970.* Cambridge: Cambridge University Press.

— and S. W. D. K. Gandah (comp.). 1980. *Une récitation du Bagré.* Paris: A. Colin.

— and S. W. D. K. Gandah. 2002. *The Third Bagre: A Myth Revisited.* Durham: Carolina Academic Press.

— and Esther Goody. 1996. 'The naked and the clothed', in John Hunwick and

Nancy Lawler (eds), *The Cloth of Many Colored Silks: Papers on History and Society Ghanaian and Islamic in Honor of Ivor Wilks*, pp. 67–89. Evanston: Northwestern University Press.

Greene, Sandra. 1996. *Gender, Ethnicity, and Social Change on the Upper Slave Coast: A History of the Anlo-Ewe*. London: James Currey.

Grindal, Bruce T. 1972. *Growing up in Two Worlds: Education and Transition among the Sisala of Northern Ghana*. New York: Holt, Rinehart and Winston.

Hagaman, Barbara L. 1977. 'Beer and matriliny: the power of women in a West African society'. PhD thesis, Northeastern University, Boston.

Hamilton, Carolyn. 1998. *Terrific Majestiy: The Powers of Shaka Zulu and the Limits of Historical Invention*. Cambridge: Harvard University Press.

Harneit-Sievers, Axel (ed.). 2002. *A Place in the World: New Local Historiographies from Africa and South-Asia*. Leiden: Brill.

Hart, Keith. 1971. 'Migration and tribal identity among the Frafras of Ghana', *Journal of Asian and African Studies*, 6, 21–36.

—. 1978. 'The economic basis of Tallensi social history in the early twentieth century', *Research in Economic Anthropology* 1, 185–216.

Hawkins, Sean. 1996. 'Disguising chiefs and God as history: questions on the acephalousness of LoDagaa politics and religion', *Africa* 66, 207–47.

—. 1997. 'To pray or not to pray: politics, medicine, and conversion among the LoDagaa of Northern Ghana, 1929–1939', *Canadian Journal of African Studies* 31, 50–85.

—. 1998. 'The interpretation of Naangmin: missionary ethnography, African theology and history among the LoDagaa', *Journal of Religion in Africa* 28, 32–61.

—. 2002. *Writing and Colonialism in Northern Ghana: The Encounter between the LoDagaa and 'the World on Paper'*. Toronto: University of Toronto Press.

Hébert, Père Jean. 1976. *Esquisse d'une monographie historique du pays Dagara. Par un groupe de Dagara en collaboration avec le père Hébert*. Diébougou: Diocèse de Diébougou.

Hien, Pierre-Claver. 1996. 'Le jeu des frontières en Afrique Occidentale. Cents ans de situations conflictuelles au Burkina Faso actuel (1886–1986)'. PhD thesis, Université Paris I.

Hilton, T.E. 1966. 'Depopulation and population movement in the Upper Region of Ghana', *Bulletin of the Ghana Geographical Association* 11, 27–47.

Holden, J. J. 1965. 'The Zaberima conquest of North-West Ghana', *Transactions of the Historical Society of Ghana* 8, 60–86.

Hubbell, Andrew. 2001. 'A view of the slave trade from the margin: Souroudougou in the late nineteenth-century slave trade of the Niger bend', *Journal of African History* 42, 25–47.

Iliasu, A. A. 1975. 'Rex V. Yagbongwura Mahama and six others', *Universitas* 5, 139–51.

Iliffe, John. 1979. *A Modern History of Tanganyika*. Cambridge: Cambridge University Press.

Ingrams, Harold. 1949. *Seven across the Sahara: From Ash to Accra*. London: John Murray.

Jewsiewicki, Bogumil and V. Y. Mudimbe, 1993. 'Africans' memories and contemporary history of Africa', *History and Theory* 32, 1–11.

Jones, W. J. A. 1938. 'The Northern Territories of the Gold Coast', *Crown Colonist*, April, 193–5.

Kambou-Ferrand, Jeanne-Marie. 1993a. *Peuples voltaïques et conquête coloniale 1885–1914, Burkina Faso*. Paris: L'Harmattan

—. 1993b 'Guerre et résistance sous la période coloniale en pays lobi/birifor (Burkina Faso) au travers de photos d'époque', in Michèle Fiéloux et al. (eds), *Images d'Afrique et Sciences sociales. Les pays lobi, birifor et dagara*, pp. 75–99. Paris: Karthala.

—. 1993c. 'Etre lobi, ça se mérite', in Michèle Fiéloux et al. (eds), *Images d'Afrique et Sciences sociales. Les pays lobi, birifor et dagara*, pp. 539–45. Paris: Karthala.

Kasanga, Kasim and Martin Avis. 1988. *Internal Migration and Urbanisation in Developing Countries: Findings from a Study in Ghana*, Department of Land Management and Development: Research Papers 1. Reading: University of Reading.

Klein, Martin A. 2001. 'The slave trade and decentralised societies', *Journal of African History* 42, 49–65.

Knösel, Didier. 2001. 'Migration, ethnische Identität und politische Macht. Die Kufule in Oronkua, Burkina Faso'. MA thesis, University of Frankfurt am Main, Department of Historical Anthropology.

Konings, Piet. 1986. *The State and Rural Class Formation in Ghana*. London: KPI.

Kopytoff, Igor, 1989. 'The internal African frontier: the making of African political culture', in Igor Kopytoff (ed.), *The African Frontier: The Reproduction of Traditional African Societies*, pp. 3–84. Bloomington: Indiana University Press.

Kpiebaya, Gregory. 1991. *Dagaaba Traditional Marriage and Family Life*. Wa: Catholic Press.

Kuba, Richard and Carola Lentz. 2002. 'Arrows and earth shrines: towards a history of Dagara expansion in southern Burkina Faso', *Journal of African History* 43, 377–406.

Kuba, Richard, Carola Lentz and Katja Werthmann (eds). 2001. *Les Dagara et leurs voisins. Histoire de peuplement et relations interethniques au sud-ouest du Burkina Faso*. Frankfurt am Main: Berichte des Sonderforschungsbereichs 268 'Westafrikanische Savanne', vol. 15.

Kuklick, Henrika. 1979. *The Imperial Bureaucrat: The Colonial Administrative Service in the Gold Coast, 1920–1939*. Stanford: Hoover Institution.

—. 1991. *The Savage Within: The British Social Anthropology, 1885–1945*. Cambridge: Cambridge University Press.

Kunbuor, Benjamin. 2003. 'Multiple layers of land rights and "multiple owners": the case of land disputes in the Upper West Region of Ghana', in Franz Kröger and Barbara Meier (eds), *Ghana's North: Research on Culture, Religion, and Politics of Societies in Transition*, pp. 101–28. Frankfurt am Main: Peter Lang.

Kuper, Adam. 1983. *Anthropology and Anthropologists*. London: Routledge.

—. 1988. *The Invention of Primitive Society: Transformations of an Illusion*. London: Routledge.

Kuukure, Edward. 1985. *The Destiny of Man: Dagaare Beliefs in Dialogue with Christian Eschatology*. Frankfurt a.M.: Peter Lang.

Labouret, Henri. 1931. *Les tribus du rameau Lobi*. Paris: L'Institut d'Ethnologie.

—. 1958. *Nouvelles notes sur les tribus du rameau Lobi: leurs migrations, leur évolution, leurs parlers et ceux de leurs voisins*. Dakar: IFAN.

Ladouceur, Paul A. 1979. *Chiefs and Politicians: The Politics of Regionalism in Northern Ghana*. London: Longman.

Lentz, Carola. 1993. 'Histories and political conflict: a case study of chieftaincy in Nandom, northwestern Ghana', *Paideuma* 39, 177–215.

—. 1994a. 'A Dagara rebellion against Dagomba rule? Contested stories of origin in north-western Ghana', *Journal of African History* 35, 457–92.

—. 1994b. 'Home, death and leadership: discourses of an educated elite from northwestern Ghana', *Social Anthropology* 2, 149–69.

—. 1995a. '"Tribalism" and ethnicity in Africa: a review of four decades of anglophone research', *Cahiers des Sciences Humaines* 31, 303–28.

—. 1995b. '"Unity for development": youth associations in north-western Ghana', *Africa* 65, 395–429.

—. 1997. 'Creating ethnic identities in north-western Ghana', in Cora Govers and Hans Vermeulen (eds), *The Politics of Ethnic Consciousness*, pp. 31–89. London: Macmillan.

—. 1998. *Die Konstruktion von Ethnizität. Eine politische Geschichte Nord-West Ghanas, 1870–1990*. Cologne: Köppe.

—. 1999. 'Colonial ethnography and political reform: the works of A.C. Duncan-Johnstone, R. S. Rattray, J. Eyre-Smith and J. Guinness on northern Ghana', *Ghana Studies* 2, 119–69.

—. 2000a. 'Of hunters, goats and earth-shrines: settlement histories and the politics of oral tradition in northern Ghana', *History in Africa* 27, 193–214.

—. 2000b. '"Tradition" versus "politics": succession conflicts in a chiefdom in north-western Ghana', in Joao de Pina-Cabral and Antónia Pedroso de Lima (eds), *Choice and Leadership in Elite Succession*, pp. 91–112. London: Berg Publishers.

—. 2000c. 'Youth associations et ethnicité au Nord-Ghana', in Coumi Toulabor (ed.), *Le Ghana de J. J. Rawlings. Restauration de l'État et renaissance du politique*, pp. 126–144. Paris: Karthala.

—. 2001a. 'Ouessa: débats sur l'histoire du peuplement', in Richard Kuba, Carola Lentz and Katja Werthmann (eds), *Les Dagara et leurs voisins. Histoire de peuplement et relations interethniques au sud-ouest du Burkina Faso*, pp. 29–61. Frankfurt am Main: Berichte des Sonderforschungsbereichs 268, vol. 15.

—. 2001b. 'Local culture in the national arena: the politics of cultural festivals in Ghana', *African Studies Review* 44, 47–72.

—. 2002. 'The time when politics came: Ghana's decolonisation from the perspective of a rural periphery', *Journal of Contemporary African Studies* 20, 245–74.

—. 2003a. 'Stateless societies or chiefdoms? A debate among Dagara intellectuals', in Franz Kröger and Barbara Meier (eds), *Ghana's North: Research on Culture, Religion, and Politics of Societies in Transition*, pp. 129–59. Frankfurt am Main: Peter Lang.

—. 2003b. 'This is Ghanaian territory: land conflicts on a West African border', *American Ethnologist* 30, 273–89.

—. 2004. 'The written word and the colonial encounter', *Journal of African History* 45, 338–9.

— and Veit Erlmann. 1989. 'A working class in formation? Economic crisis and strategies of survival among Dagara mine workers in Ghana', *Cahiers d'Études Africaines* 113, 69–111.

— and Paul Nugent. 2000. 'Ethnicity in Ghana: a comparative perspective', in Carola Lentz and Paul Nugent (eds), *Ethnicity in Ghana: The Limits of Invention*, pp. 1–28. London: Macmillan.

Lesourd, R. P. Jean. 1938. *Un peuple en marche vers la lumière. Les Dagaris.* Soisson: Imp. de l'Argue.

Levtzion, Nehemia. 1968. *Muslims and Chiefs in West Africa: A Study of Islam in the Middle Volta Basin in the Pre-Colonial Period.* Oxford: Clarendon Press.

Lobnibe, Isidor. 1994. 'A short history of Hamile from the earliest times to 1950'. BA dissertation, University of Cape Coast, Department of History.

Lonsdale, John. 1992. 'The moral economy of Mau Mau', in Bruce Berman and John Lonsdale, *Unhappy Valley: Conflict in Kenya and Africa*, pp. 315–504. London: James Currey.

—. 1996. 'Moral ethnicity, ethnic nationalism and political tribalism: the case of the Kikuyu', in Peter Meyns (ed.), *Staat und Gesellschaft in Afrika. Erosions- und Reformprozesse.* Schriften der VAD, vol. 16, pp. 93–106. Hamburg: Lit.

Lovejoy, Paul E. 1983. *Transformation in Slavery: A History of Slavery in Africa.* Cambridge: Cambridge University Press.

Mamdani, Mamood. 1996. *Citizen and Subject: Contemporary Africa and the Legacy of Late Colonialism.* Princeton: Princeton University Press.

Manoukian, Madeline. 1951. *Tribes of the Northern Territories of the Gold Coast.* London: International African Institute.

McCall, Daniel F. 1981. 'Probing Lo Bir History', in *Le Sol, la parole et l'écrit. 2000 ans d'histoire africaine. Mélanges en hommage à Raymond Maunay*, pp. 361–73. Paris: L'Harmattan.

McCaskie, Tom C. 1983. 'R.S. Rattray and the construction of Asante history: an appraisal', *History in Africa* 10, 187–206.

McCoy, Remigius F. 1988. *Great Things Happen: Personal Memoir of the First Christian Missionary among the Dagaabas and Sissalas of Northwest Ghana.* Montreal: The Society of the Missionaries of Africa.

Meyer, Birgit. 1999. *Translating the Devil: Religion and Modernity among the Ewe in Ghana.* Edinburgh: Edinburgh University Press.

Monson, Jamie. 2000. 'Memory, migration and the authority of history in southern Tanzania, 1860–1960', *Journal of African History* 41, 347–72.

Moore, Sally Falk 1986. *Social Facts and Fabrications: 'Customary' Law on Kilimanjaro, 1880–1980.* Cambridge: Cambridge University Press.

Mukassa, Der. 1987. 'L'homme dans l'univers des Dagara. Essai d'anthropologie culturelle et religieuse dagara'. Unpub. manuscript.

Naameh, Philip. 1986. 'The Christianisation of the Dagara within the horizon of the West European experience'. PhD thesis, University of Münster.

Nkrumah, Kwame. 1970. *Class Struggle in Africa.* London: Panaf.

Nugent, Paul. 2002. *Secessionists, Smugglers and Loyal Citizens on the Ghana–Togo Frontier.* Oxford: James Currey.

Oppen, Achim von. 1996. 'Village-studies. Zur Geschichte eines Genres der Sozialforschung im südlichen und östlichen Afrika', *Paideuma* 42, 17–36.

Osborn, Emily Lynn. 2003. '"Circle of iron": African colonial employees and the interpretation of colonial rule in French West Africa', *Journal of African History* 44, 29–50.

Owusu, Maxwell. 1970. *The Uses and Abuses of Political Power: A Case Study of Continuity and Change in the Politics of Ghana.* Chicago: University of Chicago Press.

Packham, E. 1950. 'Notes on the development of the native authorities in the Northern Territories of the Gold Coast', *Journal of African Administration* 2, 26–30.

Paternot, Marcel. 1949. *Lumière sur la Volta. Chez les Dagari.* Lyon: Éditions de la Plus Grande France.

Peel, J. D. Y. 1983. *Ijeshas and Nigerians: The Incorporation of a Yoruba Kingdom.* Cambridge: Cambridge University Press.

—. 1989. 'The cultural work of Yoruba ethnogenesis', in Elizabeth Tonkin et al. (eds), *History and Ethnicity*, pp. 198–215. London: Routledge.

Pels, Peter. 1996. 'The pidginization of Luguru politics: administrative ethnography and the paradoxes of indirect rule', *American Ethnologist* 23, 738–41.

—. 1997. 'The anthropology of colonialism: culture, history and the emergence of Western governementality', *Annual Review of Anthropology* 26: 163–83.

Pilaszewicz, Stanislaw. 1992. *The Zabarma Conquest of North-West Ghana and Upper Volta: A Hausa Narrative.* Warsaw: Polish Scientific Publishers.

Plange, Nii-K. 1984. 'The colonial state in Northern Ghana: the political economy of pacification', *Review of African Political Economy* 31, 29–43.

Ranger, Terence. 1983. 'The invention of tradition in colonial Africa', in Eric Hobsbawm and Terence Ranger (eds), *The Invention of Tradition*, pp. 211–62. Cambridge: Cambridge University Press.

—. 1993. 'The invention of the tradition revisited: the case of colonial Africa', in Terence Ranger and Olufemi Vaughan (eds), *Legitimacy and the State in Twentieth-Century Africa*, pp. 62–111. London: Macmillan.

Rathbone, Richard. 2000. *Nkrumah and the Chiefs: The Politics of Chieftaincy in Ghana 1951–60.* Oxford: James Currey.

Rattray, Robert S. 1932. *The Tribes of the Ashanti Hinterland*, 2 vols. Oxford: Clarendon Press.

Roberts, Richard and Kristin Mann. 1991. 'Law in colonial Africa', in Kristin Mann and Richard Roberts (eds), *Law in Colonial Africa*, pp. 3–58. London: James Currey.

Robotham, Don. 1989. *Militants or Proletarians: The Economic Culture of Underground Gold Miners in Southern Ghana, 1906–1976*, Cambridge African Monographs 12. Cambridge: University of Cambridge, Centre of African Studies.

Rohden, Frauke von. 1992. '"Fühl dich wie zu Hause, aber benimm dich nicht so" Dagara-Sprichwörter über Gastlichkeit.' Report on Student Fieldwork, Free University of Berlin, Department of Social Anthropology.

Rouch, Jean. 1990. 'Les cavaliers aux vantours. Les conquêtes zerma dans le Gurunsi, 1856–1900', *Journal des Africanistes* 60, 5–36.

Ruelle, E. 1904. 'Notes ethnographiques et sociologiques sur quelques populations noires du 2e Territoire Militaire de l'Afrique Occidental Française', *Anthropologie* 15, 657–74.

Saaka, Yakubu (ed.). 2001. *Regionalism and Public Policy in Northern Ghana*, pp. 35–65. Frankfurt am Main: Peter Lang.

Sabelli, Fabrizio. 1986. *Le pouvoir des lignages en Afrique. La réproduction sociale des communautés du Nord-Ghana*. Paris: L'Harmattan.

Sahlins, Marshall. 1963. 'Poor man, rich man, big man, chief: political types in Melanesia and Polynesia', *Comparative Studies in Society and History* 5, 285–303.

Saul, Mahir and Patrick Royer. 2001. *West African Challenge to Empire: Culture and History on the Volta-Bani Anticolonial War*. Oxford: James Currey.

Sautoy, Peter du. 1958. *Community Development in Ghana*. London: Oxford University Press.

Schildkrout, Enid.1978. *People of the Zongo: The Transformation of Ethnic Identity in Ghana*. Cambridge: Cambridge University Press.

Schott, Rüdiger. 1977. 'Sources for a history of the Bulsa in Northern Ghana', *Paideuma* 23, 141–68.

—. 1993. 'Le caillou et la boue. Les traditions orales en tant que légitimation des autorités traditionelles chez les Bulsa (Ghana) et les Lyéla (Burkina Faso)', *Paideuma* 39, 145–62.

Seavoy, Mary H. 1982. 'The Sisala xylophone tradition'. PhD thesis, University of California, Los Angeles.

Somda, Nurukyor Claude. 1975. 'La pénétration coloniale en pays Dagara, 1897–1914'. Mémoire de maîtrise, Université Paris VII.

—. 1989. 'Les origines des Dagara', *Papers in Dagara Studies* I (1).

—. 2000. 'L'esclavage. Un paradoxe dans une société égalitaire', *Cahiers du CERLESHS* 17, 267–90.

Somé, Bozi, 1969. 'Organisation politico-sociale traditionelle des Dagara', *Notes et documents voltaïques* 2, 16–41.

Somé, Magloire. 1993. *La christianisation de l'Ouest-Volta. De la révolution sociale au conflit culturel et à l'éveil politique, 1927–1960*. PhD thesis, Université de Paris IV.

—. 1996. 'Evangélisation et colonisation en Haute-Volta de 1900 à 1960', *Neue Zeitschrift für Missionswissenschaft/Nouvelle Revue de science missionaire* 52, 81–103.

Somé, Roger. 1991. 'La conception dagara de Dieu en question', *Papers in Dagara Studies* I (3), 30–43.

Somé, Valère. 2001. 'Le Dagara sous le sol de l'esclavage', *Cahiers du CERLESHS*, Numéro spécial 1, 57–97.

Songsore, Jacob. 1983. *Intraregional and Interregional Labour Migration in Historical Perspective: The Case of North-Western Ghana*. Faculty of Social Sciences, Occasional Papers 1. Port Harcourt: University of Port Harcourt.

Spear, Thomas. 2003. 'Neo-traditionalism and the limits of invention in British colonial Africa', *Journal of African History* 44, 3–27.

Spittler, Gerd. 1981. *Verwaltung in einem afrikanischen Bauernstaat. Das koloniale Französisch-Westafrika 1919–1939*. Wiesbaden: Franz Steiner.

St John-Parsons, Donald. 1958. *Legends of Northern Ghana*. London: Longman.

Staniland, Martin. 1975. *The Lions of Dagbon: Political Change in Northern Ghana*. Cambridge: Cambridge University Press.

Stoler, Ann Laura and Frederick Cooper. 1997. 'Between metropole and colony: rethinking a research agenda', in Frederick Cooper and Ann Laura Stoler (eds), *Tensions of Empire: Colonial Cultures in a Bourgeois World*, pp. 1–56. Berkeley: University of California Press.

Sutton, Inez. 1983. 'Labour in commercial agriculture in Ghana in the late nineteenth and early twentieh centuries', *Journal of African History* 24, 461–83.

—. 1989. 'Colonial agricultural policy: the non-development of the Northern Territories of the Gold Coast', *International Journal of African Historical Studies* 22, 637–69.

Tamakloe, Emmanuel Forster. 1931. *A Brief History of the Dagbamba People*. Accra: Government Printer.

Tashijan, Victoria B. 1998. 'The diaries of A. C. Duncan-Johnstone: a preliminary analysis of British involvement in the "native courts" of colonial Asante', *Ghana Studies* 1, 135–50.

Tauxier, Louis. 1912. *Le noir du Soudan. Pays mossi et gourounsi*. Paris: E. Larousse.

Tengan, Alexis B. 2000. *Hoe-Farming and Social Relations among the Dagara of Northwestern Ghana and Southwestern Burkina Faso*. Frankfurt am Main: Peter Lang.

Tengan, Edward B. 1990. 'The Sissala universe: its composition and structure', *Journal of Religion in Africa* 20, 2–19.

—. 1991. *The Land as Being and Cosmos: The Institution of the Earth Cult among the Sisala of Northwestern Ghana*. Frankfurt am Main: Peter Lang.

Thomas, Nicholas. 1994. *Colonialism's Culture: Anthropology, Travel and Government*. Cambridge: Polity Press.

Thomas, Roger. 1972. 'George Ekem Ferguson: civil servant extraordinary', *Transactions of the Historical Society of Ghana*, 13, 181–215.

—. 1973. 'Forced labour in British West Africa: the case of the Northern Territories of the Gold Coast 1906–1927', *Journal of African History* 14, 79–103.

—. 1975a. 'Military recruitment in the Gold Coast during the First World War', *Cahiers d'Études Africaines* 57, 57–83.

—. 1975b. 'Education in Northern Ghana, 1906–1940: a study in colonial paradox', *International Journal of African Historical Studies* 7, 427–67.

—. 1983. 'The 1916 Bongo "riots" and their background: aspects of colonial administration and African response in Eastern Upper Ghana', *Journal of African History* 24, 57–75.

Tonkin, Elizabeth. 1990. 'West African ethnographic traditions', in Richard Fardon (ed.), *Localizing Strategies: Regional Traditions of Ethnographic Writing*, pp. 139–51. Washington: Smithsonian Institution.

Trotha, Trutz von. 1994. *Koloniale Herrschaft. Zur soziologischen Theorie der Staatsentstehung am Beispiel des 'Schutzgebietes Togo'*. Tübingen: Mohr.

Trouillot, Michel-Rolph. 1995. *Silencing the Past: Power and the Production of History*. Boston: Beacon Press.

Tuurey, Gabriel. 1982. *An Introduction to the Mole-speaking Community*. Wa: Catholic Press.

Vail, Leroy (ed.). 1989. *The Creation of Tribalism in Southern Africa*. London: James Currey.

van Hoven, Ed. 1990. 'Representing social hierarchy: administrators-ethnographers in the French Sudan: Delafosse, Monteil and Labouret', *Cahiers d'Études Africaines* 118, 179–98.

Vansina, Jan. 1985. *Oral Tradition as History*. London: James Currey.

Ward, W. E. F. 1949. *A History of the Gold Coast*. London: Allen and Unwin.

Watherston, A. E. G. 1907–8. 'The Northern Territories of the Gold Coast', *Journal of the African Society* 7, 344–73.

Werbner, Richard. 2004. *Reasonable Radicals and Citizenship in Botswana: The Public Anthropology of Kalanga Elites*. Bloomington: Indiana University Press.

White, Hayden. 1987. *The Content of the Form: Narrative Discourse and Historical Representation*. Baltimore: Johns Hopkins University Press.

Wilks, Ivor. 1967. 'Travellers in the Gold Coast hinterland', in Philip D. Curtin (ed.), *Africa Remembered: Narratives by West Africans from the Era of Slave Trade*, pp. 153–89. Madison: University of Wisconsin Press.

—. 1989. *Wa and the Wala: Islam and Polity in Northwestern Ghana*. Cambridge: Cambridge University Press.

Worby, Eric. 1994. 'Maps, names and ethnic games: the epistemology and iconography of colonial power in North-Western Zimbabwe', *Journal of Southern African Studies* 20, 371–93.

Yelpaala, Kojo. 1983. 'Circular arguments and self-fulfilling definitions: "statelessness" and the Dagaaba', *History in Africa* 10, 349–85.

Young, Crawford M. 1986. 'Nationalism, ethnicity and class in Africa: a retrospective', *Cahiers d'Études Africaines* 103, 421–95.

INDEX